ORATORS & PHILOSOPHERS

A History of the Idea of Liberal Education

ORATORS
&
PHILOSOPHERS

A History of the Idea of Liberal Education

BRUCE A. KIMBALL

With a Foreword by Joseph L. Featherstone

Teachers College, Columbia University
New York and London

Published by Teachers College Press, 1234 Amsterdam Avenue, New York, N.Y. 10027

Library of Congress Cataloging in Publication Data

Kimball, Bruce A., 1951-
  Orators & philosophers.

  Includes indexes.
    1. Education, Humanistic—Philosophy—History.
  2. Philosophy, Ancient.   3. Philosophy, Medieval.
  4. Learning and scholarship.   I. Title.   II. Title:
  Orators and philosophers.
  LC1011.K56   1986   370.11'2   85-22272
  ISBN 0-8077-2790-3

Manufactured in the United States of America

90 89 88 87 86 85   1 2 3 4 5 6

For
George Herbert Kimball and Ann Martha Skaryd Kimball,
my first and foremost teachers

Contents

FOREWORD by JOSEPH L. FEATHERSTONE   ix

ACKNOWLEDGMENTS   xv

ABBREVIATIONS   xviii

I.   Introduction   1

II.   Foundation of the *Artes Liberales*   12

III.   Rise of the Philosophical Tradition in the High Middle Ages   43

IV.   Renaissance Humanists and Reformation Preachers   74

V.   Emergence of the Liberal-Free Ideal   114

VI.   Confrontation in America of the Oratorical and Philosophical Traditions   157

VII.   A Typology of Contemporary Discussion   205

APPENDIX I   243

APPENDIX II   255

AUTHOR INDEX   261

SUBJECT INDEX   275

ABOUT THE AUTHOR   293

Foreword

Bruce Kimball's *Orators and Philosophers: A History of the Idea of Liberal Education* comes at a perfect time. An educational reform movement dedicated to something called "excellence" is sweeping the land. The schools have been scrutinized and found wanting, lacking in, among other things, coherent standards. Almost inevitably, the reformers are moving from the schools to the colleges and universities, where, if anything, the incoherence is worse. Despite the chaos, we do have an educational system in the sense that one part links to another. And one source of our present disarray from the schools on up is the confusion over the purposes of education at any level.

Now comes Mr. Kimball, with that rarest of things in these United States of Amnesia: a historical argument. The argument is simple: we do not really understand what we mean when we invoke (as we often do) the phrase "liberal education." For all the thousands of commencement orators who use the phrase, all of us are tangled both in our own muddles and in a confusion that has its roots in the past. The first task of any real reform is to see and think clearly. Mr. Kimball can serve as our guide, if, like him, we are willing to take the history of ideas seriously.

Mr. Kimball's basic point is that "liberal education" embodies in its past two quite distinct traditions and points of view. There is the tradition of the philosophers and the tradition of the orators. The tradition of the philosophers holds that the pursuit of knowledge is the highest good: this is the line from Socrates and Plato and Aristotle to Boethius, the brilliant schoolmen of medieval Paris, the *philosophes* of the Enlightenment, T. H. Huxley, modern science, and the great research universities of the present. Its glory is the freedom of the intellect; its puzzle, as an educational philosophy, is what else to teach besides this freedom.

The tradition of the orators, on the other hand, emphasizes the public expression of what is known, the crucial importance of language, texts, and tradition—linking to and building up a community of learning and knowledge. This is the line of Isocrates, Cicero, Isidore, the *artes liberales* of the Middle Ages and the Renaissance humanists, the vision of Matthew Arnold, of some teachers of the liberal arts today, especially humanities teachers, and, of course, of many religious colleges. The glory of the orators' line is its links with the texts of the past and its focus on recreating learning communities as the central business of education; its problem, as an educational philosophy, is its dogmatic and anti-intellectual idolatry of the past and its frequent assumption that virtue resides in the texts, not in what we the living make of them.

Cicero and Socrates, and their very different, altogether opposed, ideals of education, are the founders of our feasts, and the buried divisions between them must be uncovered if we are to remake the idea of liberal education. First, though, we have to know the history, as any of our orators would insist.

It is pretty well known that orators like Isocrates, Cicero, and Quintilian were critical of the speculative, restless pursuit of truth promoted by philosophers like Socrates and Plato. Socrates and Plato, for their part, attacked the orators for their lack of concern with the radical dialectic of truth and their hand-to-mouth pragmatism. In much of today's academic world, Socrates and what Mr. Kimball calls the "liberal-free" vision of the philosophers reign supreme, especially in the great research universities that set the tone for U.S. education.

Mr. Kimball reminds us, however, that for a very long sweep of history, learned men saw that the orators were making an important point: that communicating knowledge is crucial to learning. How, for example, do we know that Plato and Socrates aren't just an amazingly successful pair of sophists, intellectual con men? We can't, unless we do what Isocrates urged us to do in ancient times: to act on the insight that "the proper use of language is the surest index of sound understanding." We have to read them and criticize what they say. We have to make some kind of public sense of them. What is expressed publicly is for all to hear and judge. The orators insisted that a community of learning would have to make such judgments. Surely this is still the test of most learning. "Words alone are certain good," Yeats said, and this is an important half-truth for those of us in education.

Beyond expression, the orators also ask that a philosophy make a difference in the world, that it enhance virtue by persuading others. They see, rightly, that all teaching is at some level a moral enterprise. The philosophers are uncertain about this. On the other hand, when the philosophers ask, soaring like predatory hawks, "what is virtue?" the orators tend to point blindly to tradition. That is their weakness: they take the virtues of their texts on faith, rather than reason. Justice Holmes once said that a gentleman can never be a philosopher, because a philosopher has to ask rude questions about implicit basic assumptions. In this sense, a well-educated modern ought never to be a gentleman in matters of the mind. Yet the orators' old complaint about the philosophers rings with justice down through the ages: a philosophy is confirmed to be true only when it is expressed or has an effect. The educated man or woman must know philosophy and express it effectively to an audience. The educated person must know how to create a community of hearers. Learning has to make a moral difference, and the circle of moral speech and concern is what the philosophers neglect, to the peril of their souls.

As Mr. Kimball says, the orators of antiquity were dogmatic: they believed the task of education was to impart the truth, not to help students seek it. They believed in absolute values of character and conduct: in fact, only the good man could become the good orator. They relied on a body of classical writings for their texts. One aim of education was to educate the good citizen to lead society, the orator capable of addressing any topic and assuming any position of leadership. The orators' education looks to define elites from among gentlemen of leisure. And yet the point of education was to develop oneself further along the path to excellence.

Such is the orators' position in its early form. It is worth elaborating, because, of course, it is not the dominant rationale for liberal education in our time. The dominant argument in our day tends to be either the philosophers'—couched in the defense of science, research, and free inquiry—or what Mr. Kimball calls an "accommodated" version of the orators'—a defense of the classics primarily as a means to developing the intellect.

It is a strange fact to emerge from this handbook of the idea of liberal education that most of today's neoconservatives defending great books and tradition and so on—the curriculum of the orators—are really closet philosophers; instead of defending the texts on the old complex grounds of the oratorical tradition, they are for the most part preaching the classics today in the name of the Socratic or scientific ideal of the free-swinging intellect. Mr. Kimball has a fresh point to make about how our neoconservatives tend to be ignorant of their own tradition, ignoring the other values the orators placed on texts and tradition apart from the development of a critical intelligence. Thus, well-known neotraditional figures like Alexander Meiklejohn and Robert Hutchins were in fact departing from the orators' tradition when they married a classics curriculum to the aim of developing the critical intellect. They were using the orators' curriculum to promote the philosophers' goals.

In doing this, didn't figures like Hutchins strengthen the old weak-headed oratory by emphasizing brains instead of dim pieties? In a way, but as Mr. Kimball points out, narrowing the tradition of the orators to critical intellect alone leaves you without some very important values, including the rationale for the great texts. Why read Plato at all? It is not easy to get a sense of this from what Mr. Hutchins said. We are asked to take too much on faith, and that is not for moderns to do.

Mr. Kimball suggests that most of the modern defenders of neoclassicism have given the store away through their ignorance of or indifference to the key value of the tradition of the orators: the creation of learning communities. It is not the dogmatism or the absolutism of the oratorical tradition that he admires—Hutchins himself is too glaring an example of how the assumed absolutes never do materialize—but rather its openness to values that are simply missing from the reigning ideals of liberal learning in our large research universities and in many of our colleges: the values of tradition, texts, language, and, above all, the continuous recreation of communities in learning. If we are to restate for our time the two great traditions in a usable way, we need to pay special attention to what our version of the orators' tradition would be.

In a conservative and nostalgic political climate such as the present, the chief attraction of the oratorical tradition will be its dogmatism and its certainty. It's a safe bet that this book will be welcomed by neoconservatives bent on reestablishing certainty in education. This is too bad, because it isn't table pounding that we need, or yet another round of smelly orthodoxy, but careful thought applied to the creation of communities and pedagogies of learning. And to tradition. Alongside the hawk-virtues of the liberated mind, our students need to reconnect to the community of the past through making communities of learning in the present. Colleges need to rethink, as Arnold put it, "the best which has been thought and said in the world." But we won't be able to renew the classics for our time by table pounding, or ukase, or committee reports: our scholars and students will need inspiration and imagination—not more courses and credits, but the path of Keats and Mandelstam—to show us how to reclaim the texts of the past as a living heritage.

In any case, it will take even more determined table-pounders than Robert Hutchins to resurrect the absolute this late in the twentieth century. Whoring after imaginary certainties won't help us renew our colleges and universities, but another look at these two opposed traditions may give us a clear sense of the complexity behind our traditions of liberal learning.

Above all, Mr. Kimball helps us see that a decent liberal education now contains—ought to contain—conflicting elements from both the philosophers and the orators. Not all mixed up in a chowder, the way most colleges are these days, but in an open tension: Socrates and his allies in modern science conjoined with the orators and their modern allies on their own ground, the public, ever-re-created space of learning communities. Socrates was right about the truth; the orators were right about community. And that fight must go on if our students are to be educated. They must learn to hold elements of the two ideals in some real tension, not a flabby compromise.

For its part, the philosophers' tradition—Mr. Kimball calls it the "liberal-free ideal"—has accommodated to the modern university by agreeing that any student is "freed" by majoring in a discipline that is all too often a mini-Ph.D. program run by specialized technicians. Surely this is not what Galileo suffered for, or why Socrates died. Trivial specialties abound. There is a parallel to the orators' weakness for table pounding, too, when today's heirs of the philosophers defend the absoluteness of critical rationality while presuming nothing to be absolute. The ideal of science detached from any obligations to human community no longer has an entirely glorious sound in the age of spaceship earth and the nuclear winter.

The liberal-free conviction that intellectual mold breaking was the highest good made excellent sense when the philosophers and their friends were on the outside of a hostile society looking in; now that they are the insiders, they must ask whether their sovereign ideal amounts to a complete educational vision or not. The answer is, for all its obvious and heroic glories, no. The splendid liberal-free vision of learning all by itself—so rare in an illiberal world—leads to anarchy and nihilism in the end. The pursuit of truth is a necessary educational ideal, but not sufficient.

That is why today we badly need to restate the position of the orators, and to establish for our time a basis for reading texts and forming communities of learning: not to supplant the free vision of the philosophers, but to engage it in a debate that will in itself be crucial for our students' education. And the narrow neoconservatism of recent past is simply not an adequate base, intellectually or spiritually. Robert Hutchins or St. John's College used to talk as though the answers resided in the texts—the sin of idolatry. The real point today's heirs of the orators have over the heirs of the philosophers—as Mr. Kimball says—is not the possession of the bare texts alone—anyone can buy the Penguin Plato—but rather the understanding that the heart of education is forming a community united in the disciplined effort of making meanings out of the texts. This is what the orators have to offer us as an era of reform sweeps from the high schools into the colleges and universities.

And what Mr. Kimball offers is this elegant historical road map of where education in the West has been. He covers all the ground, flying low, but not so low as to get tangled up in any one issue. He guides the rapid tour from the ancients to the Middle Ages to the Enlightenment and the great debates of the nineteenth century, with stop-offs at backwaters like the nineteenth-century U.S. college.

Here is a solid, a historical, context in which to place our—let's admit it—fatuous statements about liberal education. Here is a key to see that T. H. Huxley and Matthew Arnold were in fact reenacting an age-old debate between philosophers and orators in their famous interchange on education. Here is a very learned book that wears its learning lightly, and that, even as it approaches the present, takes on some of the charm of a satire or a comic novel. And here is a history of ideas that does not reify the ideas or pretend they have a life of their own, but deals with them as the orderly intellectual expression of a vast and muddled history. Here, ladies and gentlemen of learning, is a book that could change the way we think.

Its obvious audience is the circle of those concerned with reforming universities and colleges. People working in schools are less likely to see this sort of thing, which is a pity. Sometimes the most practical thing to do is theory—and history—and it would help those struggling for clarity of aim at the school level to understand that they, too, live in a distant version of the tension between philosophers and orators. The school reform movements of today are decidedly on the side of the philosophers, getting kids to think and use "higher order skills" and the like. These are superb goals, but are they enough? Those in the schools also need the wisdom of the orators to tell them that schools must also become places where students and teachers learn how to recreate learning communities, in which human speech is a test of learning and virtue.

JOSEPH L. FEATHERSTONE

Acknowledgments

THE RESEARCH FOR THIS BOOK was begun during my graduate studies at the Divinity School and the Graduate School of Education at Harvard University from 1973 to 1981. In the course of those and subsequent years of research and writing, I have learned from the work of a great number of scholars, and the extensive documentation in this work is intended both to acknowledge my enormous debt and to provide a *via* into the literature for others who may wish to pursue this subject further. Another kind of debt is owed to a number of scholars who have read chapters or drafts of this work at various points over the past ten years. Their guidance and criticism have saved it from many errors of fact, interpretation, and style, although even their much-appreciated efforts could not entirely overcome inevitable deficiencies in my own knowledge and understanding. Thus, I am responsible for the errors that may remain.

For their reading and comments, I wish to thank Eva T. H. Brann of St. John's College, Annapolis; Nathan Glazer of Harvard Graduate School of Education; Paul O. Kristeller of Columbia University; Chauncey C. Loomis of Dartmouth College; Walter McCann of Athens College, Greece; George W. MacRae, S.J., of Harvard Divinity School; Stephen G. Nichols, Jr., of Dartmouth College; Sheldon Rothblatt of the University of California, Berkeley; Frederick Rudolph of Williams College; and an anonymous reviewer from the University of Chicago. For reading and commenting on the penultimate manuscript, I am indebted to Ted Estess, John Bernard, and John McNees of the Honors Program at the University of Houston, University Park.

In addition, I wish to thank two scholars whose published writings, conversation, and astonishing network of correspondence throughout academe, here and abroad, have aided me tremendously by providing an enormous number of references, introductions, and points of information and wisdom: James Luther Adams and David Riesman, Professors Emeriti of Harvard University.

Lastly, I wish to express particular gratitude for his instruction and help over several years to Joseph L. Featherstone, who is one of the finest teachers that I have known.

Another kind of debt is financial. For their generous support, without which this book might not have been published, I am indebted to the Publications Committee, Provost George W. Magner, and the Institute for Higher Education Law and Governance and its director, Michael A. Olivas, of the University of Houston. I also acknowledge fellowship support from the Fund for Theological Education of Princeton, N.J., which first brought me to Harvard Divinity School where this research was begun, and from the Henry Luce Foundation, which provided me with a year in Japan where I was able to gain a helpful perspective on American ideas of liberal education in 1945, the point at which this study concludes. I would also like to acknowledge the generosity of Professor Stephen K. Bailey, now deceased, of Harvard Graduate School of Education, who provided some postdoctoral support during the stringent year of 1981–1982 that helped me to continue work on this project after receiving my degree. For the opportunity and financial support that allowed me to reflect upon the relationship between utility and liberal studies, I am indebted to the Board of Trustees of the State Universities and Colleges of Maryland.

Permission received from two journals to incorporate material previously published elsewhere is also gratefully acknowledged. The first chapter herein is a revised version of my article, "The 'Liberal Education' Debate and Its Historical Appeals: Toward a Sorting Out and Appraisal," which appeared in *Liberal Education* 69 (1983): 321–333. The second chapter is a revised and shortened version of "Founders of Liberal Education: The Case for Roman Orators Against Socratic Philosophers," which appeared in *Teachers College Record* 85 (Winter 1983): 225–249. Parts of the fifth and seventh chapters appeared in a different form as "Liberal vs. Useful Education: Reevaluating the Historical Appeals to Benjamin Franklin and Aristotle," *Liberal Education* 67 (1981): 286–292. The material in chapter 3 excerpted from Louis J. Paetow's translation of *La bataille des VII ars* by Henri d'Andeli is used with the permission of the University of California Press.

For his exhaustive help in checking, standardizing, and organizing the bibliographical references in the footnotes, I would like to thank Raul Garza; and for their expert typing of the manuscript, more than once, I wish to thank Pamela Chance and Evelyn Rosenthal.

Finally, I cannot conclude without thanking my dearest friend and wife, Lynne K. Karlson, for her unfailing support and care throughout the long pilgrimage of this work.

ABBREVIATIONS

AACB   *Association of American Colleges Bulletin*

Actes   *Actes du quatrième Congrès international de philosophie médiévale: Arts libéraux et philosophie au moyen âge* (Montreal: Institut d'Etudes Médiévales, 1969).

Artes   Josef Koch, ed., *Artes Liberales von der antiken Bildung zur Wissenschaft des Mittelalters* (Leiden, Neth.: E. J. Brill, 1959).

Commission   Commission Internationale pour l'Histoire des Universités, *Les universités européennes du XIVe au XVIIIe siècle: Aspects et problèmes* (Geneva: Librairie Droz, 1967).

HEQ   *History of Education Quarterly*

Itinerarium Italicum   Heiko A. Oberman, ed., with Thomas A. Brady, Jr., *Itinerarium Italicum: The Profile of the Italian Renaissance in the Mirror of Its European Transformations* (Leiden, Neth.: E. J. Brill, 1975).

JHE   *Journal of Higher Education*

JHI   *Journal of the History of Ideas*

PH   *Paedagogica Historica*

SR   *Seminar Reports, Program of General Education in the Humanities, Columbia University*

The Universities   Jozef Ijsewijn and Jacques Paquet, eds., *The Universities in the Late Middle Ages* (Louvain, Belg.: Leuven University Press, 1978).

Unless otherwise indicated, citations of Greek and Latin texts refer to the Loeb Classical Library (Cambridge: Harvard University Press), and standard notational systems, such as Stephanus for Plato and Bekker for Aristotle, are used for reference. Translations of non-English works are my own, except as noted.

In order to conserve space and make the notes more useful, bibliographical references have been incorporated into the footnotes, and a full reference is given for each source the first time that it is cited within a chapter. Cross references to sources are available through the index of authors.

ORATORS & PHILOSOPHERS

A History of the Idea of Liberal Education

I
Introduction

MY QUARREL WITH THE SPOKESMEN *for liberal education results from their misrepresentation or misunderstanding of the history of higher education and of the true nature of liberal education, [and] their unsubstantiated claims for it.*

*FRANCIS H. HORN**

*"The Folklore of Liberal Education" (1955).

THE HISTORY OF LIBERAL EDUCATION is the story of a debate between orators and philosophers. At least, if one is willing to look
at the large picture and, most importantly, to follow the words "liberal arts" or "liberal education," this is what one finds. And the truth
of this assertion points to a number of paradoxes in the twentieth-
century American debate about liberal education.

The story is, first of all, very old—not only historically, because
it begins with Isocrates and Plato, but also historiographically, because it has long been evident in the writings of modern scholars
such as Hans von Arnim, Werner Jaeger, and Henri Marrou. Yet it
is also quite new in that no volume about the historical roots of
"liberal education" in America has taken adequate account of this
background. It is paradoxical also that, on the one hand, academicians since the turn of the century have criticized the impenetrable
morass of debate on this topic. As Abraham Flexner noted in 1908,
"The college is without clear-cut notions of what a liberal education
is and how it is to be secured, . . . and the pity of it is that this is
not a local or special disability, but a paralysis affecting every college of arts in America."[1] Yet, on the other hand, this swamp can be
navigated and, indeed, mapped if one is oriented by those two well-
known, distant peaks: one Ciceronian, the other Socratic. Finally, it
is paradoxical that, precisely on a topic where academicians are forever eager to appeal to history, many erect ahistorical and relativistic conceptions of "liberal education" as cairns to mark the trail.

Given all that has been and continues to be written about "liberal education," my statements might appear brash or presump-
tuous. After all, the chaos has only worsened since the director of
the American Council on Education reported in 1921 that among the
"thousands of papers and not a few books giving individual interpretations of the college of liberal arts," there exists "no more
agreement among the writers than among the requirements of the
institutions. Moreover, it is a significant fact that nobody pays any
attention to literature of this sort when it comes to defining the college of liberal arts."[2] Nevertheless, it is the intention of this enchiridion to explain and prove the claim that the morass of modern debate
can be navigated and charted if the lineage of the discussion is
properly understood. The fundamental method will be to follow the

---

[1] Flexner was quoting the president of Cornell University. Abraham Flexner, *The American College: A Criticism* (New York: Century, 1908), p. 7.
[2] Samuel P. Capen, "The Dilemma of the College of Arts and Sciences," *Educational Review* 61 (1921): 277–278.

words "liberal education" or "liberal arts" through history and to evaluate the rationales associated with them so as to emerge from the swamp with a map, a simple typology, that will be helpful in making sense of the conflict and confusion in present discourse.

This approach, while inductive and descriptive rather than conjectural and prescriptive, comports more with the history of ideas than with the social history that has dominated the historiography of education in recent decades. The approach is not, then, *au courant*. But the surprising fact is that, despite the great volume of published material about "liberal education," little effort has been made to understand the historical meaning of the term in order to relate this legacy to the debate in contemporary America, by which I mean the last four or five decades in the United States. To be sure, there are dangers in looking into the past and abstracting general "types" from observers' statements, curricular programs, and the writings of masters in schools and colleges. Our thoughts are not necessarily the thoughts of our ancestors, and integrity of context must be respected. Still, such artificial constructs can be helpful in providing a frame of interpretation if their use is qualified and ambiguities as well as exceptions are noted.

No less surprising is the fact that a great deal of historical scholarship could be brought to bear on this topic and yet is rarely consulted. One cannot read everything, of course, but it is true that American writings on the history of liberal education too often neglect the essays from the conference at Cologne, compiled in *Artes Liberales von der antiken Bildung zur Wissenschaft des Mittelalters* (1959), from the Quatrième Congrès International de Philosophie Médiévale, published in *Actes . . . Arts libéraux et philosophie au moyen âge* (1969); or from works such as Eugenio Garin's *L'educazione in europa, 1400/1600: Problemi e programmi* (1976).[3] Similarly, in regard to the twentieth century in the United States, although the big names are always noted—Aydelotte, Meiklejohn, Hutchins; Chicago, Columbia, Harvard—much of the literature such as the publications of the Association of American Colleges, which from its inception in 1914 has dedicated itself to discussion and defense of "liberal education," has scarcely been consulted.

In view of these omissions, one may well ask preliminarily about the nature of recent discussion on liberal education, and perusal of

---

[3]An important contribution in this regard is made by David L. Wagner, ed., *The Seven Liberal Arts in the Middle Ages* (Bloomington: Indiana University Press, 1983).

American writings since the turn of the century reveals certain categories of attempts at defining the term. There exists, for example, an operational definition that can often be found in large surveys and that holds, as was stated by Louis Bénézet in 1943, that "it seems best to use 'liberal education' in the baldest possible operational sense: that is 'that kind of education which a liberal arts college program provides.' "⁴ This operational definition was employed in the 1932 yearbook of the National Society for the Study of Education, and it is still evident today in studies such as National Project IV: Liberal Education Varieties and Their Assessment, sponsored by the federal Fund for the Improvement of Post-secondary Education. In this approach, the researcher looks for institutions that claim they are, or are assumed to be, offering "liberal education" and studies them.

Alternatively, there are those who define the term by prescribing an unsystematic "basket" of all educational goods that seem important to them. Committees are especially prone to this "basket" gambit—witness the 1947 Presidential Commission on Higher Education, the 1952 Blackmer Committee, and the 1970 Four-School Study Committee. Then, too, there are those who absolutize an a priori definition by latching onto a particular understanding of liberal education and construing it as the normative definition of the term. Such is the approach employed by commentators who cite the educational upheavals of the 1960s and 1970s and then associate liberal education with "the liberation arts," "libertarian education," and "liberating education." The myopia of this definition becomes evident if we note that already in the 1920s and 1930s "ten thousand Commencement speakers annually explained that the liberal arts were the liberating arts."⁵ A further problem is revealed by the comments of those who give a countervailing twist to such references to freeing or liberating: "Liberal education, most people would agree, aims to liberate the powers of the individual by disciplining them." Jacques Maritain in 1943, William Cunningham in 1953, and Theodore deBary in 1973 each spoke in this way.⁶ Meanwhile, there

---

⁴Louis T. Bénézet, *General Education in the Progressive College* (New York: Bureau of Publications, Teachers College, Columbia University, 1943), p. 28.

⁵Jacques Barzun, "Humanities, Pieties, Practicalities, Universities," *SR* 1 (November 14, 1973): 1.

⁶Quotation is from W. Theodore deBary, "General Education and the Humanities," *SR* 1 (October 22, 1973): 1. See similar language in Jacques Maritain, *Education at the Crossroads* (New Haven, Conn.: Yale University Press, 1943), pp. 10, 11, 14; William F. Cunningham, *General Education and the Liberal College* (St. Louis: B. Herder, 1953), pp. 17–18, 77, 153.

are those who dedicate liberal education or liberal arts education, "in the original, classical sense of that term," to "the education of a citizen" according to the "highest ideals" of character and virtue.[7]

This mention of "the original, classical sense" of liberal education significantly exemplifies how definitions of the term are frequently couched in appeals to history. Perhaps most often heard is something like the view of a recent president of Barnard College, who took for granted that the "first description" of "liberal education" lay "in words attributed to Socrates in the writings of both Plato and Aristotle."[8] Attribution to the Socratic triumvirate is often expressed more generally, as a claim that "the notion of a liberal education was introduced by the Greeks," with that notion then being defined as "this ideal of pursuing knowledge for its own sake."[9] Contradicting that opinion, however, is the appeal made by other scholars not to philosophers, but to Greek and Latin orators such as Isocrates, Cicero, and Quintilian. And even greater disagreement is heard from those who believe that the idea of liberal education "is a fairly recent one and a local one" because, as President Harold Taylor of Sarah Lawrence College stated:

> Liberal education is the intellectual and cultural instrument through which the basic ideas of liberalism are transmitted and developed. . . . The central idea of liberal education is therefore the idea of individualism and individual freedom. . . . It has its origin in the Western world, in political and social changes which began in the seventeenth century with the discovery of a new universe and a new world.[10]

This view is often accompanied by mention of Benjamin Franklin's and John Dewey's ideas on education, as will become clear later on.

---

[7]Waldemar Zagars, *The Liberal Arts Education: A Popular Myth* (Gettysburg, Pa.: Baltic, 1977), pp. 21, 221.

[8]Jacquelyn A. Mattfeld, "The Predicament of Liberal Education," *SR* 5 (1977): 136. See also Alvin Johnson, *Liberal Education Fact and Fiction* (New York: New School for Social Research, 1945), pp. 1–7; Paul Hirst, "Liberal Education," in *The Encyclopedia of Education*, ed. Lee C. Deighton (New York: Macmillan, 1971), vol. 5, p. 505.

[9]Richard S. Peters, "Ambiguities in Liberal Education and the Problem of Its Content," in *Ethics and Educational Policy*, ed. Kenneth A. Strike and Kieran Egan (London: Routledge and Kegan Paul, 1978), pp. 4, 6. See J. Winfree Smith, *A Search for the Liberal College: The Beginning of the St. John's Program* (Annapolis, Md.: St. John's College Press, 1983), p. 18.

[10]Harold Taylor, "Individualism and the Liberal Tradition," in *The Goals of Higher Education*, ed. Willis D. Weatherford, Jr. (Cambridge: Harvard University Press, 1960), pp. 9–10.

Turning to explicitly historical essays written in the context of twentieth-century American education,[11] one finds similar categories of analyses. There is a group of histories, for example, that employ the operational definition described above. In 1957, G. P. Schmidt published *The Liberal Arts College: A Chapter in American Cultural History* without explaining how he identified a "liberal arts college." Apparently, he simply followed those institutions that said they were liberal arts colleges and granted what they said were liberal arts degrees. Only toward the end of the book does Schmidt state that "the liberal arts concept will not admit to definition." He allows only that it is associated with "the liberal values" and "the liberal philosophy," which concepts are never clearly explained.[12]

---

[11]The weakness and inconsistency in many lengthier historical essays about "liberal education" and "liberal arts" written in the American context are seen briefly in the following examples. In *The Seven Liberal Arts* (New York: Bureau of Publications, Teachers College, Columbia University, 1906), p. 1, Paul Abelson acknowledged and endeavored to correct this problem, but John Wise noted little improvement over forty years later in *The Nature of the Liberal Arts* (Milwaukee: Bruce, 1947), p. 13. Subsequently, Wise's historical "scholarly treatise" was touted in an essay on liberal education by Francis H. Horn, future president of the University of Rhode Island, "The Folklore of Liberal Education," *AACB* 41 (1955): 114. This opinion, however, was quite divergent from that expressed by classical scholar Lambert de Rijk, "*Enkuklios Paideia*: A Study of Its Original Meaning," *Vivarium* 3 (1965): 24–25; and revising his essay for republication, Horn later eliminated the word "scholarly," *Challenge and Perspective in Higher Education* (Carbondale: Southern Illinois University Press, 1971), p. 24. In the meantime, R. F. Butts had turned out his lengthy but polemical *The College Charts Its Course* (New York: McGraw-Hill, 1939), which E. J. McGrath, neglecting Wise who had neglected Butts, called "an invaluable source on the early beginnings of liberal education in Western culture," *Liberal Education in the Professions* (New York: Bureau of Publications, Teachers College, Columbia University, 1959), p. 9. McGrath's book was in turn cited as the normative treatment of liberal education in an avalanche of comparative studies published by the Institute of Higher Education at Teachers College, Columbia University, over the next decade. See, for example, Charles H. Russell, *Liberal Education and Nursing* (New York: Bureau of Publications, Teachers College, Columbia University, 1959); Paul L. Dressel, *Liberal Education and Journalism* (New York: Bureau of Publications, Teachers College, Columbia University, 1960); Willis J. Wager and Earl J. McGrath, *Liberal Education and Music* (New York: Bureau of Publications, Teachers College, Columbia University, 1962); Jeanette A. Lee and Paul L. Dressel, *Liberal Education and Home Economics* (New York: Bureau of Publications, Teachers College, Columbia University, 1963); William E. Simons, *Liberal Education in the Service Academies* (New York: Bureau of Publications, Teachers College, Columbia University, 1965). Butts devoted sixty of his four hundred pages to the period before 1758 and, like Wise, gave very little attention to Samuel E. Morison's *The Founding of Harvard College* (Cambridge: Harvard University Press, 1935), which Bernard Bailyn identifies as still "the leading work . . . on the idea of liberal arts education in the sixteenth and seventeenth centuries, especially as it was passed on to the American colonies" (personal correspondence, 8 February 1980).

[12]George P. Schmidt, *The Liberal Arts College: A Chapter in American Cultural History* (New Brunswick, N.J.: Rutgers Unaiversity Press, 1957), p. 238, chap. 12.

Similarly, in Willis Rudy's *The Evolving Liberal Arts Curriculum: A Historical Review of Basic Themes* (1960), "liberal arts" is defined only as "the course of study as it has developed historically in the traditional four-year American liberal arts college." Gradually, the reader comes to understand that "liberal education" is what one receives a liberal arts degree for, and that, while it is implicitly nonvocational and nontechnical, the interpretations of it can range from "pragmatist-progressivist" to "humanist-traditionalist." Explicit in Rudy's title is the presupposition that liberal arts or liberal education can and does evolve, can and does change. This is a constituent aspect of the operational definition of liberal education,[13] which is relativistic and, apparently, subject to whosoever may claim to offer "liberal education."

In a larger context, this operational definition may be found in Thomas Woody's *Liberal Education for Free Men* (1951), recently reprinted and still recommended in popular encyclopedias for further reading on liberal education. Woody's history assumes that liberal education amounts to the highest educational ideals of any particular culture at any particular time. One can therefore speak about "Chinese Modes of Liberal Learning," as well as Athenian or American, because the ideals informing liberal education change from age to age and culture to culture, a view reaffirmed by E. J. McGrath's historical essay a decade later.[14]

Opposing such relativism are historical essays presupposing that "there must be something fundamental and lasting," something permanent and absolute, underlying statements about liberal arts by the learned figures of history. Everett Martin expressed this opinion in 1926, as did Norman Foerster in 1939; but the foregoing words belong to John Wise, who embraced something akin to the "basket" definition in *The Nature of the Liberal Arts* (1947). His desideratum being fundamental continuity, Wise constructed a brief definition broad enough to include every eminent educational thinker of history and looked for continuity in Plato, Aristotle, Cicero, Quintilian, Augustine, Aquinas, the *ratio studiorum*, and John Henry

---

[13]Earl J. McGrath, "Preface," in *The Evolving Liberal Arts Curriculum: A Historical Review of Basic Themes*, Willis Rudy (New York: Bureau of Publications, Teachers College, Columbia University, 1960), p. iv; Rudy (1960), pp. 36–37, chap. 10. See also Saul Sack, "Liberal Education: What Was It? What Is It? *HEQ* 2 (1962): 210.

[14]Thomas Woody, *Liberal Education for Free Men* (Philadelphia: University of Pennsylvania Press, 1951), pp. 1–3, chap. 1; Richard R. Renner, "Liberal Education," in *Encyclopedia Americana* (Danbury, Conn.: Americana, 1978), vol. 17, p. 292; McGrath (1959), p. 18, chap. 2.

Newman. Earlier, Martin had incorporated a long list of goods in his basket definition, while mentioning Socrates, Plato, Cicero, Erasmus, Voltaire, Goethe, and Thomas H. Huxley.[15]

Another variant of the approach assuming historical continuity in liberal education might be termed the a priori definition. Here, one largely ignores how, when, or by whom the words "liberal education" or "liberal arts" were used and begins with an a priori idea of what "liberal education" ought to mean. Then one follows the development of that idea and calls it the history of liberal education. In particular, progressivists and pragmatists have tended to write in this fashion. In 1935, for example, a Bucknell professor set "liberalizing" education "on the side of dynamic achievement rather than of authoritarianism" and the "dry-rot of formalism" in all its guises. Tracing the development of various notions of individualism, egalitarianism, and freedom, the histories of L. F. Snow (1907), A. O. Hansen (1926), and R. F. Butts (1939) promoted the kind of definition that Harold Taylor attributed to the seventeenth century and that Rudy called the "pragmatist-progressivist" idea of liberal education.[16]

Related to the concern for freedom, but more narrowly drawn, is the a priori definition that says liberal education means a liberating or a freeing of the mind to pursue truth. In a brief essay written in 1944, J. H. Randall, Jr., moves from Greek *paideia* to Roman *humanitas* to *artes liberales*, while asserting that "that art is 'liberal,' whatever it may be, which *liberates* man, which releases the freedom of the mind, which effectively promotes the function that the traditional 'liberal arts' used to perform." As evident in Randall's formulations, this kind of definition tends to claim more ancient roots than the "pragmatist-progressivist" idea; and this claim has often been repeated in historical statements by distinguished educational philosophers, such as P. H. Hirst and R. S. Peters.[17] More

---

[15]Everett D. Martin, *The Meaning of a Liberal Education* (New York: W. W. Norton, 1926), p. 22; Wise (1947), pp. 7–16; Norman Foerster, "United States," in *The Meaning of Liberal Education in the Twentieth Century*, ed. Isaac L. Kandel (New York: Bureau of Publications, Teachers College, Columbia University, 1939), p. 337.

[16]Philip L. Harriman, "Antecedents of the Liberal-Arts College: To Conserve the Best Values of the Past and to Create the Most Worthy Needs of the Present," *JHE* 6 (1935): 63; Louis F. Snow, *The College Curriculum in the United States* (New York: Bureau of Publications, Teachers College, Columbia University, 1907); Allen O. Hansen, *Liberalism and American Education in the Eighteenth Century* (New York: Macmillan, 1926).

[17]John H. Randall, Jr., "Which Are the Liberating Arts?" *The American Scholar* 13 (1944): 142–143; Hirst (1971); Peters (1978).

recently, Charles Wegener incorporated aspects of both the freeing-the-intellect and the progressivist interpretations of liberal education into his own definition, which he drew from the historical context of the American research university.[18]

In fine, a brief overview of writings about "liberal education" and about its history reveals contradiction and confusion; and the more that is written, the more confounded things become. This observation presents nothing new. What is surprising is that there has been so little effort to proceed inductively by actually following the words "liberal education" or "liberal arts" in order to understand how the present state of affairs came about. One writer who did take such an approach was Sheldon Rothblatt, and his history of English "liberal education" is far more informative than any operational, basket, or a priori gambit.[19] In fact, these other approaches have little to say about the definition of "liberal education," I suggest, because they effectively ignore the fundamental question, which concerns the historical interpretation of the term.

With respect to definitions incorporating historical appeals, this relationship is obvious. If one maintains that "liberal education" appeared first "in words attributed to Socrates in the writings of both Plato and Aristotle," the question of definition is clear. Presumably, one could look back to the writings of those philosophers, see if Socrates used the words "liberal education," and ask exactly what they meant. But even when no such appeal is made, either implicitly or explicitly, contemporary definitions still fundamentally depend upon the history of the term.

Initially, this might not appear to be the case, for how can it be said that a professor or a college that invents its own definition of liberal education relies upon the lineage of the words? One reason is the fact that "liberal education" is not an arbitrary term as is, say, "alpha education." Institutions and academicians, no matter how they define liberal education, choose that term intentionally; and they do so because the words command a certain stature and respect. If the 1981 volume *The New Liberal Arts* from the Sloan Foundation had been titled *The Alpha Arts*, it would clearly have

---

[18]Charles Wegener, *Liberal Education and the Modern University* (Chicago: University of Chicago Press, 1978), p. 95, chaps. 1–2.

[19]Sheldon Rothblatt, *Tradition and Change in English Liberal Education: An Essay in History and Culture* (London: Faber and Faber, 1976). A converse example can be found in Frederick Rudolph's *Curriculum: A History of the American Undergraduate Course of Study since 1636* (San Francisco: Jossey-Bass, 1977), which is sometimes cited as a history of "liberal education," but which scarcely employs the term.

been regarded as idiosyncratic by its readers.[20] The words "liberal education" or "liberal arts" carry a certain weight, a certain respectability, even when used relativistically, and this prestige derives only from historical usage. As the director of Education Programs for the National Youth Administration grumbled in 1940:

> Does not everyone desire to share in liberal education? Does anyone venture to render an adverse judgement against anything that is liberal? With the verbal advantage that comes from the description of the traditional curriculum as made up of liberal subjects, the traditionalists lay claim to all the territory.[21]

This claim to the prestige of the term stands whether or not explicit historical attributions are made that Lao-tzu or Socrates or Isocrates or the *philosophes* or John Dewey invented liberal education.

Now, even those who appreciate the fundamental significance of the historical question may dismiss such attributions because "advocates of liberal education have usually subscribed," the popular sources tell us, ". . . to principles first clearly enunciated by Aristotle."[22] But this contention begs the question. If one presupposes rather than demonstrates that "liberal education" means a kind of education invented by Greek philosophers, then the statement that "the notion of a liberal education was introduced by the Greeks" rests on the circular reasoning that a kind of education introduced by the Greeks was introduced by the Greeks. Instead, the proper starting point would seem to be the question, When, where, and how did the term "liberal education" or "liberal arts" come into use?

To be sure, the answer, if there is one, is not going to determine the "correct" definition of liberal education today. The meanings of words change over history; and even if they did not, no law prohibits the unhistorical use of words. But since a preference exists for "liberal education" above "alpha education," it is contradictory to invoke the former term due to its implicit prestige, which derives from respect gained through past usage, and then to attempt to define it arbitrarily. I say "attempt" because, apart from the unseverable link of prestige implicitly obtaining between the his-

---

[20]James D. Koerner, ed., *The New Liberal Arts: An Exchange of Views* (New York: Alfred P. Sloan Foundation, 1981).
[21]Charles H. Judd, "The Organization of a Program of General Education in Secondary Schools and Colleges," *AACB* 26 (1940): 303.
[22]Hirst (1971), p. 505.

tory of "liberal education" and contemporary statements about it, whether those statements are historically conscious or not, it does turn out that if the history of ideas associated with the term is understood, particularly in terms of a debate between orators and philosophers, then much of the seeming relativity, arbitrariness, contradiction, and confusion in current discussion can be explained and rationalized. This being so, the historical interpretation of the term will finally be seen to shape the contours of contemporary American debate, even though such influence may not be acknowledged or understood by the discussants themselves.

The following chapters present an interpretation of the history of the ideals underlying the education that people have identified as "liberal." Given the span of centuries and the mass of evidence, the interpretation is perforce a general one. One could spend a lifetime reading—and writing—many more volumes about the history of liberal education. What I have tried to do is to gather as much of the influential testimony about liberal education as I could, to weigh it carefully, and to present an interpretation that seems to make sense overall. Nevertheless, the reader should be aware that certain conclusions have influenced the presentation. It has seemed to me that, by and large, American higher education in the second half of the twentieth century holds Socrates, rather than Cicero, as its paragon; that the purpose, rationale, structure, and content of its liberal education are, in a fundamental sense, Socratic and Platonic; and that the history of liberal education that it prefers to report concerns exclusively the philosophical ideal of liberal education: the continuing, ever-critical search for truth. The following chapters therefore try to balance what this observer considers to be a skewed understanding of the history of liberal education, an understanding that has been shaped by the particular nature of American higher education in the current era. Through this effort, it is hoped that some of the confusion that has plagued discussion about liberal education since the turn of the century may be lessened, and that the dilemmas of liberal education may be posed more firmly upon a historical basis and thereby understood more clearly than they have been in recent times.

II
Foundation
of the
Artes Liberales

*T*HUS I THINK THAT NO ONE *ought to be num-*
bered among the orators who is not pol-
ished in all those arts that are proper for a free cit-
izen.

CICERO*

*W*E ARE, THEN, EDUCATING *that perfect orator,*
who must be a good man; and therefore we
require in him not only exceptional talent for
speaking but also all virtues of the soul.

QUINTILIAN†

*De oratore.
†Institutio oratoria.

I N VIEW OF THE PRESENT DISAGREEMENT concerning the origins of "liberal education," "liberal arts," "liberal disciplines," and so forth, it may be best to begin the story by citing the most elemental facts upon which there is widespread agreement. Etymological roots of the word "liberal," used in regard to education, are found in the Latin *liberalis*,[1] an adjective applied for centuries to various words regarding education: *disciplinae liberales, studia liberalia, doctrinae liberales, litterae liberales*, and, especially, *artes liberales*. These terms abound in writings from the Renaissance, from the late Middle Ages, and on back from Isidore in the seventh century, Cassiodorus in the sixth century, Augustine in the fourth century, Quintilian in the first century C.E., and Cicero in the first century B.C.E. In fact, to the writings of Cicero has been attributed the earliest recorded use of *artes liberales*,[2] although, even if true, the attribution does not prove that he invented the term. For one thing, Cicero employs *artes liberales* in a way to suggest that it was commonly used in his day. Furthermore, there is evidence that *liberalis* had direct antecedents in Greek.

Another elemental fact about the history of the term "liberal education" is that in Roman antiquity *liberalis* denoted "of or relating to free men." Quite significantly, this denotation implied both the status of social and political freedom, as opposed to slavery, and the possession of wealth, affording free time for leisure. Thus, *liberalis* characterized the *liber*, the free citizen who was "gentlemanly or ladylike . . . magnanimous, noble, . . . munificent, generous," as well as the "studies, education, arts, professions" in which the free citizen participated. *Liberalis* descended to English where it appeared as "libral, liberal, lyberal, liberall," and other forms in the fourteenth and fifteenth centuries, with the associations to leisure still intact: "pertaining to or suitable to persons of superior social station, 'becoming a gentleman.' "[3]

---

[1]Occasionally in modern writings, as in the work of Cassiodorus and Isidore, one will find speculation linking *liberalis* to the Roman god Līber or to *līber*, meaning "book," rather than to *līber*, meaning "free person." Friedmar Kühnert, *Allgemeinbildung und Fachbildung in der Antike* (Berlin: Akademie-Verlag, 1961), pp. 4–5; Paul L. Dressel, "Liberal Education: Developing the Characteristics of a Liberally Educated Person," *Liberal Education* 65 (1979): 314.

[2]Cicero, *De inventione* 1.35; Kühnert (1961), p. 4; John F. Dobson, *Ancient Education and Its Meaning to Us* (New York: Longmans, Green, 1932), p. 127.

[3]*The Oxford Latin Dictionary*, s.v. "liberalis"; Chaim Wirszubski, *Libertas as a Political Ideal at Rome during the Late Republic and Early Principate* (Cambridge: Cambridge University Press, 1950), pp. 1–15; *The Oxford English Dictionary*, s.v. "liberal."

In addition to that lineage, the fact is undisputed that "seven liberal arts" were idealized as a normative program of education through the Middle Ages, and possibly much earlier. These *septem artes liberales* were recorded in countless medieval manuscripts and comprised three subjects concerning language—grammar, rhetoric, and logic (or dialectic)—plus four mathematical or "scientific" subjects—arithmetic, geometry, music, and astronomy. However, this does not mean that educators from Roman antiquity to the Renaissance agreed on the rationales underlying the *septem artes liberales* or even on the content of each of the individual arts. "Grammar" meant something quite different to Isidore in the seventh century than did "grammar" at the University of Paris in the thirteenth century. In view of this discontinuity, one must finally ask about the character of the original *artes liberales*, and the answer to this question requires an evaluation of the arguments of the many modern scholars who trace the foundation of "liberal education" beyond the Roman Republic to Plato's Athens.

It is another of those elemental facts that Greeks, or Athenians, of the fifth and fourth centuries B.C.E. developed the idea of educating in a cultural ideal the free citizens with leisure to study. This idea is part of the harvest of the "pedagogical century" extending from about 450 to 350 B.C.E.,[4] and one can justifiably identify the origins of "liberal education," or *artes liberales*, very broadly with the education of free Athenians during that time. However, such a broad definition is rather unsatisfying, and a problem arises when, as often happens, modern educators try to be more specific and attribute to these Athenians one particular idea or program of ideas for "liberal education." Despite warnings, many academicians make this attempt,[5] and it will be helpful to evaluate such arguments under three categories.

First is the approach presupposing that one particular rationale dominated the education of free citizens with leisure to study. That

---

[4]Richard Meister, "Die Entstehung der höheren Allgemeinbildung in der Antike," in *Erziehung und Bildung in der heidnischen und christlichen Antike*, ed. Horst-Theodor Johann (Darmstadt, W.Ger.: Wissenschaftliche Buchgesellschaft, 1976), p. 26; Frederick A. Beck, *Greek Education, 450–350 B.C.* (London: Methuen, 1964).

[5]For example: "Even at this early stage, then, [fourth century B.C.E.] the people who were most interested in the full span of subjects were philosophers; and the seven liberal arts were in essence, and always remained, a philosophers' curriculum." William H. Stahl and Richard Johnson, with E. L. Burge, *Martianus Capella and the Seven Liberal Arts* (New York: Columbia University Press, 1971), vol. 1, p. 91. Sack warned against attributing to the Greeks the primary idea of liberal education. Saul Sack, "Liberal Education: What Was It? What Is It?" *HEQ* 2 (1962): 210–224.

dominant rationale is almost always described as "this ideal of pursuing knowledge for its own sake" and then linked to Socrates, Plato, and Aristotle. Second is the effort to find an etymological bridge between *liberalis* and the Greeks. Here three possibilities are commonly advanced. One is *skholē*, the Greek word denoting "leisure, rest, ease," which came to mean "that in which leisure is employed . . . especially learned discussion, disputation, lecture." Eventually, *skholē* came also to denote the "group to whom lectures were given, [a] school," in other words, the people or institution that practices what one does with leisure. *Skholē* passed into Latin as *schola* and eventually into English as "school," and some take it to be a significant link to Greek education for leisure or "liberal education."[6] Another oft-cited etymological bridge is *eleutherios*, which can be literally translated as "fit for a free man, liberal"; and this is precisely the rendering made in the standard translations of Aristotle's discussions of education relied upon by many modern commentators on "liberal education." *Eleutherios*—especially when applied to *tekhnai*, the Greek word for *artes*—has thus been considered the most direct link to Athenian "liberal education."[7] Lastly, *artes liberales* has sometimes been regarded as a translation of the Greek term *enkuklios paideia*, meaning "general education, prior to professional studies." Since *enkuklios paideia* eventually provided the root for such English words as "encyclopedic," good reason exists for the rendering "general education"; and the *Oxford Classical Dictionary* does not differentiate between this term and the applications of *eleutherios* described above.[8]

The curious thing, however, about the last etymological approach is that *enkuklios paideia* can in no way be literally translated as *artes liberales*, and this fact has not gone unnoticed.[9] What the

---

[6]Henry G. Liddell and Robert Scott, *A Greek-English Lexicon*, rev. ed., 2 vols. (Oxford: Clarendon, 1940), s.v. "σχολή"; Jacob Klein, "The Idea of Liberal Education," in *The Goals of Higher Education*, ed. Willis D. Weatherford, Jr. (Cambridge: Harvard University Press, 1960), pp. 26–41; William K. Frankena, *Three Historical Philosophies of Education: Aristotle, Kant, Dewey* (Glenview, Ill.: Scott, Foresman, 1965), pp. 63–65.

[7]Quotation is from Liddell and Scott (1940), s.v. "ἐλευθέριος." See Andrew F. West, *Alcuin and the Rise of the Christian Schools* (New York: Charles Scribner's Sons, 1901), pp. 4–5; Henri Marrou, "Les arts libéraux dans l'antiquité classique," in *Actes* (1969), pp. 11, 31; Hans J. Mette, "ΕΓΚΥΚΛΙΟΣ ΠΑΙΔΕΙΑ," in *Erziehung und Bildung in der heidnischen und christlichen Antike*, ed. Horst-Theodor Johann (Darmstadt: Buchgesellschaft, 1976), pp. 32–33.

[8]Quotation is from Liddell and Scott (1940), s.v. "ἐγκύκλιος παιδεία." See *The Oxford Classical Dictionary*, 2d ed., s.v. "encyclopaedic learning."

[9]Raymond Klibansky, "Questions et discussions," in *Actes* (1969), p. 30.

frequent citing of *enkuklios paideia* turns into, therefore, is a third kind of appeal to the Greeks for the origins of "liberal education." It is an appeal based on the assumption that the program of seven liberal arts extended back from the Middle Ages through Roman antiquity to Plato's Athens. Thus, it presupposes a significant degree of continuity in a normative curriculum that is believed to have been established by the Greeks and renamed *septem artes liberales* by the Romans.

Needless to say, these three kinds of appeals to Athenian education—theoretical, etymological, and curricular—are by no means as distinct as just described. Whether in popular encyclopedias or academic forums, the latter two rationales are frequently swirled together, especially in regard to *enkuklios paideia*, while individuals appealing to a dominant theory of education often make an etymological argument through their choice of translations. Yet in whatever combination, none of these three appeals can bear scrutiny when set against the standard historical outline of ancient education. This can first be seen concerning the approach presupposing the existence of a dominant theory of Athenian education for free citizens with leisure to study.

Many generations prior to the "pedagogical century," the Hellenic concept of education had been founded upon the pursuit of *aretē* (excellence or virtue) defined according to the code of valor of the Attic-Ionian aristocracy.[10] Central to this program was the recitation of Homeric epic poetry, both to provide technical instruction in language and, more importantly, to inculcate the knightly mores and noble ethic of the culture. Upon the disintegration of this tradition with the rise of democracy in the fifth century B.C.E., three

---

[10]Willem J. Verdenius, *Homer, the Educator of the Greeks* (Amsterdam: North Holland, 1970), pp. 1–7, 15ff. In the following discussion of competing definitions of *aretē*, I draw from Hans von Arnim, *Leben und Werke des Dio von Prusa mit einer Einleitung: Sophistik, Rhetorik, Philosophie in ihrem Kampf um die Jugendbildung* (Berlin: Weidmannsche Buchhandlung, 1898), pp. 5–114; Werner Jaeger, *Paideia: The Ideals of Greek Culture*, trans. Gilbert Highet, 2d ed. (Oxford: Basil Blackwell, 1939), vol. 1; Henri I. Marrou, *A History of Education in Antiquity*, trans. George Lamb (New York: Sheed and Ward, 1956), pt. 1, chaps. 5–8; Everett L. Hunt, "Plato and Aristotle on Rhetoric and Rhetoricians," in *Historical Studies of Rhetoric and Rhetoricians*, ed. Raymond F. Howes (Ithaca, N.Y.: Cornell University Press, 1961), pp. 19–26; Norman Roseman, "Protagoras and the Foundations of His Educational Thought," *PH* 11 (1971): 75–89; F. C. White, "Protagoras as a Moral Educator," *PH* 15 (1975): 128–141; Beck (1964), pp. 151–183; Lambert de Rijk, "*Enkuklios Paideia*: A Study of Its Original Meaning," *Vivarium* 3 (1965): 45–57; George Kennedy, *The Art of Persuasion in Greece* (Princeton, N.J.: Princeton University Press, 1963).

principal groups responded with programs of education to prepare the free citizens for their new role in governing society.

Certain individuals, such as Gorgias, Protagoras, Prodicus, and Hippias, taught the skills of composing, delivering, and analyzing a speech. Such skills were crucial in a democratic city-state where winning votes determined the outcome of every question arising both in deliberative bodies, which were concerned with making law, and in judicial assemblies, where forensic presentations were required. These individuals acquired the name "wise man" or "teacher" (*sophistēs*), for they claimed to teach a kind of wisdom (*sophia*) or *aretē* that was political: the ideal methods for making one's point and winning arguments, that is, for participating in the democratic city-state. The sophists thus attended more to devising persuasive techniques than to finding true arguments, and this amoralism exacerbated the disintegration of the ethical tradition and led to their condemnation by Plato in *Gorgias* and by Isocrates in *Against the Sophists*.[11] Nevertheless, students flocked to the sophists as they traveled about imparting their methods of persuasion.

A different response to the cultural disintegration came from those associated with Plato (427–346), who, looking back to Socrates' never-ending quest for truth, regarded intellectual culture and philosophy as the ideal for the education of the citizen. It was with this in mind that Plato distinguished between *sophia* and *philosophia*, thereby affirming that highest truth is never attained—the search proceeds endlessly.[12] Relying upon the Socratic belief that knowledge leads directly to virtue, he translated Homeric *aretē* into the pursuit of highest knowledge through dialectic, an endeavor that liberates the mind from the chains of its shadowy cave of ignorance. Notwithstanding certain differences, this commitment to philosophy was transmitted to Plato's students, most notably Aristotle (384–322), who argued in *Nicomachean Ethics* that highest happiness is achieved in the pursuit of "theoretical knowledge or contemplation . . . for intelligence is the highest possession we have in us."[13]

Teaching next to Plato and sharing his concern over the deterioration of Athenian mores was Isocrates (436–338), who offered a third response both in his school and in his writings—chiefly *Against*

---

[11]Plato, *Gorgias* 502–522; Isocrates, *Against the Sophists* 2–11, 19–20.

[12]Plato, *Lysis* 218a, *Symposium* 203d–204b, *Phaedrus* 278d, *Republic* 394d.

[13]Aristotle, *Nicomachean Ethics*, trans. Martin Ostwald (Indianapolis: Bobbs-Merrill, 1962) 1177a11–1179a33.

the Sophists and *Antidosis*. Though often identified with the sophists, he is more properly distinguished from that group, as Plato acknowledged.[14] This is because Isocrates criticized the sophists for their emphasis on rhetorical display and technique at the expense of character ideals while he adopted, with very little analysis, the noble values of the past—the traditional standards of virtue recognized in epical heroes—as the *aretē* of his educational ideal. Isocrates thus extolled the orator who would live out the noble virtues and persuade the free citizen of the democratic city-state to adhere to them.[15]

If both Isocrates and Plato opposed the sophists, they were scarcely less critical of each other. Isocrates was profoundly skeptical of the dialectical search for truth, the central pillar of the Socratic-Platonic education. He scoffed at the distinction between *sophia* and *philosophia* and chided those who would waste time in endless speculation to arrive at wisdom. In this fashion, he denied Plato's speculative vision, and he claimed for his orator the title "philosopher" because the height of philosophy was, in his view, attained in oratorical eloquence: "to speak well and think right."[16] To all this, Plato replied by defending the worth of advanced speculation and urging Isocrates to pursue the intellectual quest involved in true philosophy.[17] Moreover, he argued again and again, in *Gorgias*, *Protagoras*, and *Phaedrus*, that rhetoric is mere sophistry if it is divorced from truth, which can be ascertained only through philosophical dialectic.

Such, in very broad terms, were the primary rationales for education of free Greek citizens with leisure to study advanced in the "pedagogical century." Subsequently, while Alexander was establishing his empire, a consensus began to emerge. More and more, the Hellenistic elite looked to the model of Isocrates for their training, as orators such as Demosthenes and Aeschines, rather than philosopher-kings, dominated public affairs. "Plato had been de-

---

[14]Plato, *Phaedrus* 278e–279a. On this important point compare Charles S. Baldwin, *Medieval Rhetoric and Poetry (to 1400) Interpreted from Representative Works* (New York: Macmillan, 1928), pp. 5–6; Donald L. Clark, *Rhetoric in Greco-Roman Education* (New York: Columbia University Press, 1957), pp. 6–7; Kennedy (1963), p. 79; George Kennedy, *The Art of Rhetoric in the Roman World, 300 B.C.–A.D. 300* (Princeton, N.J.: Princeton University Press, 1972), p. 59; Hartmut Erbse, "Platons Urteil über Isokrates," *Hermes* 99 (1971): 183–197.

[15]Isocrates, *Against the Sophists* 1–11, 19, 20, *Antidosis* 184, 252, 267–271, 274–278.

[16]Isocrates, *Against the Sophists* 8, *Antidosis* 268–277, 304–305. Quotation is from the translation of *Antidosis* 277 by George Norlin (New York: G.P. Putnam's, 1928).

[17]Plato, *Gorgias* 484d–488a, *Phaedrus* 278b–279a.

feated: posterity had not accepted his educational ideals," writes Marrou. "The victor, generally speaking, was Isocrates, and Isocrates became the educator first of Greece and then of the whole ancient world." This "victory" undergirds the ideal of Hellenistic education passed on to Rome. It also explains why, according to Jaeger, "humanistic culture" has been traced in "a direct line" through the Roman educational theorists to Isocrates, rather than to Plato or Aristotle.[18]

Several factors portended this outcome. Isocrates' view was clearly more congenial to an educational tradition based on the epical Homer and other honored poets, than was that of Plato, who was prepared to banish the poets from his ideal republic. In addition, Plato himself had moved from according scarcely any value to rhetoric in *Gorgias* toward assigning it some merit in *Phaedrus*, and this accommodation of the philosopher to the orator was subsequently acknowledged and even adopted by Aristotle, who systematized rhetoric into a "counterpart" of dialectic.[19] This is not to say that Aristotle's *Rhetoric* constitutes the synthesis of, or golden mean between, Isocrates and Plato, as some commentators would have it. The integrity of Isocrates' view was yet unappreciated by the philosophers. Nor does it mean that Plato or Aristotle were in any way won over to the oratorical ideal for education. They maintained their speculative and contemplative vision. However, the implication left by many modern statements that this philosophical ideal constituted the dominant rationale for the education of free Greek citizens with leisure to study is highly doubtful, to say the least. That approach reflects an a priori preference for the Socratic tradition to the neglect of what Hellenistic culture actually adopted from Isocrates, who "many modern scholars even maintain . . . is the father of modern liberal education."[20]

The theoretical appeal presupposing the existence of one dominant Athenian theory of "philosophical" education is thus refuted either by the evident pluralism of rationales in the late fifth and early

---

[18]Marrou (1956), p. 194; Werner Jaeger, *Paideia: The Ideals of Greek Culture*, trans. Gilbert Highet, 2d ed. (Oxford: Basil Blackwell, 1944), vol. 3, pp. 46–47. See Aubrey Gwynn, *Roman Education from Cicero to Quintilian* (London: Oxford University Press, 1926), pp. 40–41; William M. Smail, *Quintilian on Education* (Oxford: Clarendon, 1938), p. xvii.

[19]Plato, *Republic* 398a–b, 598d–602b, *Gorgias* 462b–465e, *Phaedrus* 259e–261a; Aristotle, *Rhetoric* 1354a.

[20]Costas M. Proussis, "The Orator: Isocrates," in *The Educated Man: Studies in the History of Educational Thought*, ed. Paul Nash, Andreas M. Kazamias, and Henry J. Perkinson (New York: John Wiley, 1965), p. 74.

fourth centuries, or by the preeminence of the oratorical ideal, if any is to be considered preeminent. Yet also to be considered are the three etymological appeals to Athens for the origins of the *artes liberales*. Whether or not Isocrates was the "victor" over Plato in educational theory, the palm may well go to the philosophers or the sophists if they are shown to have invented the appropriate words. To be sure, such an etymological appeal is narrow and rather uncertain at best, given the loss of many ancient writings and the textual problems in existing ones. Even so, it might serve as an important guidepost if significant differences in terminology can be found.

In regard to *skholē*, this turns out not to be the case. From its usage during the fifth and fourth centuries through the Hellenistic period down to its assimilation into Latin as *schola*, the term was employed by teachers committed to all different persuasions and curricula: the grammarians, the rhetors, the mathematicians, and the philosophers.[21] One cannot, therefore, identify *skholē* with a particular theory of education for the free citizen without making an a priori judgment that a particular theory was dominant, the argument addressed above. More important, perhaps, is the question of *eleutherios*, the word most closely linked to *liberalis* in meaning. *Eleutherios* is found in conjunction with *paideia* (education) in works by Aristotle. It was also employed by Aeschines with *paideutheis* (one who was educated) and by Isocrates with *tethrammenous* (one who has been raised), which latter reference has repeatedly been translated as "educated liberally."[22] Here again, widespread use precludes linking *eleutherios* to one particular theory of education, although it might still be asked, as it has been in the past, to which Greek school belongs *tekhnai eleutherioi*, the most literal and specific antecedent of Cicero's *artes liberales*? The rather surprising answer is that *tekhnai eleutherioi* may have appeared after the turn of the millennium and seems to be a translation of the Latin *artes liberales* into Greek, not vice versa.[23] In other words, the most precise Greek

---

[21]Liddell and Scott (1940), s.v. "σχολή"; Stanley F. Bonner, *Education in Ancient Rome: From the Elder Cato to the Younger Pliny* (Berkeley: University of California Press, 1977), p. 56.

[22]Aristotle, *Politics* 1338a32; Aeschines, *Against Ctesiphon* 154; Isocrates, *Panegyricus* 49. For translations, see *The Orations of Isocrates*, trans. J. H. Freese (London: George Bell, 1894), p. 67; George Kennedy, *Classical Rhetoric and Its Christian and Secular Tradition from Ancient to Modern Times* (Chapel Hill: University of North Carolina Press, 1980), p. 36.

[23]Klibansky (1969), p. 30; Marrou (1969), pp. 11, 31.

equivalent for "liberal arts" may have come after the Roman term, not before it. Even allowing for vagaries in the manuscript tradition, this certainly gives cause to hesitate over attributing the term to an era four or five centuries earlier.

Finally, one must consider *enkuklios paideia*, a term conducive both to an etymological and to a curricular appeal. *Enkuklios* denoted "common, general, regular" in the late fifth and early fourth centuries B.C.E.; and in conjunction with *paideia*, it can be taken to mean "general education" for the free citizen with leisure to study and thus to be the equivalent and origin of *artes liberales*. Understanding how *enkuklios* took on this meaning will be helpful both here and later in the discussion.

Until the early fifth century, the Hellenic tradition of education included two major aspects: "gymnastics," the physical training associated with the ancient obligation of military service, and "music," the study of the arts of the Muses, which were fundamental to the cultural tradition and to the rituals of the state cultus.[24] Service to the military, to the cultural tradition, and to the state cultus were the normal obligations of citizenship, and preparation for these responsibilities thus constituted the purpose of the education that was associated with the antecedents of the later term *enkuklios*. Various derivations are possible; but it seems that these antecedents, such as *kuklos*, referred to "circle," "chorus," "cycle," or the like. The root of *enkuklios* in regard to education therefore meant "belonging to a chorus," being educated "in a chorus," or education "in choric subjects," or education in a cycle of subjects or in subjects having to do with cycles, such as music and astronomy. Eventually, *enkuklios* came to mean "common, general, regular" because "musical education," or *enkuklios paideia*, broadened into a "general education" for the free citizen with leisure to study. At least, this has been the standard conclusion inferred from the fact that writers of all different sorts—Euripides, Isocrates, Plato, Aristotle, Demosthenes—employed variations of *enkuklios* to mean "common, general, regular" in the fifth and fourth centuries B.C.E. Since *enkuklios* could have obtained this meaning only through its conjunction with *paideia*, the logic goes, then the term *enkuklios paideia* must be at least contemporaneous with the above references, if not older.

---

[24] Plato, *Republic* 410a–412a. Here and below, I draw from Kühnert (1961), pp. 6–18, 42ff.; Rijk (1965), pp. 24–93; Marrou (1956), pp. 1–13, 134–141; Marrou (1969), pp. 16–18; Meister (1976), pp. 23–26; Hermann Koller, "ΕΓΚΥΚΛΙΟΣ ΠΑΙΔΕΙΑ," in *Erziehung und Bildung in der heidnischen und christlichen Antike*, ed. Horst-Theodor Johann (Darmstadt: Buchgesellschaft, 1976), pp. 3–21; Mette (1976) pp. 32–33.

The first implication regarding *enkuklios paideia* as the origin of *artes liberales* is thus clearly the same as for *skholē* and *eleutherios*: the term cannot be associated exclusively with one rationale for education of free Greek citizens with leisure to study. Rather, one must understand it to have circulated commonly among differing educators. But here surfaces a second and more arresting implication for the derivation of *artes liberales*. If *enkuklios paideia* was a common term by at least the late fourth century B.C.E., why did no sophists, philosophers, or orators writing about education during that time use the term, even though they often did employ *enkuklios* and *paideia* separately from each other? Moreover, why are the earliest uses of the term found only in Vitruvius and Quintilian of the first century C.E.?[25] These facts have led certain investigators to conclude that the term *enkuklios paideia* arose only in the second or first centuries B.C.E. Here, too, the etymological approach appears not only to fail those who would appeal to Plato's Athens for origins of *artes liberales*, but actually to contravene their arguments.

Whether *enkuklios paideia* was coined in the fifth century or in the first century B.C.E., the question about the lineage of the curriculum attributed to it remains. If the normative program of seven liberal arts was formulated in the "pedagogical century" and given the name *septem artes liberales* in Roman times, as is commonly stated, then there would still be adequate reason to say that Athenians invented the liberal arts. And if this normative program were connected with a particular school of thought, or if it implied a certain theory of education in itself, then either of these possibilities might be called the origin of the idea of liberal arts or liberal education.

Such an appeal, however, turns out to be highly problematic. Some scholars prefer to find the seven arts first organized into a normative program in the fourth or fifth centuries C.E.[26] Indeed, it has been held that the *septem artes liberales* first appear systematized in the fifth-century treatise of Martianus Capella and that Cas-

---

[25]Vitruvius actually writes about *encyclio doctrinarum omnium* rather than *enkuklios paideia* in *De architectura*, bk. 6 pref., line 4. Interestingly, Quintilian speaks in the present tense rather than in the past: "orbis ille doctrinae quem Graeci ἐγκύκλιος παιδεία vocant" (*Institutio oratoria* 1.10.1). Diogenes Laertius of the third century C.E., who in *Lives of Eminent Philosophers* repeatedly attributed the term *enkuklios paideia* to Greek writings of the fifth, fourth, and third centuries B.C.E., is unreliable.

[26]Robert R. Bolgar, *The Classical Heritage and Its Beneficiaries* (Cambridge: Cambridge University Press, 1964), p. 35; Paul O. Kristeller, *Renaissance Thought II: Papers on Humanism and the Arts* (New York: Harper and Row, 1965), p. 173; Leighton D. Reynolds and N. G. Wilson, *Scribes and Scholars: A Guide to the Transmission of Greek and Latin Literature* (London: Oxford University Press, 1968), p. 29.

siodorus in the sixth century was the first Christian to use the term.[27] Others have asserted the program of seven liberal arts to be "finally and definitely formulated" during the first century B.C.E.[28] or at various dates over the next six centuries.[29] In this way, historians have largely inclined toward attributing the formulation of the normative program of seven liberal arts to Roman antiquity rather than to Greek antiquity. But all of these judgments depend on how one defines "formulation" and "normative program."

It is probably true to say that all seven arts—the three language and the four mathematical—were known to and invented by the Greeks. The Hellenic tradition of education in "music" down to the fifth century B.C.E. seems to have involved both the recitation of ancient poetry and participation in a chorus. Commensurately, as the traditional complement of gymnastic education declined in prominence, the Pythagoreans introduced into "music" a third and mathematical interpretation. In the sixth century, Pythagoras interpreted "number" as the principle binding the world together, both cosmologically and ethically. Understanding number was thus linked to the pursuit of *sophia*; and four of the mathematical arts later mentioned by Plato—arithmetic, geometry, astronomy, music—were given special emphasis.[30] This is not to say that these disciplines had been fully elaborated. Although the Pythagoreans had developed

[27]Paul Abelson, *The Seven Liberal Arts: A Study in Mediaeval Culture* (New York: Bureau of Publications, Teachers College, Columbia University, 1906), p. 9; Dobson (1932), pp. 160–161; Gabriel Nuchelmans, "Philologia et son mariage avec Mercure jusqu'à la fin du XIIe siècle," *Latomus* 16 (1957): 90–92; Joseph M. McCarthy, *Humanistic Emphases in the Educational Thought of Vincent of Beauvais* (Leiden, Neth.: E. J. Brill, 1976), p. 85. Martianus does not actually use the term, but Cassiodorus indicates that the title of Martianus's treatise was *De septem disciplinis. Institutiones*, ed. R. A. Mynors (Oxford: Clarendon, 1937) 2.2.17. I have found no one, pagan or Christian, who used the term before Cassiodorus did.

[28]Marrou (1956), pp. 176–178; Marrou, *Saint Augustin et la fin de la culture antique*, 4th ed. (Paris: Editions E. de Boccard, 1958), pp. 211–235; Marrou, *Histoire de l'éducation dans l'antiquité*, 6th ed. (Paris: Editions du Seuil, 1965), pp. 264–267; Kühnert (1961), p. 17; Mette (1976), pp. 31–41; Francesco della Corte, *Varrone: Il terzo gran lume romano*, 2d ed. (Florence: La Nuova Italia, 1970), pp. 11, 232.

[29]Rijk (1965), pp. 90–93. Stephen d'Irsay appears to adopt all of these positions by stating: "Leur origine comme programme complet d'études remonte à Platon; mais leur définition précise fut fixée par Cicéron et les philologues de l'Empire. . . . Au IVe siècle surtout . . . [the program of seven arts] apparaît unifiée par Quintilien et Martianus Capella," in *Histoire des universités françaises et étrangères des origines à nos jours* (Paris: Editions Auguste Picard, 1933), vol. 1, pp. 34–35. Similarly does Edward K. Rand write in *Founders of the Middle Ages* (Cambridge: Harvard University Press, 1928), pp. 218–219.

[30]Plato included other mathematical sciences, such as stereometry, as well. *Republic* 522c–530d; Hans M. Klinkenberg, "Der Verfall des Quadriviums im frühen Mittelalter," in *Artes* (1959), pp. 1–6, 11; Carnes Lord, *Education and Culture in the Political Thought of Aristotle* (Ithaca, N.Y.: Cornell University Press, 1982), chap. 2.

arithmetical studies, geometry matured only with the work of Euclid in the third century B.C.E. Meanwhile, the poetic and choric interpretations of music did not at all surrender their position to the mathematical view. Astronomy was often construed as astrology and vice versa, and neither was recognized as an independent art in the monumental treatise of Varro in the first century B.C.E.[31]

Rhetoric, the oldest of the three language arts, is said to have been brought to Athens from Syracuse by sophists such as Gorgias in the latter half of the fifth century. By that time, public speaking had become a serious matter for every free citizen in the newly democratic city-states. Participation in democratic politics required skills in forensic, deliberative, and epideictic (panegyrical) rhetoric; and a fivefold division of the art, later described by Cicero, became conventional: invention, arrangement, style, memory, delivery.[32] Sophists were the ones who began to teach this discipline and to produce technical handbooks in the fifth and fourth centuries, although Socrates, Plato, and Aristotle noted that these individuals failed to identify underlying principles of organization for their supposed art. Aristotle gave himself credit for the first profound systematization in his *Rhetoric*.[33]

Sophists are also thought to have invented the interrogatory form of argumentation known as dialectic. But the term "dialectic" has been found no earlier than Plato's *Meno*,[34] and the philosophers are credited with refining dialectic into the art of logic, a more precise tool for speculation and analysis. The foundations of grammar, the third language art, have been credited to sophists such as Prodicus and Protagoras. Yet the first systematization appeared only at the turn of the first century B.C.E., so one hesitates to attribute the art to any particular school of thought from earlier centuries. Furthermore, the Stoic Chrysippus had made a considerable contribution in the intervening period.

In sum, it can be said that the subject matter of the later *septem artes liberales* was invented by the Greeks, and that their discussion about curriculum addressed primarily the topics of language and

---

[31]Corte (1970), p. 226; Cicero, *De oratore* 1.187.

[32]Cicero, *De inventione* 1.9. Aristotle (*Rhetoric* 1358a38−b33) first defined forensic, deliberative, and epideictic categories in rhetoric.

[33]Plato, *Apology* 21e, *Phaedrus* 264c, 269b−c; Aristotle, *On Sophistical Refutations* 183b35−184a10, *Rhetoric* 1354b17.

[34]Plato, *Meno* 75d; Jaeger (1939), pp. 314ff. Diogenes Laertius, who is unreliable, says that Aristotle credited the discovery of dialectic to the philosopher Zeno. *Lives of Eminent Philosophers* 8.57, 9.25.

mathematics. But whether consensus was reached on a normative program is another matter. For one thing, continuity and cohesion were prevented by the fact that masters traveled about teaching individual subjects. This happened in Isocrates' time and continued throughout the Roman era. Despite a contrary impression often left by modern commentators, no possibility existed for students to go to one place and learn seven arts from one or more masters in an association or "school."[35] Secondly, even if such institutions had existed, the arts would not have been taught in the same way or in the same order, which is to say, thirdly, that radically different interpretations of the individual arts themselves existed.

Grammar was scarcely a formal art until the second or first century B.C.E.; yet to the extent that it originated in the fifth-century study of language and literature, it certainly was elevated by sophists and orators and de-emphasized by philosophers. The roots of grammar lay in the "musical education" in ancient Greek poetry, and the teacher of grammar thus inherited a concern for ethics and history that was subsequently transmitted to the Roman *scholae*. In fact, the Greek term *grammatikē tekhnē* comes from the word for "letter" (*gramma*), and Quintilian later translated "grammar" as *litteratura* based on the Latin equivalent (*littera*) for *gramma*.[36] The link here between grammar, ethics, and history is a natural and significant one. After studying the structure of language, students received training in a canon of epic and hymnic poetry, which required *historia*. This word should be understood not in the later sense of teaching or reading the historians, but rather as an "inquiry" into the factual or mythical background, context, and allusions of a given text. Such material was presented in order to enhance students' understanding, to inculcate respect for the cultural tradition, and, usually, to impress upon them an underlying moral lesson. Gradually, the attention to *historia* was incorporated into rhetorical studies, as Cicero and Quintilian noted.[37] Over against this program stood philosophers like Plato, who stridently opposed education in much of the very literary tradition that provided the basis for the studies of grammar and rhetoric. Aristotle also cautioned against such stud-

---

[35]Marrou (1956), pp. 200ff.; Bolgar (1964), pp. 33–34; Beck (1964), p. 141; Gunther Heilbrunn, "Isocrates on Rhetoric and Power," *Hermes* 103 (1975): 156–161.

[36]Quintilian, *Institutio oratoria* 2.1.4.

[37]Cicero, *De oratore* 1. 158–159, 187, 201; Quintilian, *Institutio oratoria* 1.8.13–18, 2.4.3; Hans Wolter, "Geschichtliche Bildung im Rahmen der Artes Liberales," in *Artes* (1959), p. 65; Bonner (1977), pp. 237, 277–282, chaps. 14–17, 19.

ies, which made emotional appeals rather than logical analysis the basis of moral suasion.[38]

This conflict in attitudes carried over to the arts of dialectic and rhetoric. Plato had moved reluctantly from according scarcely any value to rhetoric in *Gorgias* toward admitting in *Phaedrus* that it might be an art worthy of study. But it still stood far below the speculative heights of dialectic in his estimation.[39] Aristotle refined the point by distinguishing between scientific "demonstration"—the method, for theoretical philosophy, of reasoning syllogistically from true premises in order to reach true conclusions known surely and abstractly—and its stepchild "dialectic"—the method, for practical philosophy, of reasoning syllogistically about human affairs in matters of opinion and contingency. Now, the term "dialectic" is used in several senses by Aristotle, his teacher, and his successors, including the sense of an open-ended inquiry into the premises of the various sciences. But one denotation that does remain firm is that "rhetoric" is the counterpart in popular discourse to "dialectic" in philosophical discourse. The rhetorical method of reasoning, Aristotle says, is the enthymeme, which has a syllogistic character that will, quite appropriately, be embellished by appeals to emotion, sensitivity, and predisposition in order to effect persuasion.[40] In this fashion, rhetoric becomes an imprecise, utilitarian, and restricted adjunct to the more penetrating investigation of larger and overarching questions of principle pursued through dialectic or logic.

The sophists and orators, on the other hand, reversed the relationship. They regarded rhetoric as the supreme art, the art that settles the great and important questions of deliberative and judicial assemblies and relies on logic or dialectic merely for the skeletal frame of its argument. From this viewpoint, rhetoric involves the

---

[38] Plato, *Republic* 377–392, 595–608; Aristotle, *Rhetoric* 1354a.

[39] Plato, *Gorgias* 462b–465e, *Phaedrus* 269–272b. In the following discussion about rhetoric and dialectic, I draw from Charles S. Baldwin, *Ancient Rhetoric and Poetic Interpreted from Representative Works* (New York: Macmillan, 1924), pp. 1–24; Richard McKeon, "The Methods of Rhetoric and Judgment," in *The Classical Tradition: Literary and Historical Studies in Honor of Harry Caplan*, ed. Luitpold Wallach (Ithaca, N.Y.: Cornell University Press, 1966), pp. 365–373; Kennedy (1963); Kennedy (1972); Kennedy (1980); and Paul O. Kristeller, *Renaissance Thought and Its Sources*, ed. Michael Mooney (New York: Columbia University Press, 1979), pt. 5.

[40] Aristotle, *Topics* 100a25–101a5, *Rhetoric* 1355b–1357b; William M. Grimaldi, *Studies in the Philosophy of Aristotle's Rhetoric* (Wiesbaden, W.Ger.: Franz Steiner, 1972), chap. 3; Larry Arnhart, *Aristotle on Political Reasoning: A Commentary on the "Rhetoric"* (DeKalb: Northern Illinois University Press, 1981), chaps. 1, 2, pp. 65–83. But see J. D. G. Evans, *Aristotle's Concept of Dialectic* (Cambridge: Cambridge University Press, 1977), pp. 3–6.

more difficult task, either in life or education, of elaborating a compelling argument based on an outline derived through the art of logic. Isocrates affirmed this while discussing curricula, and the Roman writer Varro echoed it in the first century B.C.E. Varro (116–27 B.C.E.) treated dialectic as an "eytmological science" that bridges the elementary study of language and literature in grammar and their mature study in rhetoric. In so doing, he interpreted the famous Stoic metaphor—comparing dialectic to a closed fist and rhetoric to an open hand—to mean that rhetoric develops and extrapolates the morphemes discovered by dialectic. Cicero (106–43 B.C.E.) hearkened back to this metaphor and subsumed logic under rhetoric, as did Quintilian (35–97 C.E.) in the following century.[41]

If recommendations as to the meaning and curricular value of those language arts differed greatly, the same was true for the mathematical disciplines of the later seven liberal arts. Although some sophists, such as Hippias, are reported to have mastered these disciplines, most of this group, including Protagoras, ignored or devalued mathematical arts for the sake of rhetoric. Totally opposite was the view of Plato, who, perhaps even more than Pythagoras, would have been glad to center all education before dialectic on arithmetic, geometry, astronomy, music, and other mathematical sciences. And the emphasis here would be on elevating the mind through rigorous analytic thinking, and not at all on learning useful scientific facts.[42] The latter rationale was what orators from Isocrates to Quintilian considered most important when they apologetically recommended learning something about those arts before proceeding to rhetoric.[43]

The differences here among definitions of and recommendations for arts of the same name are perfectly exemplified in the case of "music." The tension between choric and literary aspects of the art was nascent in Homeric *paideia*, and the introduction of the philosophical and mathematical interpretation engendered new conflicts. Plato, for example, specifically cited the Pythagorean tradition while associating music with astronomy and mathematics. This competition between choric, literary, and mathematical interpretations of "music" continued into and through Roman antiquity;

---

[41]Quoted phrase is translated from Corte (1970), p. 219. Isocrates, *Antidosis* 266–267; Cicero, *Orator* 32, 113, *De oratore* 2. 154–163; Quintilian, *Institutio oratoria* 12.2.10–19.

[42]Plato, *Hippias Minor* 366d–367e, *Protagoras* 318c, *Republic* 521c–531d.

[43]Isocrates, *Antidosis* 261–265; Quintilian, *Institutio oratoria* 1.10.

and the meaning of "astronomy" displayed similar ambiguity. The word in Greek comes from *aster* (star) and *nomos* (law), and as mentioned above, Plato insisted on closely associating the study of the laws of the stars with mathematics. But some incorporated astrology into astronomy or even used the word *astrologia*, as did Cicero, to refer to what others would have regarded as astronomy.[44]

No less ambiguous was the term *philosophia*. It goes without saying that the term was used in many different senses by the various philosophical schools, while it is fair to generalize that each group reserved the term to denote its own program of advanced study, which commenced after some sort of foundational education in a variety of arts. For others, however, there was a tendency either to equate philosophy with oratory, as did Isocrates; to treat it as one art among others, as did Varro; or to equate it broadly and variably with all education, as did schoolmasters in imperial Roman Gaul, where the influence of Quintilian predominated.[45] Consensus over the meaning of the term was not a legacy of Hellenistic Greece.

A final point related to the discontinuity in educational programs concerns specialization. One often reads in histories of ancient education that orators ended their program of education with specialized study in rhetoric, much as Plato and Aristotle recommended specialized study beyond a foundational curriculum in a variety of arts. However, despite the fact that rhetorical study was the crowning art for the orators, this analogy is specious on several counts. An orator's "specialization" in rhetoric lasted from about age sixteen to age twenty or so, while that contemplated by Plato or by the schools of other philosophers extended far into adulthood as followers devoted themselves for decades to a particular master.[46] In addition, the instruction in rhetoric both before and after age twenty was general in nature so as to prepare the orator to speak on any is-

---

[44]On music, see Plato, *Republic* 530d; Karl G. Fellerer, "Die Musica in den Artes Liberales," in *Artes* (1959), pp. 33–35; Edward A. Lippman, "The Place of Music in the System of Liberal Arts," in *Aspects of Medieval and Renaissance Music*, ed. Jan LaRue et al., rev. ed. (New York: Pendragon, 1972), pp. 545–559; Lord (1982), chap. 2. On astronomy, see Cicero, *De oratore* 1.187; Stahl and Johnson (1971), pp. 171–201; Jacques Fontaine, *Isidore de Seville et la culture classique dans L'espagne wisigothique* (Paris: Etudes Augustiniennes, 1959), pt. 4.

[45]Plato, *Phaedo* 61a; Isocrates, *Antidosis* 270–277; Corte (1970), pp. 226–229; T. J. Haarhoff, *Schools of Gaul: A Study of Pagan and Christian Education in the Last Century of the Western Empire* (Oxford: Clarendon, 1919), pp. 57–58, 80; Marrou (1958), pp. 193–197, 232–235; Jean-Charles Falardeau, "Perspectives d'un humanisme contemporain," in *Actes* (1969), pp. 274–275.

[46]Plato, *Republic* 539a–540a; George Kennedy, *Quintilian* (New York: Twayne, 1969), pp. 47–48, 135; Bonner (1977), p. 85.

sue, be it legal, political, military, literary, religious, or otherwise, as Quintilian noted. That sort of training can scarcely be described as "specialization." Finally, the narrow, advanced specialization pursued by philosophers was consistently criticized by sophists and orators, as Callicles and Cicero made clear.[47] Thus, important disagreements did exist about the length and breadth of education for free citizens with leisure to study.

The conclusion seems inescapable that agreement on a normative curriculum was not achieved in Greek antiquity. Great diversity existed among the prescriptions of arts for education, a condition lamented by Aristotle in the *Politics*.[48] Each of the later *septem artes liberales* may have been considered an important part of "general education" by prominent educators during this period, and each of the arts and their various permutations may have been taught. But that the Greeks before the first century B.C.E. ever agreed that precisely these seven constituted a normative curriculum for the free citizen with leisure to study has yet to be demonstrated. In view of this fact, and in view of the previously described conflict over educational rationales and the inconclusiveness of etymological appeals, one must turn to the Romans to seek the formulation of a normative "liberal education." Indeed, it appears that even those who attribute the seven liberal arts to Plato's Athens implicitly turn in this direction as well. For, without Latin antiquity to look back from, it is hard to see how anyone would arrive precisely at the *septem artes liberales* as normative for the Greeks.

The Roman Republic provides unambiguous etymological evidence, at least from the first century B.C.E. By that time, Cicero and others were employing the term *artes liberales* and the like, all clear antecedents for "liberal arts" and "liberal education" in English. The popular view,[49] however, that Varro and Cicero first or finally formulated the normative curriculum of *septem artes liberales* is rather problematic, as are attributions to figures in the subsequent two or three centuries.

The first problem is that these writers never speak about "seven liberal arts"; and it is curious that some of the same modern scholars who regard the absence of the term *enkuklios paideia* in the fifth,

[47]Quintilian, *Institutio oratoria* 12.1–2; Plato, *Gorgias* 485b–d; Cicero, *De oratore* 3. 132–140.
[48]Aristotle, *Politics* 1337a10–40.
[49]Corte (1970), pp. 11, 32; Kühnert (1961), p. 17; Marrou (1965), pp. 265–267; Marrou (1969), pp. 18–26; Mette (1976), pp. 31–41.

fourth, and third centuries B.C.E. as proof that the term was not in use, are not perturbed by the fact—even though Latin writings transmitted to us from the first century B.C.E. to the fourth century C.E. are more abundant and reliable—that the term *septem artes liberales* apparently emerges only in the fifth century C.E.[50] This fact should be disquieting because—and this raises a second problem— Varro and Cicero do not themselves list seven arts. Varro, whose encyclopedic treatise was widely read, listed nine arts: medicine, architecture, philosophy, plus six of the later seven. In works of Cicero, one must conflate scattered listings in order to arrive at a list of seven, a fact reflecting the variability in programs of Roman education. Masters still roamed around teaching their subjects individually, and Cicero himself wrote that Roman education was neither "fixed by law, publicly supported, nor standardized."[51]

The third problem with this attribution to Varro or Cicero simply confirms the foregoing: subsequent descriptions of *artes liberales* continued to vary. In the following century, Vitruvius described eleven arts for architects to study, while Seneca rejected most of the arts and held that only those conducive to virtue are "liberal" and "freeing." In the second century, Galen compiled a list of eight *artes*—the later seven plus medicine—for doctors to study, and Sextus Empiricus in the subsequent century described a system of six *artes*, assigning logic to the province of philosophy. In Augustine's writings several generations later, various enumerations of the *artes liberales* can also be found.[52] More examples could be cited, but the point should be clear that from the time of Varro different combinations of *artes liberales* were suggested, often incorporating most of the three language arts and four mathematical arts. It is by conflating these descriptions that modern scholars have argued that the norm for the entire period constituted the seven liberal arts, although this is certainly a judgment based on hindsight. In truth, it can probably never be determined when a consensus developed, but an outer limit is acknowledged by all: the appearance of *De nuptiis Philologiae et Mercurii* (On the marriage of Philology and Mercury)

---

[50] Abelson (1906), p. 9; Dobson (1932), pp. 160–161; Nuchelmans (1957), p. 90.

[51] Cicero, *De republica* 4.3; Marrou (1956), pp. 200ff.; Marrou (1969), p. 20, table 2; Corte (1970), chap. 14; Martin L. Clarke, *Higher Education in the Ancient World* (London: Routledge and Kegan Paul, 1971), pp. 7, 45.

[52] Vitruvius, *De architectura* 1.1.3–12; Maria Bellincioni, *Educazione alla sapientia in Seneca* (Brescia: Paideia, 1978), pp. 117–160. See the helpful tables and descriptions of various enumerations of liberal arts in Kühnert (1961), pp. 18–42, 50–70; Marrou (1958), pp. 195–235; Marrou (1969), pp. 9–25.

written by Martianus Capella sometime in the first quarter of the fifth century.

De nuptiis relates the story, told by an old man to his son, of how the god Mercury woos and wins Philology, an erudite young woman. At the wedding banquet in the heavens, Mercury presents his bride with seven handmaidens, each personifying one of the seven liberal disciplines, which are described in separate discourses during the banquet. Relying heavily on Varro and extolling Cicero, Martianus warns against a too intense or lengthy study of dialectic, which precedes that of rhetoric; and he praises the mathematical arts for their factual information, while largely construing geometry as geography.[53] Fundamentally, the allegory teaches that the seven liberal arts are the means to bring eloquence (Mercury) and learning (Philology) together, an aim sanctioned by the gods.[54]

None of this is original, of course, inasmuch as the wedding of eloquence to wisdom reflects the fundamental oratorical theme expressed by Quintilian, Cicero, and Isocrates. Whether one holds the normative curriculum of *septem artes liberales* to be formulated in the first century b.c.e., or in the fifth century c.e., or at some point in between, the rationale of the program was grounded in Isocratean Hellenism, which the Romans wholeheartedly perpetuated. Plato and Aristotle were certainly not excluded from the curriculum of the seven liberal arts. Platonic metaphysics, through its Neoplatonic articulation, influenced the outlook of every Roman, and Aristotle provided the basis of logic. Martianus demonstrated these influences in his treatise.[55] But the rationale behind the *septem artes liberales* involved something very different from the pursuit of critical speculation and learned contemplation, for "on the whole it was Isocrates, not Plato, who educated fourth-century Greece and subsequently the Hellenistic and Roman worlds."[56]

The relative consensus in Roman education was not achieved overnight, although the achievement itself is predictable, along with

---

[53]Martianus Capella, *De nuptiis Philologiae et Mercurii*, ed. Adolfus Dick (Stuttgart: B. G. Teubner, 1925) 1−2, 423, 588−704. In this edition, Martianus's apportionment among the first three arts is 70 pages for grammar, 60 pages for dialectic, 75 pages for rhetoric.

[54]Stahl and Johnson (1971), pp. 40−54, 83, 104−115, 125−148; Fanny LeMoine, *Martianus Capella: A Literary Re-evaluation* (Munich: Arbeo-Gesellschaft, 1972), chap. 2. *Philologia* is a term used loosely both by Martianus and others in this period, meaning wisdom, study, learning, knowledge, *paideia*. Nuchelmans (1957), pp. 84−91, 106−107.

[55]Stahl and Johnson (1971), pp. 85−90, 104−115.

[56]Marrou (1956), p. 79; Jaeger (1944), pp. 46−47; Bonner (1977), pp. 64−68, 77.

the course that it took. During the second century B.C.E., those committed to the native traditions, such as Cato the Elder, had opposed all Greek influence, and in 161 B.C.E. the Senate banned teachers of both rhetoric and philosophy from Rome.[57] But the Romans inevitably claimed the inheritance of the more sophisticated culture bequeathed to them; and being engineers, jurists, and administrators of an emerging empire, they just as inevitably felt most sympathetic toward the oratorical tradition with its concern for law, order, noble virtue, and public expression. Cicero expressed it thus:

> As do rivers out of the Apennines, the course of learning, from a single mountain ridge of wisdom, diverged, so that philosophers flowed out, so to speak, into the Greek Adriatic Sea of many ports and the orators cascaded upon our wild, craggy, inhospitable Tuscan shore.[58]

The four main currents of Hellenistic speculative thought—Epicurean, Stoic, Peripatetic, Neoplatonic—did persevere, but philosophers in the western half of the empire increasingly withdrew from ordinary culture into sects or wandering bands committed to a particular seer. This withdrawal led them to be regarded suspiciously as sophists by many Romans, and Emperor Vespasian in the first century C.E. expelled them again from Rome. Conversely, he named Quintilian to the first state professorship in rhetoric, and teachers of this art were paid the highest salaries of any instructors.[59] The orator's *schola* for students aged sixteen to twenty thus crowned a Roman educational program that was becoming normative even as Quintilian described it. The students prepared for rhetoric through four or five years in the *schola* of the *grammaticus* (grammar master), which succeeded five or six years of elementary education in the *ludus*. The techniques of *historia* and recitation were preserved from Hellenistic practice, as was the devaluation of mathematical disciplines that extended from Varro to Martianus.[60]

If both the Greek word and the Greek art *rhetorica* had thus come

---

[57]Suetonius, *De rhetoribus* 1.

[58]Cicero, *De oratore* 3.69.

[59]Quintilian, *Institutio oratoria* 12.2.6–10, 12.3.11–12; Gwynn (1926), pp. 177–184; Smail (1938), pp. xii, xxv–xxx; Clarke (1971), pp. 9–10; Bonner (1977), pp. 64–77.

[60]Corte (1970), pp. 222–226; Marrou (1956), pp. 185ff., 220ff.; Falardeau (1969), pp. 274–275. In *Institutio oratoria*, Quintilian describes the *ludus* in bk. 1, pts. 1–3, the *schola* of the grammarian in bk. 1, pts. 4–12, the *schola* of rhetoric in bks. 2–9, advanced practice in speaking in bks. 10–11, and the ideal orator in bk. 12.

to dominate education in Rome and the western provinces, *oratoria* was actually the Latin translation for the Greek word "rhetoric.[61] And it was the orator Cicero who first exemplified this Roman educational ideal for the *artes liberales*, a fact affirmed by Quintilian when he became the exemplar. Both men were beholden to Isocrates, whom Cicero called "that eminent father of eloquence" and "the master of all rhetoricians" and whom Quintilian labeled "that most brilliant instructor" whose school had turned out the greatest orators.[62] In fact, the "isocratic" tradition is said to have had its complete expression in Cicero's fullest treatment of education, *De oratore*, which in turn was the inspiration for Quintilian's *Institutio oratoria*.[63] Manifest in this lineage is the orators' perpetual conflict with the philosophers, a point requiring some elaboration.

The standard rendition of the conflict, which tends to denigrate the oratorical perspective, runs as follows.[64] Isocrates, Cicero, and Quintilian are held to be critical of the speculative and endless pursuit of truth defended by Socrates and Plato. And, in fact, Isocrates states this criticism explicitly, while Cicero rejects extraordinary complexity in issues, denigrates questions that seem to have no final answers, and criticizes philosophical contemplation pursued for its own sake. Quintilian then repeats these same arguments in *Institutio oratoria*.[65] Conversely, Socrates and Plato are rightfully regarded as critical of the orators for their lack of speculative acumen and their pragmatic outlook.

Faced with this standoff, many historians have sought, with all good intentions, to apologize for these presumably less than perspicacious orators in either of two ways. One approach seeks to find in the orators, especially Cicero, a contemplative spirit meriting the

---

[61]Haarhoff (1919), pp. 39–80; Quintilian, *Institutio oratoria* 2.14.1–3.

[62]Cicero, *De oratore* 2.10, 3.94; Quintilian, *Institutio oratoria* 2.7.11, 2.14.1, 3.1.9–12, 10.1.12, 12.10.9–12.

[63]Falardeau (1969) speaks of the tradition "*isocratique*" (p. 274). Harry M. Hubbell, *The Influence of Isocrates on Cicero, Dionysius, and Aristides* (New Haven: Yale University Press, 1913), pp. 1–40; Gwynn (1926), pp. 80–81, 186; Alain Michel, "L'originalité de l'idéal oratoire de Cicéron," *Les études classiques* 39 (1971): 311–328. Kennedy affirms the link between Quintilian and Cicero ([1969], p. 86) but questions the identification of Cicero with Isocrates ([1972], p. 279).

[64]In this account, I draw from Baldwin (1924), pp. 37–39; Baldwin (1928), pp. 2–7; Clark (1957), chaps. 1, 2; Beck (1964), chap. 8; James J. Murphy, *Rhetoric in the Middle Ages: A History of Rhetorical Theory from Saint Augustine to the Renaissance* (Berkeley: University of California Press, 1974), pp. 7–42; Kennedy (1963), pp. 15–25; Kennedy (1972), pp. 219–229, 509–513.

[65]Isocrates, *Antidosis* 268–271; Cicero, *De oratore* 1.229, 2.60–68, 156–159, 3.64; Quintilian, *Institutio oratoria*, pref. 12–20, 2.21.12–15.

name "philosophy."[66] A second and more penetrating apologetic considers the orators to be saying that communication of knowledge is important. Therefore, eloquence and expression are important. And indeed, so the apology runs, Plato is unappreciative of this consideration, despite his tentative approval of rhetoric in *Phaedrus*. This oversight, one learns, is rectified in Aristotle's *Rhetoric*, which transcends the orators' handbooks by outlining the principles of political and popular discourse in relation to those of scientific investigation. The inevitable conclusion is that oratory amounts merely to "a means to a goal"[67]—a result to be expected if one presupposes that Platonic speculation is the *summa*, in other words, that Socrates, Plato, and Aristotle are correct. Given this, the best one can do for the orators is to apologize as in the manner above. Furthermore, if one remembers that Plato was reacting against the sophists, then the lack of speculative acumen in the orators and the possibility that Isocrates might have appeared to Plato to be a sophist become all the more pronounced.

But suppose one turns the matter around. How did Isocrates know that Socrates and Plato were not sophists? Here is precisely where the Socratic bias of the standard rendition is revealed, because that question is scarcely ever entertained.[68] Yet this point is very much on the minds of the orators. In the Rome of Cicero and Quintilian, philosophers were widely suspected of sophistry, and this contributed to their expulsion in the second century B.C.E. and again in the first century C.E. This suspicion extended back to the fifth century B.C.E., when Aristophanes relegated Socrates to the *Clouds* and "philosophy" often implied withdrawal from active political life.[69] It is on the basis of this concern that the orators ask: How does one know that anything a philosopher thinks is true? How

---

[66] Alice Dermience, "La notion de 'libertas' dans les oeuvres de Cicéron," *Les études classiques* 25 (1957): 157–167; Pierre Boyancé, "Cicéron et la vie contemplative," *Latomus* 26 (1967): 3–26; Ernesto Valgiglio, "Tra scetticismo filosofico e tradizionalismo religioso," *Rivista di studi classici* 21 (1973): 234–244; Quintilian, *Institutio oratoria* 10.1.123.

[67] Kennedy (1963), p. 21.

[68] Hunt (1961, p. 21) is one who does recognize that Isocrates treated Plato as a sophist. In discussing Augustine's attention to the danger of sophistry, Murphy (1974) offers a rare acknowledgment of this point:

"An opposite vice, one to which historians of rhetoric have never given a name, depends upon the belief that the man possessed of truth will *ipso facto* be able to communicate the truth to others. . . . Its chief proponent in ancient times was the young Plato, and it would seem fair to label it the 'Platonic rhetorical heresy' just as we apply the term 'sophistry' to its opposite theory." (p. 60)

[69] Suetonius, *De rhetoribus* 1; Quintilian, *Institutio oratoria* 12.3.12; Heilbrunn (1975), pp. 159–162; Bonner (1977), pp. 64–68.

does one know that Socrates really knows the path to the true and good if he tells Glaucon that one who knows cannot communicate the path to another who is uninitiated?[70]

The orator holds that the only way to know, the only way to tell that a philosopher is not a sophist, is if the philosophy, first of all, is expressed. This is the import behind Isocrates' statement, made at the end of his career in *Antidosis*, that "the proper use of language is the surest index of sound understanding." From that point, Isocrates proceeded to deny the presupposition that would lie behind the distinction between dialectic and rhetoric later made by Aristotle: the presupposition that effective scientific contemplation can go on apart from speech. Similarly Quintilian wrote, in scorn of the sophistic philosophers of his day, that philosophy can be feigned behind a reflective posture, but eloquence cannot because it is expressed for all to hear and judge.[71]

Beyond expression, the orator also requires that the philosophy make a difference in the world, that is, have an effect—especially that it enhance virtue by persuading others. The philosophers will immediately inquire, But what is virtue? And the orators will make only dogmatic, a priori appeals and not be induced into analysis and speculation. That is the orators' weakness: reliance upon unexamined appeals to a tradition of noble virtue. But just as significant is their epistemological point scored against speculative philosophy: that such philosophy is confirmed to be true only when it is expressed or has an effect. This view is supported by none other than Socrates himself, for the oratorical criterion was precisely the one that he applied to Anaxagoras's theory of Mind. Because Anaxagoras did not demonstrate any effect of Mind upon phenomena, Socrates went elsewhere to search for true wisdom. So, too, did Isocrates criticize those seeking speculatively for uncontingent truth and ideal plans for the city-state, in the same breath that he castigated those employing amoral rhetorical devices for display.[72] Certainly, this criticism can be dismissed as "confusion apparent in the thought of Isocrates,"[73] but to do so is merely to repeat the original Socratic assumption and ignore the orators' epistemological point, whether speculative or not.

The justified fear of philosophical sophistry provides the con-

---

[70] Plato, *Republic* 532e–533a.

[71] Isocrates, *Antidosis*, trans. George Norlin (New York: G. P. Putnam's, 1928) 255–256; Grimaldi (1972), pp. 2–3; Quintilian, *Institutio oratoria* 12.3.12.

[72] Plato, *Phaedo* 97b–98c; Isocrates, *Against the Sophists* 3–8, *Antidosis* 268–271.

[73] Gwynn (1926), p. 49.

text for the claim of Isocrates, Cicero, and Quintilian that oratory stands above all other studies and is the most demanding because it requires someone "polished in all those arts that are proper for a free citizen."[74] The orator must therefore know "philosophy" and be able to express it effectively. This is a view that Cicero attributes to the Hellenic tradition antedating Socrates and Plato, who, he believes, artificially divorced eloquence from knowledge. He alleges that these two Athenians arbitrarily reduced the meaning of "rhetoric" to mere eloquence and so created "the undoubtedly absurd, useless, and reprehensible division between the tongue and the brain, that leads us to have some teaching thinking and others teaching speaking." In the same vein, Cicero states that knowledge without eloquence is better than eloquence without knowledge; but the best goal is the marriage of the two, which is oratory[75]—the wedding of expression to learning.

Having described the consensus established about *oratoria* in Roman education, its contrast with the philosophical ideal, and the rise of a normative program of *artes liberales* within the orators' milieu, I wish now to propose a general frame of reference for this education known as "liberal." Regarding the curriculum, certain characteristics have already been noted. Early in the course of study, some attention might be given to arithmetic, geometry, and astronomy as bodies of technical facts, useful for speeches, but not as formal or speculative sciences. Music is often interpreted as practical training for the ear and voice and as an aid to appreciating poetry rather than as a complement to the formal sciences. Grammar incorporates the literary tradition, including its concern for *historia* and moral instruction, while logic is subsumed under rhetoric, which crowns the program. The entire curriculum eschews specialization.

These characteristics of the course of study are significant; yet from the rationale underlying this normative, liberal arts education it is also possible to abstract a general type, a frame of reference. I call this general type the "*artes liberales* ideal" because I regard it as an ideal for those who are identified with it, specifically the orators.

---

[74]Cicero, *De oratore* 1.72. In this account, I draw from Cicero, *De oratore* 1.9–20, 3.74–78, 84–85; Prentice A. Meador, Jr., "Rhetoric and Humanism in Cicero," *Philosophy and Rhetoric* 3 (1970): 1–12; Ernesto Grassi, *Rhetoric as Philosophy: The Humanist Tradition* (University Park: Pennsylvania State University Press, 1980), chaps. 1, 2. Quintilian repeated Cicero's arguments precisely in *Institutio oratoria*, pref. 12–20, 2.21.12–15.

[75]Cicero, *De oratore* 3.59–61, 69–73, 124–125, 142–143, *De inventione* 1.1–5. See also Isocrates, *Nicocles* 5–9, *Antidosis* 244.

Moreover, it is an ideal in the sense that it is systematic and constitutes a logically coherent whole. This *artes liberales* ideal, however is not a sort of Hegelian cloud, building over the *scholae* of Rome. It has no existence of its own other than as a useful construct to denote a group of seven characteristics that are generally advanced by Roman advocates of the *artes liberales* and by later educators who hearken back to these liberal arts.

It should also be noted that although the *artes liberales* ideal emerged between the time of Varro and Martianus and had as its chief proponents Cicero and Quintilian, the ideal is not confined to them nor they to it. I do not hold that it corresponds only to figures explicitly named, or that it circumscribes all the ideas about "liberal education" held by all of these writers, or by any of them individually. Rather, the seven characteristics of the *artes liberales* ideal represent points held in common by the great majority of Roman advocates for the liberal arts, and since the *artes liberales* ideal signifies a general type abstracted from a culture, it covers a range of educators, more or less. By the same token, I do not offer this frame of reference as a fully developed philosophy of liberal arts education. In fact, it would be misleading to do so because Cicero, Quintilian, and their ancestor Isocrates are not systematic, philosophical thinkers. Moreover, the *artes liberales* ideal is by definition not a philosophy; it is simply an abstracted type: a means to think generally about a certain approach to schooling that came to dominate the education called "liberal" during Roman antiquity and that influenced the way the term "liberal education" was subsequently employed.

The first characteristic of the *artes liberales* ideal is the goal of training the good citizen to lead society. In Cicero's *De oratore* and Quintilian's *Institutio oratoria*, this fundamental purpose is manifest: to produce the active citizen who is thoroughly virtuous and universally competent, that is, the perfect orator capable of addressing any topic and assuming any position of leadership in the state.[76] This goal necessarily implies the prescription of values and standards for character and conduct, which is a second characteristic of the *artes liberales* ideal. Isocrates pronounced, Cicero elaborated, and Quintilian repeated the conviction not only that the polished orator should possess every personal and social virtue but that, in fact, "only the good man" can become a true orator.[77]

---

[76]Quintilian, *Institutio oratoria* 12.1.23−32; Cicero, *De oratore* 3.74−77, 132−139.
[77]Quintilian, *Institutio oratoria*, pref. 9−10, 2.17.31, 12.1.1−13.

Respect for commitment to the prescribed values and standards follows thirdly, while, fourthly, a body of classical texts provides the means to identify and agree upon them. Naturally, Greek literature was often cited; but by the end of the first century c.e., Vergil and Horace were also regarded as classical and became the nucleus of the corpus of Latin works recommended as both stylistic and ethical models, which explains why Martianus's *De nuptiis* is a tapestry of authoritative sources. Educators admired this command of the tradition, and the reliance upon classical texts for norms of learning and living points, in the fifth place, to identifying an elite who achieve greater merit by adopting the personal and civic virtues expressed in the texts. Appropriately, identification of an elite is intrinsic to the root meaning of *artes liberales*—the education of the free citizen who has leisure to study.

Presupposed in these five characteristics of the *artes liberales* ideal is a sixth, "a dogmatist epistemology." This is not to be understood in the sense that one "can know reality objectively," because the orators were skeptical about philosophical inquiry in this regard. Instead, their "dogmatism"[78]—their belief that truth can be known and expressed—is revealed in their relatively unspeculative attitude that the task of liberal education is to inform the student about the virtues rather than, as the Socratic tradition held, to teach the student how to search for them. The orators were thus more pragmatic than analytic, although their pragmatism did not prevent the liberal education from becoming an ideal, an end in itself, which status is a seventh characteristic of the *artes liberales* ideal. One develops oneself according to standards of excellence for the sake of that development. From Varro's translating of *paideia* as *humanitas* through Cicero's equating of *artes liberales* and *studia humanitatis*, via Quintilian's pedagogical recommendations and Martianus's listing of the seven liberal arts, the model was established for later humanists whereby they came to consider "the personal development which resulted from a study of the classics to be sufficient justification for the labour involved." Thus, the liberal arts education was established "comme un programme idéal de culture," a good in itself.[79]

If the seven characteristics of the *artes liberales* ideal dominated

---

[78]Frederick C. Copleston, *A History of Philosophy* (Westminster, Md.: Newman, 1946), vol. 1, pp. 28, 492; Corte (1970), pp. 217, 229, 231; Cicero, *De oratore*, trans. H. Rackham (London: William Heinemann, 1926), p. xi; Quintilian, *Institutio oratoria* 2.17.16–30.

[79]Quotations are from Bolgar (1964), p. 346; Marrou (1969), p. 24. See Vito R. Giustiniani, "Umanesimo: La parola e la cosa," in *Studia Humanitatis, Ernesto Grassi zum 70. Geburtstag*, ed. Eginhard Hora and Eckhard Kessler (Munich: Wilhelm Fink,

discussion about "liberal education," it is because they character-ized the oratorical tradition, which was gradually deteriorating to the sophistic in the course of Roman antiquity. In contrast to Cicero's model for the eloquent expression of truth, Quintilian's century is often cited as leaning more toward artful display, a trend that con-tinued through the period of the "Second Sophistic" or "Later So-phistic." The demise of the Republic and genesis of the Principate in the first century B.C.E. certainly contributed to this decline by di-minishing the influence of public assemblies and, hence, delibera-tive rhetoric. Although opportunities remained for practicing forensic rhetoric, a growing imperial administration gradually encroached upon the courts of law, and later appointees to these administrative posts were not expected to have training in the liberal arts. Even-tually, rhetoric was reduced to only its epideictic function—com-memorative and ceremonial.[80] In the fifth century, the extent of this decline was clearly apparent in the garish nine volumes of *De nup-tiis* by Martianus Capella.

Modern readers have often found Martianus's allegory bewil-dering, arcane, and contrived. Yet it was quickly taken up as a text-book for the *septem artes liberales* in North Africa, Spain, Italy, and Gaul. Throughout the Middle Ages, the themes and motifs from *De nuptiis* reappeared in the treatises, literature, sculpture, and paint-ing of Western Europe.[81] Aside from the wish to display his own learning, Martianus's intentions in the treatise are often understood

---

1973), pp. 23–30. On the meaning of *humanitas*, which will have import in the fu-ture, the opening passage of the relevant chapter from *Noctes atticae* by Aulus Gellius (123–169 C.E.) reads:

> *That* humanitas *does not signify what the common people think, for those who have spoken purely have used the word more particularly.*
>
> Those who have spoken Latin words and have used them properly have not intended "humanitas" to be what common people estimate and what is called *philanthropia* by the Greeks and signifies a certain skillfulness and benevolence toward all men whatever. Rather, they labeled "humanitas" approximately what the Greeks called *paideia,* which we call "learning and instruction in the good arts." And those who seek earnestly and pursue these are the most greatly hu-mane, for concern for this knowledge and training from it have been given uniquely to man of all animals and for that reason it is called *humanitas.*
>
> And thusly did the early writers use this word, especially Marcus Varro and Marcus Tullius [Cicero], as nearly all the literature attests. (13.17)

[80]Referring to the Hellenistic era, Philostratus coined the term "Second Sophis-tic" in the third century C.E. *Lives of the Sophists* 1.481. E. Patrick Parks, *The Roman Rhetorical Schools as a Preparation for the Courts Under the Early Empire* (Baltimore: Johns Hopkins Press, 1945), pp. 13–20; Fritz E. Pederson, "On Professional Qualifications for Public Posts in Late Antiquity," *Classica et mediaevalia* 31, fascs. 1–2 (1970): 161–214; Kennedy (1972), chap. 4; Murphy (1974), pp. 35–42, 50ff.

[81]LeMoine (1972), pp. 2–3; Stahl and Johnson (1971), pp. 55–79; Philippe Ver-dier, "L'iconographie des arts libéraux dans l'art du moyen âge jusqu'à la fin du quinzième siècle," in *Actes* (1969), pp. 305–355.

in two ways. In one respect, *De nuptiis* can be taken as a textbook for the preparatory education of the citizen with leisure to study; in another respect, when the description of liberal arts in the last seven books is combined with the mélange of philosophy and theology in the first two books, it can be regarded as something of an encyclopedia.

Neither the propaedeutic nor the pansophic interpretation is wholly satisfactory because the scope of Martianus's work is too wide for a school text and too narrow for an encyclopedia. Therefore, it may be best to incorporate an aspect from each interpretation by regarding this description of the *artes liberales* as the sum total of education necessary for the citizen with leisure to study. Confirmation for this view lies in the fact that Martianus stopped at seven liberal arts, explicitly excluding those practical and technical arts, medicine and architecture, that Varro had included.[82] The combination of propaedeutic and pansophic rationales also provides a way to understand how Christians accommodated the *artes liberales* and the underlying ideal to their own purposes.

After surviving persecutions in the first and second centuries, adherents of Christianity, who generally belonged to the poor and uneducated classes of society, ascended to preeminent offices of power in the empire by the late fourth century. Meanwhile, many pagan citizens, being educated in the classical tradition, tended to regard the upstart gospel as coarse and simplistic; and when the barbarian threat appeared on the horizon, they charged Christianity with undermining the moral strength and vigor of Roman civilization. Conversely, certain church leaders bore great animosity toward classical culture not only because they had been persecuted in its name but also because pagan mythology offended them both morally and theologically. This tension between Greco-Roman and Judeo-Christian ideals was experienced and addressed by many churchmen, such as Jerome (347–420), who dreamed that his love of classical letters would subject him to the divine condemnation "You are a Ciceronian, not a Christian."[83] Other leaders of the Latin church invoked pagan and Jewish myths about Plato visiting Egypt in order to support their claim that the liberal arts and all classical learning derived either directly from their Scripture or from the Egyptians, who had learned it from the Hebrews.

---

[82]Martianus Capella, *De nuptiis* 891; Kühnert (1961), pp. 50–51; Stahl and Johnson (1971), p. 97; LeMoine (1972), pp. 5–6.

[83]Jerome, *Epistulae* 22.30. On the Christian appropriation of classical culture, I draw from Gerard L. Ellspermann, *The Attitude of Early Christian Writers Toward Pa-*

This myth was also cited, though later qualified, by Augustine (354–430), who proposed much of what would become the medieval resolution of this conflict. Two of Augustine's important works in this regard were *De doctrina christiana* (On Christian learning) and *De civitate Dei* (City of God), which were written over the first three decades of the fifth century as the Roman Empire crumbled. Frequently citing Cicero, Augustine adopted the forms of classical erudition, thus legitimating their use by other Christians at the same time that he met pagan critics on their own ground. In this fashion, he argued that Christianity had not caused the decline of the empire. Rather, fundamental pride and love of praise—the antithesis of the Christian virtue of humility—had rotted out the civilization. At the same time, he admonished Christians that their faith and classical culture shared many of the same values, and for this reason the latter could not be completely condemned.[84]

While the problem of moral corruption by pagan literature could thus be answered so far as some were concerned, the problem of theology remained, and here entered the combination of pansophic and propaedeutic rationales. The *septem artes liberales* came to be adopted as all the education necessary for the study of higher truth in Scripture. In this way, the Church informed the late sophistic liberal arts with a reinvigorated sense of inherited truth and virtue, an inheritance derived from a textual tradition and meant to be eloquently expounded. The Christian adoption of classical forms thus elevated the sophistic *artes liberales* of late antiquity closer to the oratorical model advanced by Cicero and received from Isocratean Hellenistic civilization. Notable evidence for this development can be found in Augustine's essay on Christian preaching in Book 4 of *De doctrina christiana*, in which he explains and defends the wedding of eloquence and wisdom.[85]

It is true that Augustine also became a Neoplatonic "Christian

---

gan *Literature and Learning* (Washington, D.C.: Catholic University of America Press, 1949); B. Carmon Hardy, "*Et vocasti in hereditatem tuam*: Secular Knowledge and the Early Christians," *PH* 8 (1968): 19–41; Peter R. Brown, *Augustine of Hippo: A Biography* (Berkeley: University of California Press, 1967); Kennedy (1980), chap. 7; George A. Kennedy, *Greek Rhetoric Under Christian Emperors* (Princeton, N.J.: Princeton University Press, 1983), chap. 4.

[84]In *De civitate Dei*, see especially bks. 1, 8, 18.

[85]Augustine, *De doctrina christiana* 4.5.7–4.6.10. See Sister Thérèse Sullivan, S. *Avreli Avgvstini Hipponiensis Episcopi "De Doctrina Christiana," Liber Qvartvs, A Commentary, with a Revised Text, Introduction, and Translation* (Washington, D.C.: Catholic University of America Press, 1930); Marrou (1958), pt. 3, chap. 6; Murphy (1974), pp. 57–64, 285–290; W. R. Johnson, "Isocrates Flowering: The Rhetoric of Augustine," *Philosophy and Rhetoric* 9 (1976): 217–231.

philosopher" in the sense offered by Etienne Gilson, but there is little justification for considering him to be a Socratic who regarded the "liberal arts as philosophical liberation," as some modern scholars have done.[86] Augustine was trained as a rhetor; and language, not dialectic or mathematics, was for him the focus of the *artes liberales*. He sought at times to make an Aristotelian distinction between scientific "logic" and discursive "dialectic," but he did not do so consistently, which reflects the fact that, as he himself suggested, he learned his philosophy from Cicero, not Plato or Aristotle. And his notion of that word was linked more to *sophia*, a cycle of studies or divine truth securely grasped, than to *philosophia*, the speculative search for truth.[87] Consistent with this outlook, Augustine divides *philosophia* according to the Stoic division—logic, ethics, physics—that Cicero had endorsed, though he attributes it to Plato.[88]

Augustine's writings contain varying enumerations of the liberal arts. But in *De ordine*, he lists Martianus's seven while citing Varro, and he affirms the etymological foundation of the arts by writing that in order to master the "liberal arts," one must have "leisure which is the privilege of advanced age or some happy circumstances."[89] Meanwhile, in the first four books of *Confessiones*, he answers affirmatively, though with reservations, the larger question of whether the pagan arts are compatible with and complementary to Christian truth. Each of these points anticipates the fact that the meaning of liberal education for subsequent generations would be dictated by Cassiodorus and Isidore, rather than the philosopher Boethius.

---

[86]Etienne Gilson, *The Spirit of Mediaeval Philosophy*, trans. A. H. Downes (New York: Charles Scribner's Sons, 1936), p. 37; Peter H. Baker, "Liberal Arts as Philosophical Liberation: St. Augustine's *De magistro*," in *Actes* (1969), pp. 469–479; Edmund J. Dehnert, "Music as Liberal in Augustine and Boethius," in *Actes* (1969), pp. 987–991.

[87]Augustine, *Confessiones* 3.4; Guy-H. Allard, "Arts libéraux et langage chez Saint Augustin," in *Actes* (1969), pp. 481–492; Marrou (1958), pp. 193–197, 232–275. *Curiositas*, in Augustine's view, implies a vain and dangerous motive for study. *Confessiones* 10.35.

[88]Augustine, *De civitate Dei* 8.4, 11.25; Cicero, *Academica* 1.5.19–21.

[89]"Privilegio aetatis aut cujuslibet felicitatis otiosus." Augustine, *De ordine* 2.16.44, in *Patrologiae Cursus Completus Series Latina*, ed. J. P. Migne (Paris: Garnier Fratres, 1845), vol. 32. See Marrou (1958), pp. 189–192; Marrou (1969), table 5.

III
Rise of the Philosophical Tradition in the High Middle Ages

*T*HE SEVEN LIBERAL ARTS *do not sufficiently divide theoretical philosophy.*

THOMAS AQUINAS*

*P*ARIS AND ORLEANS *are at odds . . .*
Do you know the reason for the discord?
It is because they differ about learning;
For Logic, who is always wrangling,
Calls the authors authorlings
And the students of Orleans mere grammar-boys.

HENRI D'ANDELI†

Expositio super librum Boethii De trinitate.
† *La bataille des VII ars.*

DURING THE PERIOD OF TRANSITION in Western Europe between late antiquity and the Middle Ages, the understanding of the *artes liberales* and *disciplinae liberales* was fundamentally shaped for subsequent centuries by the comprehensive handbooks of three writers: Martianus, Cassiodorus, and Isidore. The treatise of the first, as noted previously, was a pagan work that Christians nonetheless cited, taught, and finally claimed as their own. Thus, Saint Gregory of Tours in the sixth century urged leaders of the Church to study the "seven disciplines" of "our Martianus."[1]

One who had already followed this advice was Cassiodorus (c. 484–c. 584), who, after a full career as administrator, politician, and diplomat, founded a monastery called Vivarium near the heel of the Italian peninsula to be a center of Christian scholarship eclipsing all that had preceded it. For the instruction of the monks he wrote *Institutiones*, which comprises a first book of "divine readings" and an accompanying book of "human readings," the latter being described as a long appendix to aid the monks in their study of scripture and the Church Fathers. These "human readings" consist of the *septem artes liberales*, the study of which is defended in the preface by citations of Proverbs 9:1, "Wisdom has built a home for herself and hewn out seven columns," and Exodus 25:37, "You shall make seven lamps and put them so they light out against it."[2] These citations, plus Cassiodorus's derivation of *liberalis* from *liber* (book), were subsequently repeated and elaborated in connection with references to Egyptian papyrus, for Egypt was regarded as the homeland of learning, where Plato, according to myth, had visited and studied with the Egyptians or the Hebrews.[3]

Through these scriptural citations and mythical references, Cassiodorus offered an apology to rigorists of the Church, who, despite the writings of Jerome, Augustine, and others, had never calmed

---

[1]Gregory of Tours, *Historia francorum*, trans. O. M. Dalton (Oxford: Clarendon, 1927) 10.18, 31.

[2]Cassiodorus, *Institutiones*, ed. R. A. Mynors (Oxford: Clarendon, 1937) 1.21.1, 1.27.2, 2.pref.2; Leslie W. Jones, "The Influence of Cassiodorus on Mediaeval Culture," *Speculum* 20 (1945): 433–442; James J. O'Donnell, *Cassiodorus* (Berkeley: University of California Press, 1979), chaps. 6, 7.

[3]Cassiodorus, *Institutiones*, 2.pref.4; 2.2.22; Isidore, *Etymologiarum sive originum, libri XX*, ed. W. M. Lindsay (Oxford: Clarendon, 1911) 6.13.3; Simone Viarre, "A propos de l'origine égyptienne des arts libéraux: Alexandre Neckam et Cassiodore," in *Actes* (1969), pp. 583–591; Silvestro Fiore, "La théorie de Bernard Sylvestris *Aegyptus parturit artes* et les préceptes persans du Damdad Nask," in *Actes* (1969), pp. 575–581; O'Donnell (1979), p. 158–159.

themselves about the moral and theological offenses of pagan culture. One alternative for this group inspired with *contemptus mundi* was to enter the monasteries, a not uncommon choice by the end of the fifth century. There they sought to draw the line starkly: the believer must choose between Scripture and pagan literature, including the liberal arts. Paradoxically, an authority appealed to along these lines was a pagan himself—Seneca the Younger, who had argued in a letter that the only arts that are truly "liberal" or "free" are those devoted to virtue. This letter was later transcribed and circulated under the title *Liber de septem artibus liberalibus*.[4] The rigorist critique, though never entirely compelling even in the monasteries, as demonstrated by Cassiodorus's example at Vivarium, nevertheless remained an important issue for all. Throughout the Middle Ages, fear of corruption by the liberal arts was to be matched by a reluctant or enthusiastic acceptance of their necessity for the literate Christian. In the words of Ermenric of Ellwangen in the ninth century, "Since even as dung spread upon the field enriches it to good harvest, so the filthy writings of the pagan poets are a mighty aid to divine eloquence."[5]

Cassiodorus had put it more delicately, but the point was the same: the accommodation of the *artes liberales* to Christian purposes. And this was based upon the oratorical tradition of liberal education. For dialectic, Cassiodorus offered a description drawn from Aristotle and Cicero, largely amounting to a series of definitions, while for rhetoric, he relied heavily on the Ciceronian *compendia* handed down from antiquity. Regarding both those arts, he cited Varro in connection with the metaphor of the closed fist and open hand. The four mathematical disciplines were given less attention than the three language arts, and were presented either as sets of facts useful for scriptural allegory or as evidence of the harmonic influence of divine guidance in the world, but not as a means

---

[4]Jacques Chailley, "La danse religieuse au moyen âge," in *Actes* (1969), pp. 357–380; Etienne Gilson, "La philosophie et les arts libéraux," in *Actes* (1969), pp. 269–270; Pierre Riché, *Education and Culture in the Barbarian West from the Sixth through the Eighth Centuries*, trans. John J. Contreni (Columbia: University of South Carolina Press, 1976), chap. 3; José A. Fránquiz, "The Place of Seneca in the Curriculum of the Middle Ages," in *Actes* (1969), pp. 1065–1072.

[5]Quoted in Helen Waddell, *The Wandering Scholars*, rev. ed. (London: Constable, 1934), p. xx; Jean LeClercq, *The Love of Learning and the Desire for God: A Study of Monastic Culture*, trans. Catharine Misrahi, 2d ed. (New York: Fordham University Press, 1974), chap. 7; Robert Bultot, "*Grammatica, ethica*, et *contemptus mundi* aux XIIe et XIIIe siècles," in *Actes* (1969), pp. 815–827.

of instructing the mind in mathematical or formal reasoning.[6] The general lines of Cassiodorus's approach, as well as much of his actual text, were incorporated into the third popular medieval handbook of the seven arts.[7]

That treatise, the *Etymologiae* or *Origines*, was written by Isidore (570–636), the bishop of Seville, who was the author most read in the early Middle Ages. And the first three books of *Etymologiae*, describing the *septem artes liberales*, were the most frequently cited of his writings. Isidore devoted three times as much attention to the language arts as he did to mathematics. He also equated *logica* with *dialectica* and seemed to prefer the Stoic-Augustinian division of *philosophia* to the Aristotelian.[8] But of all the arts, the fundamental one for Isidore was grammar, into which he incorporated "prose," "poetry," "fables," and "history." The etymological investigation of words in order to explain their meaning and their referents constituted for him the archetype of all other arts and, indeed, all other fields of knowledge. In justifying his preference for this etymological grammar above dialectic, whose speculative methods could lead to entertaining thoughts contrary to Christian teaching, he elsewhere stated, "Better to be grammarians than heretics."[9]

If the interpretation of the liberal arts by Martianus, Cassiodorus, and Isidore favored the oratorical above the philosophical, a thread of the latter tradition nevertheless extended into the early

---

[6]James J. Murphy, ed., *Three Medieval Rhetorical Arts* (Berkeley: University of California Press, 1971), pp. viii–xiii; Karl G. Fellerer, "Die Musica in den Artes Liberales," in *Artes* (1959), pp. 33–43; Hans M. Klinkenberg, "Der Verfall des Quadriviums im frühen Mittelalter," in *Artes* (1959), pp. 8–20; Edward A. Lippman, "The Place of Music in the System of Liberal Arts," in *Aspects of Medieval and Renaissance Music*, ed. Jan LaRue et al., rev. ed. (New York: Pendragon, 1972), pp. 550–559. In Mynors's edition of Cassiodorus's *Institutiones*, the distribution of attention to the seven disciplines is grammar 4 pages, rhetoric 12 pages, and dialectic 22 pages, for a total of 38 pages; arithmetic 11 pages, music 9 pages, geometry 3 pages, and astronomy 5 pages, for a total of 28 pages.

[7]The citing of the Varronian metaphor by Cassiodorus (*Institutiones* 2.3.2) and Isidore (*Etymologiarum sive originum* 2.23) is a specific example of the continuity being described here.

[8]Isidore, *Etymologiarum sive originum* 2.22, 24; Jacques Fontaine, *Isidore de Seville et la culture classique dans l'Espagne wisigothique* (Paris: Etudes augustiniennes, 1959), pp. 3–4, 13–15, 593–645. The division of Isidore's attention to the arts in Lindsay's edition is one book of 62 pages on grammar, one book of 42 pages on rhetoric and dialectic, and one book of 37 pages on the four mathematical disciplines.

[9]"Meliores esse grammaticos quam haereticos" (or: "Grammarians are better than heretics"). Isidore, *Sententiarum libri tres* 3.3.11, in *Patrologiae Cursus Completus Series Latina*, ed. J. P. Migne (Paris: Garnier Fratres, 1850), vol. 83; Isidore, *Etymologiarum sive originum* 1.5, 38–44; Fontaine (1959), pp. 27–209.

Middle Ages. Evidence for this persistence appears in the writing of Boethius (480–524), a minister to the Ostrogoth king in Italy. Boethius took upon himself the breathtaking task of translating, commenting upon, and reconciling the works of Plato and Aristotle, an assignment indicative of his intellectual orientation. Upon his imprisonment and early death, he had barely managed to begin the enterprise, having completed the translation and commentary of only two of Aristotle's six treatises on logic. Yet this work, plus half of Plato's *Timaeus*, was to provide the sum total of classical Greek philosophy known to the early Middle Ages.[10] Boethius supplemented those two treatises on logic with his own *De differentiis topicis*, which subordinated the "topics" of rhetoric to those of dialectic.[11]

This medieval philosopher meanwhile began translating and composing treatises on the mathematical liberal arts, and the introduction to *De institutione arithmetica* neatly conveys the contrast in form and content between Boethius's work and the handbooks of Martianus, Cassiodorus, and Isidore. Acknowledging the leadership of Pythagoras, Boethius cites the four mathematical disciplines—"like a place where four roads meet" (*quasi quadruvio*)—as the sole path to philosophy. In this way, while relying on an antecedent root, he coined the term *quadrivium* for future masters of the liberal arts. Boethius then announces that the common denominator of the four quadrivial studies is *quantitas abstracta*,[12] an assertion that comports with his analysis of *scientia musica* and his explanation that sensory observation is merely the occasion for gathering mathematical knowledge. Contrary to Augustine, he approves *musica* for its

---

[10]Pierre P. Courcelle, *"La consolation de Philosophie" dans la tradition littéraire: Antécédents et postérité de Boèce* (Paris: Etudes augustiniennes, 1967), chap. 6; Edward K. Rand, *Founders of the Middle Ages* (Cambridge: Harvard University Press, 1928), chap. 5. However much more profound Boethius's writings may have been compared to Cassiodorus's, the orientation of the former was less influential than that of the latter in the early Middle Ages. See *The Seven Liberal Arts in the Middle Ages*, ed. David L. Wagner (Bloomington: Indiana University Press, 1983) and my brief review in *Educational Studies* 16 (1985): 99–103.

[11]Michael C. Leff, "Boethius' *De differentiis topicis*, Book IV," in *Medieval Eloquence: Studies in the Theory and Practice of Medieval Rhetoric*, ed. James J. Murphy (Berkeley: University of California Press, 1978), pp. 3–24; Henry Chadwick, *Boethius: The Consolations of Music, Logic, Theology, and Philosophy* (Oxford: Clarendon, 1981), pp. 111–120.

[12]Boethius, *De institutione arithmetica, libri duo, De institutione musica, libri quinque. Accedit geometria quae fertur Boetii*, G. Friedlein (Leipzig: B. G. Teubner, 1867) 1:1; Chadwick (1981), pp. 69–107. The *Arithmetic* is a translation from the Greek of the *Introduction to Arithmetic* by Nicomachus of Gerasa, and *quadruvium* is a translation of *tessares methodoi* (four methods).

mathematical and speculative import, not its emotional, ethical, or aesthetic sense of the divine.[13]

The *quadrivium* is, therefore, the path to philosophy for Boethius, and the Platonic nature of that *via* is confirmed by his *De consolatione Philosophiae* (The consolation of Philosophy). Book 1 opens with its author languishing in prison, bemoaning the loss of his possessions, youth, and health. Philosophia appears to him as a robed woman of dignified mien. Low on her tunic is written the Greek letter Pi, representing practical philosophy, and a series of steps leads to the Greek letter Theta, representing theoretical philosophy, high on the tunic. Invoking a Platonic metaphor, she tells Boethius, "You have forgotten what you truly are," and reminds him that fortune, health, and youth are transitory and that a man is fundamentally rational. In Book 2, Philosophia warns about "the sweetness of Rhetoric's persuasion which proceeds on the correct track only when it does not desert my instruction." She eventually outlines a speculative dialectic that, by elevating his mind to the contemplative vision of philosophy, can liberate him from prison.[14]

The significance of this outlook, however, was lost on future generations. Although Boethius's commentary on Aristotle's logical treatises was employed in the schools, *De consolatione* was neglected for three centuries. The Platonic admonition that one should speculatively search for highest truth was rejected along with the philosophers' favorite means to pursue this course: mathematics and dialectic.

This rejection and loss of Athenian philosophical works was not due simply to a medieval preference for rhetoric, just as the fact that the foregoing writers lived in Italy, southern Gaul, and Spain was not coincidental.[15] In 476, barbarian conquerors deposed the last Roman emperor, and the Western Empire was divided into small kingdoms until 533, when Justinian achieved some success in re-

---

[13]Boethius, *De institutione musica* 1.1–2; Fellerer (1959), pp. 33–40; Klinkenberg (1959), pp. 1–6; Edmund J. Dehnert, "Music as Liberal in Augustine and Boethius," in *Actes* (1969), pp. 987–991; Calvin Bower, "Boethius and Nicomachus: An Essay Concerning the Sources of the *De institutione musica*," *Vivarium* 16 (May 1978): 1–45.

[14]Boethius, *De consolatione Philosophiae* 1.1, 1.6, 2.1, 3 song 9; Klinkenberg (1959), pp. 1–32; Courcelle (1967), chap. 1, pp. 17–28.

[15]For the following, I draw from Beryl Smalley, *The Study of the Bible in the Middle Ages*, 2d ed. (Oxford: Basil Blackwell, 1952); T. J. Haarhoff, *Schools of Gaul: A Study of Pagan and Christian Education in the Last Century of the Western Empire* (Oxford: Clarendon, 1919); Pierre P. Courcelle, *Late Latin Writers and Their Greek Sources*, trans. Harry E. Wedeck (Cambridge: Harvard University Press, 1969), pp. 410–421; Riché (1976), chaps. 1–7; Pierre Riché, *Les écoles et l'enseignement dans l'occident chrétien de*

uniting it. Despite that restoration, education began nearly two centuries of decay. In the most Romanized areas, teaching in the liberal arts lingered on, but in the farther territories of Britain, northern Gaul, and Germany, communities rapidly returned to clan life. As decades passed, with repeated invasions and migrations uprooting and impoverishing the nobles and their institutions, the classical education became more and more difficult to find.

Where it did continue to some degree was in private tutorials in the homes of noble families who still remembered the ideal of eloquent *learning*; in parish and episcopal schools, though these flickered on and off; and most of all, in monasteries such as the Vivarium of Cassiodorus or Monte Cassino of Benedict. Institutions of this latter sort, being small, self-sufficient, and enclosed, were best suited to preserve liberal education throughout the barbarian occupation of Western Europe. To be sure, the monasteries themselves did not lack critics, even despisers, of classical culture. But the continuing threat of invasion, the widespread circulation of the Cassiodorian and Isidorian treatises, and the practice of Benedict's rule helped soften these objections, and, in any case, Christians tended to view classicism as a lesser threat than barbarism.

Similar to the secluded monasteries and the Italian and Iberian peninsulas in their relative isolation from tribes invading out of the north and east, Ireland and Wales also preserved elementary instruction in the *artes liberales*. For two hundred years following the Roman evacuation in the fifth century, the Jutes, Angles, and Saxons slowly pushed the indigenous Celts westward across the British Isles. These invaders did not value Latin culture; hence literary education retired to the monasteries in Wales, where abbots' biographies report that they studied the *disciplinae liberales*, and in Ireland, where the subject matter of arithmetic, grammar, and rhetoric was drawn from the comprehensive handbooks of the liberal arts. By the seventh century, Ireland had become one of the chief repositories of liberal studies in all of Europe, and clerics from other kingdoms traveled there to study.[16]

---

la fin du Ve siècle au milieu du XIe siècle (Paris: Aubier Montaigne, 1979), pp. 11–46; O'Donnell (1979), chap. 6.

[16] For the discussion of Wales, Ireland, and Irish missionaries, I draw from Charles H. Talbot, ed. and trans., *The Anglo-Saxon Missionaries in Germany, Being the Lives of SS. Willibrord, Boniface, Sturm, Leoba, and Lebuin together with the "Hodoeporicon" of St. Willibald and a Selection from the Correspondence of St. Boniface* (New York: Sheed and Ward, 1954); Max L. Laistner, *The Intellectual Heritage of the Early Middle Ages, Selected Essays*, ed. Chester G. Starr (Ithaca, N.Y.: Cornell University Press, 1957), chap. 6; Robert R. Bolgar, *The Classical Heritage and Its Beneficiaries* (Cambridge: Cam-

The Irish schools gradually found themselves in a position to begin sending missionaries back into barbarian Europe, and these teachers first went to England, where monastic schools were established for teaching the traditional letters. Out of this movement arose the impetus for monks to accept the children of princes and nobles in "exterior" monastic schools for training in the liberal arts. Meanwhile, Irish monks commenced traveling to Gaul. One such was Columban (d. 615), who established several monasteries on his way to Italy, where he founded the monastery at Bobbio. Through these Irish efforts and also those by Italian monks heading northward, the centers of literary culture in Ireland, Italy, and Spain began to reestablish a tenuous network across barbarian Europe.

By the beginning of the eighth century, Irish missionaries had yielded the leadership in liberal education to their Anglo-Saxon students, who appropriated the meager remnants of the *artes liberales*, comprising grammar, hymnic poetry, *historia*, prosody, and arithmetic. In one respect, the elementary level of this schooling reflected the general decline in learning, for, in this epoch, progress was made even by the simple reading and copying of *florilegia*— "bouquets" of excerpts from ancient authors.[17] The meagerness of the curriculum stemmed also from the continuing rigorist fear of contamination by pagan learning, a fear which is expressed in writings by Aldhelm and Bede and which extended to the oratorical and philosophical traditions. In the final analysis, however, Christian teachers concluded not only that some classical learning was helpful to the faith, but also, when forced to choose between the two traditions, that it was "better to be grammarians than heretics." Here is seen influence from works on the liberal arts by Augustine, Cassiodorus, and Isidore. When Bede's colleagues and students educated Alcuin (730–804) at the cathedral school of York, they relied on these authors, whose teachings were then carried by Alcuin to the court of Charlemagne.

In Gaul, the chaos of civil war and repeated invasions continued into the first half of the eighth century until the Franks quashed internal rebellions and repulsed the Saracens driving north from

---

bridge University Press, 1964), chaps. 1–2; Manuel C. Díaz y Díaz, "Les arts libéraux d'après les écrivains espagnols et insulaires aux VIIe et VIIIe siècles," in *Actes* (1969), pp. 42–46; LeClercq (1974), chap. 7; Riché (1976), chaps. 8–10; Fergal McGrath, *Education in Ancient and Medieval Ireland* (Dublin: Studies "Special Publications," 1979), chaps. 7–9.

[17]On the *florilegia* and their subsequent influence, see R. H. Rouse, "Florilegia and Latin Classical Authors in Twelfth- and Thirteenth-Century Orléans," *Viator* 10 (1979): 131–160.

Spain. Beyond achieving relative stability through these military exploits, the Frankish nobility also contributed to the late eighth-century Carolingian Renaissance by breaking the traditional practice of educating children at home under tutors. Instead, they began to entrust their children to the monks for education, following the model of "exterior" schools advanced at certain Anglo-Saxon monasteries. This development laid the ground for a renewal of education, which resulted from the consolidation of the Frankish Empire under Charlemagne, who established a palace school and called Alcuin to be the master.

Arriving in 782 from York, the English scholar recommended that learning in the palace school and throughout the empire be based on the *septem artes liberales* as enumerated in his *Grammatica*, and Charlemagne responded with proclamations to spread learning by strengthening existing schools and establishing new ones. Alcuin went on to teach the *artes* at Tours for the last eight years of his life. His legacy was passed on to the ninth century by his students and colleagues, many of whom attained eminence at important schools in Europe. Meanwhile, monastic schools like St. Gall were founded or chartered under the authority of Charlemagne and devoted themselves to the primary scholarly task of the era: collecting, copying, and commenting upon texts, chiefly in the disciplines of the *trivium*.[18]

The term *trivium* for the three language arts came into use among Alcuin's circle of scholars in the Carolingian era,[19] and this fact is just as telling about them as the coining of *quadrivium* is about Boethius. On the one hand, the Carolingians demoted the mathematical arts, teaching them before rhetoric and interpreting them, not in terms of *quantitas abstracta*, but as information useful for allegorical

---

[18]Eleanor S. Duckett, *Alcuin, Friend of Charlemagne: His World and His Work* (New York: Macmillan, 1951), chaps. 6–7; Luitpold Wallach, *Alcuin and Charlemagne: Studies in Carolingian History and Literature* (Ithaca: Cornell University Press, 1959), chap. 5; Lambert de Rijk, "On the Curriculum of the Arts of the Trivium at St. Gall from c.850–c.1000," *Vivarium* 1 (1963): 35–86; Leighton D. Reynolds and N. G. Wilson, *Scribes and Scholars: A Guide to the Transmission of Greek and Latin Literature* (London: Oxford University Press, 1968), chap. 3; Gérard Mathon, "Les formes et la signification de la pédagogie des arts libéraux au milieu du IXe siècle: L'enseignement palatin de Jean Scot Erigène," in *Actes* (1969), pp. 47–57; LeClercq (1974), chaps. 7–8.

[19]The fundamental source on the appearance of the terms *trivium* and *quadrivium* is Pio Rajna, "Le denominazioni *trivium* e *quadrivium*," *Studi medievali* 1 (1928): 4–36. Bonner implies that an earlier association between these words and the *artes* can be found in the fact that Roman teachers would stand at a streetcorner—*trivio* or *quadrivio*—to gather and teach their students. Stanley F. Bonner, *Education in Ancient Rome From the Elder Cato to the Younger Pliny* (Berkeley: University of California Press, 1977), pp. 116–117.

exegesis or liturgical practice.[20] On the other hand, they necessarily concentrated on the study of texts and language and thus emphasized the study of grammar in the traditional handbooks. For instance, their reliance on Martianus is shown by their preference for odd and contorted phraseology.[21]

Pulled from the encyclopedias, the Latin treatises of Donatus (c. 350 c.e.) and Priscian (c. 525 c.e.) had already become the standard textbooks in grammar, while for dialectic, which was treated superficially and generally subordinated to rhetoric, the handful of Boethian translations and commentaries on Aristotle comprised the sum of available learning. The height of the *trivium*, and thus of the seven arts, was rhetoric, although even here important texts were lacking. There was, however, a revival of Quintilian,[22] a development consonant with the thoroughly Ciceronian character of Alcuin's treatise on rhetoric and with the general liaison established between *historia* and *ethica*. As Pierre Riché has repeatedly noted, "Carolingian culture under Charlemagne remained, as in the past, literary and rhetorical."[23]

With this in mind, I propose that, here again, the *artes liberales* ideal serves as an abstracted type systematizing the ideas generally associated with the words "liberal education" and "liberal arts" in the early Middle Ages, including the Carolingian era. In terms of curriculum, the *artes liberales* ideal, due to its foundation in the or-

---

[20]Alcuin, *Disputatio de rhetorica et de virtutibus*, trans. Wilbur S. Howell (Princeton, N.J.: Princeton University Press, 1941), lines 18–22; Klinkenberg (1959), pp. 8–27; Fellerer (1959), pp. 33–43; Díaz (1969), pp. 37–46; Eugenio T. Toccafondi, "Il pensiero di San Tommaso sulle arti liberali," in *Actes* (1969), pp. 639–651; Lippman (1972), pp. 552–559.

[21]William H. Stahl and Richard Johnson, with E. L. Burge, *Martianus Capella and the Seven Liberal Arts* (New York: Columbia University Press, 1971), vol. 1, pp. 30, 60–67; Charles S. Baldwin, *Medieval Rhetoric and Poetry (to 1400) Interpreted from Representative Works* (New York: Macmillan, 1928), chap. 5; Fritz Schalk, "Zur Entwicklung der Artes im Frankreich und Italien," in *Artes* (1959), pp. 137–138. Others argue that this interest in Martianus was "scholastic" and dialectical rather than rhetorical and literary: John O. Ward, "The Commentator's Rhetoric: From Antiquity to the Renaissance: Glosses and Commentaries on Cicero's *Rhetorica*," in *Medieval Eloquence: Studies in the Theory and Practice of Medieval Rhetoric*, ed. James J. Murphy (Berkeley: University of California Press, 1978), p. 44.

[22]Paul Lehmann, "Die *Institutio oratoria* des Quintilianus im Mittelalter," *Philologus* 89 (1934): 354–360; Bolgar (1964), pp. 110–117; James J. Murphy, *Rhetoric in the Middle Ages: A History of Rhetorical Theory from Saint Augustine to the Renaissance* (Berkeley: University of California Press, 1974), pp. 124–127.

[23]Riché (1976), p. 499; Riché (1979), pp. 111–118; Wilbur S. Howell, ed. and trans., *The Rhetoric of Alcuin and Charlemagne* (Princeton, N.J.: Princeton University Press, 1941), pp. 22–33; Wallach (1959), chap. 6; Hans Wolter, "Geschichtliche Bildung im Rahmen der Artes Liberales," in *Artes* (1959), pp. 64–78.

atorical tradition, is implied by the above description of studies and by the frequent Carolingian references to commentaries on Cicero that emphasized the importance of uniting eloquence and wisdom.[24] More specifically, the seven characteristics of the *artes liberales* ideal may also be identified in this period.

First is the aim of training the good citizen and leader of society, a goal demonstrated by Alcuin's *Disputatio de rhetorica et de virtutibus*. Alcuin incorporated into this work a theory of kingship for Charlemagne just as Cicero and Quintilian had sought to mold the consummate orator and governor through their writings. Moreover, those who studied the *artes liberales*, whether monks or not, tended to be drawn from the wellborn and, in any case, to enter the ranks of leadership in medieval society after their liberal education.[25] Schooling therefore involved the prescription of values and standards for personality formation and civic responsibility as well as the expectation of commitment to the same, the second and third characteristics of the *artes liberales* ideal. That such values and standards were intended to mold character is demonstrated clearly by Alcuin's *Disputatio*, where the discussion of rhetoric culminates in a consideration of the cardinal virtues.[26] Fourthly, and following necessarily, is the reliance on authoritative texts, a body of classical authors, as the source of the teachings of the *artes*. Indeed, the "authorities" were the *auctores*—this is the etymological root—and these authors provided moral and literary instruction simultaneously.[27]

The identification of an elite who achieve merit as a consequence of their education in the *artes liberales* constitutes a fifth characteristic. This point is shown not only by the special privileges and immunities legally granted to teachers of the liberal arts, but also by the various kinds of "secret language" employed by those with a literary education in order to reserve their learning from the untutored. Bede developed a finger language for this purpose, and the seventh-century schoolmaster Aenas is said to have recommended

---

[24]Gabriel Nuchelmans, "Philologia et son mariage avec Mercure jusqu'à la fin du XIIe siècle," *Latomus* 16 (1957): 84–97; Mathon (1969), pp. 48–58; Cora E. Lutz, ed., *Remigii Autissiodorensis commentum in Martianum Capellam* (Leiden: E. J. Brill, 1962), pp. 16–24).

[25]Wallach (1959), chap. 4; John W. Baldwin, *The Scholastic Culture of the Middle Ages, 1000–1300* (Lexington, Mass.: D. C. Heath, 1971), pp. 36, 47, 55; Riché (1976), pp. 48, 205–206, 284, 447–499.

[26]Alcuin, *Disputatio de rhetorica et de virtutibus*, lines 1187–1368.

[27]Ernst R. Curtius, *European Literature and the Latin Middle Ages*, trans. Willard R. Trask (New York: Pantheon, 1953), pp. 48–61; Jacques Paquet, "Aspects de l'université médiévale," in *The Universities* (1978), pp. 3–25.

that the learned use cryptography "so as not to enable the young and fools to understand mysteries which are to be known only by the initiated."[28]

Underlying those five characteristics is, sixthly, the presupposition of early medieval scholars of the certainty and ultimacy of their learning, an assumption revealed in their reluctance to ask critical questions of epistemology and ontology. In words attributed to schoolmaster Aenas, "The more one defends his own curiosity, the more he finds himself in error."[29] Masters attended to grammar and rhetoric because they were, with Isidore, convinced that "language was a natural, necessary phenomenon, the study of which could reveal metaphysical truth."[30] Conversely, they displayed little interest in searching for new knowledge. The Stoic and Aristotelian schemata of *philosophia* were known, but they stimulated no speculation about what the lost sciences, beyond the seven liberal arts, might have contained.[31] The scholars' attitude was thus dogmatic; they devoted themselves to preserving and transmitting the inherited wisdom unchanged and uncorrupted, a devotion shown by their reliance upon devices and aids for memorization that rhetors had developed in antiquity.[32]

With respect to the seventh characteristic of the *artes liberales* ideal, it must be said that medieval educators decidedly accommo-

---

[28]Quoted in Riché (1976), p. 477. See Pearl Kibre, *Scholarly Privileges in the Middle Ages: The Rights, Privileges, and Immunities of Scholars and Universities at Bologna, Padua, Paris, and Oxford* (Cambridge: Mediaeval Academy of America, 1962), pp. 3–8.

[29]Quoted in Riché (1976), p. 475.

[30]Jeremy Y. Adams, "The Political Grammar of Isidore of Seville," in *Actes* (1969), p. 764. See Díaz (1969), p. 42.

[31]Boethius had, in various places, followed the Aristotelian tradition in distinguishing practical philosophy from speculative (theoretical) philosophy, with the latter divided into *naturalis, mathematica,* and *theologica* subsections (*De trinitate* 2 lines 1–20). Cassiodorus had discussed this (*Institutiones* 2.3.4) as had Isidore (*Etymologiarum sive originum* 2.24.10–12). But Isidore seemed to prefer the Stoic-Augustinian division (2.24.3–8) which Alcuin then described at the beginning of his *De dialectica.* However, the Carolingians exhibited no effort to fill out the missing parts of the various schemata, thus effectively equating *philosophia* with the seven liberal arts. Margaret T. Gibson, "The *Artes* in the Eleventh Century," in *Actes* (1969), pp. 121–124; James A. Weisheipl, "Classification of the Sciences in Medieval Thought," *Mediaeval Studies* 27 (1965): 57–67; Richard P. McKeon, "The Organization of Sciences and the Relations of Cultures in the Twelfth and Thirteenth Centuries," in *The Cultural Context of Medieval Learning: Proceedings of the First International Colloquium on Philosophy, Science, and Theology in the Middle Ages,* ed. John E. Murdoch and Edith D. Sylla (Boston: D. Reidel, 1975), pp. 151–186; Paul O. Kristeller, *Renaissance Thought and Its Sources,* ed. Michael Mooney (New York: Columbia University Press, 1979), p. 230.

[32]Frances A. Yates, *The Art of Memory* (Chicago: University of Chicago Press, 1966), chaps. 1–3.

dated the *artes liberales* to preparation for explicating divine texts, rather than devoting them to personal refinement according to an idealistic notion of the perfect orator. The biblical verses from Cassiodorus were often cited both to defend the liberal arts and to emphasize their subservience to Scripture.

If the artificial construct of the *artes liberales* ideal, linked to the oratorical tradition and accommodated to Christian purposes, can therefore be abstracted from the bulk of discussion and teaching of liberal education in the early Middle Ages, the philosophical tradition was not entirely forgotten. Johannes Scotus Erigena (c. 810–c.877) headed the Carolingian palace school in the mid-ninth century and brought a Neoplatonic perspective to the study of the liberal arts. He wrote a commentary on *De nuptiis*, which, without neglecting the Ciceronian theme of uniting eloquence and wisdom, argued that the arts are not merely instrumental for the study of Scripture but also worthy of study in their own right as theoretical philosophy, concluding finally that "No one enters into heaven except through philosophy."[33] Erigena, however, was a relatively isolated case and not seminal for a renaissance of philosophy.[34] Neither, paradoxically enough, was the revival of Boethius.

The style of Boethius's *De consolatione Philosophiae*, combining prose and poetry in an allegorical format, made it congenial to the literary tradition of education; and a number of scholars wrote commentaries upon it during this period. By and large, they misinterpreted the allegory, skewing it away from its speculative and contemplative import. The commentary of Remigius (841–908) was chief among these misguided efforts. Remigius was an eminent teacher of his day with a scholarly lineage extending back directly to Alcuin. Emphasizing the marriage of eloquence and wisdom, he

---

[33]Johannes Scotus Erigena, *Annotationes in Marcianum*, edited with an introduction by Cora E. Lutz (Cambridge: Mediaeval Academy of America, 1939), p. xvi, sect. 53.15; Mathon (1969), pp. 47–64; Michael Masi, "Boethius and the Iconography of the Liberal Arts," *Latomus* 33 (1974): 57–75. See Stahl and Johnson (1971), p. 63n., on the authenticity of Erigena's commentary.

[34]A revisionist view, emphasizing the philosophical influence of Erigena and Boethius on Remigius and others, can be found in Margaret T. Gibson, "The Continuity of Learning, circa 850–circa 1050," *Viator* 6 (1975): 1–13; and John Marenbon, *From the Circle of Alcuin to the School of Auxerre: Logic, Theology, and Philosophy in the Early Middle Ages* (Cambridge: Cambridge University Press, 1981), chaps. 3–4. The latter argues that Erigena was more representative of and less outstanding in his age. Cf. John J. Contreni, *The Cathedral School of Laon from 850 to 930: Its Manuscripts and Masters* (Munich: Arbeo-Gesellschaft, 1978), pp. 95–134; Riché (1979), pp. 111–118, 261–263.

wrote a commentary on Martianus that had great influence through the twelfth century. Similarly, his commentary on Boethius came to be regarded as the authoritative interpretation by scholars in the eleventh century. Therein he mistakenly equated Philosophia with scriptural truth and, following Alcuin, construed the steps on Philosophia's robe to signify the seven liberal arts leading up to that divine wisdom. The contemplative liberation achieved through theoretical philosophy was lost to Remigius and his readers, as it had been to Alcuin.[35]

In the course of the ninth century, the Carolingian Empire broke into several kingdoms, and because of the destruction from new barbarian invasions the tenth century has traditionally been characterized as an epoch of "iron and lead." Early evidence for this cultural degeneration can be found in a letter to the bishops of England from King Alfred the Great, who complained that no one could read Latin anymore, let alone scholarly books. By the last quarter of the century, however, learning and teaching of the *artes liberales*, especially in the *trivium*, were reviving at Bobbio, Rheims, St. Gall, and elsewhere with the help of the Ottonian emperors.[36] In the eleventh century, a period of economic revival in Western Europe, as well as the beginnings of urbanization and the incorporation of cities and towns under charters, contributed to the founding of schools. These took several forms. Monastic schools like Monte Cassino and Bec grew in stature; some urban schools were begun, especially in northern Italy, where the study of law was rekindled. But the growth occurred primarily in the cathedral and parish schools, which greatly expanded in number and size between 1050 and 1150 with the encouragement of the papacy and Church councils.[37]

This growth was not merely quantitative; it also comprised the enhancement of intellectual activity and excitement at the schools.

---

[35] Lutz (1962), pp. 5–6, 16–24, 40–50; Courcelle (1967), pp. 29–66, 241–300.

[36] Francis P. Magoun, Jr., "Some Notes on King Alfred's Circular Letter on Educational Policy Addressed to His Bishops," *Mediaeval Studies* 10 (1948): 93–105. On the tenth century and cultural revival, see Luitpold Wallach, "Education and Culture in the Tenth Century, *Medievalia et Humanistica* 9 (1955): 18–22; Benny R. Reece, *Learning in the Tenth Century* (Greenville, S.C.: Furman University Press, 1968), pp. 1–33; Rijk (1963), pp. 44–86; Gibson (1975); Riché (1979), pp. 137–186; Cora Lutz, *Schoolmasters of the Tenth Century* (Hamden, Conn.: Archon, 1977).

[37] John R. Williams, "The Cathedral Schools of Rheims in the Eleventh Century," *Speculum* 29 (1954): 661–677; Maria G. Merello-Altea, *Scienza e professione legale nel secolo XI* (Milan: Giuffre, 1979), pp. 1–29; Riché (1979), pp. 335–344.

The presence of more and more masters and students within schools, as well as traveling between them, allowed for and promoted intellectual debate. Out of this context emerged the movement later known as "scholasticism," a word that would assume strongly negative connotations in later centuries. Here, however, it should be understood as a generic term for the "teaching of the schools" and, therefore, as being intrinsically linked to the type of study promoted there. The scholastics employed a dialectical method that systematized subject matter into genera and species by identifying and categorizing points of consistency and, when faced with a *contrarium*, searching for a *solutio* by making new *distinctiones* (categories) or citing an *exceptio*. Refined in the fields of theology and law, this method presupposed that traditional authorities "are different but not contradictory."[38]

Gerbert at Bobbio and Rheims in the tenth century, Beranger of Tours in the eleventh century, and Anselm (1033–1104) were early advocates of submitting all to dialectic. However, the archetypal scholastic was Abelard (1079–1144), who attained great fame, especially in the schools of Paris, for his combative and abrasive debates and lectures. Abelard applauded the Boethian position that mathematics is the foundation of the liberal arts, and subordinated the other six arts to logic, which he considered the primary instrument of philosophy. In so doing, Abelard, and like-minded schoolmen, initiated the move from "symbolic theology," for which the liberal arts education provided material for allegorical exegesis of the Bible, to "dialectical theology," for which the liberal arts education aimed to instruct the mind in the analytical and critical method of seeking *distinctiones* when facing a *contrarium*. The same method inspired the studies of civil and canon law.[39]

The expansion of schools was not the sole stimulus of this in-

---

[38]"Diversi sunt sed non adversi." For standard statements on this dialectical method and the emergence of scholasticism, see Joseph de Ghellinck, *Le mouvement théologique du XIIe siècle*, 2d ed. (Bruges, Belg.: Editions "De Tempel," 1948), pp. 517–523; Henri de Lubac, "A propos de la formule: *diversi sed non adversi*," *Recherches de science religieuse* 40 (1952): 27–40; David Knowles, *The Evolution of Medieval Thought* (New York: Random House, 1962), chaps. 8, 9.

[39]The quoted terms appear in Ludwig Hödl, "Die dialektische Theologie des 12. Jahrhunderts," in *Actes* (1969), pp. 137–147. See Mary M. McLaughlin, "Abelard's Conceptions of the Liberal Arts and Philosophy," in *Actes* (1969), pp. 523–530; G. R. Evans, *Old Arts and New Theology: The Beginnings of Theology as an Academic Discipline* (Oxford: Clarendon, 1980), chaps. 1–3; Stephan Kuttner, "The Revival of Jurisprudence," in *Renaissance and Renewal in the Twelfth Century*, ed. Robert L. Benson and Giles Constable (Cambridge: Harvard University Press, 1982), pp. 299–323.

tellectual excitement. Scholasticism was significantly influenced by the rediscovery and translation of the lost philosophical learning of Greek antiquity, especially the corpus of Aristotle. From points of contact between Western Europeans and Middle Eastern culture— Syria, Sicily, Spain, Constantinople—the remaining four treatises on logic, which Boethius had not translated, arrived in mid-twelfth century. Together, these were called the "New Logic" in contradistinction to the two treatises known via Boethius, which were labeled the "Old Logic." By the end of the twelfth century, Aristotle's natural and metaphysical philosophies had been recovered, and the *Politics, Ethics, Economics,* and *Rhetoric* by the first half of the thirteenth century. Meanwhile, Arabic, Jewish, and other Greek writings on mathematics and natural science streamed into Western Europe, stimulating a revolution.

For the liberal arts of the twelfth century, this revolution amounted to a challenging of the oratorical tradition and a shifting toward the philosophical, a transition that came about gradually and unevenly. The *auctores* still persevered, proclaiming the nuptial tie between eloquence and wisdom. Martianus influenced many twelfth-century writers, while Quintilian rose in popularity at schools like Chartres. *Florilegia* appeared in greater numbers and thereby disseminated the classical authors, albeit in an excerpted, excised, mutilated form.[40] Nevertheless, writers of a type of introductory tract called *didascalicon* or *accessus ad auctores* (introduction to the authors) increasingly adopted a concern for classifying the writings prescribed for the *artes* according to certain systematic divisions of *philosophia*, usually derived from the Stoics, via Augustine and Isidore, or from Aristotle, via Boethius. In pedagogical practice, the *accessus* had long had the role of preparing students for reading a given work by briefly explaining the *auctor's* identity and purpose, the subject of the work, and its place among the literary classics. In this sense, the *accessus* was not unrelated to the tradition of *historia.* However, in the twelfth century these introductions began to move away from the task of relating a given work to classical writings and toward asking, "Which branch of philosophy should it be put un-

---

[40]Priscilla S. Boskoff, "Quintilian in the Late Middle Ages," *Speculum* 27 (1952): 71–72; Nuchelmans (1957), pp. 99–100; Murphy (1974), pp. 106–132; Rouse (1979), pp. 131–160. On the perseverance of the oratorical tradition in the twelfth century, see Philippe Delhaye, "L'enseignement de la philosophie morale au XIIe siècle," *Mediaeval Studies* 11 (1949): 77–99; Delhaye, "*Grammatica* et *ethica* au XIIe siècle," in *Artes* (1959), pp. 91–93; Delhaye, "La Place des arts libéraux dans les programmes scolaires du XIIIe siècle," in *Actes* (1969), pp. 161–173.

der?" The twelfth-century *Dialogus super auctores* by Conrad of Hirsau perfectly exemplifies this shift in purpose.[41]

Accompanying and, indeed, enhancing this transition, a pronounced concern arose to inquire both about the missing content of certain branches of philosophy, whose existence had been known of for centuries, and about the systematization of philosophy in all its branches. This concern was reflected in twelfth-century iconography portraying various arrangements of the divisions of philosophy and the seven arts. Meanwhile, the seven arts, in practice, continued to be taught as the sum of "philosophy" and to constitute the totality of "liberal education."[42] This rather ambiguous situation, indicative of the changing nature of the rationale underlying the terms, is typified in writings by Hugh of St. Victor.

Hugh began teaching at the school of the Parisian abbey of St. Victor about 1125 and composed there his *Didascalicon*, an introductory manual for the *artes*. In accord with the scholastic movement, Hugh demonstrates an intense interest in the classification of philosophy, adapting and augmenting the Aristotelian-Boethian division of philosophy, but also citing the Stoic-Isidorian division. At the same time, he employs the Aristotelian distinctions between demonstrative, probable, and sophistic arguments, while he uses *logica* both in its Stoic-Isidorian sense, as a division of philosophy equivalent to the *trivium*, and in its sense of being an art within the *trivium*.[43] On the other hand, once beyond the discussion about systems of dividing up philosophy, he states matter-of-factly that the *septem artes liberales* constitute *philosophia*, and he describes these secular letters as reference material for use in symbolic theology

---

[41]"Cui parti philosophiae subponatur?" Quoted in Leslie G. Whitbread, "Conrad of Hirsau as Literary Critic," *Speculum* 47 (1972): 234–245. E. A. Quain, "The Medieval *accessus ad auctores*," *Traditio* 3 (1945): 215–264. A comprehensive treatment of the *accessus* is found in R. B. Huygens, *Accessus ad auctores: Bernard d' Utrecht, Conrad d'Hirsau* (Leiden, Neth.: E. J. Brill, 1970).

[42]Weisheipl (1965), pp. 62–67; Adolf Katzenellenbogen, "The Representation of the Seven Liberal Arts," in *Twelfth-Century Europe and the Foundations of Modern Society*, ed. Marshall Clagett, Gaines Post, and Robert Reynolds (Madison: University of Wisconsin Press, 1961), pp. 39–55; Philippe Verdier, "L'iconographie des arts libéraux dans l'art du moyen âge jusqu'à la fin du quinzième siècle," in *Actes* (1969), pp. 305–355.

[43]Hugh of St. Victor, *Didascalicon*, translated with an introduction by Jerome Taylor (New York: Columbia University Press, 1961) 1, 2.16, 2.30, pp. 7–19; Roger Baron, *Science et sagesse chez Hugues de Saint-Victor* (Paris: P. Lethielleux, 1957), pp. 49–82; Baron, "L'insertion des arts dans la philosophie chez Hugues de Saint-Victor," in *Actes* (1969), pp. 551–555; Robert Javelet, "Considérations sur les arts libéraux chez Hugues et Richard de Saint-Victor," in *Actes* (1969), pp. 557–568.

about divine letters. Appropriately, Hugh supports his division of the liberal arts by citing Isidore more than anyone else, borrowing most of his approach to grammar from Isidore's *Etymologiae*, stressing beautiful language from the *auctores*, linking *historia* and moral training to grammar and rhetoric, and making *musica* a "handmaid to language" rather than to mathematics.[44]

Such ambiguity of terms, which attests to the ambivalence present in liberal education at the time, was not confined to Hugh of St. Victor or to *philosophia*. The use of other terms likewise demonstrates the twelfth-century challenge to the oratorical view of *artes liberales*. The word *moderni* (moderns), for example, had had a long history since being coined from *modo* (now) in late antiquity. But in the twelfth century, talk about the contrast between *antiqui* and *moderni* heightened considerably, and the latter term came to denote those who embraced the intellectual changes and new educational practices, which were focused primarily on dialectic. Revealed in the occasional phrase *subtilitas modernorum* (subtlety of the moderns), there existed no small ambivalence toward the *moderni*, ranging from admiration for their new learning to scorn for the pride and superficiality of those *moderni* who neglected grammar and rhetoric or pursued dialectic merely in order to advance their careers.[45] Significantly, this kind of double-edged response appeared repeatedly at the school at Chartres, an important witness to the difficult and dramatic transition being made in liberal education.[46]

---

[44]Hugh of St. Victor, *Didascalicon* 1, 2.6–30, 3.4, 5, 6, pp. 32–39; Wolter (1959), pp. 50–83; Fellerer (1959), pp. 43–47; Enzo Liccaro, "Alcune osservazioni su Ugo di San Vittore grammatico e stilista," in *Actes* (1969), pp. 797–804; Maxwell S. Luria, "Some Literary Implications of Hugh of St. Victor's *Didascalicon*," in *Actes* (1969), pp. 541–549; Hödl (1969), pp. 137–147.

[45]John of Salisbury repeatedly contrasts the "ancients" with the "moderns" in *Metalogicon*, trans. Daniel D. McGarry (Berkeley: University of California Press, 1955) 1 prologue. H. R. Jauss, "Antiqui/moderni (Querelle des anciens et des modernes)," in *Historisches Wörterbuch der Philosophie*, ed. Joachim Ritter (Stuttgart: Schwabe, 1971), vol. 1, pp. 410–414; J. O. Ward, "The Date of the Commentary on Cicero's 'De Inventione' by Thierry of Chartres (ca. 1085–1160?) and the Cornifician Attack on the Liberal Arts," *Viator* 3 (1972): 219–247; Wilfried Hartmann, " 'Modernus' und 'antiquus': Zur Verbreitung und Bedeutung dieser Bezeichnungen in der wissenschaftlichen Literatur vom 9. bis zum 12. Jahrhundert," in *Antiqui und Moderni: Traditionsbewusstsein und Fortschrittsbewusstsein im späten Mittelalter*, ed. Albert Zimmermann (Berlin: Walter de Gruyter, 1974), pp. 21–39; Elisabeth Gössmann, " 'Antiqui' und 'Moderni' im 12. Jahrhundert," in Zimmermann (1974), pp. 40–57.

[46]The renowned metaphor *"nani gigantum humeris insidentes"* attributed to Bernard of Chartres in John of Salisbury's *Metalogicon* (3.4) is similarly ambiguous in meaning. On the one hand, it implies progress because the *moderni* advance beyond the *antiqui*. George Sarton, "Query no. 53—'Standing on the Shoulders of Giants,' "

While rising to prominence early in the eleventh century, the school at Chartres had devoted itself to training clerics in morality and divinity and to teaching the seven *artes*, with most attention given to the *trivium*.[47] Then, during the lifetime of John of Salisbury (1115–1180), bishop of Chartres for his last four years, a different notion came to hold sway; and this transition is reflected in John's *Metalogicon*. In certain respects, his bent is oratorical. He opposes those who "make things new and innovate"; relies prominently on Quintilian, Isidore, and Cassiodorus; does not attempt to systematize philosophy as did Hugh of St. Victor; and, in other of his writings, advocates that the educated person must have read the *poetas*, *historicos*, and *oratores*. In fact, in *Metalogicon*, he asserts that anyone "who would eliminate the teaching of eloquence from philosophical studies, [thereby] begrudges Mercury his possession of Philology, and wrests from Philology's arms her beloved Mercury" and so destroys "*omnia liberalia studia*."[48] Yet John is clearly sympathetic to the rising tide of philosophy. Three of the four books of *Metalogicon* are devoted to the logical art of the *trivium*, specifically to Aristotle's work, which is much praised. John attends to both the Old and New Logic, although he does not really understand the more "logical" parts and devotes most of his attention to aspects relating directly to rhetorical argument. Furthermore, he praises Abelard, among other teachers of his youth, as one who elevated the liberal arts to their proper stature in the schools.[49]

John's teaching and writing demonstrate that liberal education and its rationale were being transformed. Meanwhile, the educa-

---

Isis 24 (1935): 107–109. On the other hand, the *moderni* are dwarfs compared to the *antiqui*. Raymond Klibansky, "Standing on the Shoulders of Giants," *Isis* 26 (1936): 147–149. Writings of the twelfth and thirteenth centuries reveal this two-sided interpretation of the metaphor. Edouard Jeauneau, " '*Nani gigantum humeris insidentes*': Essai d'interprétation de Bernard de Chartres," *Vivarium* 5 (1967): pp. 79–99.

[47]Loren C. MacKinney, *Bishop Fulbert and Education at the School of Chartres* (Notre Dame, Ind.: Mediaeval Institute, University of Notre Dame, 1957), chap. 2; Raymond Klibansky, "The School of Chartres," in Clagett, Post, and Reynolds (1961), pp. 3–14. R. W. Southern ("The Schools of Paris and the School of Chartres," in Benson and Constable [1982], pp. 113–137) argues that Chartres had little influence as a school after about 1124.

[48]John of Salisbury *Metalogicon* 1.1, 3–5; Daniel D. McGarry, ed. and trans., *The Metalogicon of John of Salisbury: A Twelfth-Century Defense of the Verbal and Logical Arts of the Trivium* (Berkeley: University of California Press, 1955), pp. 36–72; Wolter (1959), pp. 50–83; Mary B. Ryan, "John of Salisbury's Theory of Rhetoric," *Studies in Medieval Culture* 2 (1966): 56–62; Ward (1972), pp. 218–238.

[49]John of Salisbury, *Metalogicon* 1.5, 2.3; Brian P. Hendley, "John of Salisbury's Defense of the *Trivium*," in *Actes* (1969), pp. 753–762; Murphy (1974), pp. 127–130.

tional institutions themselves underwent radical change. Encouraged by the Third and Fourth Lateran Councils in 1179 and 1215, various cathedral, collegiate, and urban schools grew into universities. In a sentence, these institutions appeared when masters or students incorporated themselves and took one of the standard names for a guild, very often *universitas*, a term originally bearing no connotation of breadth of curriculum or scholarship.[50] The actual institution of teaching and learning was called the *studium*, or *studium generale* if its influence was especially significant,[51] although neither of these terms should be pressed very hard in light of the marked diversity among the early *studia* and the decades involved in regularizing their practices. Nevertheless, it is fair to generalize about two points.

First is the struggle of the guilds in the late twelfth and early thirteenth centuries to free themselves from the economic and political control of local officials, both ecclesiastical and municipal. In whatever country or city, the guilds had to establish and reestablish their right to run their own affairs. The popes and monarchs helped greatly in this struggle, granting to scholars the privileges and immunities normally reserved for clerics.[52] Second is the long debate that ensued over the power to bestow the *licentia docendi*, the "license for teaching" that had traditionally been granted by local ecclesiastical officials, notably the chancellor of the cathedral. This entitlement to teach in the area under the purview of that episcopal school essentially constituted the degree for study in the liberal arts, and the power to grant it and charge fees for it became a matter of fierce contention between the masters and episcopal officials. Here, too, the popes, not reluctant to extend their influence over local ec-

---

[50]*Universitas* was only one among several terms that referred to a guild, others being *corpus, communitas, collegium, societas*. Pierre Michaud-Quantin, *Universitas: Expressions du mouvement communautaire dans le moyen-âge latin* (Paris: J. Vrin, 1970), chap. 1. The fundamental and indispensable source on the founding of the universities is Hastings Rashdall, *The Universities of Europe in the Middle Ages*, ed. F. M. Powicke and A. B. Emden, 3 vols. (Oxford: Clarendon, 1936).

[51]Various explanations have been offered for what qualified a *studium* to be called *generale*, including the attracting of students from a wide geographic area, the recognition of its *licentia* over a wide area, and the teaching of one or more graduate disciplines in addition to the liberal arts. Gordon Leff, *Paris and Oxford Universities in the Thirteenth and Fourteenth Centuries: An Institutional and Intellectual History* (New York: John Wiley, 1968), pp. 17–19; G. B. Hackett, ed. *The Original Statutes of Cambridge University: The Text and Its History* (Cambridge: Cambridge University Press, 1970), pp. 176–177; Alan B. Cobban, *The Medieval Universities: Their Development and Organization* (London: Methuen, 1975), pp. 23–36.

[52]Gaines Post, "Parisian Masters as a Corporation, 1200–1246," *Speculum* 9 (1934): 421–445; Kibre (1962), chaps. 1–4, 9; Leff (1968), pp. 15–34, 82–97.

clesiastical prerogatives, favored the guilds of the young *studia* in a battle that continued well into the fourteenth century.[53]

Meanwhile, the universities had grown into venerable and venerated institutions. About twenty had been founded and were still functioning at the turn of the century,[54] including Salamanca, Lisbon, Valladolid, and Coimbra in the Iberian peninsula; Bologna, Padua, Naples, Vicenza, Arezzo, and Siena in Italy; Paris, Orléans, Angers, Toulouse, and Montpellier in France; and Oxford and Cambridge in England. (None yet existed in Germany and central Europe.) Cathedral, collegiate, and parish schools did carry on independently; but these were largely reduced to offering preparatory training, after which the student went on to the *studium* of liberal arts. In addition to the right to grant the *licentia docendi*, a true university was expected to have at least one higher faculty of law, medicine, or theology above the faculty of arts, a degree from the latter being the *sine qua non* of entrance to any of the others. The steps leading to being graduated—reaching the grade of—a master of arts varied greatly from university to university and from generation to generation. Nevertheless, a generalized pattern of requirements can be posited for the liberal arts course in the thirteenth century.[55]

By and large, a student began his candidacy to become a

---

[53]Gaines Post, "Alexander III, the *Licentia Docendi*, and the Rise of the Universities," in *Anniversary Essays in Mediaeval History by Students of Charles Homer Haskins*, ed. Charles H. Taylor (Boston: Houghton Mifflin, 1929), pp. 255–278; Cobban (1975), pp. 27–32; Astrik L. Gabriel, "The Conflict between the Chancellor and the University of Masters and Students at Paris during the Middle Ages," in *Die Auseinandersetzungen an der Pariser Universität im 13. Jahrhundert*, ed. Albert Zimmermann (Berlin: Walter de Gruyter, 1976), pp. 106–154. Acrimony over the *licentia docendi* even heightened as the license of the most prestigious *studia* came to be credited throughout Western Europe. Since this recognition was desired by all the arising universities, the *ius ubique docendi* (right of teaching everywhere) was formally instituted, and the power to grant this right was accorded to certain existing universities *ex post facto* by papal or royal decree and then, selectively, to new universities.

[54]Cobban (1975), pp. 116–121; Helene Wieruszowski, *The Medieval University: Masters, Students, Learning* (Princeton, N.J.: D. Van Nostrand, 1966), chaps. 7–8. The paucity of sources about many *studia* makes their status unclear, as does the fact that they often closed down or moved away for years at a time.

[55]Hackett notes that "the system of promotion to degrees and studies" is "the most obscure and intractable area of the organization of the *studium*" ([1970], p. 119). In the following postulation, I draw from Rashdall (1936); James A. Weisheipl, "Curriculum of the Faculty of Arts at Oxford in the Early Fourteenth Century," *Mediaeval Studies* 26 (1964): 143–185; Nancy G. Siraisi, *Arts and Sciences at Padua: The Studium of Padua before 1350* (Toronto: Pontifical Institute of Mediaeval Studies, 1973), chaps. 3–4; Leff (1968), pp. 147–160. Excerpts from significant documents are readily available in translation from Lynn Thorndike, *University Records and Life in the Middle Ages* (New York: Columbia University Press, 1944) and Wieruszowski (1966).

baccalaurius[56] at about age 14 or 15—though there were many exceptions, younger and older—and spent three to five years hearing the *lectiones* (readings or lectures) of the masters on prescribed books and topics in the *artes*. The candidate also attended and began to participate in logical disputations such as *sophismata*, thereby drilling in the scholastic method of dialectic. Finally, after honing his technique and acumen in *responsiones* with his master, the candidate was prepared to swear that he had completed the foregoing studies and to demonstrate his skills in a series of debates before a board of masters. If he succeeded at that trial, the faculty of arts awarded the title *baccalaurius*, and the student was allowed to wear the *cappa*, the sign of this achievement.

The young bachelor continued at the *studium* for another one to three years, for a total of about six. He heard again the *lectiones* and sophistical exercises previously attended, and he delivered "extraordinary" or "cursory" lectures during afternoons and holidays, usually on the lesser texts and arts. Finally came the *examinatio* for the license, including his swearing to having completed his studies, his presiding at a debate in which he had to "determine" the resolution, and his being presented by the masters to the chancellor to receive the *licentia*. Receipt of the license did not, however, make him a master of arts until he subsequently was admitted to the guild. This occasionally required participating in another series of debates and disputations. Absolutely obligatory, however, was the swearing of allegiance and obedience to the rules of the *universitas* and the hosting of a feast for his new confreres in the guild.

The content and rationale of these years of study in the *artes liberales* had slowly been changing through the twelfth century, just as the entire realm of scholarship and learning had been transformed. Not only had the treatises of Martianus, Cassiodorus, and Isidore been eclipsed by the influx of newly translated works, especially those concerning logic, natural sciences, and mathematics, but the thinking of Aristotle had caused a revolution in how one did philosophy and related it to theology. Aristotle's writings were at first received with open arms due to his longstanding prestige and his popularity among twelfth-century scholastics, who were greatly

---

[56]The origin of *baccalaurius* (or *baccalaureus*) and its relationship to the English term *bachelor* are matters of some debate. By the thirteenth century, the latter term was commonly applied in England to any young warrior who was nearing the attainment of knighthood and intimate in the household of his lord. J. M. Bean, " 'Bachelor' and Retainer," *Medievalia et Humanistica*, New Series 3 (1972): 117–131.

stimulated by the Old Logic and even more by the New Logic. Soon the attitude changed. The texts of Aristotle and other ancient writers, often accompanied by or woven into commentaries of Islamic scholars and thus tinged with their concepts, terms, and references, came to be viewed as vehicles of heterodoxy. No less disturbing, as more of the corpus was translated, was the emerging recognition of Aristotle's rationalism and humanism and his rejection of Platonic metaphysics, all of which made his work suspect in the eyes of many churchmen.

A battle naturally ensued among academicians, and thick in the fray were the mendicant orders, the Franciscans and Dominicans. Friars of these orders had risen to prominence in the universities during the first half of the thirteenth century, despite a series of conflicts with the guilds of masters.[57] Like the Cistercians in the twelfth century, both of these orders of monks, while originally infused with rigorist hostility toward the pagan liberal arts, eventually embraced them[58]—though with very different kinds of affection. The Franciscans and their associates, including Bonaventure (1221–1274), Robert Grosseteste (1170–1253), and Roger Bacon (1219–1292), emphasized the antecedent tradition: Platonic, Augustinian, spiritualist, stressing truths of revelation above conclusions from reason, and subsuming philosophy into theology. The Dominicans, notably Albert the Great (1200–1280) and Thomas Aquinas (1224–1274), sought to reconcile orthodoxy with the new learning in a different synthesis: Aristotelian, empirical, distinguishing logical

---

[57]The conflicts arose because the teaching friars enjoyed the privileges and immunities of the masters, but refused to join the masters in abandoning the *studium* when the guilds sought to assert themselves against municipal or royal intrusion. The *solutio* reached by the papacy was that the friars had to obey the rules of the guild, but the masters could not expel or exclude a friar because he did not obey. This "resolution" was due, in part, to the fact that the friars answered to the papal see, which did not want its authority compromised by their obligations to an *universitas*. Leff (1968), pp. 34–36, 103–105, 272–294; Astrik L. Gabriel, *Garlandia: Studies in the History of the Mediaeval University* (Notre Dame, Ind.: Mediaeval Institute, University of Notre Dame, 1969), chap. 10.

[58]Thorndike (1944), pp. 30–31; Nicholas M. Haring, "The Liberal Arts in the Sermons of Garnier of Rochefort," *Mediaeval Studies* 30 (1968): 47–69; Delhaye (1969), pp. 169–171. The continuing rigorist sentiment is demonstrated by the biographer of the prominent twelfth-century Cistercian monk, Ailred of Rievaulx: "Accordingly, therefore, our master Christ in his school did not teach grammar, rhetoric, dialectic; rather he taught humility, meekness and justice. Nor did our master Christ in his school teach those arts that they call liberal, but that are neither free (*libere*) nor liberating and indeed may instruct greatly in sin" (my translation). Charles H. Talbot, ed. *Ailred of Rievaulx: De Anima* (London: Warburg Institute, University of London, 1952), p. 17 n. 8.

method from revelation, and separating philosophy from theology. The specific doctrinal and metaphysical issues are not important here; what is significant is how this debate influenced the arts curriculum.

There was first an inconsequential attempt, chiefly at Paris in the first half of the thirteenth century, to proscribe the offending texts of Aristotle from being taught by masters in the liberal arts. These proscriptions were largely ignored and by 1255 were finally rescinded. More persistent was the resistance to overhauling the longstanding schema of the *septem artes liberales*. The traditionalists sought to preserve the frame of seven arts as the propaedeutic *philosophia* for Christian theology, along with a corresponding emphasis on moral training conveyed by grammar and rhetoric.[59] These tendencies are seen in the early *De artibus liberalibus* by Grosseteste and the *Reductio artium ad theologiam* (Restoration of the arts to theology) by Bonaventure, the latter preserving the Stoic-Augustinian-Isidorian divisions of philosophy. This approach of retaining the seven-part frame necessarily implied an expansion of the traditional *artes* as they bulged to incorporate more and more of the new learning. And that result indicated a lack of empathy with the Aristotelian method of devising new classifications for newly discovered knowledge. The traditional approach appears also in the renowned encyclopedia of Vincent of Beauvais, whose Dominican affiliation signals the danger of generalizing too starkly about the position taken by the orders of friars in this debate.

Still, it was the Dominican Thomas Aquinas who pronounced the inevitable conclusion that "the seven liberal arts do not sufficiently divide theoretical philosophy." Two things were implied there: that a new understanding of *artes liberales* was required, and that this understanding would spring from the philosophical tradition.[60] Satisfying these requirements demanded that consensus be reached on defining and categorizing "philosophy," even as the

---

[59]Here and below, I draw from Daniel A. Callus, ed., *Robert Grosseteste: Scholar and Bishop: Essays in Commemoration of the Seventh Century of His Death* (Oxford: Clarendon, 1955), pp. 1–23; Leff (1968), pp. 187–240, 270–309; Fernando Gneo, "La *Reductio artium ad theologiam* secondo S. Bonaventura," in *Actes* (1969), pp. 631–638; Antonio Tognolo, "Il *De artibus liberalibus* di Roberto Grossatesta," in *Actes* (1969), pp. 593–597; McKeon (1975), pp. 151–186; Joseph M. McCarthy, *Humanistic Emphases in the Educational Thought of Vincent of Beauvais* (Leiden, Neth.: E. J. Brill, 1976), pp. 14–109.

[60]"Septem liberales artes non sufficienter dividunt philosophiam theoricam." Thomas Aquinas, *Expositio super librum Boethii De trinitate* (Leiden, Neth.: E. J. Brill, 1955), ques. 5, ans. 1, resp. 3. For the interpretation of the thirteenth- and early fourteenth-century liberal arts, I rely on Louis J. Paetow, *The Arts Course at Medieval Universities with Special Reference to Grammar and Rhetoric* (Champaign: University of

battle over Aristotle's import to theology raged through the thirteenth century. By combining, not altogether intentionally, the Stoic-Augustinian-Isidorian division of philosophy into logic, ethics, and physics with the various divisions of philosophy made by Aristotle at various points in his writings, academicians reached accord on a categorization of *philosophia* into natural, moral, and metaphysical divisions.[61] Albert, Thomas, and others then proceeded to outline a five-step program of intellectual formation leading to theology: (1) *trivium*, (2) *quadrivium*, (3) natural philosophy, (4) moral philosophy, and (5) metaphysics.[62] Like Abelard, who did not know the New Logic, Aquinas made logic the heart and soul of the *artes liberales*, which were stripped of direct connection to ethics and oriented purely to intellectual formation.[63]

These developments were most pronounced at Paris, where curricular records of 1215, 1231, 1252, and 1255 clearly reveal the ascendance of logic as the paradigmatic *scientia speculativa* among the liberal arts. Due to Dominican and Aristotelian influences, Paris emphasized logic as the core of preparatory instruction, especially for highest philosophy, or metaphysics. This trend was less evident at Bologna and its neighbors, although Naples and the Dominican *studium artium* in Florence did follow the Parisian example.[64] Oxford

---

Illinois Press, 1910); Delhaye (1949), pp. 77–99; Delhaye (1959), pp. 91–93; Delhaye (1969), pp. 161–173; Weisheipl (1964), pp. 143–185; James A. Weisheipl, "Developments in the Arts Curriculum at Oxford in the Early Fourteenth Century," *Mediaeval Studies* 28 (1966): 151–175; Leff (1968), pp. 116–184; Heinrich Roos, "Le *trivium* à l'université au XIIIe siècle," in *Actes* (1969), pp. 193–197; Palémon Glorieux, *La faculté des arts et ses maîtres au XIIIe siècle* (Paris: J. Vrin, 1971), pp. 1–58; Siraisi (1973), chaps. 2–3. Appropriately, Olaf Pederson remarks that, by the beginning of the thirteenth century, the root sense of "free" in liberal arts was understood as liberation from "the slavery of the soul, vegetating in the shadow of its ignorance." "Du quadrivium à la physique: Quelques aperçus de l'évolution scientifique au moyen âge," in *Artes* (1959), pp. 107–123.

[61] Weisheipl (1965), pp. 54–90.

[62] Mary H. Mayer, *The Philosophy of Teaching of St. Thomas Aquinas* (Milwaukee: Bruce, 1929), chap. 6; Toccafondi (1969), pp. 639–651; Gérard Verbeke, "Arts libéraux et morale d'après Saint Thomas," in *Actes* (1969), pp. 653–661.

[63] Mariateresa B. Fumagelli, "Note per una indagine sul concetto di retorica in Abelardo," in *Actes* (1969), pp. 829–832; Mariano Traina, "La dialettica in Giovanni Duns Scoto," in *Actes* (1969), pp. 923–930; Pierre Michaud-Quantin, "L'emploi des termes *logica* et *dialectica* au moyen âge," in *Actes* (1969), pp. 855–862; Leff (1978), pp. 3–24; Norman Kretzmann, "The Culmination of the Old Logic in Peter Abelard," in Benson and Constable (1982) pp. 488–511.

[64] Charles T. Davis, "Education in Dante's Florence," *Speculum* 40 (1965): 425–433; Michael B. Crowe, "Peter of Ireland: Aquinas's Teacher of the *Artes Liberales*," in *Actes* (1969), pp. 617–626. Excerpts from the curricular records may be found in Rashdall (1936); Thorndike (1944); Wieruszowski (1966).

records indicate that there, too, logic dominated the *trivium*. In mathematics, however, a different trend is noteworthy.

The quadrivial studies[65] were generally taught at Paris as lesser arts in "extraordinary" or "cursory" lectures because the *quadrivium* was regarded as preparatory to natural philosophy, and this association with nature gained it little respect there. However, Oxford was dominated by the Franciscans, whose Platonic outlook lent a different yet still philosophical orientation to the liberal arts. For Oxonians like Roger Bacon, mathematics became the paradigmatic preparation for climbing to the heights of philosophy. Natural philosophy, or physics, was demoted below the *quadrivium*, while those four arts were studied for their theoretical interest and not simply to provide resource material for allegorical exegesis in symbolic theology. Of course, such changes were not uniform, and different rationales for the *quadrivium* often went hand in hand. For example, interest in Greek and Arabic natural science (an interest demonstrated by Adelard of Bath even before the founding of Oxford as an *universitas*) led to an expansion of the content of the quadrivial arts with the inclusion of "intermediary sciences" such as optics. Meanwhile, concern for training the mind in a formal and mathematical method prompted the development of *musica speculativa* as another *scientia speculativa*.[66]

If Paris devoted itself to logic and Oxford was noted for quadrivial studies, neither were the Italian universities unaffected by the newly arriving scientific and philosophical knowledge. The study of medicine, whether in its own graduate faculty at Salerno, or included in the arts curriculum in Bologna or Padua, demonstrated its capacity to stimulate interest in natural philosophy and the *quadrivium*, if not scholastic speculation outright.[67] Nonetheless, Bologna

---

[65]For the following, I draw from Callus (1955), pp. 22–23; Weisheipl (1965), pp. 72–90; Pearl Kibre, "The *quadrivium* in the Thirteenth Century Universities (with Special Reference to Paris)," in *Actes* (1969), pp. 175–191; John E. Murdoch, "*Mathesis in philosophiam scholasticam introducta*: The Rise and Development of the Application of Mathematics in Fourteenth-Century Philosophy and Theology," in *Actes* (1969), pp. 215–249; Guy Beaujouan, "The Transformation of the Quadrivium," in Benson and Constable (1982) pp. 463–487.

[66]Fellerer (1959), pp. 33–49; Graziella Federici, "L'inserimento della' perspectivá tra le arti del quadrivio," in *Actes* (1969), pp. 969–974; F. Joseph Smith, "A Medieval Philosophy of Number: Jacques de Liège and the *Speculum musicae*," in *Actes* (1969), pp. 1023–1039; Jean Gagné, "Du *quadrivium* aux *scientiae mediae*, in *Actes* (1969), pp. 975–986; Andrew Hughes, *Medieval Music: The Sixth Liberal Art (A Bibliography)*, rev. ed. (Toronto: University of Toronto Press, 1980), pp. 24–29.

[67]Paul O. Kristeller, "Beitrag der Schule von Salerno zur Entwicklung der scho-

and other universities in its sphere upheld the memory and much of the practice of the oratorical liberal arts, albeit gradually giving ground in the course of the thirteenth century. As should be expected, this attitude expressed itself in greater attention to rhetoric than could be found at Oxford or, especially, Paris.[68]

There are good historical and geographical reasons for the difference. Italy was the ancient home of the study of law and of literary Latin culture, which had never been completely extinguished there, and this heritage had prompted the formation of new rhetorical arts. In the ninth and tenth centuries, *ars dictaminis* had begun to develop, and this "art of letter-writing" was associated with legal practice because of the need for a carefully regulated style for governmental and contractual correspondence. The first systematic treatise on this new art issued from Monte Cassino in the late eleventh century, and in the following century, a notarial discipline (*ars notaria*) began to emerge, later followed by *ars arengandi* (art of pleading at law) and *ars praedicandi* (art of preaching), the latter inspired by the fourth book of Augustine's *De doctrina christiana*.

These new arts were thus rooted in the *trivium*. In fact, one of the titles applied to someone trained in law (*legis lator*) in northern Italian schools was adapted directly from *artis lator*, signifying one trained in trivial studies at the same schools. This does not mean that the new disciplines straightforwardly represented an expression of the "liberal arts" in the oratorical tradition, for they were as often as

---

lastischen Wissenschaft im 12. Jahrhundert," in *Artes* (1959), pp. 84–90; Siraisi (1973), chaps. 4–5. On the subsequent relation of medicine and the *artes*, see Pearl Kibre, "Arts and Medicine in the Universities of the Later Middle Ages," in *The Universities* (1978), pp. 213–227.

[68]For the following discussion of rhetoric, I draw from H. M. Willard, "The Use of Classics in the *Flores rhetorici* of Alberic of Monte Cassino," in *Anniversary Essays in Mediaeval History by Students of Charles Homer Haskins*, ed. Charles H. Taylor (Boston: Houghton Mifflin, 1929), pp. 351–364; Helene Wieruszowski, "*Ars Dictaminis* in the Time of Dante," *Medievalia et Humanistica* 1 (1943): 95–108; Harry Caplan, "Classical Rhetoric and the Mediaeval Theory of Preaching," in *Historical Studies of Rhetoric and Rhetoricians*, ed. Raymond F. Howes (Ithaca, N.Y.: Cornell University Press, 1961), pp. 71–89; R. J. Schoeck, "On Rhetoric in Fourteenth-Century Oxford," *Mediaeval Studies* 30 (1968): 214–225; Roos (1969), pp. 193–197; Murphy (1974), chap. 5; James R. Banker, "The *Ars Dictaminis* and Rhetorical Textbooks at the Bolognese University in the Fourteenth Century," *Medievalia et Humanistica*, New Series 5 (1974): 153–168; Rouse (1979), pp. 131–160. The writings of Alexander Neckham (1157–1271), a teacher in England and Paris, are occasionally cited as evidence of the literary bent of rhetoric at these places, but this is an anomalous case. J. Reginald O'Donnell, "The Liberal Arts in the Twelfth Century with Special Reference to Alexander Nequam (1157–1217)," in *Actes* (1969), pp. 127–135; Murphy (1974), pp. 127, 274.

not taught outside the arts faculties, as happened with *ars notaria* at Bologna. Furthermore, as these genres became systematized into *artes*, they acquired the schematic and categorical character of scholastic inquiry, an orientation antagonistic to reliance on literary *auctores*. It was precisely this development that led Guido Faba, when studying law at Bologna early in the thirteenth century, to feel that he was losing his rhetorical eloquence and thus to return to teach in the arts faculty.[69] Nevertheless, just as Cicero, Quintilian, Isidore, and Alcuin had all included the study of law prominently in their writings on rhetoric, so Bologna and its neighbors, such as Padua, Toulouse, and Arezzo, taught *ars dictaminis* in their arts faculties through much of the thirteenth century, thereby preserving some interest in expression and style. That the *auctores* were relied upon is shown by the use of the informal name *auctorista* for a master teaching rhetoric in Italian universities.[70] These new arts, therefore, helped to preserve greater attention to rhetoric and literary studies than could be found elsewhere.

It remains to ask about the fate of *grammatica*, and here arises a paradox, for rather than a diminution of interest in grammar in the arts faculties of Paris, Oxford, and other northern universities, one discovers instead tremendous activity.[71] Some background will help to explain this. Among the early advocates of dialectic, Anselm had analyzed the use of words and their syntax in order to account for apparent inconsistencies in arguments, and had thereby introduced the consideration of grammatical arguments into the study of logic. Abelard then raised provocative questions about the signification of

---

[69]Thorndike (1944), pp. 41–46; Louis J. Paetow, ed. and trans., *The Battle of the Seven Arts: A French Poem by Henri d'Andeli* (La bataille des VII ars) (Berkeley: University of California Press, 1914), pp. 13–30; Charles B. Faulhaber, "The *summa dictaminis* of Guido Faba," in *Medieval Eloquence: Studies in the Theory and Practice of Medieval Rhetoric*, ed. James J. Murphy (Berkeley: University of California Press, 1978), pp. 85–88; Merello-Altea (1979), pp. 9–29, 48–52.

[70]Helene Wieruszowski, "Arezzo as a Center of Learning and Letters in the Thirteenth Century," *Traditio* 9 (1953): 342–383; Giuseppe Billanovich, "Auctorista, humanista, orator," *Rivista di cultura classica e medioevale* 7 (1965): 146ff.; Siraisi (1973), chap. 2; Manlio Bellomo, *Saggio sull' universitá nell' etá del diritto comune* (Catania: Giannótta, 1979), chaps. 3, 10.

[71]For the following treatment of speculative grammar, I draw from Louis M. Regis, "L'être du langage et l'humanisme médiéval et contemporain," in *Actes* (1969), pp. 281–294; Heinrich Roos, "Die Stellung der Grammatik im Lehrbetrieb des 13. Jahrhunderts," in *Artes* (1959), pp. 94–106; Roos (1969), pp. 193–197; Marcia L. Colish, "Eleventh-Century Grammar in the Thought of St. Anselm," in *Actes* (1969), pp. 785–795; Ada Lamacchia, "I *modi significandi* di Martino di Dacia," in *Actes* (1969), pp. 913–921; Paetow (1910), chap. 2. The scholarly literature on the speculative grammar

words and their relationship to the thing signified. Gradually, this kind of inquiry was addressed even by those committed to literary grammar and the *auctores*, such as Alain de Lille (d. 1202), a teacher at Orléans. Alain applied a schematic and hence "logical" frame to grammar, while he also wrote an allegory about the seven liberal arts building a vehicle to conduct the student to higher philosophy.[72]

Anselm's investigation culminated in the thirteenth-century search for a universal grammar that was thought to underlie the different grammars of all languages. The study was known as *grammatica speculativa*, another of the *scientiae speculativae*, and its masters in the arts faculties were generally paid more than twice as much as teachers of literary grammar. Correspondingly, the traditional handbooks of Priscian and Donatus, which taught by examples drawn from classical writings, were eclipsed by new textbooks emphasizing schematic and "logical" rules for grammatical usage. In particular, the *antiqui grammatici*—as Priscian and Donatus were sometimes called—were pushed aside by what were called *modi significandi moderni* (or, more often, just *modi significandi*), meaning "modes of signifying." Treatises on this subject sought to analyze and describe the parts of speech and syntax according to the relationship between "modes of being," "modes of signifying," and "modes of understanding." When this was accomplished, the *oratio perfecta* was expected to arise from *grammatica speculativa*.

The *auctores* and their advocates did not go down without a fight, as is attested by John of Garland's *Morale scolarium*, written in 1241. Educated at Oxford, John taught at Toulouse and Paris before eventually returning to England, and each of his writings defends the value of classical authors, fine literary style, and the study of grammar and rhetoric. In the prologue of *Morale scolarium*, John recounts the Christian appropriation of the oratorical tradition, declaring, "Thus he [God] provided philosophers as well as prophets, the former to endow the Church with the ornament of Latin language, the latter to witness to the truth." After a first chapter titled "Plea for Morality and for the Liberal Arts," John entreats, "Let

---

is extensive and growing. See E. J. Ashworth, *The Tradition of Medieval Logic and Speculative Grammar from Anselm to the End of the Seventeenth Century* (Toronto: Pontifical Institute of Mediaeval Studies, 1978).

[72] Alain de Lille, *Anticlaudianus*, translated with an introduction by James J. Sheridan (Toronto: Pontifical Institute of Mediaeval Studies, 1973), sects. 2, 7, pp. 10–31; Santo Arcoleo, "Filosofia ed arti nell' *Anticlaudianus* di Alano di Lilla," in *Actes* (1969), pp. 569–574; Cesare Vasoli, "*Ars grammatica* e *translatio teologica* in alcuni testi di Alano di Lilla," in *Actes* (1969), pp. 805–813.

books be brought forth and worthy poems be read," and proceeds to enumerate the *septem artes liberales*, subsequently denigrating the handbooks in *grammatica speculativa* that had come to replace Priscian and Donatus.[73]

Even more graphic is *La bataille des VII ars*, a poetic ballad written by Henri d'Andeli in the second quarter of the thirteenth century depicting a mythical battle fought between the *studia* of Paris and Orléans. From the latter, a center of law and letters, which is losing students and regarded by Parisian scholars as a place for "authorlings" and "mere grammar-boys," Grammar leads forth her army of "good author knights." From Paris, where "Logic has the students,/Whereas Grammar is reduced in numbers," Plato and Aristotle lead forth their troops against the army from Orléans. Then the battle unfolds:

> Aristotle, who was unhorsed,
> Made Grammar tumble backwards.
> Then pricked forward master Persius,
> Sir Juvenal and Sir Horace,
> Virgil, Lucan, and Statius,
> and Sedulius, Propertius, Prudentius,
> Arator, Homer, and Terence:
> All smote Aristotle,
> Who stood firm as a castle on a hill.
> Priscian with his two nephews
> tried to beat out his eyes,
> When Sophistical Refutations and the Two Logics,
> On Interpretation and the Topics,
> The books of Nature, Ethics,
> Madame Necromancy, Medicine,
> and Sir Boethius and Sir Macrobius
> Dressed in caitiff garb,
> and Porphyry, came on a run
> To bring aid to Aristotle.

Logic finally wins the day, and Grammar flees from the field to "Egypt, where she was born,"[74] a reference recalling the Christian apology for pagan learning.

---

[73]John of Garland, *Morale scolarium*, translated with an introduction by Louis J. Paetow (Berkeley: University of California Press, 1927), prologue, sect. 1, sect. 2 line 26, sect. 14, pp. 82–96, 98–106, 120–127.

[74]Henri d'Andeli, *The Battle of the Seven Arts: A French Poem by Henri d'Andeli:* (La bataille des VII ars), translated with an introduction by Louis J. Paetow (Berke-

With the *auctores* retreating in confusion, the new consensus over liberal arts bequeathed to the fourteenth century becomes apparent. *Philosophia* is no longer equated with the seven liberal arts but has risen above them and is divided into natural, moral, and metaphysical philosophies. Where Aristotle reigns without rival, as at Paris, logic is both *fundamentum* and *summa* of the arts; where the Platonic heritage is remembered, as at Oxford, mathematics holds sway. In either case, it is a philosopher's curriculum of liberal education, dedicated to *scientiae speculativae* inquiring after knowledge. The concern for moral training is de-emphasized, while rhetoric practically drops from sight. Only near the home of Latin literature does this latter discipline remain strong, and there the study leans increasingly away from *auctores* and toward technical and schematized *artes*, preparatory for the academic study of law. Grammar is even more sharply torn from classical writings and transformed into a linguistic and formalized tool for specialized research.

Implied in the last development, as it has been throughout the emergence of the *studia*, is a growing emphasis on specialized graduate faculties and a commensurate diminution of arts education as a whole. This change in emphasis resulted, on the one hand, because the graduate faculties incorporated much of the newly received learning, which so excited the masters of the time, and, on the other hand, because the specializations of theology, medicine, and law clearly constituted the path to a successful career in the late medieval world. Prompted by these factors, many students were as eager to prepare themselves quickly in order to move on to advanced studies, as were their teachers to push them. This attitude led to the gradual narrowing and shortening of the arts curriculum, as seen notably at Paris in the thirteenth century and increasingly at Bologna and Oxford in the fourteenth.[75] The laments of John of Garland and Henri d'Andeli were no more effective in their day than the warning of John of Salisbury against early tendencies in these directions had been in the late twelfth century. The orators had fled to Egypt, and philosophers determined liberal education.

---

ley: University of California Press, 1914), lines 1–45, 205–223, 407, pp. 13–30. See chap. 3, n.3 above.

[75]James A. Weisheipl, "The Place of the Liberal Arts in the University Curriculum during the XIVth and XVth Centuries," in *Actes* (1969), pp. 209–213; Alexander Murray, *Reason and Society in the Middle Ages* (Oxford: Clarendon, 1978), chaps. 9, 12; John M. Fletcher, "The Teaching of Arts at Oxford, 1400–1520," *PH* 7 (1967): 417–421; Vern L. Bullough, "Achievement, Professionalization, and the University," in *The Universities* (1978), pp. 497–510; Evans (1980), chaps. 1–3.

IV
Renaissance Humanists and Reformation Preachers

*T*HE HIGHEST SUBJECT *in the liberal arts and learning is that moral philosophy which brings a remedy for the deadly diseases of the soul.*
JUAN LUIS VIVES*

*A*ND THIS CANNOT BE DENIED—*dialectic, instead of being useful to theology, is rather an obstacle to theological studies.*
MARTIN LUTHER†

*W*HERE ARE THE PREACHERS, *jurists and physicians to come from, if grammar and other rhetorical arts are not taught?*
MARTIN LUTHER‡

Introduction to Wisdom.
† Letter to George Spalatin.
‡ "A Sermon on Keeping Children in School."

In 1300, THERE EXISTED in Western Europe between fifteen and twenty functioning universities; and over the following two centuries scores more were planned, founded, or actually opened for lectures. Many failed when funds or students did not materialize. Some *studia* were moved, some were refounded, others merged, many were forgotten; and the number approached seventy by the year 1500. Concurrently, scholastic trends in the arts curriculum were extended further. At Oxford, for example, disputations in logic and speculative grammar more and more crowded out other studies, except for mathematics, physics, and some *ars dictaminis*.[1] In general, too, the arts course became shorter as students were graduated to bachelor at a much younger age.[2]

Meanwhile, spirited controversy regarding the study of dialectic and its application to theology was sparked by the "nominalist" theory of William of Occam (1285–1349).[3] Anticipating later empiricist philosophy, this Franciscan challenged the "realism" of his contemporaries: the belief that universal ideas of individual entities do objectively exist. Rather, Occam and his followers held such universals merely to be names and not to exist in their own right, a position that wreaked havoc upon metaphysical and epistemological presuppositions of orthodox doctrine. This nominalist view—the *via moderna*, as it came to be called—gained a significant following at

[1]Brother Bonaventure, "The Teaching of Latin in Later Medieval England," *Mediaeval Studies* 23 (1961): 1–16; John M. Fletcher, "The Teaching of Arts at Oxford, 1400–1520," *PH* 7 (1967): 417–454. An argument has been made for the vitality of rhetoric at fourteenth-century Oxford; R. J. Schoeck, "On Rhetoric in Fourteenth-Century Oxford," *Mediaeval Studies* 30 (1968): 214–225. But see the interpretation of James A. Weisheipl, "Curriculum of the Faculty of Arts at Oxford in the Early Fourteenth Century," *Mediaeval Studies* 26 (1964): 143–185; Weisheipl, "Developments in the Arts Curriculum at Oxford in the Early Fourteenth Century," *Mediaeval Studies* 28 (1966): 151–175.

[2]Some universities, like Paris, had originally prohibited students from becoming a master of arts before the age of 20. By the fourteenth century, this restriction was not being observed, and students often began the arts course at the age of thirteen or fourteen. By the sixteenth century, the entrance age had risen to fourteen or fifteen, and then to about fifteen or sixteen in the next century. Astrik L. Gabriel, *Student Life in Ave Maria College, Mediaeval Paris: History and Chartulary of the College* (Notre Dame, Ind.: Mediaeval Institute, University of Notre Dame, 1955), pp. 185–188; Kenneth Charlton, "Ages of Admission to Educational Institutions in Tudor and Stuart England: A Comment," *History of Education* 5 (1976): 221–226; Richard L. DeMolen, "Ages of Admission to Educational Institutions in Tudor and Stuart England," *History of Education* 5 (1976): 207–219; Lawrence Stone, "Ages of Admission to Educational Institutions in Tudor and Stuart England: A Comment," *History of Education* 6 (1977): 9; David Cressy, "School and College Admission Ages in Seventeenth Century England," *History of Education* 8 (1979): 167–177.

[3]On the *via antiqua* and *via moderna* and the debate in the universities, I draw from Gordon Leff, *Paris and Oxford Universities in the Thirteenth and Fourteenth Cen-*

the universities of Krakow, Leipzig, Heidelberg, Paris, and Oxford, while the "realists"—those who followed the *via antiqua*—continued to dominate Cologne, Prague, and the Italian *studia*.

The very intensity of this controversy contributed to the arguments' becoming increasingly arcane and ingrown, deteriorating to syllogistic and linguistic exercises. The *sophismata* decayed to sophistry, and critics began speaking of the schoolmen as "dunces" in ridicule of John Duns Scotus (1266–1308), who became the official doctor of the Franciscans, and who attracted more followers between 1350 and 1650 than did even Thomas Aquinas. This derisive epithet was applied not only to the Occamists specifically, but to all the scholastics, whose endless cycle of criticism and disputation, though belonging to an ancient philosophical tradition, constituted something relatively "modern" or "of now." The reaction against everything associated with the *via moderna* stood prominently in the minds of Renaissance humanists when they, though riding a new wave themselves, took the name *antiqui*.

By 1300, economic and political conditions in Italy allowed for the initiative of entrepreneurship while sustaining the wealth of royal, ducal, and ecclesiastical patrons, all of which promoted a general flowering of literary culture south of the Alps. Early contributors included Dante Alighieri (1265–1321), whose allegorical, encyclopedic *Il convivio* had been influenced by Martianus through the work of Alain de Lille. But the foundation of a movement was laid by Petrarch (1304–1374), who largely ignored the interests of the schoolmen in philosophy, logic, and professional studies, resurrecting instead the literary model of ancient Latin rhetors with Cicero as his main guide. In short, he taught his disciples to close their *Organon* and open their Tully, and they did. His intellectual descendants included two of the most prominent Renaissance educators, Guarino da Verona (1370–1460) and Vittorino da Feltre (1378–1446), who were greatly influenced by the rediscovery of the full text of Quintilian's *Institutio* in 1416 and Cicero's *De oratore* in

---

turies: An Institutional and Intellectual History (New York: John Wiley, 1968), pp. 240–255, 294–308; Carlo Giacon, "La *suppositio* in Guglielmo di Occam e il valore reale delle scienze," in *Actes* (1969), pp. 939–947; Howard Kaminsky, "The University of Prague in the Hussite Revolution: The Role of the Masters," in *Universities in Politics: Case Studies from the Late Middle Ages and Early Modern Period*, ed. John W. Baldwin and Richard A. Goldthwaite (Baltimore: Johns Hopkins University Press, 1972), pp. 79–106; Astrik L. Gabriel, " 'Via Antiqua' and 'Via Moderna' and the Migration of Paris Students and Masters to the German Universities in the Fifteenth Century," *Miscellanea Mediaevalia* 9 (1974): 339–483.

1422. Naturally, these Roman orators were already well known and admired by the humanists, and the fact is undisputed that they served as paragons of culture and education for the Renaissance movement.

The humanists heartily condemned the scholastic *moderni* and applied the adjective "middle" to an age that they considered a period of darkness after the glorious antiquity of Rome—a culture that was being reborn, they felt, through their efforts. Out of this commitment to classical Latin, the humanists substituted the term *orator* for *auctorista*, which they considered a medieval corruption.[4] Yet, ironically, they were oblivious of their own debt to the renaissance of the twelfth century that had precipitated the search for lost texts of classical humanism. And the use of such ambiguous terms as "Renaissance" or "humanism" now requires some clarification.

Without retracing the protracted and tortuous debate over defining "Renaissance" initiated by Burckhardt's provocative study of 1860,[5] one can say that some scholars attribute to the Renaissance a revival of Platonism or deem it the starting point for experimental science, the Enlightenment, nineteenth-century liberalism, or modernity in general. But this is not the approach taken here, for I rely on the view that the Renaissance can be identified with no particular revival of philosophy because the leaders of the movement were decidedly unphilosophical. Instead, what united the Renaissance humanists was primarily their common commitment to an educational ideal based on the classical literature of antiquity, especially the writings of Cicero and Quintilian.[6] Appropriately, this under-

---

[4]Giuseppe Billanovich, "Auctorista, humanista, orator," *Rivista di cultura classica e medioevale* 7 (1965): 143–163; Cesare Vasoli, "La première querelle des 'anciens' et des 'modernes' aux origines de la Renaissance," in *Classical Influences on European Culture, A.D. 1500–1700*, ed. Robert R. Bolgar (Cambridge: Cambridge University Press, 1976), pp. 67–80.

[5]Jakob C. Burckhardt, *Die Kultur der Renaissance in Italien* (Basel, 1860), translated by S. G. Middlemore (London: C. K. Paul, 1878). In the following discussion, I rely on Herbert Weisinger, "The Renaissance Theory of the Reaction Against the Middle Ages as a Cause of the Renaissance," *Speculum* 20 (1945): 461–467; Wallace K. Ferguson, *The Renaissance in Historical Thought: Five Centuries of Interpretation* (Boston: Houghton Mifflin, 1948), chap. 9; William J. Bouwsma, *The Culture of Renaissance Humanism* (Washington, D.C.: American Historical Association, 1973); and Paul O. Kristeller, "Studies on Renaissance Humanism during the Last Twenty Years," *Studies in the Renaissance* 9 (1962): 7–30, which according to Heiko A. Oberman is the best general introduction to Renaissance thought (*Itinerarium Italicum* [1975], pp. ix-xxviii).

[6]Vito Giustiniani, "Umanesimo: La parola e la cosa," in *Studia Humanitatis, Ernesto Grassi zum 70. Geburtstag*, ed. Eginhard Hora and Eckhard Kessler (Munich: Wilhelm Fink, 1973), p. 25; Denys Hay, "England and the Humanities in the Fifteenth Century," in *Itinerarium Italicum* (1975), p. 321. Paul O. Kristeller has been the

standing of "humanism" coincides with the original meaning of *humanitas*, defined by Varro, Cicero, and Gellius as "learning and instruction in the *bonae artes*."[7]

For their program of education, the Renaissance humanists took the name *studia humanitatis* or *studia humaniora*, terms that Cicero and Gellius had coined and equated with *artes liberales* and that, by the fifteenth century, had come to mean the disciplines of grammar, rhetoric, poetry, and history, often combined with moral philosophy. From here a line of continuity can be traced back through Henri d'Andeli, Alcuin, and Isidore, although this lineage must not be overemphasized because the motivation had changed. Apart from its commitment to moral instruction of the good citizen, Renaissance humanism was devoted to continual refinement of the human personality. With this orientation, the Renaissance scholars, though Christian, advanced classical study for its own sake rather than emphasizing its instrumentality for the study of theology, and they cited the necessity of leisure for the pursuit of classical study.[8] Because all this recalls the oratorical tradition and the *artes liberales* ideal, it should not be surprising, despite the circulation of Cicero's *Academica*,[9] that the same criticisms that were directed against the Hellenistic Roman archetype were, and continue to be, made against the Renaissance humanists. Being "conspicuously deficient in all that

---

chief advocate for this view. Kristeller (1962), p. 22; Kristeller, *Medieval Aspects of Renaissance Learning, Three Essays*, ed. and trans. Edward Mahoney (Durham, N.C.: Duke University Press, 1974), p. 369. For opposing and alternative views, see Ernst Cassirer, *The Individual and the Cosmos in Renaissance Philosophy*, trans. Mario Domandi (Oxford: Basil Blackwell, 1963); James E. Biechler, "Review of *The Pursuit of Holiness in Late Medieval and Renaissance Religion*," *Theological Studies* 35 (1974): 756; George M. Logan, "Substance and Form in Renaissance Humanism," *Journal of Medieval and Renaissance Studies* 7 (1977): 1–34.

[7]Aulus Gellius, *Noctes atticae* 13. 17. See chap. 2, n. 79 above. Analogous to the way in which the Greek and Roman orators regarded the quadrivial arts as sets of useful facts rather than as formal mathematical disciplines, the Renaissance humanists prompted a shift from the late medieval perspective of viewing the liberal arts as formal disciplines to one of regarding them as subject matters. Richard McKeon, "The Transformation of the Liberal Arts in the Renaissance," in *Developments in the Early Renaissance*, ed. Bernard S. Levy (Albany: State University of New York Press, 1972), pp. 161–169.

[8]Paul O. Kristeller, *Studies in Renaissance Thought and Letters* (Rome: Edizioni di Storia e Letteratura, 1956), pp. 572–574; Kristeller, *Renaissance Thought: The Classic, Scholastic, and Humanist Strains*, rev. ed. (New York: Harper and Row, 1961), pp. 10, 100–110, 131–132; Giustiniani (1973), pp. 23–30; Sem Dresden, "The Profile of the Reception of the Italian Renaissance in France," in *Itinerarium Italicum* (1975), p. 186.

[9]Cicero's *Academica* is credited with stimulating skepticism, outside of the humanist movement, during the Renaissance era. Charles B. Schmitt, *Cicero Scepticus: A Study of the Influence of the "Academica" in the Renaissance* (The Hague: Martinus Nijhoff, 1972), chaps. 1–2.

concerns philosophical speculation," they have been charged with an eclectic approach to moral instruction, an inclination to formalism, and dogmatic obsequiousness to cited authorities.[10]

For better or worse, this Renaissance movement incorporating characteristics of the *artes liberales* ideal was transmitted to other European lands during the fifteenth and sixteenth centuries, and different interpretations of this dissemination are possible. Some make typological distinctions by describing the northern Renaissance as "Christian humanism" and the southern as "classical humanism." Others see in it a process of attrition whereby, as in the Low Countries, the import of Italian humanism was greatly reduced in stature.[11] In any case, the educational program could not be separated from the humanist influence because the program was conceptually integral to the humanist movement and, secondarily, because more humanists earned their living by teaching than by any other pursuit.

Late in the fourteenth century, Pier Paolo Vergerio (1349–1420) wrote one of the first Renaissance treatises on education, *De ingenuis moribus et liberalibus adolescentiae studiis* (On the upright character and liberal studies of youth), which achieved a great popularity that extended through the sixteenth century. A master at Padua, Vergerio clearly connected the humanist educational plan to "liberal education" when he wrote, "we call those studies *liberal* which are worthy of a free man; those studies by which we attain and practise virtue and wisdom."[12] Vergerio argued against the scholastic emphasis on logic in the arts curriculum and made a firm connection between high morality and the learning of classical letters. Meanwhile, scholars traveling back and forth between the Byzantine Em-

---

[10]The quotation is from William H. Woodward, *Desiderius Erasmus concerning the Aim and Method of Education* (Cambridge: Cambridge University Press, 1904), p. 36. See Frederick Eby and Charles F. Arrowood, *The History and Philosophy of Education, Ancient and Medieval* (New York: Prentice-Hall, 1940), p. 921; Paul O. Kristeller, *Renaissance Thought II: Papers on Humanism and the Arts* (New York: Harper and Row, 1965), pp. 36–37.

[11]Cf. Robert R. Bolgar, *The Classical Heritage and Its Beneficiaries* (Cambridge: Cambridge University Press, 1964), p. 305; Oberman (1975), p. xxiii; Jozef Ijsewijn, "The Coming of Humanism to the Low Countries," in *Itinerarium Italicum* (1975), p. 275.

[12]Vergerio is quoted from the translation of *De Ingenuis Moribus* in *Vittorino da Feltre and other Humanist Educators: Essays and Versions*, William H. Woodward (Cambridge: Cambridge University Press, 1897), p. 102. See Eugenio Garin, *L'educazione in Europa, 1400/1600: Problemi e programmi*, rev. ed. (Rome: Editori Laterza, 1976), pp. 117–127. Better translations (in Italian) and some Latin texts of humanist educators are available in *Il pensiero pedagogico dello Umanesimo*, ed. and trans. Eugenio Garin (Florence: Giuntine, Sansoni, 1958).

pire and Italian cities stimulated philological studies, invigorating the pursuit of Greek letters.

The two leading educators of the fifteenth century, who were close friends and did the most to establish the humanist ideal in schools, were Guarino da Verona and Vittorino da Feltre. The former, having taught at Florence, Venice, and Padua, served as a master of rhetoric at Ferrara, where he promoted the study of Greek and Latin. The latter spent many years as a student and teacher at the University of Padua before establishing his school for the Gonzaga family, rulers of Mantua. He framed the curriculum around the *septem artes liberales* reinterpreted according to the humanist ideal that he found in Quintilian. This reliance on the *Institutio oratoria* and a complementary interpretation of philosophy as a practical guide for life, reminiscent of the view of Isocrates, were shared by his humanist contemporaries and transmitted to their fifteenth-century successors.[13]

The *studia humanitatis* (or *artes liberales, studia litterarum, bonae artes, humanae artes*, and *studia humaniora*, as they were also known) had thus made inroads into the arts curricula of Italian universities and city schools by the middle of the fifteenth century. Venice, Ferrara, Mantua, Padua, and Florence were among the leaders in this promotion of Greek and Latin literature, to which the Bolognese attention to rhetoric contributed as well.[14] Humanist studies were also being advanced at the University of Rome, where the masters of rhetoric included Lorenzo Valla (1407–1457). In his *Dialecticae disputationes contra aristotelicos* and *De linguae latinae elegentia*, Valla advocated the writing style of classical *auctores* by way of attacking the scholastic preoccupation with logic. The latter treatise, in particular, was much admired and widely consulted. It epitomizes the

---

[13]William H. Woodward, *Studies in Education during the Age of the Renaissance, 1400–1600* (Cambridge: Cambridge University Press, 1906), pp. 26–47; Woodward (1897), pp. 48–78; Jean Giraud, "Victorin de Feltre (1378–1447?)" *PH* 11 (1971): 369–387; Garin (1976), pp. 127–134.

[14]The schools of Florence were relatively late in embracing humanism. Charles T. Davis, "Education in Dante's Florence," *Speculum* 40 (1965): 425–433. Here and below, I draw from Eugenio Garin, "La concezione dell'università in Italia nell'età del Rinascimento," in *Commission* (1967), pp. 84–93; Jacques Le Goff, "La conception française de l'université à l'époque de la Renaissance," in *Commission* (1967), pp. 94–100; James R. Banker, "The Ars Dictaminis and Rhetorical Textbooks at the Bolognese University in the Fourteenth Century," *Medievalia et Humanistica*, New Series 5 (1974): 153–168; Adriano Franceschini, *Nuovi documenti relativi ai docenti dello studio di Ferrara nel sec. XVI* (Ferrara: SATE, 1970), pp. xvii-xix; Robert N. Swanson, *Universities, Academics, and the Great Schism* (London: Cambridge University Press, 1979), pp. 202–207.

humanist effort both to reinstate the practice of relying on examples of great classical writing in the teaching of grammar and rhetoric and to oust the *grammatica speculativa* from the schools of northern Europe, where the speculative grammar had become established.[15]

The developments in Italy should not, however, lead one to generalize too quickly about areas north of the Alps. For some of the same political and economic reasons cited earlier, Renaissance humanism flourished earlier and more strongly in Italy, and the spread of its influence northward and into the universities is a matter of some ambiguity and contention. Certain historians hold that humanism did not enter the universities in the fifteenth century, even going so far as to say, "The fact is, humanism was an anti-university movement." Others take the opposite view, citing expanded attention to grammar, rhetoric, and the new sciences, and the number of humanist teachers at colleges and schools.[16] These interpretive contradictions, crucial to the understanding of liberal education during the period, must be appreciated in light of four factors.[17]

First is the matter of defining "Renaissance humanism," for if one regards it as a forerunner of the Enlightenment, then one is more inclined to deny its influence in the institutions of a pre-Enlightenment world, namely the universities. On the other hand, if one holds to the definition offered here—an educational ideal based on classical letters—then one tends to see greater penetration into the universities of the fifteenth century. A second factor in the conflict-

[15]Wilhelm Kölmel, "*Scolasticus Literator* Die Humanisten und ihr Verhältnis zur Scholastik," in *Historisches Jahrbuch*, ed. Johannes Spörl (Munich: Karl Alber, 1973), vol. 93, pp. 311–327; Lisa Jardine, "Lorenzo Valla and the Intellectual Origins of Humanist Dialectic," *Journal of the History of Philosophy* 15 (1977): 143–164.

[16]For examples of the former, see Louis J. Paetow, *The Arts Course at Medieval Universities: With Special Reference to Grammar and Rhetoric* (Champaign: University of Illinois Press, 1910), pp. 61–66; Ernest C. Moore, *The Story of Instruction*, vol. 2, *The Church, the Renaissances and the Reformations* (New York: Macmillan, 1938), p. 141; James A. Weisheipl, "The Place of the Liberal Arts in the University Curriculum during the XIVth and XVth Centuries," in *Actes* (1969), p. 216. For the latter, see Kristeller (1961), p. 102; Helene Wieruszowski, *The Medieval University, Masters, Students, Learning* (Princeton, N.J.: D. Van Nostrand, 1966), pp. 115–116; Sven Stelling-Michaud, "Quelques remarques sur l'histoire des universités à l'époque de la Renaissance," in *Commission* (1967), p. 72.

[17]For the following, I draw from Gabriel (1955), chap. 10; Lewis W. Spitz, *Conrad Celtis, the German Arch-Humanist* (Cambridge: Harvard University Press, 1957), pp. 3–8; Astrik L. Gabriel, *The College System in the Fourteenth-Century Universities* (Baltimore: privately printed, 1962), pp. 1–6; Andrzej Wyczański, "Le rôle de l'université à l'époque de l'humanisme," in *Commission* (1967), p. 135; Karl A. Sprengard, "Die Bedeutung der Artistenfakultät für die Entwicklung der modernen Philosophie des XIV. und XV. Jahrhunderts," in *Actes* (1969), pp. 691–699; Alan B. Cobban, *The Medieval Universities: Their Development and Organization* (London: Methuen, 1975), chap. 6;

ing interpretations relates to the curricular interest of the humanists and scholastics. Since the former focused on the *artes* of grammar and rhetoric, while incorporating poetry and history and attending also to ethics, and the latter concentrated on logic and philosophy, their interests were in some sense competitive but not necessarily mutually exclusive. In fact, members of both camps were known to quarrel more with their own colleagues than with their supposed opponents (which, as will be seen, Conradus Celtis discovered at Leipzig). Therefore, the continuing strength of the scholastic *artes* and philosophies at the universities in the fifteenth century does not necessarily preclude the presence of the humanist *artes liberales* at the same time.

Third is the matter of defining "studies." The humanist educational ideal was originally adopted in extracurricular and adjunct institutions, while the diminution of ecclesiastical power, the rise of the bourgeoisie, and the laicization of universities progressed over the course of the Renaissance. These changes subsequently encouraged individuals to establish residential colleges and schools next to universities. These new establishments offered some lecturing and tutoring based on the humanist educational ideal. In addition to this complement to the formal university curriculum, the humanist movement influenced secondary education, which was not yet highly organized but for that very reason allowed free reign to tutors to incorporate the *studia liberalia* or *studia humanitatis*, as they did in fifteenth-century Venice. Hence, the fact that a university's statutes may not have formally required teaching of the *studia humanitatis* does not mean that such teaching did not take place in and around the university. Finally, even where universities did not officially promote the oratorical *artes liberales*, it was academicians from universities who traveled about and did just that. This fact, too, is cited both by those modern scholars who find humanist influence in the universities and by those who do not. Bearing these four points in mind, let us review briefly the geographical extension of that influence.

After Italy, the area next transformed by the Renaissance is often said to be the Germanies and central Europe. As early as 1445, Enea Silvio de Piccolomini, later Pope Pius II, went to Vienna to promote

---

James B. Ross, "Venetian Schools and Teachers, Fourteenth to Early Sixteenth Century: A Survey and a Study of Giovanni Battista Egnazio," *Renaissance Quarterly* 24 (1976): 522–530; Laetitia Boehm, "Humanistische Bildungsbewegung und mittelalteriche Universitätsverfassung: Aspekte zur frühneuzeitlichen Reformgeschichte der deutschen Universitäten," in *The Universities* (1978), pp. 329–345.

the humanist letters and, about this same time, wrote a tract for the king of Bohemia and Hungary describing the humanist approach to the liberal arts and philosophy and quoting extensively from Quintilian. Inspired by such visits and scholarship, the University of Vienna gradually expanded the study of Latin literature in the arts curriculum, a change subsequently adopted at Prague and then Krakow.[18] Even more significant than this kind of influence, however, were visits made to Italy by northern scholars who returned home proclaiming the humanist gospel.

Many did not intend this when beginning their travels to Padua, Bologna, Pavia, Ferrara, or Siena to study Roman and canon law; but others had the notion very much in mind. Such a one was the Dutch humanist Rodolphus Agricola (1443–1485). Educated in northern universities, he spent ten years at Italian schools in classical studies before returning north and eventually inspiring Heidelberg with the humanist spirit. No less noteworthy was Conradus Celtis (1459–1508), who, disappointed by the scholasticism of Cologne, went to study at Heidelberg in 1485 and, after Agricola died, moved to Erfurt, where he taught the future lights of its Renaissance circle. After traveling south to study humanist classics in several Italian centers, he returned north and lectured at a number of German universities before finally arrving in 1491 at Ingolstadt, where it had become the fashion to sponsor a university poet. There Celtis wrote his *Oratio,* the first plan for university reform composed by a humanist. The *Oratio* did not attack the liberal arts course but sought to revitalize it according to the Renaissance educational ideal that Celtis had seen in Italian schools.[19] Carrying on this tradition in the faculty at Ingolstadt was Johann Reuchlin (1455–1522), who in his later years advanced the study of Greek and Hebrew at Tübingen.

The fact that Reuchlin was graduated a master of arts from the University of Basel is telling because that *studium* had become one

---

[18]Aeneas Silvius Piccolomini, *De liberorum educatione,* trans. Joel S. Nelson (Washington, D.C.: Catholic University of America Press, 1940), chaps. 1–3; Woodward (1897), pp. 138–158; Lynn Thorndike, *University Records and Life in the Middle Ages* (New York: Columbia University Press, 1944), documents 132, 163; Alphons Lhotsky, *Die Wiener Artistenfakultät, 1365–1497* (Vienna: Hermann Böhlaus, 1965), pp. 133–145. On the extension of influence from Vienna through Prague to Krakow, see Paul W. Knoll, "The World of the Young Copernicus: Society, Science, and the University," in *Science and Society: Past, Present, and Future,* ed. Nicholas H. Steneck (Ann Arbor: University of Michigan Press, 1975), pp. 27–34.

[19]Spitz (1957), pp. 1–31; Spitz, "The Course of German Humanism," in *Itinerarium Italicum* (1975), pp. 374, 402; Agostino Sottili, "La natio germanica dell'Università di Pavia nella storia dell'umanesimo," in *The Universities* (1978), pp. 347–364.

of the principal centers of humanism north of the Alps after its founding in 1460. But more significantly, Basel demonstrates how the universities founded by the bourgeoisie in this period were relatively free of Church influence, with its accompanying scholastic emphasis, and thus more open to the humanist impulse. Where the bourgeoisie were frustrated in their efforts to change the medieval university studies, adjunct institutions such as gymnasia, academies, and *studia particularia* were formed to meet the desire for education according to the humanist ideal. Schools at Chelmo, Torun, and Braunsberg in fifteenth-century Prussia were founded under such circumstances.[20]

Another factor contributing to the rise of humanism in central Europe, Germany, and Poland lay in the fragmentation of those areas into many small principalities. This pluralism encouraged diversity and competition among the reigning princes and nobles and thus helped to produce the humanist orientation that developed at Krakow, Erfurt, and Nuremberg by the late fifteenth century. Similarly, when Frederick the Wise planned the foundation of the University of Wittenberg, he hoped to elevate the cultural life of his Saxon electorate above that of its neighbors. The founding document of 1502 specifically prescribed that the *studia humaniora* be taught, and by 1512, humanism had become the acknowledged educational ideal of many of the masters.[21]

By that time, too, the atmospere of the University of Leipzig had changed greatly from its portrayal in *Manuale scholarium*, which first appeared in print in 1481. This handbook's poor Latin reveals a decided lack of humanist influence. In 1518 that text was eclipsed by the *Paedologia* of Petrus Mosellanus (1493–1524), who became professor of Greek at Leipzig and achieved fame throughout Europe for this colloquy. Imbued with the scholarly and aesthetic tenents of the humanist ideal, Mosellanus was the first to base a colloquy on the classical Latin style of the "New Learning," and he noted that the authors to be read by the beginning student in the arts curriculum of Leipzig were Cicero, Terence, Vergil, Prudentius, and Erasmus. The 1519 timetable of lectures for the faculty of arts at Leipzig con-

---

[20]Lewis W. Spitz, *The Religious Renaissance of the German Humanists* (Cambridge: Harvard University Press, 1963), pp. 20–40; Stelling-Michaud (1967), pp. 75, 82; Brygida Kurbis, "Discussion," in *Commission* (1967), p. 134; Wolfgang Rother, "Zur Geschichte der Basler Universitätsphilosophie im 17. Jahrhundert," *History of Universities* 2 (1982): 153–155.

[21]Maria Grossmann, *Humanism in Wittenberg, 1485–1517* (Nieuwkoop, Neth.: B. De Graaf, 1975), pp. 42–46, 55; James H. Overfield, "Scholastic Opposition to Hu-

firms the new humanist orientation.[22] Overall then, the influence of Renaissance humanism and its educational ideal arrived in Germany by the late fifteenth and early sixteenth centuries. So, too, did it come to the Low Countries. In the mid-fifteenth century, Rodolphus Agricola had felt himself a stranger among barbarians after returning home from Italy. Very soon, however, the University of Louvain incorporated the study of Latin poets and orators in the arts curriculum, and by 1500 town schools in communities such as Bruges, Ghent, and Deventer were striving to bring the humanist model of education northward. A stay in Italy had become a *sine qua non* for those wishing to call themselves educated.[23]

As in Germany, humanism in France gained acceptance first in secular courts and bourgeois urban centers, then gradually in the universities. In the fifteenth century, the strength of scholasticism forced the French bourgeoisie to form their own colleges and urban humanist schools outside of the universities. Some change in this pattern was anticipated when jurisdiction over the University of Paris was transferred to the Parlement in 1461. Since this naturally reduced clerical authority, a precondition to laicization of the university, the building of new institutions by the bourgeoisie gradually abated. In the first half of the fifteenth century about twenty-five colleges appeared, in the second half only three. Similarly, eight new universities were founded in France before 1463, then no more for several centuries. This does not mean that humanist studies were promptly transferred from the academies and colleges to the older, established universities. Even after 1530, when the Royal Lectureships were founded at Paris to advance humanist scholarship, the instructional level of these *lecteurs royaux* was often elementary. The acceptance of humanism was gradual; thus, the sixteenth rather than the fifteenth is commonly regarded as the century of Renaissance in France.[24]

---

manism in Pre-Reformation Germany," *Viator* 7 (1976): 391–420; Michal Patkaniowski, "Periodizzamento, giurisprudenza umanistica, influssi italiani a Cracovia," in *Commission* (1967), pp. 128–129.

[22]*Manuale scholarium*, translated with an introduction by Robert F. Seybolt (Cambridge: Harvard University Press, 1921), pp. 9–13; Petrus Mosellanus, *Paedologia in puerorum usum conscripta*, translated with an introduction by Robert F. Seybolt as *Renaissance Student Life* (Urbana: University of Illinois Press, 1927), pp. xi–xix; Alfred O. Norton, *Readings in the History of Mediaeval Universities* (Cambridge: Harvard University Press, 1909), pp. 132–134.

[23]Ijsewijn (1975), pp. 198–200, 223; Astrik L. Gabriel, "Intellectual Relations between the University of Louvain and the University of Paris in the 15th Century," in *The Universities* (1978), pp. 87–88.

[24]Le Goff (1967), pp. 94–100; Dresden (1975), pp. 119–192; Anthony Grafton, "The

Little different was the fifteenth-century situation in the Iberian peninsula. There the Aristotelian philosophical tradition and its accompanying scholasticism remained strong, as at Salamanca and Coimbra, despite visits by Italian humanists and their gifts of humanist texts to Spanish princes and authors. At the very end of the century, the most famous Spanish humanist, Juan Luis Vives (1492–1540), was exposed to a bit of humanist influence in his youth only because he was tutored at home. He soon left his native land for Paris, Louvain, and finally Oxford, where in 1522 he accepted a lectureship in Latin, Greek, and rhetoric.[25]

The year 1520 is sometimes regarded as the culmination of a four-decade introduction of the humanist educational ideal to the British universities. The way for this transition had been prepared in adjunct and lower schools, where contributions to endowments had begun to arrive from secular rather than ecclesiastical sources, freeing those schools from the clerical constraints to adhere to the scholastic model.[26] In contrast, where clerics continued to dominate education, as in parts of western England, there was a corresponding emphasis on *scientia grammatica*, logic, and Aristotle in the *artes liberales*.[27] Hand in hand with this change in the lower schools went the laicization of the student population, which was increasingly composed of the sons of the nobility, gentry, and bourgeoisie, due both to the changing economic conditions already experienced in Italy and to the expanded need for civil servants brought on by the rise of the bureaucratic state. Most significant for cultivation of the humanist ideal in the liberal arts, however, was the rise of the col-

---

Classical Teaching of the *Lecteurs Royaux* at Paris: A Reconsideration" (Paper presented at Symposium, Innovation and Tradition: The Universities of Early Modern Europe, conducted by the Warburg Institute (University of London, March 1979).

[25]Hastings Rashdall, *The Universities of Europe in the Middle Ages*, ed. F. M. Powicke and A. B. Emden (Oxford: Clarendon, 1936), vol. 2, chap. 7; Woodward (1906), pp. 180–182; Marian L. Tobriner, ed., *Vives' Introduction to Wisdom: A Renaissance Textbook* (New York: Teachers College Press, 1968), pp. 11–32; Martin L. Clarke, *Classical Education in Britain, 1500–1900* (Cambridge: Cambridge University Press, 1959), pp. 22–31. See note 43 in this chapter.

[26]On this four-decade introduction, I draw from Roberto Weiss, *Humanism in England During the Fifteenth Century*, 2d ed. (Oxford: Basil Blackwell, 1957); Weiss, "Learning and Education in Western Europe from 1470–1520," in *New Cambridge Modern History: The Renaissance, 1493–1520*, ed. G. R. Potter (Cambridge: Cambridge University Press, 1957), pp. 95–126; W. A. Pantin, "The Conception of the Universities in England in the Period of the Renaissance," in *Commission* (1967), pp. 109–112; Cobban (1975), chap. 6; Hay (1975), pp. 305–370.

[27]Nicholas Orme, *Education in the West of England, 1066–1548: Cornwall, Devon, Dorset, Gloucestershire, Somerset, Wiltshire* (Exeter: University of Exeter Press, 1976), pp. 23–26.

lege tutorial system. Begun informally as a way of supplementing the university lectures, tutoring existed as a necessary complement to the lectures during the fifteenth century, and eventually usurped their place as the primary means of instruction in the universities. These institutional and curricular changes provided the avenues whereby the ideas of certain humanists entered English academic life, particularly those of Desiderius Erasmus, who visited England between 1510 and 1515.

Throughout Europe, Erasmus (1469–1536) achieved fame for his humanist learning, displayed in such celebrated books as *Adagia* (Proverbs) and *Moriae encomium* (The praise of folly), and for his vastly improved editions of the Church Fathers and Greek New Testament.[28] He thereby established himself as the arbiter of scholarship in both divine and classical letters. In so doing, he probably contributed more than any other individual to making the humanist ideal normative for education, that is, for the "liberal studies" he described in *De ratione studii* (On the right plan of study) and *Declamatio de pueris statim ac liberaliter instituendis* (Declamation that children ought to be educated liberally and from early youth). Accordingly, it is possible to abstract from these and other Erasmian writings, as exemplars of humanist defense of the *studia humanitatis*, the oratorical frame of seven characteristics constituting the *artes liberales* ideal.

Erasmus, first of all, derived from his erudition little appreciation of speculative and critical philosophy. In educational theory, for example, he relied directly on Quintilian and wrote his *Institutio principis christiani* (Education of a Christian prince) as the counterpart to a treatise by Isocrates. His often platitudinous writings on education, coupled with his appeal to the authority of the Bible and classical authors, point to an epistemological dogmatism underlying the identification of definite standards for personality formation, a second characteristic of the *artes liberales* ideal. The Erasmian stan-

---

[28]Here and below, I draw from Woodward (1904), chaps. 2–3; Desiderius Erasmus, *The Education of a Christian Prince*, translated with an introduction by Lester K. Born (New York: Columbia University Press, 1936; New York: W. W. Norton, 1968), pp. 30, 135, 199; Johan Huizinga, *Erasmus of Rotterdam*, trans. F. Hopman (New York: Charles Scribner's Sons, 1924); Hellmuth Exner, *Der Einfluss des Erasmus auf die Englische Bildungsidee* (Berlin: Junker und Dünnhaupt, 1939); Desiderius Erasmus, *Declamatio de pueris statim ac liberaliter instituendis* (Etude critique), translation and commentary by Jean-Claude Margolin (Geneva: Librairie Droz, 1966), pp. 41–82; Myron P. Gilmore, "Italian Reactions to Erasmian Humanism," in *Itinerarium Italicum* (1975), pp. 61–118. A good brief overview can be found in Martin L. Clarke, "The Educational Writings of Erasmus," *Erasmus in English* 8 (1976): 23–31.

dards were of two kinds: aesthetic norms that he found in certain literary classics and moral norms that he found in Jesus, and Erasmus tried to harmonize those norms in what he called the "philosophy of Christ."

While that terminology further confirms his skewing of "philosophy" away from the speculative tradition, it also demonstrates, thirdly, his straightforward appeal to a classical corpus in two respects. Erasmus judged pagan books by a Christlike moral standard and, conversely, adopted the philological principles of humanist erudition for interpreting sacred texts. In this fashion, he tried to reconcile the literary, aesthetic, and moral norms through his notion of *humanitas*: the program of scholarship and virtue by which one seeks to form the good citizen, a fourth characteristic of the *artes liberales* ideal. This intention to form the good citizen appears in the prescriptions in *Enchiridion militis christiani* (Handbook for the Christian knight); and, in line with Alcuin and the ancient orators, it is also shown by the *Institutio*, which was written to convey how a monarch should be educated to become his own archetypal good citizen.

These same norms, however, present a paradox when considered in relation to two other characteristics of the *artes liberales* ideal: respect for commitment to the absolutes and designation of an elite. Despite his firm convictions, Erasmus was relatively tolerant and broadminded in an age when most of his contemporaries embraced the bibliolatry of the Reformers or the inviolability of the Church. He held an optimistic faith that all could achieve his ethic of *humanitas* and become good Christian citizens in order to resolve social and political problems. Harmony, he hoped, could be achieved in one true religion, one classical culture, and one exquisite language. This tolerant, even egalitarian piety reflects his youthful education under the Brethren of the Common Life, and it would seem to contravene the *artes liberales* ideal except that Erasmus adopted those views precisely because he retained the absolute standards of Jesus and Cicero. Consequently, his feelings of tolerance and Christian brotherhood were upheld as tenets of his authorities. When the basis of that code was challenged, Erasmus could become as intolerant and condescending as any of his humanist contemporaries who reserved the *studia humanitatis* for an elite. He did not hesitate to pour vitriolic abuse upon Martin Luther when he finally concluded that Reformer to be an enemy of the true faith.[29]

---

[29]Preserved Smith, *Erasmus: A Study of his Life, Ideals, and Place in History* (New York: Harper and Brothers, 1923), pp. 52, 443; Albert Hyma, *The Youth of Erasmus*, 2d

This fundamental respect for commitment and the concomitant elitism were not untroubling to Erasmus. His writings reveal an inner conflict that calls into question his affinity to the seventh characteristic of the *artes liberales* ideal: the regard for this liberal training and its refinement in prescribed virtues as an end in itself. Erasmus experienced great tension between his Christian commitment to humility and the humanist value assigned to pride and praise, between the Christian desire for pure, simple belief and the humanist respect for sophisticated refinement. He thus recognized a central difficulty of Renaissance humanism in the clash between ethical and aesthetic standards, a tension that was particularly pronounced in the ideal of the courtier.[30]

While this conflict may indeed have compromised an idealistic conception of endless refinement through the *artes liberales* for Erasmus, his curricular prescription for "liberal studies" nonetheless confirms his allegiance to the oratorical tradition. In considering what it meant to be *liberaliter educatum,* he recalled in the *Declamatio*:

> The most miserable time of my youth was when [we] boys were flayed by 'modi significandi' . . . and at the same time were taught nothing but to speak poorly. Truly, the teachers obscured grammar by introducing dialectical and metaphysical difficulties so that they would not appear to be teaching childish things.[31]

Later in the *Declamatio* and in the *De ratione studii,* he recommended for study essentially the offerings of the *septem artes liber-*

---

ed. (New York: Russell & Russell, 1968), chaps. 9–10, 12; James D. Tracy, *Erasmus: The Growth of a Mind* (Geneva: Librairie Droz. 1972), pp. 9–10, 103–105.

[30]The humanist conflict between aesthetic and ethical standards may be seen clearly in *Il cortegiano* (The courtier) by Baldassare Castiglione (1478–1529). Castiglione advises that a gentleman should never admit ignorance or lack of skill but rather choose an opportunity to speak or act so that others will believe he is more competent than he actually is. From that point, the courtier ought to move skillfully the engagement to a different matter where he has greater knowledge or skill. Recognizing that some might consider such deceit improper, Castiglione argued:

> And where you have a jewell that unset seemeth faire, afterwarde when it commeth to a goldsmithes handes that in well setting it maketh it appear much more fairer, will you not say that the goldsmith deceiveth the eyes of them that looke on it? And yet for that deceite, deserveth he prayse. (*The Book of the Courtier,* trans. Sir Thomas Hoby [1561; reprint, New York: E. P. Dutton, 1928], p. 132)

This "deceite" should not call into question the basic "seriousness' and "integrity of purpose" with which Castiglione approached his work. Fritz Caspari, *Humanism and the Social Order in Tudor England* (Chicago: University of Chicago Press, 1954; New York: Teachers College Press, 1968), p. 153. Rather, it means "the ethical objection is refuted by an aesthetic argument." John S. White, *Renaissance Cavalier* (New York: Philosophical Library, 1959), p. 38

[31]Erasmus, *Declamatio* 514f, 504d.

ales, but with an emphasis on literary grammar and rhetoric. He reinterpreted logic as an auxiliary to rhetoric rather than to philosophy, and gave scant attention to the elementary quadrivial studies, which were recommended merely as useful sets of facts.[32]

This curricular framework had thus not been forgotten and was actually being reoriented toward the resurrected ideal of the Roman orators. At late fifteenth-century Erfurt, one of the first universities in central and northern Germany to introduce humanist studies into the curriculum, it was the recommendation of the *antiqui* to lecture from Martianus's exposition of grammar that brought them into battle with Erfurt scholastics, who preferred that grammar be taught as a branch of logic.[33] And when the Spaniard Vives, who himself recommended the reading of Martianus, wrote *De tradendis disciplinis* (On the disciplines to be transmitted) in 1531, he prescribed a curriculum of "liberal training" that comprised subjects of the seven liberal arts realigned from the scholastic to the humanist perspective.[34] Meanwhile, the traditional handbooks continued to be consulted. Martianus, Cassiodorus, and Isidore each appeared in at least six editions during the sixteenth century. It is no surprise, then, that the Protestant reformer Philipp Melanchthon (1497–1560) encountered the curricular framework of the *trivium* and *quadrivium* in his early studies at Heidelberg and Tübingen, even while the scholastic emphasis was rapidly giving way to the humanist. Nor is it surprising that when Melanchthon became a master and then began to teach at the University of Wittenberg, he incorporated the humanist orientation into his own lectures on the *artes liberales.*[35]

The Protestant Reformation is often considered in the light of various developments: the preceding revival of Augustinianism, the

---

[32]Desiderius Erasmus, *De ratione studii,* in *Opera Omnia Desiderii Erasmi Roterdami Recognita et Adnotatione Critica Instructa Notisque Illustrata* (Amsterdam: North-Holland, 1969), order 1, vol. 2, pp. 136–146.

[33]Pantin (1967), pp. 103–104; Emil Lucki, "Concern of the Synods for the Liberal Arts during the First Century of the Renaissance, 1350–1450," in *Actes* (1969), pp. 731–733. Insight into the role of Martianus's exposition of grammar can be found in Cora E. Lutz, "Aesticampianus' Commentary on the *De Grammatica* of Martianus Capella," *Renaissance Quarterly* 26 (1973): 157–166.

[34]Juan Luis Vives, *De tradendis disciplinis,* translated with an introduction by Foster Watson (Cambridge: Cambridge University Press, 1913), pp. ci–clv, bks. 3–5; Tobriner (1968), pp. 36–64. Cf. William Sinz, "The Elaboration of Vives' Treatises on the Arts," *Renaissance Studies* 10 (1963): 68–90.

[35]Hans Ahrbeck, "Melanchthon als Praeceptor Germaniae," in *Philipp Melanchthon Forschungsbeiträge zur vierhundersten Wiederkehr seines Todestages dargeboten in Wittenberg 1960,* ed. Walter D. Elliger (Göttingen, W. Ger.: Vandenhoeck & Ruprecht,

emergence of nominalism and mysticism as alternatives to the Thomistic synthesis, the corruption of the Church in times of social oppression, the appearance of nationalism and royal power. However, the central issue of concern here is the interaction of Reformation thought with Renaissance humanism and therefore with the oratorical tradition and the *artes liberales* ideal.[36] Although the Protestant and Catholic Reformations often dominate discussion of Western Europe in the sixteenth century, it is no less significant that the Renaissance reached its apogee in the sixteenth century. It was in the course of this century that French, English, and central European universities embraced the humanist gospel.

Scholarly opinion on the relationship between the Reformation and the Renaissance has tended to polarize between—to state the matter starkly—those who view the Reformation as essentially medieval and thus in opposition to and opposed by the Renaissance humanists, and those who believe that the Reformation was the religious complement of the Renaissance, that the Reformation and Renaissance were two branches of the same movement. Now, the theology of Renaissance humanists differed significantly from that of the reformers in that the former practiced more tolerance and held a higher opinion of the capacity and worth of human beings, especially the intellect, than did the latter. Furthermore, the majority of Renaissance humanists in Europe, whether teaching inside or outside the universities, did not follow Luther into revolt and after 1520 consistently opposed him. Nonetheless, these two movements are profoundly linked by their mutual opposition to scholasticism, for educators from both parties favored the study of rhetoric over logic. The Protestant Reformers, like the Renaissance humanists, sided not with the speculative tradition of the philosophers but with the orators, whose purpose had always been to argue persuasively

---

1961), pp. 140–146; Wilhelm Maurer, "Melanchthon als Humanist," in Elliger (1961), pp. 116–132.

[36]In the following analysis, I draw from Smith (1923), pp. 1–3, 320–324; E. Harris Harbison, *The Christian Scholar in the Age of the Reformation* (New York: Charles Scribner's Sons, 1956), pp. 123, 145–163; Roland H. Bainton, "Interpretations of the Reformation," *American Historical Review* 66 (1960): 74–84; Ernst Troeltsch, "Renaissance and Reformation," in *The Reformation Basic Interpretations*, ed. and trans., Lewis W. Spitz, 2d ed., (Lexington, Mass.: D.C. Heath, 1972), pp. 25–43; Kristeller (1965), pp. 77–82; William J. Bouwsma, "Renaissance and Reformation: An Essay in Their Affinities and Connections," in *Luther and the Dawn of the Modern Era: Papers for the Fourth International Conference for Luther Research*, ed. Heiko A. Oberman (Leiden, Neth.: E. J. Brill, 1974), pp. 129, 133–147; Heiko A. Oberman, "Headwaters of the Reformation: *Initia Lutheri-Initia Reformationis*," in Oberman (1974), pp. 40–88.

for a high tradition of true civic virtue. Underlying this outlook was a distrust of the scholastic assumption that life could be explained by deductions from abstract principles. The humanists, largely for aesthetic reasons, and the Reformers, with their fervent pietism, were impressed rather by the power of the *logos* to convince and to persuade.

Following Lorenzo Valla, they rejected the dry, ethereal rules of the *grammatica speculativa* and "artificial logic" taught by the scholastics; and they advocated instead the study of "natural logic" as it existed in the actual argumentation of great rhetors and prophets from the past. While thus incorporating the study of logic into and under rhetoric, these two groups placed emphasis upon learning and applying the tools of philology in order to determine the most accurate readings of classical and canonical texts. Moreover, the humanists and reformers agreed on the point made by Vives, that "the highest subject in the liberal arts and learning is that moral philosophy which brings a remedy for the deadly diseases of the soul."[37] This sharply contrasted with the scholastic view of the arts curriculum as primarily a program for studying logical method and metaphysics in preparation for systematic theology and other specialized studies. When these points are combined with the admiration expressed by both Martin Luther (1483–1546) and John Calvin (1509–1564) for classical authors, especially Cicero and Quintilian, it is not surprising to learn that nearly all of the top two-dozen leaders of the Protestant revolt had counted themselves Renaissance humanists.[38]

Having castigated scholastic institutions, Luther, in 1524, appealed to mayors and aldermen to rejuvenate education; and in sermons and letters he recommended the "liberal arts," asking; "Where are the preachers, jurists and physicians to come from, if grammar and other rhetorical arts are not taught?"[39] Melanchthon assumed

---

[37]Juan Luis Vives, *Introduction to Wisdom*, translated by Richard Morison (1540) with an introduction by Marian L. Tobriner (New York: Teachers College Press, 1968), p. 204.

[38]Martin Luther, "Letter to George Spalatin, Wittenberg, February 22, 1518," in *Luther's Works, Letters*, ed. Gottfried G. Krodel (Philadelphia: Fortress, 1967), vol. 48, p. 58; Lewis W. Spitz, "Headwaters of the Reformation: *Studia Humanitatis,* Luther Senior et *Initia Reformationis,*" in *Luther and the Dawn of the Modern Era: Papers for the Fourth International Conference for Luther Research,* ed. Heiko A. Oberman (Leiden, Neth.: E. J. Brill, 1974), pp. 89, 101–107; Henk J. de Jonge, "The Study of the New Testament in the Dutch Universities, 1575–1700," *History of Universities* 1 (1981): 113–114.

[39]Martin Luther, "A Sermon on Keeping Children in School," in *Luther's Works,*

leadership in this effort and provided the model of school organization (*Schulordnung*), whereby the Latin grammar school became normative for Protestant municipal schools throughout central Europe. Melanchthon's students became teachers in nearly every college and gymnasium in Germany after passing through the Wittenberg arts curriculum, which Melanchthon had revised in 1533, taking Cicero and Quintilian as guides for *eloquentia* and elevating rhetoric above philosophy.

With Wittenberg as the model, other universities were reformed on the basis of the "melanchthonischen Synthese von Reformation und Humanismus," including Tübingen in 1535, Leipzig in 1539 and 1559, Greifswald in 1539, and Rostock in 1563; and new ones were founded in the same spirit, including Königsberg in 1544, Jena in 1558, Leyden in 1574, and Franeker in 1585.[40] Beyond inspiring these activities, Wittenberg attracted many students from surrounding lands, such as young nobles from Bohemia and Poland. As the sixteenth century progressed, however, Lutheranism became more and more strict and tended to favor princes above nobility. Such attitudes estranged some of the non-German students, including the Bohemians and Poles, who began moving to other Protestant centers, especially Strasbourg.[41]

The founder of the noted school at Strasbourg, Johannes Sturm (1507–1589), had been educated by the Brethren of the Common Life, who provided him, as they did Erasmus and the rest of Europe, with an early model of how simple piety could be combined with clas-

---

The Christian in Society, ed. Robert C. Schultz (Philadelphia: Fortress, 1963), vol. 46, p. 252.

[40]Quotation is from Gustav A. Benrath, "Die deutsche evangelische Universität der Reformationszeit," in *Universität und Gelehrtenstand, 1400–1800*, ed. Hellmuth Rössler and Günther Franz (Limburg an der Lahn, W. Ger.: C. A. Starke, 1970), p. 70. Charles L. Robbins, *Teachers in Germany in the Sixteenth Century, Conditions in Protestant Elementary and Secondary Schools* (New York: Bureau of Publications, Teachers College, Columbia University, 1912), pp. 40–46; Gustav M. Bruce, *Luther as an Educator* (Minneapolis: Augsburg, 1928; Westport, Conn.: Greenwood, 1979), chaps. 7–12; Ahrbeck (1961), pp. 142–146; Maurer (1961), pp. 116–132; M. Steinmetz, "Die Konzeption der deutschen Universitäten im Zeitälter von Humanismus und Reformation," in *Commission* (1967), pp. 114–127; Gerald Strauss, "The State of Pedagogical Theory c. 1530: What Protestant Reformers Knew about Education," in *Schooling and Society, Studies in the History of Education*, ed. Lawrence Stone (Baltimore: Johns Hopkins University Press, 1976), pp. 69–94; Strauss, *Luther's House of Learning: Indoctrination of the Young in the German Reformation* (Baltimore: Johns Hopkins University Press, 1978), pp. 6–13.

[41]H. de Chelminska, "Sturm et la Pologne," in *L'humanisme en Alsace* (Paris: Société d'Edition "Les Belles-Lettres," 1939), pp. 52–53, 60; D. Stremooukhoff, "Les humanistes tchèques à l'Académie de Strasbourg," in *L'humanisme en Alsace* (1939),

sical studies. After a liberal arts education at Louvain and further study and then teaching at Paris, he came to Strasbourg, where, in 1538, he established his school under the motto *sapiens et eloquens pietas* (wise and eloquent piety), which he drew from Cicero just as the Carolingians had done. For the next forty-four years he served as rector of the secondary school (gymnasium) and the higher school of public lectures (academy), which achieved university status in 1621. Like that of Melanchthon, Sturm's program of eloquent piety was based on the humanist liberal arts and was adopted as a model for Latin schools throughout Poland, England, and Germany, as well as in Leyden, Franeker, Edinburgh, and Geneva.

The transmission to the Calvinist center of Geneva is especially significant. As Sturm's school came under the influence of strict Lutheranism in the late sixteenth and early seventeenth centuries, the Bohemians and Poles again redirected their pilgrimages, this time to the Reformed Church schools and universities that had arisen in Geneva, Basel, and Zurich and to Huguenot schools in France. Since these foreign students were still seeking the same humanist education, their migration reflects the fact that Calvin's *collège* at Geneva, founded in 1559, was based on Sturm's school and that Huguenot colleges and other French Protestant schools were in turn modeled after Geneva or Strasbourg. The Genevan pattern was sustained and further disseminated by Calvin's successor, Theodore Beza (1519–1605), who corresponded with Protestant educators throughout Europe.[42] Thus, the broad dissemination of a humanist arts education from Lutheran to Calvinist to Huguenot institutions can be traced to contacts between students and educators—and it also extended to the educational efforts of the Catholic Reformation.

Partly reacting to the Protestant revolt, the Council of Trent (1546–1563), in an effort to combat widespread ignorance among Catholic clergy, recommended that seminaries be established in every diocese, where students aspiring to the priesthood could be educated in the liberal arts. The most effective and far-reaching re-

---

pp. 42–44; František Hrubý, *Étudiants tchèques aux écoles protestantes de l'Europe occidentale à la fin du 16ᵉ et au début du 17ᵉ siècle* (Brno, Czech.: Universita J. E. Purkyne, 1970), pp. 11–14, 25–31.

[42]Howard C. Barnard, *The French Tradition in Education, Ramus to Mme. Necker de Saussure* (Cambridge: Cambridge University Press, 1922), chap. 3; J. Rott, "L'humanisme et la réforme pédagogique en Alsace," *L'humanisme en Alsace* (1939), pp. 73ff.; E. Hoepffner, "Jean Sturm et l'enseignement supérieur des lettres à l'école de Strasbourg," in *L'humanisme en Alsace*, (1939), pp. 86–88; Gérard Mathon, "Les formes et la signification de la pédagogie des arts libéraux au milieu du IXᵉ siècle: L'enseignement palatin de Jean Scot Érigène," in *Actes* (1969), p. 58.

sponse to this acknowledged need was embodied in the Society of Jesus founded by Ignatius of Loyola (1493–1556). In 1547 in Messina, the Jesuits opened their first college for secular students, and it provided the model for the curriculum of the Roman College, which was incorporated into the 1551 Constitutions of the Society. That model was elaborated in the *ratio studiorum* of 1586, which was amended in 1591 and finalized in 1599.[43] Meanwhile, the Society experienced phenomenal success in founding institutions. Upon the death of Loyola in 1556, the Jesuits had established 35 colleges across Western Europe. In 1599, there were 245; in 1626, 444. Each of them, whether standing alone or situated at a university, modeled their liberal arts education upon the curriculum of the Roman College and the *ratio studiorum*. This can be seen, for example, in the lectures and readings assigned at Ingolstadt, which became for Catholics in central Europe what Wittenberg was to Protestants.[44]

Despite the creedal distinctions and the diversity among national cultures that began to undermine the cultural unity of Europe in the sixteenth century, the arts curricula maintained a fairly uniform pattern for liberal education. For texts, Cicero and Aristotle were the two indispensable sources, while a number of standard humanist colloquies were widely utilized. The *Paedologia* (1518) of Petrus Mosellanus had appeared in 64 editions by 1706, and similar colloquies of Erasmus (1519), Vives (1539), and Corderius (1564) went through more than 100 editions each.[45] The order of the liberal arts

---

[43] Allan P. Farrell, *The Jesuit Code of Liberal Education: Development and Scope of the Ratio Studiorum* (Milwaukee: Bruce, 1938); George E. Ganss, *Saint Ignatius' Idea of a Jesuit University: A Study in the History of Catholic Education (Including Part IV of the Constitutions of the Society of Jesus)* (Milwaukee: Marquette University Press, 1954), pp. 10–11, chap. 3; Richard L. Kagan, "Universities in Castille, 1500–1810," in *The University in Society*, ed. Lawrence Stone (Princeton, N.J.: Princeton University Press, 1974), vol. 2, pp. 367–382.

[44] By mid-seventeenth century, the Jesuits provided half of the college-level instruction in Spain. In Italy, where universities had long been accustomed to the atmosphere of Renaissance humanism, the Society achieved great influence by orienting its colleges toward secondary or even primary education. Northward, in central Europe, the followers of Loyola came to dominate liberal arts education in almost every Catholic college, with the notable exception of the University of Salzburg, which was confided to the Benedictines. In addition to sources cited above in this regard, see Henri de Vocht, "Les débuts de l'enseignement classique dans la Compagnie de Jésus et leurs rapports avec l'humanisme," *Les études classiques* 13 (1945): 193–209; Denys Hay, "Schools and Universities," in *The New Cambridge Modern History: The Reformation, 1520–1559*, ed. G. R. Elton (Cambridge: Cambridge University Press, 1958), pp. 415, 430, 431; Ernst Schubert, "Zur Typologie gegenreformatorischer Universitätsgründungen: Jesuiten in Fulda, Würzburg, Ingolstadt, und Dillingen," in *Universität und Gelehrtenstand, 1400–1800*, ed. Hellmuth Rössler and Günther Franz (Limburg an der Lahn, W. Ger.: C. A. Starke, 1970), pp. 85–99.

[45] Mosellanus, *Paedologia*, pp. xi–xiv; Bolgar (1964), p. 435.

likewise remained fundamentally consistent, as shown by these documents and programs: Melanchthon's tract *De artibus liberalibus* and the revised Wittenberg arts curriculum from mid-century, Sturm's plan of studies for his gymnasium and academy, Calvin's *Ordre du Collège* of 1559, the curriculum of the French Protestant colleges of the sixteenth century, and the Jesuit *ratio studiorum*, originating in the colleges of Messina and Rome.[46] When these curricular plans are considered together and allowance is made for some discontinuity, the general outline of the liberal arts can be delineated as follows.

Before arrving at any sort of formal school, the small fraction of children bound for higher education were expected to have learned reading, writing, and counting, usually from the local clergy. Nevertheless, these *petits*, or "petties," as they came to be called in English, often did not have sufficient grounding to begin studying grammar and so had to be given even the most elementary training—a task known as "petty" instruction and despised by the grammar master, to whom the responsibility fell. Between the ages of six and ten, depending how early and how far he studied as a "pettie," the student entered what might be called the college, gymnasium, secondary school, or grammar school. At this level, the child studied the *trivium*, and it was this "debasement" of the *trivium* that eventually led to the demeaning connotation of the term "trivial."[47] Under the influence of Renaissance humanism, grammar came to mean training in both language and literature, more and more often including Greek in addition to Latin as time passed. In grammar and in rhetoric, which followed, the universal paragons were Cicero and Quintilian. Completing the curriculum at this level were poetry and history, another indication of the influence of the *studia humanitatis*.

---

[46]For these curricular programs, see Woodward (1906), pp. 144–162, 230–246; Barnard (1922), pp. 40–49, 91–94; Farrell (1938), pp. 29ff., 357ff.; Ganss (1954), pp. 33, 47–58, 85–111, 153; Gabriel (1955), pp. 185–188; Stephen d'Irsay, *Histoire des universités françaises et étrangères des origines à nos jours* (Paris: Editions Auguste Picard, 1933–35) vol. 1, pp. 313–315; Hay (1958), pp. 415–423; Robert R. Bolgar, "Education and Learning," in *The New Cambridge Modern History: The Counter-Reformation and Price Revolution, 1559–1610*, ed. R. B. Wernham (Cambridge: Cambridge University Press, 1968), pp. 427–452; Astrik L. Gabriel, *Garlandia: Studies in the History of the Mediaeval University* (Notre Dame, Ind.: Mediaeval Institute, University of Notre Dame, 1969), pp. 97–116; Jurgen Herbst, "The First Three American Colleges: Schools of the Reformation," *Perspectives in American History* 8 (1974): 30–35; Anton Schindling, *Humanistische Hochschule und freie Reichsstadt; Gymnasium und Akademie in Strassburg, 1538–1621* (Wiesbaden, W. Ger.: Franz Steiner, 1977), pp. 162–289.

[47]In fifteenth-century English, "trivial" education usually meant "belonging to the *trivium* of medieval studies." When these studies were adopted in the lower school

In fact, this influence is demonstrated by the incorporation of poetry and history not only into grammar but also into rhetoric as examples of the "natural logic" embodied in human communication, in contrast to the "artificial logic" of scholasticism.

Having spent four to seven years at the lower school, which may have included an introduction to dialectic, mathematics, and Hebrew, the student of age ten to fifteen entered the next level of education. Often this was the arts faculty of a university, which, especially in Germany, was coming to be called the faculty of philosophy, although it might just as often be a higher division of the Protestant or Catholic college or academy. At this level, the student spent about six to ten years continuing Latin and Greek grammar and rhetoric with varying amounts of Hebrew while also pursuing studies in logic; in remnants of the *quadrivium*; in "physics," or natural philosophy; in economics, politics, and ethics as divisions of moral philosophy; and in the beginnings of metaphysics. If attending a university, the student would then become a master of arts, and the prestige of the degree was an incentive to prefer a university over independent colleges or academies. But either route provided access to a teaching career or to the graduate faculties of universities controlled by powers friendly to one's academy or college.

If the composition and order of the liberal arts were essentially consistent, great discontinuity existed in the stratification of the program. The lines between "petty schools," grammar schools, colleges, and universities varied with local conditions and over time. In general, it may be said that higher-level institutions were loath to assume preparatory teaching duties and eager to slough them off if the opportunity arose. Hence, arts faculties happily yielded the teaching of trivial subjects to the proliferating colleges and gymnasia, which in turn gladly surrendered the petty subjects to *les petites écoles*. On the other hand, where universities did not exist or were hostile to a given college, then the latter's curriculum expanded to include most of the seven liberal arts and natural, moral, and metaphysical philosophy.

This program of liberal arts education, significantly influenced

---

curriculum and made preparatory to the formal university arts course, "trivial" came to mean "such as may be met with anywhere, common, commonplace, ordinary, everyday, familiar" and then passed into its more pejorative meaning today, "of small account, little esteemed, paltry, poor, trifling, inconsiderable, unimportant, slight." *The Oxford English Dictionary*, s.v. "trivial."

by Renaissance humanism, thus gained acceptance in colleges, schools, and gymnasia while it still struggled for official recognition. In France, for example, one can find abundant evidence of contradictory attitudes toward humanist studies: that the universities, led by Paris, embraced humanism in the sixteenth century, and also that they firmly rejected it. The latter attitude is seen in the supremacy of Aristotle asserted by the Parisian arts faculty in 1534 and maintained in the philosophy course through the mid-seventeenth century.[48] The contradiction depends in part on whether one is talking about the formal lectures or the extracurricular teaching at colleges located at the universities. Also to be taken into account is the fact that opponents to humanism within universities were influenced, on the one hand, by national and religious politics, because the *studia humanitatis* were initially associated with the Protestant reformers, and on the other hand, by institutional politics, because considerable jealousy was provoked by the creation of the Royal Lectureships in 1530. Thus, objection to the *studia humanitatis* did not necessarily signify objection in principle to humanism. Such ambiguity only worsened the conflict that occurred at French universities, which increasingly surrendered their autonomy to the throne. Commensurately, they lost their vitality and yielded leadership in education to the colleges founded by the bourgeoisie; by the Huguenots, who established thirty-five colleges by 1610; and by the Jesuits, who brought their plan of study to Paris in 1564 at the Collège de Clermont. By 1600, these groups had transmuted the standard of liberal arts education in France to their own humanist model, as seen in the reformed statutes of the University of Paris granted by Henri IV.

Persecution eventually forced the Huguenots and Jesuits to flee from France to the Low Countries, where humanists had been active at the University of Louvain since late in the fifteenth century. Such activity was furthered in 1517 through a bequest to support eight students plus three professors—one in Greek, one in Latin, and one in Hebrew—in the Collegium Trilingue at Louvain. Organized by Erasmus, this humanist institution became a beacon for subsequent programs at the Collège de France and colleges of Oxford. In

---

[48]Cf. Barnard (1922), pp. 5–18, 95–108, 189–196; d'Irsay (1933), pp. 259–273, 358; Farrell (1938), pp. 31, 39, 376ff.; Le Goff (1967), pp. 97–98, 138; Anthony Grafton, "Teacher, Text, and Pupil in the Renaissance Classroom: A Case Study from a Parisian College," *History of Universities* 1 (1981): 37–53; Laurence B. Brockliss, "Philosophy Teaching in France, 1600–1740," *History of Universities* 1 (1981): 131–152.

this fashion, the humanist ideal again penetrated the liberal arts, first through its embodiment in a college foundation, and then by transmission across national and religious boundaries. Paradoxically, the transmission was later reversed when Louvain became the refuge of English Catholic scholars after the 1559 Acts of Supremacy under Elizabeth forced many of these scholars to migrate to the Continent.[49]

That migration typifies the English situation through the tumultuous sixteenth and seventeenth centuries,[50] when fierce sectarian conflict between Catholics, Anglicans, and Puritans exacerbated the fight for political power among the interests of church, monarchy, gentry, and parliament. Despite this turmoil, which resulted in repeated injunctions being directed against the schools and universities, essential uniformity in the content and rationale of liberal education was maintained through the support of a consensus existing among academicians and political authorities. This is not to say the situation was static. Rather, a progressive norm of teaching the humanist liberal arts, more and more infused with a gentlemanly ideal, slowly evolved.

For grammar schools, John Colet initiated the trend in 1511 by establishing St. Paul's School with a new curriculum of humanist studies that was opposed by the average churchman of the day. The universities had previously been forced to begin their arts course with elementary grammar because of the lack of preparation among their entering students, but this primary training now began to be assumed by the grammar schools, which in turn bemoaned the fact that they had to teach the "petties." Gradually, Colet's approach— relying on Cicero, Quintilian, and Erasmus for models of Latin

---

[49]Henri de Vocht, *History of the Foundation and the Rise of the Collegium Trilingue Lovaniense, 1517–1550,* 4 vols. (Louvain, Belg.: Bibliothèque de l'Université, 1951–1955), vol. 1, pp. 1–7, 46ff., 99–236, and vol. 2, pp. 349–363; Arthur C. Beales, *Education Under Penalty: English Catholic Education from the Reformation to the Fall of James II, 1547–1689* (London: Athlone Press, 1963), pp. 16, 28–38, 148, 273–274.

[50]In the following discussion, I draw from Ruth Kelso, *The Doctrine of the English Gentleman in the Sixteenth Century* (Urbana: University of Illinois Press, 1929), pp. 121–122; Robert Walcott, *The Tudor-Stuart Period of English History (1485–1714): A Review of Changing Interpretations* (New York: Macmillan, 1964); Kenneth Charlton, *Education in Renaissance England* (London: Routledge and Kegan Paul, 1965), pp. 98, 105–128; Joan Simon, *Education and Society in Tudor England* (Cambridge: Cambridge University Press, 1966), pp. 73ff., 299–305; Hay (1975), p. 367. In sixteenth- and seventeenth-century England, the Stoic metaphor comparing rhetoric to an open hand and dialectic to a closed fist (described in chapter 2) once again became enormously popular. Wilbur S. Howell, *Logic and Rhetoric in England, 1500–1700* (Princeton, N.J.: Princeton University Press, 1956), pp. 4, 66–145.

grammar and rhetoric, teaching Greek, and, eventually, introducing Hebrew—became the norm. This preparation came to require about seven years—usually between the ages of seven and fifteen—and often culminated with an introduction to logic as an auxiliary to rhetoric, as the humanists advised. In the course of the sixteenth century the program was popularized by university graduates who went to outlying areas and taught grammar according to models drawn from ancient classics. The ideal of the grammar master thus became "the *bonus orator* of Quintilian,"[51] and this paragon is found, importantly, in the *The Scholemaster* (1570) of Roger Ascham, one of the most acclaimed books on education in Renaissance England. Following Sturm closely, Ascham (1515–1568) drew his educational precepts from humanist principles and techniques, such as the method of double translation, which had been employed by Vives.[52] Very soon, *The Scholemaster* was being cited throughout England, a fact confirming that the third quarter of the sixteenth century marks the entrance of Renaissance humanism, by practically anyone's definition, into English trivial education.

This preparatory curriculum of letters provided the foundation for the humanist studies developing in the liberal arts of Cambridge and Oxford, the only universities in England until the nineteenth century.[53] Erasmus had stimulated humanist scholarship at the former, during his visit early in the sixteenth century; and soon thereafter, Richard Foxe planned for the latter a college congenial to the new learning, an effort that resulted in the founding of Corpus

---

[51]Foster Watson, *The English Grammar Schools to 1660: Their Curriculum and Practice* (Cambridge: Cambridge University Press, 1908), p. 6

[52]Roger Ascham, *The Scholemaster, 1570*, ed. R. C. Alston (Menston, Eng.: The Scholar Press, 1967), fols. 33v–35v; Lawrence Ryan, *Roger Ascham* (Stanford, Cal.: Stanford University Press, 1963). Ascham's program was congruent with that of St. Paul's as well as those of English Catholic colleges in exile, Sandwich School in Kent, St. Bees School in Cumberland, and others. This uniformity was enhanced by the adoption of Lily's Latin grammar—compiled by William Lily and Erasmus for St. Paul's School—as the standard grammar for the realm. Donald L. Clark, *John Milton at St. Paul's School: A Study of Ancient Rhetoric in English Renaissance Education* (New York: Columbia University Press, 1948), chap. 5; John H. Brown, *Elizabethan Schooldays: An Account of the English Grammar Schools in the Second Half of the Sixteenth Century* (Oxford: Basil Blackwell, 1933), p. 83; Robert Middlekauf, *Ancients and Axioms: Secondary Education in Eighteenth Century New England* (New Haven, Conn.: Yale University Press, 1963), pp. 1–6; Beales (1963), pp. 132ff., 273–274; David Cressy, *Education in Tudor and Stuart England* (New York: St. Martin's Press, 1975), pp. 72–73, 80–84; Thomas W. Baldwin, *William Shakespere's Small Latine & Lesse Greeke* (Urbana: University of Illinois Press, 1944), vol. 2, chap. 31.

[53]In the following discussion, I draw from Norman Wood, *The Reformation and English Education: A Study of the Influence of Religious Uniformity on English Education*

Christi College. The prompting of humanists also led in the 1530s to the issuing of royal injunctions that called for a reduction in scholastic textbooks and the introduction of college lectures on Greek and Latin to complement the prescribed university course in rhetoric, logic, arithmetic, geography, music, and philosophy. In the 1540s, Henry VIII advanced this trend by establishing Regius professorships and by founding Christ Church, Oxford, and Trinity College, Cambridge. The movement continued with the promulgation of new university statutes in 1549 and then the Elizabethan statutes of 1564 for Oxford and 1570 for Cambridge.

Meanwhile, the establishment of the Anglican church bolstered the humanist attack on scholasticism, since the break from Rome eliminated many opportunities for careers in doctrinal theology and canon law. This decline in professional opportunities reduced the demand for those graduate disciplines, which had historically reinforced scholasticism in the universities, and led to more attention being focused on the arts curriculum, which had slowly been shifting away from logic toward rhetoric. The shift can be seen in the fleshing out of rhetorical study according to the fivefold Ciceronian division and in the revising of pedagogy toward more modeling on classical letters and less teaching by scholastic abstractions.[54] Grammar was also expanded through the addition of classical literature and the study of Greek. Quadrivial disciplines were amplified, with some mention of sonorous music, and the study of logic and the three philosophies was continued—in theory.

---

in the Sixteenth Century (London: George Routledge, 1931), pp. 88–92; Clarke (1959), pp. 16–31, 61; Craig R. Thompson, *Universities in Tudor England* (Washington, D.C.: Folger Shakespeare Library, 1959), pp. 2–3; Simon (1966), pp. 73–132, 253–305; Fletcher (1967), pp. 421–429; Hugh F. Kearney, *Scholars and Gentlemen: Universities and Society in Pre-Industrial Britain, 1500–1700* (London: Faber and Faber, 1970), pp. 34, 71–96; John M. Fletcher, "Change and Resistance to Change: A Consideration of the Development of English and German Universities during the Sixteenth Century," *History of Universities* 1 (1981): 1–36.

[54]Some have argued that a revival of scholasticism took place in English universities in the late sixteenth and early seventeenth centuries. But this means that the logic of Aristotle usurped that of Peter Ramus whose logical method had eclipsed that of Aristotle. It should not be understood as an antihumanist revival. In this respect, the difference between the Ramist and scholastic perspectives was negligible. Howell (1956), pp. 142–172, 342, 373; William T. Costello, *The Scholastic Curriculum at Early Seventeenth Century Cambridge* (Cambridge: Harvard University Press, 1958); Charlton (1965), pp. 145–168; Richard L. Greaves, *The Puritan Revolution and Educational Thought: Background for Reform* (New Brunswick, N.J.: Rutgers University Press, 1969), p. 103; Anton Antweiler, "Scholastik als Psychologisches Phänomen," in *Actes* (1969), pp. 1087–1103; Walter J. Ong, *Ramus, Method, and the Decay of Dialogue, from the Art of Discourse to the Art of Reason* (Cambridge: Harvard University Press, 1958), chaps. 1, 8, 12.

One must say "in theory" because the university statutes, which especially cite the scholastic inheritance as forming part of the curriculum, were coming to be ignored. Particularly neglected was the requirement that, after four years of work for the Bachelor of Arts degree, students had to read and lecture in advanced dialectic and the three philosophies—natural, moral, and metaphysical—for some additional years to become a Master of Arts. Already in the fifteenth century, this requirement was not being fulfilled, and the easy granting of dispensations for actual study by the bachelors led in the sixteenth and seventeenth centuries to the degeneration of this requirement for the M.A. into simply a few years of residence at the university and then into merely the passage of time—as the modern M.A. of Cambridge and Oxford came to signify. Commensurately, the colleges assumed more and more responsibility for instruction.

By the beginning of the seventeenth century, students at Oxford and Cambridge generally took up residence in the colleges, and these institutions had assumed the primary responsibility for supervising and teaching them. The university merely registered and examined the students and granted the degrees. Many university professorships became sinecures as young tutors did nearly all the instruction. Because the tutors individually prescribed the texts for their own tutees, their employment as teachers introduced more diversity and secularization into the arts education and a corresponding expansion of humanist influence. This pattern is clearly evident in *Directions for a Student in the Universitie*, produced in 1649 by John Merryweather, tutor at Magdalene College, Cambridge, as the plan of liberal education for his students. The mornings were devoted primarily to logic and the three philosophies, and afternoons, to the oratorical humanities, with especial reliance on Cicero. Little different was the 1657 program of Thomas Barlow, tutor and later provost of Queen's College, Oxford, in its combination of scholastic and humanistic studies that had become the norm for the liberal arts.[55]

Also to the American colonies in the seventeenth and eighteenth centuries came these *artes liberales*—a transmission best

---

[55]Samuel E. Morison, *The Founding of Harvard College* (Cambridge: Harvard University Press, 1935), pp. 60–78; Kearney (1970), pp. 104–123; Cressy (1975), pp. 132–134; Jefferson Looney, "Undergraduate Education at Early Stuart Cambridge," *History of Education* 10 (1981): 9–19. In the past, the *Directions* of John Merryweather have been attributed to Richard Holdsworth of Emmanuel College and dated before 1640.

understood in its broader context. By this, I do not mean to interpret education in the widest sense, including all those institutions that transfer culture,[56] but to take into account certain aspects of institutional and social context that directly informed the educational program described as "liberal."

In 1647, when Massachusetts enacted a statute requiring towns to maintain schools, nine were already operating in that colony. Beyond elementary education in reading, writing, and counting, these Latin schools faithfully adopted the program from Britain. The authority of this source was acknowledged also in the 1684 Rules and Regulations of Hopkins Grammar School in New Haven and in the statutes ordaining the grammar school at the College of William and Mary in Virginia:

> In this Grammar School let the Latin and Greek tongues be well taught. As for the Rudiments and Grammars, and Classick Authors of each tongue, let them teach the same Books which by Law or Custom are used in the Schools of England.[57]

The colonial school curriculum, like that in England, was guided by the purpose of preparing students for admission to college; and there were only three colleges operating in the American colonies before 1740: Harvard, William and Mary, and Yale. In reports of the Harvard laws from 1642, 1655, 1686, and 1702, it is consistently specified that a boy desiring admission must demonstrate ability to speak and write Latin prose and poetry, comprehension of Greek and its grammar, and familiarity with standard classical authors, especially Cicero and Vergil in Latin and Isocrates and the New Testament in Greek—"Then may hee bee admitted into the Colledge, nor shall any claime admission before such qualifications." Chartered in 1693, William and Mary differed scarcely at all from Harvard in its entrance requirements, as seen in the statutes of 1727–1728, which demanded that prospective students "must first undergo an Examination before the President and Masters and Ministers skilful in the

---

[56]See Bernard Bailyn, *Education in the Forming of American Society: Needs and Opportunities for Study* (Chapel Hill: University of North Carolina Press, 1960), especially pp. 15–21.

[57]Edgar W. Knight, *A Documentary History of Education in the South before 1860*, vol. 1, *European Inheritances* (Chapel Hill: University of North Carolina Press, 1949), p. 511; Lawrence A. Cremin, *American Education: The Colonial Experience, 1607–1783* (New York: Harper and Row, 1970), pp. 181–186, 503ff.; Middlekauf (1963), pp. 6–9, 76.

learned Languages; whether they have made due Progress in their Latin and Greek."[58] In Connecticut, a college later to be named after Elihu Yale was begun in 1701, and the trustees' decree of that year, as well as transcriptions of the college laws from 1702 and 1726, indicates that entrance requirements were entirely conventional.[59]

These first three colleges were very similar in their organization,[60] academic exercises, and graduation practices, with significant parallels to longstanding practice in Europe.[61] And the essential congruence of the four-year liberal arts curricula at Harvard, William and Mary, and Yale can be demonstrated no less clearly. The arts curriculum at Harvard actually began as a three-year course, even though it was modeled directly after the four-year program found in the colleges at Cambridge and Oxford, from which many of the Puritan colonists were graduated. In 1652, the course was expanded to four years, with the extra year devoted mainly to an initial review of the grammar and authors that the student was supposed to have learned in grammar school. This curriculum was reaffirmed in President Chauncy's Laws of 1655 and "A Particular Account of the Present Stated Exercises Enjoyned the Students" of 1723.

Through the early eighteenth century, freshmen at Harvard, Monday through Thursday, reviewed Latin, continued Greek, and commenced the study of logic and Hebrew. Since the course was essentially cumulative, sophomores continued those subjects and

---

[58]Laws and statutes quoted from Knight (1949), p. 513; Edwin C. Broome, *A Historical and Critical Discussion of College Admission Requirements* (New York: Macmillan, 1903), pp. 18–29; Morison (1935), p. 333.

[59]Richard Warch, *School of the Prophets: Yale College, 1701–1740* (New Haven, Conn.: Yale University Press, 1973), p. 187. Outside of Puritan New England and Anglican Virginia, New Netherland (later to become the colonies of New York and New Jersey) completed an "identical transfer of the institutional life of the parent country." This "institutional life" reflected the practice of the Calvinist Reformed church, prescribed at the Synod of Dort and derived from Strasbourg and Geneva. Thus, the foundation of elementary schooling in reading, writing, and arithmetic undergirded the "trivial" or Latin school in the Dutch city of New Amsterdam, as well. William H. Kilpatrick, *The Dutch Schools of New Netherland and Colonial New York* (Washington, D.C.: Government Printing Office, 1912), pp. 19–21, 95–97, 220–223. Similarly, in the French Catholic educational system of Quebec, variation in the approach to the *artes liberales* is not to be found in the handful of *petites écoles* begun in 1635, nor in *les écoles latines* of both Catholics and Huguenots, nor in the Jesuit Collège de Québec organized on the *ratio studiorum* in 1655. Louis-Philippe Audet, *Histoire de l'éducation au Québec: L'organization scolaire sous le régime français, 1608–1760* (Montreal: Centre de Psychologie et de Pédagogie, 1966), pp. 19–29.

[60]On the incorporation and organization of the three colleges with external boards of trustees, see Jurgen Herbst, *From Crisis to Crisis: American College Government, 1636–1819* (Cambridge: Harvard University Press, 1982), pp. 1–61.

[61]On the continuity of the academic exercises of recitation, lecture, declamation,

broached physics (or natural philosophy), which third-year students—then referred to as junior sophisters—also studied, along with ethics (or moral philosophy) and metaphysics. In addition to a review of Latin, Greek, Hebrew, logic, and physics, senior sophisters briefly addressed arithmetic, geometry, and astronomy. Throughout the four years, Fridays were devoted primarily to rhetoric and Saturdays to divinity, while history and geography were also intermittently included. Such were the B.A. requirements. The three-year demands for the M.A. very quickly degenerated to the level of those at Cambridge and Oxford. For assigned reading during the substantive four years of study in the liberal arts at Harvard, the books differed little from those being assigned to students at Oxford and Cambridge, at Paris and Leyden, or in Germany. The humanist influence was still balanced by a scholastic element through the late seventeenth century, a fact revealed by the lists of commencement theses and by the presence of Duns Scotus in the library and in a portrait in Harvard Hall.[62] And this "Liberall Education" of Harvard became the archetype for subsequent colonial colleges.

In the 1660s, the Virginia Assembly petitioned the Crown for "a colledge of students of the liberall arts and sciences," but approval was obtained only when the Assembly sent to England the spirited clergyman James Blair. Blair had been educated at Marischal College, Aberdeen, and Edinburgh University, and he secured a charter for the College of William and Mary in 1693, and was named its first president. This has led some to find pronounced similarities between the early William and Mary and Scottish universities. However, it is difficult to confirm these analogies because the college, library, and founding records were consumed by fire in 1705, and the institution was rebuilt only in 1723. Soon thereafter, Professor

---

and disputation, and of the graduation exercises, see Mary L. Smallwood, *An Historical Study of Examinations and Grading Systems in Early American Universities: A Critical Study of the Original Records of Harvard, William and Mary, Yale, Mount Holyoke, and Michigan from Their Founding to 1900* (Cambridge: Harvard University Press, 1935), chap. 2; Morison (1935), pp. 135–137; Morison, *Harvard College in the Seventeenth Century* (Cambridge: Harvard University Press, 1936), vol. 1, pp. 159–193, and vol. 2, app. B; George S. Pryde, *The Scottish Universities and the Colleges of Colonial America* (Glasgow: Jackson, 1957), pp. 5ff.; Warch (1973), chaps. 8, 9.

[62]The last of Harvard's "in course" M.A.'s was granted in 1872. Louis F. Snow, *The College Curriculum in the United States* (New York: Bureau of Publications, Teachers College, Columbia University, 1907), pp. 18–30; Colyer Meriwether, *Our Colonial Curriculum, 1607–1776* (Washington, D.C.: Capital, 1907), pp. 49–62; Edward K. Rand, "Liberal Education in Seventeenth Century Harvard," *The New England Quarterly* 6 (1933): 525–551; Morison (1935), pp. 36–90, 337; Morison (1936), vol. 1, pp. 139–175, 189, 256.

Hugh Jones wrote: "The Nature of the Country scarce yet admits of the Possibility of reducing the *Collegians* to the nice Methods of Life and Study observed in *Oxford* and *Cambridge*; tho' by Degrees they may copy from thence many useful Customs and Constitutions."[63] Confirmation that William and Mary followed Harvard in looking to England can be found in the college statutes of 1728. These describe first the grammar school, where "the Latin and Greek tongues" were mastered, and beyond that:

> In the Philosophy School we appoint Two Masters or Professors. . . . One of these Masters shall teach Rhetorick, Logick, and Ethicks. The other Physicks, Metaphysicks and Mathematicks. . . . [W]e do, according to the Form and Institution of the Two famous Universities in England, allot Four Years before they attain to the Degree of Bachelor and Seven Years before they attain the Degree of Master of Arts.[64]

Yale was established in 1701, based upon the conviction that "the Liberal & Relligious Education of Suitable youth is under the blessing of God, a chief & most probable expedient." Every member of the original "board of Collegiate Undertakers" that met at Saybrook, Connecticut, had graduated from Harvard, as did the rectors and presidents of Yale through its first half century. Although most of these men feared the latitudinarianism of their alma mater, they essentially replicated the Harvard curriculum at Yale, as shown by testimony from members of the classes of 1713 and 1714, by the Trustees' decrees of 1701 and 1718, and by the "orders and Appointments to be observed in ye Collegiate School in Connecticut" of 1726. All undergraduates studied rhetoric, ethics, and divinity on Friday and Saturday of each week. Monday through Thursday, "while ye students are freshmen, they commonly recite ye grammars," emphasizing Greek and Hebrew and reviewing Latin. The sophomores attended to "Logick," and the "Junior Sophisters" studied "physics" with some "Metaphysics." The senior sophisters recited a few texts in arithmetic, geometry, and astronomy. As at

---

[63]Quotations are from Knight (1949), pp. 371, 489. See Louis Shores, *Origins of the American College Library, 1638–1800* (Nashville: George Peabody College, 1934), p. 6; Morison (1935), pp. 134–135; Pryde (1957), pp. 1–16; Rena Vassar, "The College Battle: Political Factionalism in the Founding of the College of William and Mary," *PH* 4 (1964): 444–456; Douglas Sloan, *The Scottish Enlightenment and the American College Ideal* (New York: Teachers College Press, 1971a), pp. 20–21 n. 39.

[64]Knight (1949), pp. 513, 515.

other colleges, the course at Yale was cumulative, so the upper classes continued to practice grammar, conduct disputations and recitations, study literature and ethics, and attend to geography and history. In theory, this program leading to the B.A. was to be followed by three years of further study for the M.A., but the latter never became more than a shadow of its ideal and soon deteriorated to the English custom.[65]

The curriculum of liberal education transmitted to the first three colonial colleges was thus far different from the scholastic course of the medieval *universitas*. The humanist influence had led to an emphasis upon classical letters, which came to occupy the bulk of the program as they subsumed the study of logic, pushed to the side "speculative grammar" and quadrivial studies, and edged the three philosophies out to a phantom course for the M.A. The remnants of the philosophies were to be found primarily in the study of ethics and divinity, and this fact points to an important social ideal influencing students of the liberal arts: the ideal of gentility.

During the late Middle Ages, nobles had nurtured an ideal of the "verray, parfit, gentil knight," whereby qualities of valor, chivalry, and fighting prowess had been associated with nobility of blood.[66] This ideal essentially conflicted with the goals and pursuits of the schoolmen, although seven perfections of the knight had been enumerated as analogous to the seven liberal arts in the twelfth and thirteenth centuries. With the rise of Italian humanism, writers such as Baldassare Castiglione recommended learning to the knight and thus combined the roles of soldier and scholar, although Castiglione advised in *Il cortegiano* (The courtier) that the knight pretend his attainments had not arrived by study for "that may bee saide to be a

---

[65]Franklin B. Dexter, ed., *Documentary History of Yale University, Under the Original Charter of the Collegiate School of Connecticut, 1701–1745* (New Haven, Conn.: Yale University Press, 1916), pp. 27–28; Snow (1907), pp. 27–38; Warch (1973), pp. 187–234, 243. The curriculum plan of the Collège de Québec in the French Catholic colonies to the north is strikingly similar to that of the Protestant English colleges of America. Audet (1966), pp. 31–35.

[66]Geoffrey Chaucer, "The General Prologue," *The Canterbury Tales*, line 72, in *The Works of Geoffrey Chaucer*, ed. F. N. Robinson, 2d ed. (Boston: Houghton Mifflin, 1957). In this discussion, I rely upon Kelso (1929), pp. 111–116; Morison (1935), pp. 50–53; Edwin H. Cady, *The Gentleman in America: A Literary Study in American Culture* (Syracuse, N.Y.: Syracuse University Press, 1949), pp. 3–11; Fritz Schalk, "Zur Entwicklung der Artes in Frankreich und Italien," in *Artes* (1959), pp. 139–144; Jack H. Hexter, *Reappraisals in History: New Views on History and Society in Early Modern Europe* (Evanston, Ill.: Northwestern University Press, 1961), p. 67; Simon (1966), pp. 63–65, 334–360; Caspari (1968), pp. 8–14, 259ff.; Kearney (1970), pp. 24, 39–41; Cobban (1975), pp. 231–233.

verie arte that appeareth not to be arte . . . and such bent studie taketh away the grace of every thing."[67] As the Renaissance humanists pushed northward, the writings of Castiglione and Erasmus were enthusiastically received in England, and the *noblesse de l'épée* was transformed into *noblesse de la robe*. This transformation involved converting the standard of nobility of blood, linked to valorous excellence, into one of nobility of merit based on courtly competence, educational attainment, and moral worth. Here was the meeting ground of the knightly ideal, the Renaissance humanist program, and the Christian ethical standard that together composed the ideal of the gentleman.

In England, its earliest and foremost expression came in Thomas Elyot's *The Boke Named the Gouernour* (1531), which combined Castiglione's doctrine of courtesy with the educational theories of Erasmus and so recommended "what the 'orator' was to Cicero or Quintilian—the *beau idéal* of the man of education and affairs."[68] Elyot's plan of "the education or fourme of bryngynge up the chylde of a gentilman, which is to haue auctorite in the publike weale,"[69] consisted of Greek and Latin grammar and rhetoric, logic as an aid to exposition, geography and law for their utility in statecraft, poetry and history for their didactic moral lessons, and philosophy, by which he meant almost exclusively moral philosophy or ethics. Together with a complement of gentlemanly exercises, these studies formed a program that was justified by, and predominantly employed, works from Erasmus, Quintilian, Cicero, Isocrates, and Demosthenes. Appearing in eight editions over its first fifty years, *The Gouernour* spawned a progeny of similar writings on the ideal of the gentleman. These works had varying emphases, but all shared the same intent of balancing the doctrine of courtesy epitomized in the writing of Castiglione, the humanist educational ideal expressed by Erasmus, and a program of personal virtue consonant with Chris-

---

[67]Castiglione, *The Book of the Courtier*, p. 46.

[68]Barnard (1922), p. 116. On the English and colonial gentleman, I draw from Foster Watson, *The Beginnings of the Teaching of Modern Subjects in England* (London: Sir Isaac Pitman, 1909), pp. xxvi–xxxii; John E. Mason, *Gentlefolk in the Making: Studies in the History of English Courtesy Literature and Related Topics from 1531 to 1774* (Philadelphia: University of Pennsylvania Press, 1935), pp. 180–181; Louis B. Wright, *The Cultural Life of the American Colonies, 1607–1763* (New York: Harper and Row, 1957), pp. 128–130; Caspari (1968), pp. 2–4, chaps. 4, 6; Oscar Handlin and Mary F. Handlin, *The American College and American Culture: Socialization as a Function of Higher Education* (New York: McGraw-Hill, 1970), pp. 8–10; Cremin (1970), pp. 68ff.

[69]Sir Thomas Elyot, *The Boke Named the Gouernour*, edited by Henry H. S. Croft from the first edition of 1531 (1883; reprint, New York: Burt Franklin, 1967), bk. 1, chap. 4.

tian ideals. The treatises stood prominently on the bookshelves of early American colonists, who aspired to the pretensions of gentlemanly status. Since the books varied in recommending more or less courtly, pious, or literary pursuits, Puritan Bostonians and Anglican Virginians could suit their taste.[70]

The gentlemanly ideal began to reshape the regnant curriculum of liberal arts in the first half of the sixteenth century, when young gentlemen inundated colleges throughout Europe.[71] This deluge resulted in the curricular recommendations of the courtesy books being applied to the liberal arts of the academies, colleges, and universities. In England, Elyot's program of education was highly influential, being taken up by subsequent figures such as Roger Ascham, James Cleland, Henry Peacham, and John Whitgift, archbishop of Canterbury. A normative curriculum for the gentleman, never exactly repeated but always approximated, thus emerged.[72]

In grammar, the study of Greek and Latin through the reading of easy authors was recommended, as well as some attention to modern languages, especially French and Italian. Rhetoric and oratory—the principles and practice drawn from Hermogenes, Quintilian, Erasmus, Isocrates, Demosthenes, and Cicero—were emphasized as useful tools in politics. The rationale of utility also justified recommendations for learning geography and history. An

---

[70]I do, however, disagree with the sharp differentiation sometimes made in regard to the colonies themselves—the South being described as the home of the "fine gentleman" or "cavalier" and New England being singularly associated with the Puritan or Christian gentleman. Certainly, Massachusetts was not Virginia; but it is dangerous to drive this wedge between northern and southern conceptions of the gentleman. Although the cavalier or fine gentleman is often characterized as impious or willing to sacrifice moral principle for display, in contrast to the Puritan or Christian gentleman, the very concept of gentleman had at its core the notion of moral virtue. The Renaissance humanists condemned impious holdovers from the chivalric tradition, such as dueling, and they made recommendations of virtue central to their writings. Morality was a cornerstone no less of the "fine gentleman" than of the Christian one. Cady (1949), chaps. 1–3; Wright (1957), p. 127; George C. Brauer, Jr., *The Education of a Gentleman: Theories of Gentlemanly Education in England, 1660–1775* (New York: Bookman, 1959), p. 53; Michael V. Belok, "The Courtesy Tradition and Early Schoolbooks," *HEQ* 8 (1968): 306–309; Kearney (1970), pp. 39ff.; Garin (1976), pp. 241ff.

[71]Mark H. Curtis, *Oxford and Cambridge in Transition, 1558–1642: An Essay on Changing Relations Between the English Universities and English Society* (Oxford: Clarendon, 1959), chap. 4; Hexter (1961), pp. 4, 50; Lawrence Stone, "The Educational Revolution in England, 1560–1640," *Past and Present* 28 (1964): 41–80; Caspari (1968), chap. 6.

[72]Woodward (1906), pp. 295–322; Kelso (1929), pp. 118, 127–138; Caspari (1968), chap. 4; Kearney (1970), pp. 37ff., 107–123; Patricia-Ann Lee, "Some English Academies: An Experiment in the Education of Renaissance Gentlemen," *HEQ* 10 (1970): 284.

acquaintance with law was thought desirable,[73] often as a part of politics, economics, and ethics, which together constituted the medieval divisions of moral philosophy. An introduction to logic and metaphysical and natural philosophy was also considered valuable, as were, again with an eye to utility, arithmetic and astronomy. Some study of divinity was necessary, more if one were especially devout, while those headed for court were advised to learn dancing, music, and other gentle pursuits. Disagreement naturally existed over such issues as the stature of modern languages and the total amount of learning necessary,[74] but academic professionalization in the arts curriculum had certainly subsided, making a nonspecialized liberal education the mark of a gentleman.

With learning and gentility thus allied in England, it follows directly that Virginia and New England made the association as well. Apart from their course of study, the organization of colonial colleges under external boards of trustees, which placed governance in the hands of leaders of society rather than schoolmen, strengthened the alliance in America between liberal education and the ideals of Christian gentility. From this perspective, the three central themes that Lawrence Cremin identifies in colonial education—piety, civility, and learning—are especially meaningful, for they suggest the religious, courtly, and humanist impulses underlying gentlemanly education.[75] The reading of history and geography—gentlemanly subjects found among the *artes liberales* at the Collège de Québec as well as Protestant English colleges—verifies this, as does the eighteenth-century custom at Harvard and Yale of ranking students ac-

---

[73]Located in London apart from the universities and colleges, the Inns of Court, where barristers in common law were trained, provided a complement to the gentlemanly education of Oxford and Cambridge. This appears to have been the case as early as 1470, when Lord Chief Justice John Fortescue wrote, "truly, in the greater as well as the smaller Inns, beyond the school of law, there is also a *gymnasium* for all the pursuits that are fitting for nobles." *De laudibus legum angliae*, ed. S. B. Grimes (Cambridge: Cambridge University Press, 1942), chap. 19. In the sixteenth century, young gentlemen often left Oxford and Cambridge after a year or two and went to the Inns to acquire a superficial acquaintance with the common law and a profound understanding of "the pursuits that are fitting for nobles." Wilfred R. Prest, *The Inns of Court under Elizabeth and the Early Stuarts, 1590–1640* (London: Longman, 1972), chap. 7.

[74]Gentlemen held a deep fear of pedantry, doubtlessly passed down from the medieval tradition of knighthood, and the frequent accusations of gentlemanly ignorance made by educators through this period were always met by the counterattack that such educators were pursuing obscure erudition and that a gentleman had no use for arcane learning. Brauer (1959), pp. 52–103.

[75]Cremin (1970), p. 192 and passim; Wallace Notestein, *The English People on the Eve of Colonization, 1603–1620* (New York: Harper and Row, 1954), pp. 130–131; Handlin and Handlin (1970), p. 11.

cording to the social status estimated to be commensurate with their background.[76]

Through the early eighteenth century, therefore, the "liberall arts & sciences" in colonial Virginia, Connecticut, and Massachusetts were remarkably similar to those of Renaissance England. The same heritage, the same books, the same pedagogy, and even some of the same teachers were known and respected on both sides of the Atlantic. And from this program of "liberall arts & sciences" for the Christian gentleman, one can abstract the seven characteristics of the *artes liberales* ideal, a frame not named as such in the historical context, but serving here as an artificial construct whereby this "Liberal & Relligious Education" is to be aligned with the oratorical tradition.

First, there is the fundamental assumption that truth can be known and expressed, a dogmatism underlying the belief that the task of liberal education is to transmit wisdom rather than to teach the student how to search for it. Being more pragmatic than speculative or analytic, the liberal arts master presented to his students a view of life and the world that was to be appropriated and repeated, not challenged. The seventeenth-century Harvard pedagogy reveals this outlook in its prescription of learning *technologia,* comprehensive sytems of the arts and sciences that had to be memorized and recited.[77] The nature of the pedagogical norm is also shown by the strident attacks made against the dominant dogmatic appeal to authorities. In his *Positions* of 1581, Richard Mulcaster argued, "It is no proufe, bycause Plato praiseth it, bycause *Aristotle* alloweth it, bycause *Cicero* commendes it, bycause *Quintilian* is acquainted with it, or any other else . . . that therefore it is for vs to vse." Francis Bacon echoed this attack in *Novum Organum* (The new organon).[78] Merely the shells remained of the critically disputational— one might say Socratic—approach that Abelard, Occam, and other schoolmen had enlivened centuries earlier.

Secondly, the purpose of knowing and conveying the truth is to train the *bonus orator* of Isocrates and Quintilian, the statesman who could and would serve society in any capacity of leadership.[79] Not

[76]Morison (1935), pp. 50–51; Morison (1936), vol. 1, pp. 150, 265, 272; Pryde (1957), p. 9; Audet (1966), pp. 31f.

[77]On this pedagogy and *technologia,* see Morison (1936), vol. 1, pp. 148–256.

[78]Richard Mulcaster, *Positions Wherein Those Primitive Circumstances Be Examined, Which Are Necessarie for the Training Up of Children* (1581; reprint, London: Longmans, Green, 1888), p. 11; Francis Bacon, *Novum Organum; or, True Suggestions for the Interpretation of Nature,* ed. Thomas Fowler, 2d ed. (Oxford: Clarendon, 1889) 1. 84.

[79]In the following discussion, I rely on Kelso (1929), pp. 116, 146; Cady (1949), pp.

so coincidentally, the English courtesy books stressed the mastery of oratory, an important acquirement with which the young gentlemen could do themselves honor and fulfill their role in the commonwealth. The clear prescription of values and standards for character formation follows thirdly and necessarily, and those norms are derived, fourthly, from a body of classical texts. Personal refinement and civic virtues were to be cultivated through gentlemanly education, as the Renaissance courtesy books outlined; and the study of history was universally recommended because it was thought particularly effective in this respect. Similarly, the popularity of the colloquies of Mosellanus, Erasmus, Vives, and Corderius through the eighteenth century stemmed from their combining intellectual refinement with moral lessons communicated in good, classical Latin. Of course, these and other "modern" classics were complemented by the Greek and Roman *auctores,* as well as the Bible.

The goal of training the *bonus orator* also implies a fifth characteristic of the *artes liberales* ideal: the clear identification of a liberally educated elite. Certainly, Oxford, Cambridge, and Harvard had always educated the clerical elite for Church and State. However, this task gained new significance in the seventeenth and eighteenth centuries because the influx of gentry led to the predominance in the colleges of "the ruling *élite,*" who took up places previously occupied by poor boys and clerics.[80] Furthermore, as the gentlemanly ideal infused the liberal arts, it enhanced, in the sixth place, the respect for commitment to the pretensions of "Good Breeding," by which was attained the proper "nobility of mind," and the disapprobation of tolerance toward those without the acquirements of polite and liberal learning. As Samuel Johnson, first president of King's College of New York, remarked in 1759, Hebrew was "a gentleman's accomplishment."

Lastly, the seventh characteristic of the *artes liberales* ideal—the regard for liberal education in the established virtues as an end in itself—can be identified, though not without some qualification on two counts: the utility of the liberal arts for the Puritans, who held to the ultimacy of religious aims for all education, and the utility of the liberal arts for political and social advancement. Either point would seem to compromise an idealist notion of liberal education.

3–6, 40; Brauer (1959), chaps. 1–3, 5; Simon (1966), pp. 63–64, 295ff., 353; Caspari (1968), pp. 25, 256–279; Kearney (1970), pp. 15–98, 136.

[80]Quotations are from Kearney (1970), p. 115; Morison (1936), vol. 1, p. 200; Hexter (1961), pp. 50–53, 65.

However, the usefulness of the program in these respects did not preclude its being regarded as a goal in its own right as well. The "Liberal & Relligious Education of Suitable youth" became intrinsically linked with the gentlemanly ideal in the course of the sixteenth and seventeenth centuries, and the two proceeded in tandem. The gentlemanly ideal thus did not exclude but actually incorporated piety. Similarly, since the gentlemanly ideal did not contravene political and social advancement but actually required it, so too did the rationale for the liberal arts. In this way, liberal education in the early American colonies, as in England, became "without losing its usefulness as a preparatory study . . . an end in itself."[81]

---

[81]Curtis (1959), p. 123. For comments concerning the utility of this liberal education, see Watson (1908), pp. 534–536; Bailyn (1960), p. 19; Middlekauf (1963), p. 3; Tobriner (1968), pp. 49–50; Greaves (1969), pp. 104–113.

V

Emergence
of the
Liberal-Free Ideal

*I*N THE WARMTH *of the innovating and reforming
spirit . . . they (Milton, Locke, Rousseau, and
. . . others who have written on the subject) censure modes of treatment which are right, they recommend methods which really cannot be reduced to
practice, and which, if they could, would be useless
or pernicious. . . . I mean then, in the following
Treatise, to speak in favor of that ancient system of
education, which consists in a classical discipline and
which has produced in our nation many ornaments
of human nature.*

VICESIMUS KNOX*

*Liberal Education; or, A Practical Treatise on the Methods of Acquiring Useful
and Polite Learning (1789).

WITH THE RISE OF EXPERIMENTAL SCIENCE and the dawning of the Enlightenment, the catalysis for renewing philosophical activity and precipitating a different ideal that would come to be linked with the words "liberal education" commenced as well. This evolution of a different conceptual species of liberal education is, however, denied by some modern scholars, who argue instead that the scientists, freethinkers, and *philosophes* of the seventeenth and eighteenth centuries shared an identical view of liberal arts with the Renaissance humanists. But while it is true that both groups celebrated and promoted the study of the "ancients" and believed that "liberal studies . . . are called this because they render man free," the Renaissance humanists maintained that the "*studia humanitatis* . . . were bound to an image of a man and his function, to a conception of his place in the world and in society." Thus, the *artes liberales* "make men free" as they become "bound by a common bond, with a common culture, members of a more universal *res publica.*"[1] In this way, freedom for the Renaissance humanists implied discipline according to specific cultural conventions; and that conception is far different from the individualistic, open-ended sense of freedom popularized in the Enlightenment.

This distinction between meanings of the term "free" is reflected in the etymological development of "liberal" in the vernaculars, as evident, for example, in English. In sixteenth-century England, the word was applied to the activities of gentlemen who were free by virtue of having leisure, in line with the historical tradition of *liberalis*. "Liberal" also meant "free from restraint, free in speech or action"; but this was usually intended in a pejorative sense of "unrestrained by prejudice or decorum, licentious." Only in the eighteenth century did this latter meaning take on the positive connotations of "free from narrow prejudice, open-minded."[2] The distinction holds as well for Renaissance Latin. When eulogizing Guarino da Verona in 1460, one of his disciples proclaimed in

---

[1] I am quoting and disagreeing with Eugenio Garin, *L'educazione in Europa, 1400/1600: Problemi e programmi*, rev. ed. (Rome: Editori Laterza, 1976), pp. 16–21, 241–245, 259–281. See also Vito R. Giustiniani, "Umanesimo: La parola e la cosa," in *Studia Humanitatis, Ernesto Grassi zum 70. Geburtstag*, ed. Eginhard Hora and Eckhard Kessler (Munich: Wilhelm Fink, 1973), p. 27; Girolamo Arnaldi, ed., *Le origini dell'università* (Bologna: Il Mulino, 1974), p. 14; George M. Logan, "Substance and Form in Renaissance Humanism," *Journal of Medieval and Renaissance Studies* 7 (1977): 1–34.

[2] *The Oxford English Dictionary*, s.v. "liberal"; Sheldon Rothblatt, *Tradition and Change in English Liberal Education: An Essay in History and Culture* (London: Faber and Faber, 1976), chap. 3.

Latin, "So many men whom nature made barbarian he liberated from barbarity of language!" This sense of liberation and freedom stems from the oratorical tradition, and involves something very different from the famous line of Rousseau, "Man is born free, and everywhere he is in chains," or of Kant, "Dare to know! Have courage to make use of your own understanding."[3]

One must likewise distinguish between the relationships of humanists and freethinkers to the ancients. Renaissance figures extolled classical authors, especially Cicero and Quintilian; and the eighteenth-century modernists were also gentlemen, members of the leisure class raised on great works of the past. They admired the ancients, the orators included. But their "folk hero" was Socrates with his uncompromising, never-ending search for truth. He was constantly held up as the model teacher and thinker because the freethinkers identified philosophy with criticism. In fact, "it was this critical activity which, they thought, gave them the right to call themselves philosophers."[4] Closely associating philosophy, criticism, and antiquity, they concluded that the Socratic habit of criticism was the greatest legacy of antiquity.

It goes without saying that the Renaissance humanists had not ignored Socrates or Plato. In fact, they had advanced and promoted the study of Plato's writings. But quoting the Philosopher is rather different from incorporating the inquisitiveness of his philosophy, and determining how the *auctores* were read is just as important as knowing which *auctor* was read. For example, it is reported that Edward Gibbon "devoured" Cicero with "voracious" pleasure in the

---

[3]The eulogy of Guarino is quoted and translated from Garin (1976), p. 128. Jean-Jacques Rousseau, *Du contrat social; ou, Principes du droit politique,* in *Oeuvres complètes,* ed. Bernard Gagnebin and Marcel Raymond (Paris: Gallimard, 1964), vol 3, bk. 1, chap. 1; Immanuel Kant, *Beantwortung der Frage: Was ist Aufklärung?* in *Werke,* ed. Ernst Cassirer (Berlin: Bruno Cassirer, 1922), vol. 4, p. 169.

[4]Paul Hazard, *The European Mind, 1680–1715,* trans. J. Lewis May (New Haven, Conn.: Yale University Press, 1952), p. 141. See Peter Gay, *The Enlightenment: An Interpretation* (New York: Alfred A. Knopf, 1966), vol. 1, pp. 81–82, 121–132; Elaine Limbrick, "Montaigne and Socrates," *Renaissance and Reformation* 9 (1973): 46–57. (Kant, however, excluded "the Socratic dialogue" from moral education. Immanuel Kant, *The Metaphysical Principles of Virtue* [*Part II of the Metaphysics of Morals*], trans. James Ellington [New York: Bobbs-Merrill, 1964], 4. 479). This does not mean that the *philosophes'* Socrates was an accurate reflection of the Platonic Socrates or that the latter was the direct source of the liberal-free ideal, despite its foundation in the philosophical tradition. Indeed, some have linked the "liberal" tradition in ancient Greek thought—an evolutionary, egalitarian, progressive, pragmatic view of the world—to the sophists rather than to Socrates and Plato. Eric A. Havelock, *The Liberal Temper in Greek Politics* (New Haven, Conn.: Yale University Press, 1957), pp. 30, 80–81; Frederick A. Beck, *Greek Education, 450–350 B.C.* (London: Methuen, 1964), pp. 149–150.

eighteenth century, and that Johannes Sturm admired and incorporated Socrates into his teaching in the sixteenth. But these two should not be confused. The former discovered in the Orator the basis of an attack on the *artes liberales* of his day, while the latter cited the Philosopher apodictically to recommend certain Christian virtues.[5]

Whether or not one agrees that the emergence of experimental science "outshines everything since the rise of Christianity and reduces the Renaissance and Reformation to the rank of mere episodes, mere internal displacements within the system of Medieval Christendom,"[6] it scarcely needs repeating that the development of the modern world was profoundly shaped by the growth of science. Neither is there any need to reiterate the well-documented progression of the "New Philosophy" or "New Science" from Nicholas Oresme to Charles Darwin. However, in view of the preceding arguments concerning humanism, it should be acknowledged that the Renaissance was at least a beginning point for the rise of experimental science. Some, in fact, have gone further, arguing for the "unity" between humanist and scientific endeavors or stressing the Renaissance attitude of innovation that promoted scientific experimentation. Others have talked about the early scientists' use of original texts of ancient science or about the roots of seventeenth-century scientific societies in Renaissance literary societies. Nevertheless, the fundamental alliance between humanists and early sci-

---

[5]E. Hoepffner, "Jean Sturm et l'enseignement supérieur des lettres à l'Ecole de Strasbourg," in *L'humanisme en Alsace* (Paris: Société d'Edition "Les Belles-Lettres," 1939), p. 87; Gay (1966), pp. 55–57.

[6]Herbert Butterfield, *The Origins of Modern Science, 1300–1800*, rev. ed. (New York: Macmillan, 1957), p. 7 and chap. 10. Concerning the origins of experimental science and the contribution of the Renaissance, I draw from Martha Ornstein, *The Rôle of Scientific Societies in the Seventeenth Century* (1913; reprint, Chicago: University of Chicago Press, 1938), pp. 73–139; Hans Baron, "Towards a More Positive Evaluation of the Fifteenth Century Renaissance," *JHI* 4 (1943): 21–49; Alastair C. Crombie, "The Significance of Medieval Discussions of Scientific Method for the Scientific Revolution," in *Critical Problems in the History of Science*, ed. Marshall Claggett (Madison: University of Wisconsin Press, 1959), pp. 79–101; Olaf Pederson, "Du quadrivium à la physique: Quelques aperçus de l'évolution scientifique au moyen âge," in *Artes* (1959), pp. 107–123; Marie (Boas) Hall, *The Scientific Renaissance, 1450–1630* (New York: Harper and Row, 1962), pp. 18–19; Joan Gadol, "The Unity of the Renaissance: Humanism, Natural Science, and Art," in *From the Renaissance to the Counter Reformation: Essays in Honor of Garrett Mattingly*, ed. Charles H. Carter (New York: Random House, 1965), pp. 29–55; Cesare Vasoli, "La première querelle des 'anciens' et des 'modernes' aux origines de la Renaissance," in *Classical Influences on European Culture, A.D. 1500–1700*, ed. Robert R. Bolgar (Cambridge: Cambridge University Press, 1976), pp. 67–80; Vasoli, "The Contribution of Humanism to the Birth of Modern Science," *Renaissance and Reformation*, n.s., 3, no. 1 (1979): 1–15.

entists was actually a negative one: both groups opposed the scholastic practices and authorities.

In saying this, I am de-emphasizing any direct contribution Renaissance humanism might have made to the advancement of the mathematical-mechanical model of the world which Copernicus (1473–1543), Kepler (1571–1630), and Galileo (1564–1642) did so much to promote and which was so instrumental in launching the New Science. True, the effort to find mathematical harmony in astronomy has been linked to the resurgence of Platonism in the Renaissance, and early scientists were often teachers and students in humanist circles. However, it is more significant that the converse is not true: the leading humanists were singularly undistinguished in natural, experimental sciences.[7]

The reason for this important distinction lies in the fact that Renaissance humanism was committed to recapturing ancient tradition and appreciating its literary achievements. In contrast, Copernicus, Kepler, and Galileo challenged conventional beliefs in astronomy and mechanics, and the New Science developed a methodology that was critical and open-ended. As John Donne wrote in verse, "New Philosophy calls all in doubt."[8] As befitting to its very nature, the New Science was put forward with a certain tentativeness even as Cartesian rationalism and British empiricism began to unfold its deeper philosophical implications and, paradoxically, the *Philosophiae Naturalis Principia Mathematica* of Isaac Newton (1642–1727) earned for it reliability, acceptance, and thereby a presumption of being true knowledge.[9]

From a beginning point in the Renaissance, therefore, the New Philosophy gradually matured, ultimately gaining enthusiastic ac-

---

[7]Edwin A. Burtt, *The Metaphysical Foundations of Modern Physical Science: A Historical and Critical Essay*, rev. ed. (New York: Harcourt, Brace, 1932), pp. 36–50; Paul O. Kristeller, "The Place of Classical Humanism in Renaissance Thought," *JHI* 4 (1943): 59–63; Harcourt Brown, "The Renaissance and Historians of Science," *Studies in the Renaissance* 7 (1960): 27–40.

[8]John Donne, "An Anatomie of the World: The First Anniversary," in *The Complete Poetry and Selected Prose of John Donne*, ed. Charles M. Coffin (New York: Random House, 1952), line 205; A. R. Hall, *The Scientific Revolution, 1500–1800: The Formation of the Modern Scientific Attitude*, 2d ed. (London: Longmans Green, 1962), pp. 32–33.

[9]Indeed, the presumption of truly knowing the secrets of nature was such that Halley wrote, in praise of Newton, "it is not right for a mortal to approach the gods more closely." Edmund Halley, "In Viri Praestantissimi Isaaci Newtoni Opus Hocce Mathematico-Physicum: Seculi Gentisque Nostrae Decus Egregium," in *Isaac Newton's Philosophiae Naturalis Principia Mathematica*, ed. Alexandre Koyré and I. Bernard Cohen, 3d ed. (1726; reprint, Cambridge: Harvard University Press, 1972), vol. 1, p. 14, line 48.

claim in the Enlightenment. Out of this revival of the philosophical tradition, with its fascination for Socratic criticism and mathematical laws, can be abstracted the characteristics of another ideal type that would come to be associated with "liberal" studies in contradistinction to the *artes liberales* ideal. I call this the "liberal-free ideal" because it served as an underlying cultural ideal and because it is systematic in the sense of comprising a logically coherent whole. Here again, the standard qualifications are in order. In proposing that this liberal-free ideal emerged between, say, the time of Descartes and Hobbes and that of Kant and Priestley, I do not mean that any particular figure described it in those terms. By the same token, although early scientists, "moderns," and Enlightenment freethinkers contributed, the liberal-free ideal is not confined to them or they to it. Rather, I maintain that this coherent set of seven characteristics can be abstracted from the writings of certain thinkers of this period, and that it gradually began to appear in statements and programs of education described as "liberal" by later advocates who would hearken back to those same thinkers.

Foremost among the seven characteristics of the liberal-free ideal is an emphasis on freedom, especially freedom from a priori strictures and standards. The writings of John Locke (1632–1704) had great influence in this regard, especially his *Two Treatises of Government* (1690), wherein he asserted, "what State all Men are naturally in . . . is a *State of perfect Freedom* to order their Actions, as they think fit." Based upon that premise, Locke subsequently promoted liberty as a fundamental human right. Jean-Jacques Rousseau (1712–1778) then incorporated it into the liberal tradition through his writings: metaphysically, in the theology of the Savoyard Vicar, who maintains that all action originates "in the will of a free being"; politically, in *Du contrat social*, with its defense of the unalienable right to freedom; and educationally, in *Emile*, which encourages the infant, child, and adolescent to fulfill their needs as they perceive them. Certainly many *philosophes* in the eighteenth century had reservations about the extent of Rousseauan liberation; nonetheless, they still applauded freedom, first and foremost.[10]

---

[10]John Locke, *Two Treatises of Government . . . Printed for Awnshan and J. Churchill at the Black Swan, 1968*, ed. Peter Laslett, rev. ed. Cambridge: Cambridge University Press, 1967), 2.2.4; Jean-Jacques Rousseau, *Du contrat social*, bk. 1, chap. 4; Rousseau, *Emile; ou, de l'éducation*, in *Oeuvres complètes*, vol. 4, bk. 1, pp. 253–254, bk. 2, pp. 310–312, bk. 4, pp. 586–587; Gay (1966), p. 3. There are profound tendencies toward totalitarianism in Rousseau's thought, but the promotion of individualistic freedom was later understood to be his primary influence on "liberal education" both by supportive Progressivists and by acerbic critics like Irving Babbitt.

The desire for freedom is particularly linked to an emphasis on intellect and rationality, a second characteristic of the liberal-free ideal. When Diderot called for an "Age of Reason" he was calling also for an age of freedom, because effective use of the philosopher's intellect required freedom and vice versa. "Free-Thinking," which seemed to place no a priori bounds on the intellect, was intoxicating, and "the rise and growth of a sect call'd Free-Thinkers" was applauded by its members and deplored by their scholastic contemporaries. The fascination with the power of human reason and mathematical laws is, of course, a well-known theme in treatments of the Enlightenment, and deservedly so.[11] Newton and Descartes were perhaps the foremost progenitors of the mathematical rationalism underlying the Age of Reason, although it was the latter who more fully elaborated its philosophical implications.

In *Discours de la méthode*, René Descartes (1596−1650) intended to clear away the scholastic reliance on authority by systematically searching for a new criterion of certainty. This he found in logical relationships perceived "clearly and distinctly" in the mind. His deducing of the cosmos from that starting point needs no exposition here, except to note his overriding confidence in this purely rationalistic approach, as is demonstrated by his basically Socratic view that evil arises from ignorance, his denigration of emotions as essentially confused ideas, and his distrust of sensory experience, which he thought to be transmitted to the mind through the pineal gland in a confused way.[12] Such confidence, plus a respect for the mathematical model of the world, led subsequently to the enthroning of reason as sovereign of the Enlightenment, notwithstanding the romantic reaction of Rousseau and others.[13]

Thirdly, the liberal-free ideal incorporates a critical skepticism, even though some freethinkers, converted to the new faith of nat-

---

[11]Anthony Collins, *A Discourse of Free-Thinking Occasion'd by the Rise and Growth of a Sect call'd Free-Thinkers* (London: n. p., 1713); Gay (1966), pp. 20, 31, 83, 129; Hazard (1952), pp. 145−184; Friedrich A. Hayek, *New Studies in Philosophy, Politics, Economics, and the History of Ideas* (London: Routledge & Kegan Paul, 1978), pp. 119−132. Certainly, closed deductive metaphysical systems, which seem to allow very little freedom, were built also by "moderns" such as Descartes, Spinoza, and Leibniz. Ernst Cassirer, *The Philosophy of the Enlightenment*, trans. Fritz C. A. Koelln and James P. Pettegrove (Princeton, N.J.: Princeton University Press, 1951), pp. 6−7, 45ff.

[12]René Descartes, *Discourse on the Method*, pt. 4; *The Passions of the Soul*, articles 16−32, 48; *Rules for the Direction of the Mind*, rule 12; *Meditations on First Philosophy*, meditations 5, 6; *Notes Directed Against a Certain Programme*, pp. 442−443, in *The Philosophical Works of Descartes*, trans. Elizabeth S. Haldane and G. R. Ross (Cambridge: Cambridge University Press, 1911), vol. 1.

[13]The development of a reaction against the intellectualism of the *philosophes* is

ural science, presumed to reach final answers in their inquiries. But this response generally missed the point of the scientific method: that any conclusions inferred become new hypotheses and are always subject to challenge and criticism. The method depends fundamentally on an attitude of skepticism. Descartes, with his method of doubting, and Locke, through his attack on the existence of innate ideas, had contributed to the theoretical background, but only with David Hume (1711–1776) were the implications fully articulated. Arguing in *An Inquiry Concerning Human Understanding* that empirical factuality rests merely on past observation that a certain effect follows a certain cause, Hume made clear that the New Science could never provide certainty.[14] The same experimental results obtained a thousand times are under no logical necessity to repeat themselves on a subsequent trial.

As "certainty is the mother of intolerance," so tolerance became a fourth characteristic of the liberal-free ideal. Appearing at the turn of the eighteenth century, this was "a new virtue," for the notion of tolerance had previously implied weakness or cowardice, that is, lack of commitment to one's professed beliefs.[15] The new virtue thus depended centrally on the epistemology of skepticism, as Locke demonstrated forcefully about religion.[16] If standards cannot finally be proven right or wrong, then no viewpoint can be considered absolute, and the freethinkers were quick to embrace the idea. A tendency toward egalitarianism, a fifth characteristic of the liberal-free

---

often attributed to inspiration from Rousseau, whose influence was criticized so severely by Irving Babbitt, *Rousseau and Romanticism* (Boston: Houghton, Mifflin, 1919), chap. 2. It must be granted that for Rousseau reason acts primarily as the servant of desire, that moral judgments arise from sentiment rather than from reason, and that his arguments were more passionate than systematic. Rousseau, *Emile; ou, de l'éducation,* pp. 203–244; Jean Starobinski, "The Accuser and the Accused," *Daedalus* 107 (Summer 1978): 41. For testimony against those who "accuse the psychology of the eighteenth century of being wholly intellectualistic and of limiting its analysis primarily to the realm of ideas and theoretical knowledge, while neglecting the force and specific quality of emotional life," see Cassirer (1951), pp. 104ff.; Peter Gay, *The Enlightenment: An Interpretation* (New York: Alfred A. Knopf, 1969), vol. 2, pp. 187–207.

[14]David Hume, *An Inquiry Concerning Human Understanding,* in *The Philosophical Works of David Hume* (Edinburgh: Adam Black and William Tait, 1826), vol. 4, sects. 6–7; Kingsley Martin, *French Liberal Thought in the Eighteenth Century: A Study of Political Ideas from Bayle to Condorcet,* ed. J. P. Mayer, 2d ed. (London: Phoenix, 1962), pp. 13–16, 35–53, 117–123, 177–183; A. R. Hall (1962), pp. 32–33.

[15]Quotations are from Hazard (1952), pp. 343–344. Gay (1966), p. 163; Gay (1969), p. 399.

[16]Locke's *Epistola de Tolerantia* appeared in 1689, but his epistemological argument is developed more fully in *A Second Letter Concerning Toleration* (1690), in *The Works of John Locke* (1823; reprint, Aalen, W. Ger.: Scientia Verlag, 1963), vol. 6, pp. 61–137.

ideal, follows also from the relativizing of standards and norms, although this connection was not immediately emphasized. Rather, on the principle of "Natural Lawes," Thomas Hobbes (1588–1679), among others, based the belief that "Nature hath made men so equall," a notion greatly respected by Enlightenment thinkers. While differing from Hobbes in evaluating the state of nature, Locke and Rousseau also advanced "this equality of men by nature."[17] Thus, by the time Hume debunked as convenient fictions the theories of natural law and social contract to which the proposition of equality had been linked, the notion was well entrenched in "enlightened" discourse.

A sixth characteristic of the liberal-free ideal necessarily accompanies this tolerance and egalitarianism: emphasis upon volition of the individual rather than upon the obligations of citizenship found in the *artes liberales* ideal. Contributing to this ethic of individualism, Locke, in his writings on education, stressed each child's personal nature, to which the teacher is to respond in order to awaken motivation to learn, rather than resorting to compulsion. Rousseau advanced the same theme in his letter about educating young children in *La nouvelle Héloïse*. He then elaborated the idea in *Emile* by implicitly describing human developmental stages, thus associating a concept of personal growth with the emphasis upon the individual.[18]

The concern for individual growth reinforces the seventh characteristic of the liberal-free ideal: its standing as an ideal, an end in itself. Freedom of intellect realized in the pursuit of knowledge becomes a goal that is sought for its own sake. Since conclusions are always subject to criticism, it is not the truth that is finally desirable, but the search. Hence, Gotthold Lessing, a prominent German writer of the Enlightenment, maintained that if God were to offer him the truth with one hand and the search for truth with the other, he would choose the latter. Similar, in a sense, was the view of Immanuel Kant (1724–1804).

---

[17]Thomas Hobbes, *Leviathan; or, The Matter, Forme and Power of a Commonwealth, Ecclesiastical and Civil*, ed. C. B. Macpherson (1651; reprint, Baltimore: Penguin, 1968), pt. 1, chap. 13; Locke, *Two Treatises of Government*, 2.2.4; Judith N. Shklar, "Jean-Jacques Rousseau and Equality," *Daedalus* 107 (Summer 1978): 13–26. Appropriately, *eleutheria* in "philosophical" Athens implied equalitarian or democratic rule while *libertas* in "oratorical" Rome did not. Chaim Wirszubski, *Libertas as a Political Ideal at Rome during the Late Republic and Early Principate* (Cambridge: Cambridge University Press, 1950), pp. 9–15.

[18]Jean-Jacques Rousseau, *Julie; ou, La nouvelle Héloise*, in *Oeuvres complètes*, vol. 2, pt. 5, letter 3; John Locke, *Of the Conduct of the Understanding*, ed. Francis W. Gar-

Commentators have said that Kant was "insistent on autonomy, freedom, and individuality" in his educational philosophy, but as stated previously, it is not the intention here to circumscribe perfectly a particular individual with the liberal-free frame. For example, one can scarcely argue that Kant was a skeptic, even though he believed himself shaken from "dogmatic slumber" by Hume and held that noumena can never be known directly.[19] Yet, there is justification for attributing to Kant great influence in upholding the free and never-ending search for truth at the close of the eighteenth century. As he wrote: "I am myself by inclination a seeker after truth. I feel a consuming thirst for knowledge and a restless passion to advance in it, as well as satisfaction at every forward step." This outlook can also be found in the developmental aspect of his thought, which presupposes that progress can be made toward realizing transcendental ideals through advancing rationalization. This presupposition was shared generally by Enlightenment thinkers, as revealed in their philosophy of history and in the experimental science they found so congenial.[20]

Turning from this set of ideas that can be abstracted from discussion in the seventeenth and eighteenth centuries and that would gradually begin to be associated with education called "liberal," one finds in the curriculum of the time, especially in Britain, three different sorts of liberal studies predominating. There remained a residue of the scholastic program, emphasizing the study of logic and a philosophical approach that reasoned from a priori principles down to the particulars of experience. In addition, there were the *studia humanitatis*, which in some cases still preserved the humanistic tradition of the orators, although just as often had deteriorated, under the influences of scholasticism and institutional constraints, to the

---

forth (New York: Teachers College Press, 1966), sect. 4; Locke, *Some Thoughts Concerning Education*, in *The Works of John Locke*, vol. 9, sects. 66, 167–168.

[19]Immanuel Kant, *Prolegomena to Any Future Metaphysics*, translated with an introduction by Lewis W. Beck (New York: Bobbs-Merrill, 1950), 4.260; Kant, *Critique of Pure Reason*, trans. Norman K. Smith (New York: Macmillan, 1929) A10, B14–18; A22–41, B37–58; A76–83, B102–116. The commentators' quotation is from William K. Frankena, *Three Historical Philosophies of Education: Aristotle, Kant, Dewey* (Glenview, Ill.: Scott, Foresman, 1965), p. 92.

[20]Quoted in Ernst Cassirer, *Rousseau, Kant, Goethe: Two Essays*, trans. James Gutman, Paul O. Kristeller, and John H. Randall, Jr. (Princeton, N.J.: Princeton University Press, 1945), pp. 1–2, Cassirer (1951), pp. 49ff., 209–228; William H. Walsh, *Kant's Criticism of Metaphysics* (Edinburgh: Edinburgh University Press, 1975), app.; Butterfield (1957), chap. 12; Alfred C. Ewing, *A Short Commentary on Kant's Critique of Pure Reason* (Chicago: University of Chicago Press, 1938), chaps. 4, 5.

point of teaching classical languages and literature by dry grammatical and rhetorical rules. Thirdly, there arose what might be termed the liberal-free subjects, including primarily the natural and experimental sciences and modern languages, a set of subjects that developed in two ways. One variant merely seized upon the findings of the New Science and taught them apodictically; the other incorporated with those findings the experimental method and attitude.

These three programs and their variants were combined and promoted in different ways in a range of academic institutions and forums of educational discussion—a range wider than had previously existed. Grammar schools and independent classical schools filled the lower level, and above them, various sorts of independent academies and tutors stood as alternatives to the universities. These included academies established by the religious minorities of a country or principality—called dissenting or nonconformist academies in Britain—which floated or foundered with varying degrees of buoyancy depending on the tolerance of the government. In the universities, the residential colleges and tutors, the lectureships and professorial chairs, and the officially required courses and exams for the liberal arts degree were often linked together very loosely, as at Cambridge and Oxford during the late seventeenth and eighteenth centuries. And while critics of the traditional studies generally stood outside of the institutions, they did contribute to the discourse concerning liberal education through their writings and correspondence. Considered together, these educational programs and advocates exhibit a variety of opinion on liberal education.

Amid the variety of issues, a central question is whether the kind of thinking and subjects associated here with the liberal-free ideal infiltrated the universities in the seventeenth and eighteenth centuries. As in the debate over when and where Renaissance humanism entered the universities, there is much disagreement on this point among present-day scholars. Some affirm such infiltration to have occurred, while others deny it.[21] For one scholar, Cambridge's

---

[21]Compare the views of Herbert McLachlan, *English Education Under the Test Acts, Being the History of the Non-conformist Academies, 1662–1820* (Manchester, Eng.: Manchester University Press, 1931), chaps. 1, 2; P. Allen, "Scientific Studies in the English Universities of the Seventeenth Century," *JHI* 19 (1949): 219–253; Nicholas Hans, *New Trends in Education in the Eighteenth Century* (London: Routledge and Kegan Paul, 1951), pp. 37–38, 47–49, 54ff.; W. A. Pantin, "The Conception of the Universities of England in the Period of the Renaissance," in *Commission* (1967), pp. 105–106; Hugh F. Kearney, *Scholars and Gentlemen: Universities and Society in Pre-Industrial Britain, 1500–1700* (London: Faber and Faber, 1970), pp. 151–152, 165; Richard S. Tompson, *Classics or Charity? The Dilemma of the 18th Century Grammar School* (Manchester, Eng.: Manchester University Press, 1971), p. 23.

appointment of the eminent Newton is evidence of openness to science; for another, the very eminence and uniqueness of Newton demonstrate how much the university resisted science. The Dissenting Academies are regarded as modernist by some and mainstream by others. The ambiguity of the evidence, leading to contradictory interpretations, is heightened by the fact that the critics of education were not of one mind. Critics such as Locke and Priestley, though perhaps associated with liberal-free subjects and thinking, nevertheless held that Greek and Latin "are languages of great use and excellency; and a man can have no place among the learned, in this part of the world, who is stranger to them." Furthermore, those who strongly attacked the schoolmen often drew on scholastic arguments in doing so.[22] Consequently, many different shades of interpretation can reasonably be argued about the nature of liberal education over this period. My own preference is for a more traditional view—anti-revisionist, if one prefers. On balance, it appears to me that the universities resisted the entrance of liberal-free subjects, just as they had Renaissance humanist studies two or three centuries earlier.

Consider the attitude of proponents of the New Philosophy and New Science toward the schools. Most stood with Francis Bacon, outside the established institutions, objecting to their scholastic and gentlemanly preoccupations. Hobbes had been bored by the Aristotelianism of Oxford and wanted his own doctrine taught in the universities rather than that of the ancients. Descartes did not find the study of rote syllogisms or ancient authorities helpful in pursuing truth, and Locke thought the disputations of the universities were useless.[23] These attacks on the schoolmen persisted in the eighteenth century, as when Gibbon derided the universities for their dogmatism and Hume suggested that their libraries be weeded out:

> When we run over libraries, persuaded of these principles, what havoc must we make? If we take in our hand any volume, of divinity or school metaphysics, for instance; let us ask, *Does it con-*

---

[22]Quotation is from Locke, *Some Thoughts Concerning Education*, sect. 168. See Joseph Priestley, *Miscellaneous Observations Relating to Education, More Especially as It Respects the Conduct of the Mind*, 2d ed. (Birmingham, Eng.: M. Swinney, 1788), sect. 3; James P. Ferguson, "The Image of the Schoolmen in 18th Century English Philosophy, with Reference to the Philosophy of Samuel Clarke," in *Actes* (1969), pp. 1199–1206.

[23]Hobbes, *Leviathan*, pp. 727–728; Descartes, *Rules for the Direction of the Mind*, rules 3, 7, 14; Locke, *Of the Conduct of the Understanding*, sects. 7, 29, 31.

tain any abstract reasoning concerning quantity or number? No. *Does it contain any experimental reasoning concerning matter of fact and existence?* No. Commit it then to the flames; for it can contain nothing but sophistry and illusion.[24]

The New Philosophers were equally critical of the adulation of Greek and Latin letters. They did not disdain the vernacular: Descartes, Rousseau, and Voltaire wrote important works in French; Bacon, Hobbes, Locke, and Hume in English; Lessing and Kant in German. And they criticized the pedantic approach to teaching literary classics: Descartes, in the *Discours*; Locke, in *Some Thoughts Concerning Education*; and Rousseau, who mourned the two years he spent "to learn, along with Latin, all the useless stuff that accompanies it under the name of education."[25] Led by Bacon and Hobbes and backed by the Royal Society of London in the late seventeenth century, the critics eventually assailed both the Ciceronian and scholastic rhetorical theories and developed a simplified approach to rhetoric based on a rejection of all artificialities, whether owed to scholastic abstractions or to classical conventions. In eighteenth-century England, this activity contributed to reducing rhetoric from the elaborate, fivefold, Ciceronian definition to simply the form and style of expression.[26] The marriage of eloquence and wisdom was thereby annulled. These New Philosophers fundamentally rejected the oratorical conception of liberal learning—the appropriation of a high tradition of the persuasive and beautiful expression of true, civic virtue.

In consequence of these attitudes, and notwithstanding such mid-seventeenth century efforts at reform as those of Samuel Hartlib, John Milton, and their small circle, the freethinkers, experimenters, modernists, and *philosophes* basically worked outside of the educational institutions. Until late in the seventeenth century, scientists usually conducted research as individuals, scattered with their helpers in private workshops and homes. Gradually, formal insti-

---

[24]Hume, *An Inquiry Concerning Human Understanding*, sect. 12, pt. 3.

[25]Descartes, *Discourse on the Method*, pt. 1; Locke, *Some Thoughts Concerning Education*, sects. 168–169; Jean-Jacques Rousseau, *Confessions*, in *Oeuvres complètes*, vol. 1, bk. 1, p. 12.

[26]Wilbur S. Howell, *Logic and Rhetoric in England, 1500–1700* (Princeton, N.J.: Princeton University Press, 1956), pp. 388–390; Howell, *Eighteenth-Century British Logic and Rhetoric* (Princeton, N.J.: Princeton University Press, 1971), pp. 76, 145ff.; Karl R. Wallace, "Francis Bacon on Understanding, Reason, and Rhetoric," *Speech Monographs* 38 (1971): 79–91; Peter France, *Rhetoric and Truth in France: Descartes to Diderot* (Oxford: Oxford University Press, 1972).

tutions to support these endeavors were established apart from the universities in the form of scientific societies dedicated to the New Philosophy. These included the Royal Society of London in 1622, the French Académie des Sciences in 1666, and, subsequently, the Societas Regia Scientarum in Berlin. Shortly thereafter, free journals arose to publish their findings. In 1682, Leibniz founded *Acta Eruditorum* in Leipzig; and Holland, ever a tolerant land and thus mother of new ventures, gave birth to others. These seventeenth-century efforts then became the models for similar enterprises in the eighteenth and nineteenth centuries.[27]

Meanwhile, the universities had declined. By the beginning of the eighteenth century, the disease of sophistic scholasticism had thoroughly infected the thirty-two universities of the Holy Roman Empire; and hope for future reform lay mainly in the founding of Halle (1694), Göttingen (1734), and Erlangen (1743).[28] Nor was the French experience very different.[29] In England, there was some evidence of openness to the New Philosophy before the Restoration of 1660, but from that date until the nineteenth century, Oxford and Cambridge returned to the dessicated scholastic-humanist tradition. The universities thereby excluded not only much of the work of English scientists, of whom the percentage graduating from English universities steadily decreased through the eighteenth century, but also the best of classical scholarship, wherein the advances were

[27]Stephen d'Irsay, *Histoire des universités françaises et étrangères des origines à nos jours* (Paris: Éditions Auguste Picard, 1933—35), vol. 2, pp. 56—57, 89—90; Ornstein (1938), chaps. 3—7; M. B. Hall (1962), pp. 238—246; A. R. Hall (1962), chap. 7; Kurt Müller, "Zur Entstehung und Wirkung der wissenschaftlichen Akademien und gelehrten Gesellschaften des 17. Jahrhunderts," in *Universität und Gelehrtenstand, 1400—1800,* ed. Hellmuth Rössler and Günther Franz (Limburg an der Lahn, W. Ger.: C. A. Starke, 1970), pp. 127—143.

[28]Notker Hammerstein, "Zur Geschichte der Deutschen Universität im Zeitalter der Aufklärung," in *Universität und Gelehrtenstand 1400—1800,* ed. Hellmuth Rössler and Günther Franz (Limburg an der Lahn, W. Ger.: C. A. Starke, 1970), pp. 145—172; R. Steven Turner, "University Reformers and Professional Scholarship in Germany, 1760—1806," in *The University in Society,* ed. Lawrence Stone (Princeton, N.J.: Princeton University Press, 1974), pp. 495—532; Charles E. McClelland, "The Aristocracy and University Reform in Eighteenth Century Germany," in *Schooling and Society: Studies in the History of Education,* ed. Lawrence Stone (Baltimore: Johns Hopkins University Press, 1976), vol. 1, pp. 153—154; McClelland, *State, Society, and University in Germany, 1700—1914* (Cambridge: Cambridge University Press, 1980), pts. 1, 2; R. J. Evans, "German Universities after the Thirty Years War," *History of Universities* 1 (1981): 169—189.

[29]d'Irsay (1935), p. 90—103, 112—142; Boguslaw Lésnodorski, "Les universités au siècle des lumières," in *Commission* (1967), pp. 143—159; Jacques Le Goff, "La conception française de l'université à l'époque de la Renaissance," in *Commission* (1967),

largely unrelated to university studies.[30] This judgment does not mean that England or Europe was neatly divided into "Ancients" and "Moderns." Such a dichotomization can, of course, be easily criticized, as it already has been.[31] But it is fair to generalize that the revival and invigoration of critical and speculative philosophy in the early modern period occurred apart from the universities and what they called "liberal education."

A central reason for this can be found in Benedict Spinoza's view that ecclesiastical control of the educational institutions restrained intellectual freedom, for theological creeds did not encourage the clerics to doubt. Not that the scientists wanted to doubt on that score. Many, such as Newton and Boyle, sincerely embraced the Faith and firmly believed that reason and science were entirely consonant with religious truth—a view that led eventually to Deism.[32] Still, from even before Galileo's censure, through Spinoza's condemnation by both Jews and Christians, to Bishop Stillingfleet's opposition to Locke, and beyond, the clergy dug in their heels against the New Philosophy. This resistance carried over to the grammar schools and universities, about which countless authorities, in making a general assessment of the period, maintain that the curriculum, institutional structure, and pedagogy stagnated or decayed over the sixteenth, seventeenth, and much of the eighteenth centuries.

Despite this deterioration, the resistance of the universities was not at all passive. They had enough stamina to join the churches in their energetic condemnation of the New Philosophy and the freethinkers—at least, this is the traditional interpretation, which has not gone unchallenged. Just as Newton's presence at Cambridge has been used to support opposing arguments, so the official sanction

---

pp. 94–100; Laurence B. Brockliss, "Philosophy Teaching in France, 1600–1740," *History of Universities* 1 (1981): 131–168.

[30]Martin L. Clarke, *Greek Studies in England, 1700–1830* (Cambridge: Cambridge University Press, 1945), chap. 3; Clarke, *Classical Education in Britain, 1500–1900* (Cambridge: Cambridge University Press, 1959), pp. 68–73; Hans (1951), pp. 31–36; Kearney (1970), pp. 141ff., 157ff.; Howell (1971), chap. 1.

[31]Cf. Richard F. Jones, *Ancients and Moderns: A Study of the Rise of the Scientific Movement in Seventeenth-Century England*, 2d ed. (St. Louis: Washington University Press, 1961), and Allen G. Debus, *Science and Education in the Seventeenth Century: The Webster-Ward Debate* (New York: American Elsevier, 1970). See also Kearney (1970), chap. 10.

[32]Cassirer (1951), pp. 39–45; Stuart Hampshire, *Spinoza* (Harmondsworth, Eng.: Penguin, 1951), pp. 42–44, 200–209; Gerald R. Cragg, *The Church and the Age of Reason, 1648–1789* (Harmondsworth, Eng.: Penguin, 1960), pp. 74–78; Martin (1962), pp. 123–131; A. R. Hall (1962), pp. 103–105.

of Cartesian textbooks at the turn of the eighteenth century is dismissed or lauded, depending upon the degree of decay attributed to the universities. And the same sort of conflicting interpretations can be found about the fact that Locke's *Essay Concerning Human Understanding* was known and read by students and faculty at Oxford and Cambridge, yet was proscribed from being taught.

Beyond these curricular matters, the role of various intellectual movements in the universities is similarly ambiguous. In the latter half of the seventeenth century, the Cambridge Platonists attacked the materialism of Hobbes and the mechanistic rationalism of Descartes and thus the mathematical-mechanical model of the world. From within the University of Cambridge, these Platonists defended a spiritualist view of the cosmos as the basis for Christian morality. Therefore, they would seem to qualify as critics of the New Philosophy. However, they are also characterized as the moderates and "latitudinarians"—the relatively tolerant and broad-minded Christians—of the era, who argued that the requirements of reason and faith are entirely compatible. In the following century, the Scottish Common Sense philosophers strongly opposed the skepticism of Berkeley and Hume and held that philosophy must be grounded in certain assumptions about the world that are common to all people and taken to be true. Members of this Common Sense school such as Thomas Reid and George Campbell held chairs of honor in the Scottish universities, and their ally James Beattie received a pension from the king and a doctorate from Oxford for attacks on Hume of the most polemical and shallow kind. On the other hand, Reid and Campbell contributed to breaking the study of logic away from both scholasticism and humanist rhetoric and uniting it with scientific inquiry; and Reid has been viewed as a moderate whose party advanced the cause of the Enlightenment.

Such ambiguity notwithstanding, it must finally be said that the universities by and large opposed freedom of thought and the new learning. Proposals for reform did not come from within the universities, even if some members of the faculties recognized the merit in the New Philosophy.[33] As late as 1765 at Cambridge, reputed to

[33]Joseph Priestley, like other new scientists and philosophers, would seem to endorse this assessment. See Joseph Priestley, *An Examination of Dr. Reid's "Inquiry into the Human Mind on the Principles of Common Sense," Dr. Beattie's "Essay on the Nature and Immutability of Truth," and Dr. Oswald's "Appeal to Common Sense on Behalf of Religion,"* 2d ed. (London: J. Johnson, 1775). For varying interpretations of evidence cited about the intellectual climate of the universities, compare Clarke (1959), pp. 65–69; Cragg (1960), pp. 68–78; Frederick C. Copleston, *A History of Philosophy*

have far outstripped Oxford in scientific and mathematical accomplishments, an Anglican bishop, Richard Watson, could still be appointed professor of chemistry, although, as he later stated, he did not know anything about chemistry and had never received any training in it.

Exceptions did exist, with certain Italian universities first embracing some of the new learning.[34] Leadership was then assumed, predictably, by the universities in Holland, where neutrality in politics and religion was maintained in order to promote commerce. These, in turn, were partly responsible for sparking interest in the New Philosophy at Scottish universities after the Restoration of 1660 and for increasing it after the Revolution of 1689. Enrollments at universities in Scotland were less aristocratic, including more middle-class and poor boys, than those in England, and the percentage of English scientists who had graduated from Scottish universities steadily increased in the course of the eighteenth century. Yet even in these relatively progressive environments, interest in the New Philosophy had relatively little effect on the liberal arts curriculum. The first year was devoted to Latin and Greek grammar and literature drawn from the orators and rhetors, the second year to more of the same plus logic and elementary mathematics, the third year to further repetition plus some ethics, and the fourth year to review and a modicum of natural philosophy and metaphysics.

The Scottish and Dutch universities heavily influenced another group of exceptions, the Dissenting Academies, which enjoy the reputation of having provided the most modern and progressive education then available in England. In fact, one historian speaks of "a seed of modern liberal education" being sown by these Dissenting Academies in the fertile soil of the "liberalizing ideas" of Dutch and Scottish educators.[35] The Puritan influence contributed to this, as did the example of Samuel Hartlib, even though his own acad-

---

(Westminster, Md.: Newman, 1962), vol. 5, chaps. 3, 17; Gay (1969), pp. 24–25, 155–158; Vivian H. Green, *The Universities: British Institutions* (Baltimore: Penguin, 1969), pp. 41–42, 232–236; J. David Hoeveler, Jr., *James McCosh and the Scottish Intellectual Tradition: From Glasgow to Princeton* (Princeton, N.J.: Princeton University Press, 1981), chap. 4.

[34]For the following discussion about the new learning in the universities and Dissenting Academies, I draw from d'Irsay (1935), pp. 1–23; Clarke (1959), chap. 11; Vern L. Bullough, "Educational Conflict and the Development of Science in the Renaissance," *Bucknell Review* 15 (1967): 35–45; Green (1969), chap. 5; Karl A. Sprengard, "Die Bedeutung der Artistenfakultät für die Entwicklung der modernen Philosophie des XIV. und XV. Jahrhunderts," in *Actes* (1969), pp. 691–699; Kearney (1970), pp. 129–135, 156; Hoeveler (1981), chap. 2.

[35]Hans (1951), p. 57. On the Academies, see McLachlan (1931), pp. 19–32; Rich-

emy had failed. Nevertheless, during the initial period of academy founding, between 1670 and 1720, the Dissenters largely followed the models of Oxford and Cambridge, from which they had been excluded. Only gradually in the eighteenth century did the mathematical and experimental sciences begin to earn a place in the curriculum of these academies, and even then, these liberal-free subjects were generally not considered a part of "liberal education"—a fact reflecting the ambivalence in outlook to be found even at these most "enlightened" places of English higher education during this period of transition. Not until the second half of the eighteenth century did a "subtle but noticeable shift" in the meaning of "liberal" education begin to occur.[36]

Less or no change took place at other educational institutions in England. University lectures on the new learning that might have occurred were never given official sanction. Instruction in the liberal-free subjects was usually offered privately for a fee, rather than supported by university or college endowments. The situation of Gresham College typifies the extracurricular nature of these liberal-free subjects. Though sometimes held up as an example of Oxford and Cambridge professors lecturing on the New Philosophy, Gresham offered no degrees and was located in London, far from the liberal arts curricula in the two universities. In contrast, *Directions for Younger Scholars* by Thomas Barlow, tutor at Oxford in the last half of the seventeenth century, demonstrates the mix of scholastic and humanist studies actually current at that institution, as does *Of Education Especially of Young Gentlemen* (1673) by Obadiah Walker, who also tutored at Oxford. The latter account of the gentleman's standard course, reprinted at least six times by 1699, criticized excessive enthusiasm for science while defining "liberty of spirit" as magnanimity rather than freedom from restraint.[37]

---

ard L. Greaves, *The Puritan Revolution and Educational Thought: Background for Reform* (New Brunswick, N.J.: Rutgers University Press, 1969), p. 92; Green (1969), pp. 44—47, 228—232; Charles Webster, ed., *Samuel Hartlib and the Advancement of Learning* (Cambridge: Cambridge University Press, 1970), pp. 7—10, 71—75.

[36] Rothblatt (1976), pp. 27, 76, 98ff.

[37] Barlow and Walker are discussed in Kearney (1970), pp. 146—159. Here and below, I draw from John W. Adamson, *Pioneers of Modern Education, 1600—1700* (Cambridge: Cambridge University Press, 1921), chap. 10; Hans (1951), pp. 63—67, 117—121; John L. Mahoney, "The Classical Tradition in Eighteenth Century English Rhetorical Education," *History of Education Journal* 9 (1958): 95: Fritz Caspari, *Humanism and the Social Order in Tudor England* (Chicago: University of Chicago Press, 1954; New York: Teachers College Press, 1968), p. 299; Patricia-Ann Lee, "Some English Academies: An Experiment in the Education of Renaissance Gentlemen," *HEQ* 10 (1970): 273—286; Rothblatt (1976), p. 25, chaps. 3, 6, 7.

The tutors' approach, very similar to that of Sir Philip Sidney's education a century earlier, was carried forward into Georgian society, where "liberal" implied gentility and "liberal arts" meant a gentleman's education. When some independent academies were established as alternatives to the two universities and incorporated scientific subjects or modern languages, their "liberal education" still consisted of classical letters in Cicero and Aristotle. Meanwhile, other "courtly academies" were founded, and the colleges at the universities generally became even more socially exclusive. In 1721, Nathan Bailey published the first edition of *An Etymological English Dictionary* (which would appear in thirty editions by 1802, as well as in German translation), and he distinctly associated "liberal education" with polite society. This view was repeated in the latter half of the eighteenth century by Vicesimus Knox, fellow of St. John's College, Oxford, whose *Liberal Education: Or, a Practical Treatise on the Methods of Acquiring Useful and Polite Learning* went through eleven editions by 1795. Knox wrote:

> In the warmth of the innovating and reforming spirit . . . they (Milton, Locke, Rousseau, and . . . others who have written on the subject) censure modes of treatment which are right, they recommend methods which really cannot be reduced to practice, and which, if they could, would be useless or pernicious. . . . I mean then, in the following Treatise, to speak in favor of that ancient system of education, which consists in a classical discipline and which has produced in our nation many ornaments of human nature.[38]

At the beginning of the nineteenth century, the Oxford statutes required for the B.A. that "always and for every degree, an examination in Humane Literature is to be set on foot, and especially one in the Greek and Roman writers, three of whom at fewest, of the best age and stamp, are to be used." This attention to "Humane Literature" signifies, in fact, a heightening of interest in classical studies that occurred at both Oxford and Cambridge at this time. Simultaneously, German universities were advancing their idea of *neuhumanistische* scholarship, and "humanism" first appeared as an

---

[38]Vicesimus Knox, *Liberal Education; or, A Practical Treatise on the Methods of Acquiring Useful and Polite Learning*, 10th ed. (London: Charles Dilly, 1789), vol. 1, pp. 1−3; William E. Axon, ed., *English Dialect Words of the Eighteenth Century as Shown in the "Universal Etymological Dictionary" of Nathaniel Bailey* (London: Trübner, 1883), pp. v−viii.

English word, expressing an educational emphasis on Greek and Latin letters in contradistinction to more utilitarian and scientific training.[39] In the lower schools in England, a similar situation obtained, as seen in a well-known juridical verdict of 1805 that, according to traditional and contemporary usage, "Grammar School" meant a school "for teaching grammatically the learned languages" and therefore the master of a grammar school could not be obligated to teach the vernacular. Small wonder that, after surveying the scene for curricular models in 1828, the Corporation and faculty of Yale College concluded, "In the British Isles, in France, Germany, Italy and, indeed in every country in which literature has acquired distinction and importance, the Greek and Roman classics constitute an essential part of liberal education."[40]

That the New Haven college should look across the Atlantic for leadership in education is, as shall be seen, illustrative of the development of early American colleges. I say this because, having adhered to a more traditional interpretation concerning the entrance of experimental science and "modern" subjects—as a rough and tentative proxy for the liberal-free ideal—into British education, I am also frankly timid about subscribing to the revisionist or modernist interpretations of the history of American undergraduate education that have become increasingly popular in recent decades. Nevertheless, it must be acknowledged that scientific subjects were not entirely excluded from the nine colleges founded in colonial times, each by the dominant Protestant sect in its locale: Harvard (1636), Congregational; William and Mary (1693), Anglican; Yale (1701), Congregational-Presbyterian; Princeton (1746), Presbyterian; Columbia (1754), Anglican; Pennsylvania (1755), Anglican-Presbyterian; Brown (1765), Baptist; Rutgers (1766), Dutch Reformed; Dartmouth (1769), Congregational.

In 1711, William and Mary established the first chair of mathematics and natural philosophy in America, and by 1776 five other

[39]Statute quoted in Clarke (1959), pp. 98, 104–131. Raymond Klibansky, "Questions et discussions," in *Actes* (1969), pp. 301–302; Carl Diehl, *Americans and German Scholarship, 1770–1870* (New Haven, Conn.: Yale University Press, 1978), chap. 1; McClelland (1980), pp. 99–131; Martha McMackin Garland, *Cambridge before Darwin: The Ideal of a Liberal Education, 1800–1860* (Cambridge: Cambridge University Press, 1980), chap. 1.

[40]*Reports on the Course of Instruction in Yale College by a Committee of the Corporation and the Academical Faculty* (New Haven, Conn.: Hezekiah Howe, 1828), p. 34; *The Attorney-General v. Whiteley, July 20th, 22d, 1805* 11 *Vesey Junior* 241.

colleges had followed suit. Harvard appointed Isaac Greenwood, who brought with him the Newtonian outlook of *A Course in Experimental Philosophy*, and then John Winthrop, who taught for four decades as the second professor of mathematics and natural philosophy. At Yale, efforts in this same direction were initiated by Samuel Johnson, tutor between 1716 and 1719, and expanded upon by President Thomas Clap and others in the years prior to the Revolution.[41]

Around the College of New Jersey, later to be known as Princeton, swirled two eddies of influence that sent waves into all colonial colleges, but especially into that Presbyterian college. On one side frothed the Great Awakening and the turbulence of revivalist groups, which, despite a degree of anti-intellectualism, encouraged pluralism and diversity in education through their schismatic tendencies. On the other side churned the activity of the Dissenting Academies and Scottish universities, whose relative sympathy to liberal-free subjects has previously been mentioned. Although its first four presidents held closely to the scholastic-humanist course of studies and the curriculum was not broadened until John Witherspoon's tenure (1768–1794), these factors did influence Princeton. In 1771, a professorship in mathematics and natural philosophy was established, and the curriculum of the following year included geography, history, astronomy, and French. Meanwhile, Rutgers, chartered as Queen's College in 1766, adhered to the model of its New Jersey neighbor rather closely.[42]

At Columbia, founded as King's College, the influence of the new learning is sometimes located in the use or presence of texts reflecting Cartesian and Lockean philosophy, as well as in the gradual incorporation of "observation and experiment" into the course of

---

[41]Robert Freeman Butts, *The College Charts Its Course: Historical Conceptions and Current Proposals* (New York: McGraw-Hill, 1939), pp. 60–66; Theodore Hornberger, *Scientific Thought in the American College, 1638–1800* (Austin: University of Texas Press, 1945), pp. 25–26, 44–51; Carl A. Hangartner, "Movements to Change American College Teaching, 1700–1830" (Ph.D. diss., Yale University, 1955), pp. 128–136; Richard Warch, *School of the Prophets: Yale College, 1701–1740* (New Haven, Conn.: Yale University Press, 1973), pp. 72, 195, 214–215; Brooks M. Kelley, *Yale: A History* (New Haven, Conn.: Yale University Press, 1974), pp. 70–82.

[42]Thomas J. Wertenbaker, *Princeton, 1746–1896* (Princeton, N.J.: Princeton University Press, 1946), chap. 3; Hangartner (1955), pp. 48–63; George P. Schmidt, *Princeton and Rutgers: The Two Colonial Colleges of New Jersey* (Princeton, N.J.: D. Van Nostrand, 1964), p. 34; Richard P. McCormick, *Rutgers: A Bicentennial History* (New Brunswick, N.J.: Rutgers Unversity Press, 1966), chap. 1; Douglas Sloan, *The Scottish Enlightenment and the American College Ideal* (New York: Teachers College Press, 1971a), pp. 33, 64–72, 110–112; Sloan, "Harmony, Chaos, and Consensus: The American College Curriculum," *Teachers College Record* 73 (1971b): 227–232; Sloan, ed. *The Great*

natural philosophy.[43] Even more sympathy for educational innovation is usually attributed to the "College, Academy and Charitable School" founded in Philadelphia. This attribution is supported by the college's association with Benjamin Franklin, whose 1749 *Proposals Relating to the Education of Youth in Pennsylvania* argued for curricular utility and for employment of "Apparatus for Experiments in Natural Philosophy," and whose 1751 "Idea of the English School" is often cited for its counter-classical influence and promotion of study in the vernacular. In addition, William Smith, who was named the first provost, had written *A General Idea of the College of Mirania*, which resembled the reformed course of study in Scottish universities and incorporated much of the educational thinking of the Enlightenment. Further proof for this receptiveness to the new learning resides in the nature of Pennsylvania commencement "Exercises" and the later appointment of Benjamin Rush as the first professor of chemistry in America.[44]

The foregoing constitutes a sketchy outline of the kind of evidence usually put forth to show that "the 'New Learning' made itself felt throughout the [colonial] curriculum, dignifying induction at the expense of deduction, ethics at the expense of theology and English at the expense of Latin." Often accompanying this interpretation are the assertions that teaching faculties became more specialized and departmentalized and that scholastic disputations in Latin yielded to forensic disputations in English.[45] Now, all this sort of change could be admitted, and for present purposes the more

Awakening and American Education: A Documentary History (New York: Teachers College Press, 1973), pp. 19–27, 41, 128; David C. Humphrey, "Colonial Colleges and English Dissenting Academies: A Study in Transatlantic Culture," *HEQ* 12 (1972): 184–187; Howard Miller, *The Revolutionary College: American Presbyterian Higher Education, 1707–1837* (New York: New York University Press, 1976), chap. 1, p. 94.

[43]David C. Humphrey, *From King's College to Columbia, 1746–1800* (New York: Columbia University Press, 1976), pp. 164–180.

[44]Benjamin Franklin, *Proposals Relating to the Education of Youth in Pennsylvania* (Philadelphia: B. Franklin, 1749), pp. 6–9, 13–14; Franklin, "Idea of the English School, sketched out for the Consideration of the Trustees of the Philadelphia Academy," appended to the Reverend Richard Peters's *A Sermon on Education, Wherein Some Account Is Given of the Academy Established in the City of Philadelphia* (Philadelphia: Franklin and Hall, 1751), pp. 1–8; Edward P. Cheyney, *History of the University of Pennsylvania, 1740–1940* (Philadelphia: University of Pennsylvania Press, 1940), pp. 28–29; Terry W. Smith, " 'Exercises' Presented during the Commencements of the College of Philadelphia and Other Colonial Colleges," *PH* 7 (1967): 182–222; Louis F. Snow, *The College Curriculum in the United States* (New York: Bureau of Publications, Teachers College, Columbia University, 1907), chaps. 3, 4. (Snow vastly overrates the influence of William Smith's essay but still helps to trace out the lines of influence.)

[45]Quotation is from Frederick Rudolph, *Curriculum: A History of the American Undergraduate Course of Study since 1636* (San Francisco: Jossey-Bass, 1977), pp. 37.

specific question would still have to be asked: was this new learning actually considered part of "liberal education"? There will come a time to consider this point, but here it scarcely need be addressed because—contrary to the impression often left by modernist interpretations—the New Philosophy and the Enlightenment made relatively little impact on the colonial colleges. They remained heavily insulated from the revival of the philosophical tradition, wedded as they were to the continuing scholastic-humanist tradition accommodated to Christian purposes.

The differences among the interpretations advanced by historians are largely a matter of context. Yes, as Frederick Rudolph notes, for example, the 1642 student would find some change in the 1764 curriculum.[46] But relative to the scientific knowledge of the mid-eighteenth century, the faculties of the colleges were not especially learned, and the pedagogy and facilities were little influenced by the new developments of the day. As in Europe, the real business of enlightened thinking took place outside of the educational institutions.

Leading colonial minds had very early been recruited into the Royal Society of London, and these included some colonial educators, such as Increase Mather and John Winthrop. However, the colleges themselves left the pursuit of knowledge to external associations like the American Philosophical Society, which was organized by Benjamin Franklin and merged in 1769 with a similar organization in Philadelphia to form the American Philosophical Society Held at Philadelphia for Promoting Useful Knowledge. Two years later, the Society's membership included 248 colonists and Europeans, and it had swelled to 650 before the turn of the century, by which time the American Academy of Arts and Sciences had been founded in Boston. These were the American institutions steeped in the liberal-free ethos of the Enlightenment.[47] The scientific and experimental method was employed by "amateurs," not academic and professional scientists in the colleges.

James J. Walsh, *Education of the Founding Fathers of the Republic: Scholasticism in the Colonial Colleges, a Neglected Chapter in the History of American Education* (New York: Fordham University Press, 1935), chap. 3; Joe W. Kraus, "The Development of a Curriculum in the Early American Colleges," *HEQ* 1 (June 1961): 70–71. On specialization, see Hangartner (1955), chaps. 1, 2; Samuel E. Morison, *Three Centuries of Harvard, 1636–1936* (Cambridge, Mass.: Belknap, 1936), pp. 89–90.

[46]Rudolph (1977), p. 53. On the nature and prevalence of rote recitations in the antebellum college curriculum, see Appendix 1 herein.

[47]Allen O. Hansen, *Liberalism and American Education in the Eighteenth Century*

Exceptions usually involved professors in medical schools, who constituted the vast majority of academicians trained outside the colonies. Indeed, one national study of 124 noted American college professors—out of the some 210 who taught between 1750 and 1800—found that, apart from those teaching medicine, only two were educated in Europe. Even where the medical school was prominent, as in Philadelphia, the scientific activity revolved around the American Philosophical Society rather than the college. Certainly, this might be expected in that city, given that Philadelphia was the home of the Society. Yet, in the national study, of 124 professors only fifteen were found to belong to the Society, most of those from the College of Philadelphia. And when the American Academy of Arts and Sciences and the American Academy of Fine Arts were considered as well, the number of member college professors rose to a mere twenty-four.[48]

Beyond simply not participating, the sectarian colleges maligned the new critical philosophy and experimental method, even as they began to embrace the scientific findings that could be incorporated into a natural theology. In this way, the denunciations voiced by the colleges moved from a late seventeenth-century and early eighteenth-century condemnation of deism and the corresponding growth of human self-reliance—justification by reason rather than justification by faith—to the fear of "an inextricable skepticism," which beset, for example, President Samuel Johnson of King's College about John Locke and his intellectual descendants. This fear, Walter Minto, the new professor of mathematics and physics at Princeton, tried to assuage in the 1780s. But it was still expressed by Charles Nisbet, who became president of Dickinson

(New York: Macmillan, 1926), pp. 62, 105–107; Frank Klassen, "Persistence and Change in Eighteenth Century Colonial Education," HEQ 2 (June 1962): 92–93; Joseph C. Kiger, American Learned Societies (Washington, D.C.: Public Affairs Press, 1963), chap. 1; Ralph S. Bates, Scientific Societies in the United States, 3d ed. (Cambridge: MIT Press, 1965), pp. 2–12; George F. Frick, "The Royal Society in America," in The Pursuit of Knowledge in the Early American Republic: American Scientific and Learned Societies from Colonial Times to the Civil War, ed. Alexander Oleson and Sanborn C. Brown (Baltimore: Johns Hopkins University Press, 1976), pp. 70–73; Alexandra Oleson, "Introduction: To Build a New Intellectual Order," in Oleson and Brown (1976), pp. xv–xxv; John C. Greene, "Science, Learning, and Utility: Patterns of Organization in the Early American Republic," in Oleson and Brown (1976), pp. 1–3.
[48] Hornberger (1945), pp. 66–74; William L. Sachse, The Colonial American in Britain (Madison: University of Wisconsin Press, 1956), pp. 55–63; William D. Carrell, "American College Professors: 1750–1800," HEQ 8 (1968): 291–292; Sloan (1971a), pp. 226–236.

College in 1800 and abhorred the "monstrous and misshapen pro-
ductions" of "the spirit of free inquiry."[49]

From New England to the Old South, the classical curriculum
and its tradition persisted. In fact, there is evidence that the study
of humanist classics increased after the mid-eighteenth century,
particularly in the belles lettres—orations, history, poetry, and literature—which were directed toward instilling "virtue and morality" through education. That these studies served to identify an elite
who pursued them for their own sake—for their adornment—is
avowed by Daniel Calhoun: "For many [colonial] students, perhaps
for most, liberal education served no functions of any specific use to
society. Latin and Greek and philosophy, and the having attended
some higher school, were marks of prestige and breeding."[50] Such
a generalization is not at all extreme, especially in view of the uniformity of the colonial curriculum. This program of liberal arts varied little—from Thomas Clap's Yale catalog of 1743 to that of Ezra
Stiles in 1778, or from Dartmouth in New Hampshire to the University of North Carolina (1789), the first degree-granting state university.[51]

Apart from divinity, freshmen devoted nearly all their time to
Greek grammar for "testament" and Latin grammar in orations, plus
some arithmetic. Sophomores continued these studies while under-
taking rhetoric, including perhaps some belles lettres in the vernacular, and picking up logic and advanced arithmetic or algebra.
Juniors continued Latin, Greek, and rhetoric and passed through algebra, geometry, and perhaps trigonometry or "fluxions," along with
a course in natural philosophy. Seniors reviewed the previous three

---

[49]Samuel Johnson, Elementa Philosophica: Containing Chiefly, Noetica, or Things
Relating to the Mind or Understanding: and Ethica, or Things Relating to the Moral Be-
haviour (Philadelphia: B. Franklin and D. Hall, 1752), tract 1, p. 6; Samuel Miller,
Memoir of the Rev. Charles Nisbet, D.D., Late President of Dickinson College, Carlisle (New
York: J. Leavitt, 1840), p. 269.

[50]Daniel H. Calhoun, The Intelligence of a People (Princeton, N.J.: Princeton
University Press, 1973), p. 40. Robert Middlekauf, "A Persistent Tradition: The
Classical Curriculum in Eighteenth Century New England," William and Mary Quarterly, 3d series, 18 (1961): 56–60; Klassen (1962), pp. 83–99; Richard M. Gummere,
The American Mind and the Classical Tradition: Essays in Comparative Culture (Cambridge: Harvard University Press, 1963), chap. 1; Edwin A. Miles, "The Old South and
the Classical World," North Carolina Historical Review 48 (1971): 258–275; Phyllis Vine,
"The Social Function of Eighteenth-Century Higher Education," HEQ 16 (1976):
409–424.

[51]Snow (1907), pp. 41–45, 54, 79–82; Leon B. Richardson, History of Dartmouth
College (Hanover, N.H.: Dartmouth College, 1932), vol. 1, pp. 248–249; Kraus (1961),
pp. 68–75; Gummere (1963), chap. 4; Kelley (1974), pp. 70–83.

years, studied metaphysics, took the crowning course in moral philosophy from the president, and received more exposure to natural philosophy in the spring term if there was time. This generalized frame of studies was pursued through the long-standing practice of recitations and declamations, with the lecture format slowly creeping in.

Meanwhile, the first chair of mathematics and natural philosophy established in America—at William and Mary in 1711—folded. The first professor to hold it was practically a vagabond; the second held class for a year or two and then left Virginia still retaining the appointment. By this time nearly twenty years had passed, and the scientific stimulation at colonial William and Mary afterward was minimal. At Harvard, Professor Isaac Greenwood apparently taught his natural philosophy course in sixteen lectures. His successor, John Winthrop, covered the lever, pulley, inclined plane, screw, wedge, gravity, attraction and cohesion, laws of motion, magnetism, electricity, fluids, optics, astronomy, and other mechanics in thirty lectures. Small wonder that science instruction in the eighteenth century has repeatedly been called "little more than a series of definitions."[52]

Compared to Harvard, Yale remained more conservative theologically and educationally. The syllogistic disputation was promoted in New Haven until almost 1790; and despite assertions about Newton's early presence in the Yale curriculum, President Theodore Dwight Woolsey remarked in the mid-nineteenth century that, even in the 1770s, to have exposed students directly to Newton's *Principia* "must have been a very rare thing."[53] No different was the case at King's College. There, President Samuel Johnson (1754–1763) had described a very broad and progressive curriculum in early advertisements. In practice, however, he was devoted to the traditional classics and "polite learning," a commitment appropriate for King's College, whose students were mainly drawn from the well-to-do, that is, Anglican burghers and gentlemen. Nor was the oratorical tradition broken by Johnson's successor, Myles Cooper (1763–1775), with his *Plan of Education*. Rather, the dominance of classical letters in-

---

[52]Quoted from Cheyney (1940), p. 83; Stanley M. Guralnick, *Science and the Antebellum American College* (Philadelphia: American Philosophical Society, 1975), p. 14. Hornberger (1945), pp. 25–51; Hangartner (1955), pp. 128–136.

[53]Theodore Dwight Woolsey, *An Historical Discourse Pronounced before the Graduates of Yale College, August 14, 1850; One Hundred and Fifty Years After the Founding of that Institution* (New Haven: B.L. Hamlen, 1850), p. 61. Cf. Warch (1973), pp. 215, 229; Kelley (1974), pp. 41, 81.

creased while natural philosophy and mathematics were largely ignored.[54]

At the College of New Jersey, President Aaron Burr (1748–1757)
instituted a classical orientation in the curriculum that is apparent
in the commencement theses for the period, which were classified
according to the divisions of the *septem artes liberales*. The two subsequent presidents essentially preserved the program, though add-
ing some study of English letters. It is to the next, John Witherspoon,
that a relatively broad curriculum is often attributed; and this view
may be admitted, especially in a context where the College of Rhode
Island, for example, still grouped its commencement theses under
the headings of the *septem artes liberales*. But compared to the intellectual activity outside of the colleges, the curriculum of the College
of New Jersey, like that of its neighbor, Rutgers, was far from enlightened.[55] The judgment about liberal education depends on the
contextual standard, and this applies especially to the college in
Philadelphia.

From Benjamin Franklin's *Proposals* and "Idea of the English
School" and from William Smith's *College of Mirania*, many "liberal" or "progressive" ideas can be derived, and some historians
have located in them the fount of modernity for the liberal arts. Yet,
Franklin's English school is not concerned with "liberal education,"
and his *Proposals*, which does address "liberal education," com-
mends *"most ornamental"* as well as *"most useful"* studies. While arguing for the study of English, Franklin is "not here speaking against
Greek and *Latin* . . . two of the best languages that ever were, the
most expressive, copious, beautiful." He repeatedly quotes *Observations on Liberal Education in All Its Branches* (1742) by George Turnbull, who orients "liberal education" toward "the nobility and
Gentry" of "Good Breeding" in order to produce a "liberal Character" evincing "Courage, Firmness, and manly Vigour." Similarly,
Franklin's "Idea of the English School," together with Richard Peter's *A Sermon on Education*, to which it was appended, makes clear
that the study of Greek and Latin grammar and "classicks" is the key
constituent for an education that is to be called "liberal."[56]

---

[54]Humphrey (1976), pp. 79–100, 158, 164–176; Snow (1907), pp. 56–59.

[55]Walter C. Bronson, *The History of Brown University, 1764–1914* (Providence, R.I.:
Brown University, 1914), pp. 101–106; Cheyney (1940), p. 86; Wertenbaker (1946), p.
93; Gummere (1963), p. 64; Sloan (1971a), pp. 62–64, 112–113.

[56]Franklin (1749), pp. 10, 11, 14, 18, 29–32. Franklin's "Idea of the English School"
does not recommend the classics but neither does it mention "liberal" education (pp.
1–8). This omission is underscored by the fact that it was appended to the Reverend
Richard Peters's *A Sermon on Education, Wherein Some Account Is Given of the Acad-*

Similarly, William Smith's *College of Mirania*, in and of itself, might be called a significant forerunner of progressive liberal education. In 1756, however, during his tenure as provost, Smith published a more conventional curricular plan that reflected the actual three-year course in the College of Philadelphia. Maintaining the distinction implied by Franklin's "Idea," Smith did not mention the English school since it was not concerned with liberal education. Instead, he attended to forming young men of affairs through what was substantially the scholastic-humanist curriculum of the day.[57] Thus, at the colonial college often cited as having the most scientific or progressive influence, the term "liberal education" still followed the classical languages and letters, with characteristics of the oratorical tradition predominant.

The Revolution brought change. In fact, it was precisely this rebellion that kindled Enlightenment influence in America, particularly in education, and weakened the Georgian theory of liberal education in England. Equality, liberty, learning, progress, experimentation, and science were associated in the minds of the Revolutionary leaders; and one can trace the specific transmission of many of these conceptual associations from Adam Smith, Locke, Rousseau, and Helvétius to key figures in the American independence movement: Franklin, Jefferson, Rush, Adams, Paine. Not surprisingly, this Enlightenment ethos also prompted suspicion of authority and tradition, as well as attacks on the gentlemanly virtues and classical education that conveyed them.[58] Consequently, the Revolution can be considered the catalyst for engendering the liberal-free ideal in America.

---

emy Established in the City of Philadelphia (Philadelphia: Franklin and Hall, 1751), delivered at the opening of the Academy in 1751. The Academy consisted of a Latin grammar school (classroom) and an English grammar school (classroom). The latter is described by Franklin, while Peters speaks of Greek and Latin grammar and "classicks" and mathematics as the "Liberal Arts and Sciences" and the study of them as "liberal education." Peters also defends the study of English grammar, but this is "for the use of those who may not be inclined to learn Latin" (pp. 22–23, 26, 30). The subsequent elevation in status of the Latin school above the English was clearly indicated by and provided for in the Constitutions of the Academy.

[57] Lawrence Cremin, *American Education: The Colonial Experience, 1607–1783* (New York: Harper & Row, 1970), pp. 378–383. Important proponents of the view that the College of Philadelphia was modern and progressive include Snow (1907), chap. 3; Butts (1939), passim; Hornberger (1945), pp. 28–29. Others have relied on their authority: Cheyney (1940), pp. 85–87; Smith (1967), p. 199.

[58] Donald G. Tewksbury, *The Founding of American Colleges and Universities Before the Civil War, with Particular Reference to the Religious Influences Bearing upon the College Movement* (New York: Bureau of Publications, Teachers College, Columbia Uni-

Not that theories of education put forward by the rebels neglected the oratorical tradition. In republican writings on freedom, equality, individualism, pursuit of knowledge, and technological progress—advanced in the context of national systems of education by Benjamin Rush, Noah Webster, Robert Coram, and others—characteristics of the *artes liberales* ideal still appear prominently. Indeed, Thomas Jefferson's notion of *aristoi* arose from the tradition of the virtuous gentleman, and his plan for universal education involved reconciling democracy and civility, as did Washington's farewell address to the American people. This dialectic of "civility liberalized"—to use Lawrence Cremin's apt phrase—is further demonstrated by the Americans' tremendous interest in the ancient writings of the Greeks and, most especially, of the Romans.[59] "Civility liberalized" therefore bespeaks the emerging confrontation between the two countervailing ideals of liberal education, as seen in writings from the Revolution and the young Republic.

This confrontation is reflected in the semantic development of "liberal," especially concerning the term's initially pejorative connotation of "free" or "unrestrained." The early battle over whether this sense of "liberal" would be viewed with approbation occurred in the field of religion, for theologians had always been particularly sensitive to semantic perturbations that could, in the long run, weaken orthodox doctrine. Much criticism was therefore directed against the "liberality" of "liberal Christians," whose rejection of

versity, 1932), pp. 60ff., 142; Agatho Zimmer, *Changing Concepts of Higher Education in America Since 1700* (Ph.D. dissertation, Catholic University of America, 1938), pp. 38–62; Gordon C. Lee, ed., *Crusade Against Ignorance: Thomas Jefferson on Education* (New York: Bureau of Publications, Teachers College, Columbia University, 1961), chap. 1; Paul Nash, "Innocents Abroad: American Students at British Universities in the Early Nineteenth Century," *HEQ* 1 (June 1961): 32–44; Hyman Kuritz, "Benjamin Rush: His Theory of Republican Education," *HEQ* 7 (1967): 432–451; Wilhelm Sjöstrand, *Freedom and Equality as Fundamental Educational Principles in Western Democracy: From John Locke to Edmund Burke* (Stockholm: Almqvist & Wiksell, 1973); Rothblatt (1976), pp. 117ff.; Henry S. Commager, *The Empire of Reason: How Europe Imagined and America Realized the Enlightenment* (New York: Doubleday, 1977). These leaders of the early Republic constituted an elite, yet their relatively egalitarian commitments are shown by their favoring mass schooling far more than did elites in Britain. Carl F. Kaestle, " 'Between the Scylla of Brutal Ignorance and the Charybdis of a Literary Education': Elite Attitudes Toward Mass Schooling in Early Industrial England and America," in *Schooling and Society: Studies in the History of Education*, ed. Lawrence Stone (Baltimore: Johns Hopkins University Press, 1976), pp. 177–191.
    [59]Cremin (1970), p. 419. Edwin H. Cady, *The Gentleman in America: A Literary Study in American Culture* (Syracuse, N.Y.: Syracuse University Press, 1949), chap. 5; Lee (1961), pp. 81–103; Michael V. Belok, "The Courtesy Tradition and Early Schoolbooks," *HEQ* 8 (1968): 306–309; Edwin A. Miles, "The Young American Nation and the Classical World," *JHI* 35 (1974): 259–274; Eva T.H. Brann, *Paradoxes of Education*

sectarianism arose out of gentlemanly Christian charity and evolved into an epistemological critique of dogmatic orthodoxy.[60]

In education, the dialectical ambiguity of "liberal," straddling the *artes liberales* and liberal-free senses, was expressed at a very early date in the series of tractates published as *Cato's Letters*, especially in Number 71, "Polite Arts and Learning naturally produced in Free States and marred by such as are not free." Written in England and immensely popular in America, these tractates helped convey that dialectic across the Atlantic. Other conduits were provided by expatriate Englishmen, such as Joseph Priestley. Expounding on "liberal education" toward the end of the eighteenth century, this Unitarian chemist declared that "a man's great object be the *pursuit of truth* and the *practice of virtue*." Accordingly, he held that "liberal philosophical science" or "natural philosophy" or "experimental philosophy" should be part of "liberal education," while he also asserted that a "liberal scholar" requires "sufficient *leisure* for reading" and that "the study of the Latin and Greek tongues is still of great importance to persons of any *liberal profession*."[61]

In the United States, the confrontation between the *artes liberales* and liberal-free ideals appeared in two prize-winning essays

---

in a Republic (Chicago: University of Chicago Press, 1979), pp. 79–102; Meyer Reinhold, *Classica Americana: The Greek and Roman Heritage in the United States* (Detroit: Wayne State University Press, 1984), pp. 23–49, 95–97, 156–157.

[60]The American "liberal Christians," while denying themselves to be Arminian or deistic, at least at the outset, began using the word "liberal" to mean "broadminded" and "unsectarian." In their view, this was merely a charitable and genial response to the increasing pluralism in Christianity that had, ever since the Reformation, put in doubt the idea that one sect had the only true doctrine while all others were in error. Opponents recognized that a danger lay in the incipient relativism, which could, in the long run, undermine all claims to truth. And, in fact, the tolerance originating out of the geniality of "liberal Christians" evolved into an epistemological challenge to orthodoxy. Of course, the two themes were intertwined and could not easily be separated, as was demonstrated in William Ellery Channing's 1806 defense of liberal Christians:

> You complain that our standard is not *particular* enough. But this is the distinguishing feature of our liberality. The greater variety of sentiments with which a system will harmonize, or the fewer its fundamentals, the more worthy it is of liberal minds. (Quoted in C. Conrad Wright, *The Liberal Christians: Essays on American Unitarian History* [Boston: Beacon, 1970], p. 30)

Alan Heimert, *Religion and the American Mind from the Great Awakening to the Revolution* (Cambridge: Harvard University Press, 1966), pp. 5–23; Andrew Delbanco, *William Ellery Channing: An Essay on the Liberal Spirit in America* (Cambridge: Harvard University Press, 1981), chap. 3.

[61]Priestley (1788), pp. xiv, 19, 23–27, 45; *Cato's Letters*, Number 71, Saturday, March 31, 1722, "Polite Arts and Learning naturally produced in Free States and marred by such as are not free," in *The English Libertarian Heritage from the Writings of John Trenchard and Thomas Gordon in the "Independent Whig" and "Cato's Letters,"* ed. David L. Jacobson (New York: Bobbs-Merrill, 1965), pp. 186–192.

from a contest, sponsored in 1795 by the American Philosophical Society, that called for descriptions of "the best system of liberal Education and literary instruction adapted to the genius of the Government of the United States." Both authors, Samuel Knox and Samuel H. Smith, expressed respect for classical letters and "modern" studies, concern for inculcating civic virtue and pursuing knowledge, and appreciation that advances in natural science and technology could produce more leisure for cultural refinement and reflection. They were commensurately ambiguous in using the term "liberal" to mean "magnanimous" or "gentlemanly" and to convey a sense of freedom or liberation.[62] What must be remembered about such sources as Priestley, the American Philosophical Society, and the like is that they represent the enlightened, or liberalized, point of view. If they still honored classical letters in the oratorical tradition, the educational institutions did so all the more.

Grammar schools faced mounting attacks on their resistance to change. By and large, they did not respond, although slight alterations were made in their curricula in order to meet college admissions standards, which had expanded to require elementary arithmetic, as well as Latin and Greek, by 1800. In the colleges, scarcely more of an influx of liberal-free subjects was evident. Nearly one-half of the curriculum was commonly devoted to Latin and Greek letters; one-quarter to moral philosophy, logic and rhetoric; and one-quarter to belles lettres, history, and natural philosophy.[63]

On the other hand, some efforts to deviate from the inherited

---

[62]On Samuel H. Smith, "Remarks on Education: Illustrating the Close Connection Between Virtue and Wisdom. To which is Annexed a System of Liberal Education. Which, Having received the Premium Awarded by the American Philosophical Society, December 15, 1797, is Now Published by Their Order" (Philadelphia, 1798), see Hansen (1926), pp. 139–140; Frederick Rudolph, ed., *Essays on Education in the Early Republic* (Cambridge, Mass.: Belknap, 1965), p. 167. On Samuel Knox, "An Essay on the Best System of Liberal Education, Adapted to the Genius of the Government of the United States. Comprehending also, an Uniform General Plan for Instituting and Conducting Public Schools, in This Country, on Principles of the Most Extensive Utility. To Which is Prefixed, an Address to the Legislature of Maryland on That Subject" (Philadelphia, 1799), see Rudolph (1965), pp. 282–290, 301–315.

[63]Edwin C. Broome, *A Historical and Critical Discussion of College Admission Requirements* (New York: Macmillan, 1903), p. 39; Snow (1907), pp. 82–140; Klassen (1962), pp. 83–99; Robert Middlekauf, *Ancients and Axioms: Secondary Education in Eighteenth Century New England* (New Haven, Conn.: Yale University Press, 1963), p. 154; David W. Robson, "College Founding in the New Republic, 1776–1800," *HEQ* 23 (1983): 323–341. Southern colleges continued to hold more closely to the gentlemanly ideal and traditional curriculum, even during the Revolutionary period. Robert P. Thomson, "Colleges in the Revolutionary South: The Shaping of a Tradition," *HEQ* 10 (1970): 399–412.

liberal arts can be cited, such as the 1779 curriculum reform at William and Mary, the ambitious 1784 plan for Columbia College, and the appointment of European university graduates to the faculty at Pennsylvania. Noteworthy attempts were made at Presbyterian schools and colleges such as Princeton, where Samuel S. Smith, first as an instructor, and after 1794, as president, tried to introduce more scientific and modern studies into the curriculum. Certain states chartered public universities—Georgia (1785), North Carolina (1789), Vermont (1791), South Carolina (1801), Ohio (1802)—often in the name of egalitarianism, a sentiment contributing to a general decline in academic standards over the same period.[64]

A kind of "cultural nationalism" has also been attributed to these decades, as Americans looked homeward to promote science and progress equal to that in Europe. This motivation intensified after the War of 1812, and some historians find American scientists after 1815 increasingly engaged in the pursuit of knowledge for its own sake. The 1820s have been called a time of "revolution" in scientific interest in colleges, and the 1830s, a promotional period for "free learning" in the lower schools, while the next two decades are regarded by some as the key period in the professionalization of American science and academe.[65] Evidence for the "liberalizing" influence of these phenomena on college curricula in the first half of the nineteenth century—as a rough and tentative proxy for the liberal-free ideal—can be solicited from many quarters.

R.F. Butts described fifteen examples in this regard, including prominently the revisions of the B.A. course made at Union College during the presidency of Eliphalet Nott from 1804 to 1866. Other "vigorous exponents of these liberalizing changes" were Thomas C. Brownell at Washington College, Philip Lindsley at the University

---

[64]Hangartner (1955), pp. 19, 33; Merle Bowman, "The False Dawn of the State University," *HEQ* 1 (June 1961): 6–22; Oscar Handlin and Mary F. Handlin, *The American College and American Culture: Socialization as a Function of Higher Education* (New York: McGraw-Hill, 1970), pp. 19–21; Sloan (1971a), chaps. 5, 7; Miller (1976), pp. 180–185.

[65]Elizabeth B. Cowley, *Free Learning* (Boston: Bruce Humphries, 1941), pp. 9–13; Brooke Hindle, *The Pursuit of Science in Revolutionary America, 1735–1789* (Chapel Hill: University of North Carolina Press, 1956), pp. 248–251, 382–386; George H. Daniels, *American Science in the Age of Jackson* (New York: Columbia University Press, 1968), p. 3; Daniels, "The Process of Professionalization in American Science: The Emergent Period, 1820–1860," in *Science in America since 1820*, ed. Nathan Reingold (New York: Science History Publications, 1976), pp. 63–75; Guralnick (1975), pp. viii, xi, chap. 2; Martin Finkelstein, "From Tutor to Specialized Scholar: Academic Professionalization in Eighteenth and Nineteenth Century America," *History of Higher Education Annual* 3 (1983): 106–115.

of Nashville, Amos Eaton at Rensselaer Polytechnic Institute, James Marsh at the University of Vermont, Jacob Abbott at Amherst College, and Thomas Jefferson, James Madison, and others on the 1818 commission planning the University of Virginia. Meanwhile, the naming of Benjamin Silliman as professor of chemistry at Yale stimulated colleges such as Rutgers to make similar appointments.[66] By 1835 several young faculty members had returned to Harvard from advanced study at German universities, where they had steeped themselves in the attitude of free inquiry prevalent during the early nineteenth century.[67] The future model for American higher education resided in those German institutions, and the proposals of these young academicians and the 1825 reform at Harvard were prophetic in their call for departmentalization of faculty, teaching by lectures, election of courses by students, instruction in modern languages, and sectioning of students by ability and progress. In fact, according to one study, such pedagogical changes were introduced throughout American colleges during the period between 1800 and 1870.[68]

These initiatives were augmented by the influence of German professors who came to teach in the United States, and in the second quarter of the nineteenth century, President Francis Wayland at Brown University argued strongly on behalf of introducing useful and scientific studies into the college curriculum. Meanwhile, Henry P. Tappan, chancellor of the University of Michigan from 1852 to 1863, tried to introduce the German university model of free research. Such efforts resulted in the tightening of academic standards through the introduction of written examinations and the refinement of grading systems and in the expansion of college en-

---

[66]Quotation is from George M. Dutcher, *An Historical and Critical Survey of the Curriculum of Wesleyan University and Related Subjects* (Middletown, Conn.: Wesleyan University Press, 1948), p. 8. Butts (1939), chaps. 6, 8; McCormick (1966), pp. 44–45; Roland G. Paulston, "The Report of the Rockfish Gap Commission: A Proposal for a New American Higher Learning," *PH* 8 (1968): 108–119; Rudolph (1977), pp. 62–63, 85–94.

[67]Turner (1974), p. 495; Carl Diehl, "Innocents Abroad: American Students in German Universities, 1810–1870," *HEQ* 16 (1976): 321–341; McClelland (1980), pts. 1, 2.

[68]Morison (1936), pp. 229–238; M. St. Mel Kennedy, "The Changing Academic Characteristics of the Nineteenth-Century American College Teacher [1800–1870]," *PH* 5 (1965): 360–371. On the question of whether Americans really understood and embraced the methods of the German university early in the nineteenth century, cf. Richard J. Storr, *The Beginnings of Graduate Education in America* (Chicago: University of Chicago Press, 1953), chaps. 3–5, with the reinterpretation of Diehl (1978), chaps. 3–5.

trance requirements to include geography, English grammar, and beginning algebra in the 1820s and 1830s and history and beginning geometry in the 1840s and 1850s. These developments led to the publication of new textbooks, such as *Common School Grammar: A New and Practical System of English Grammar*, which was dedicated

> To You, Fellow Citizens of the United States, of every rank and condition in life, who spurn not the idea of improvement; who do not discard truths, merely because newly discovered, for ancient errors, because *'Sanctioned by long established usage.'*[69]

This sentiment and the changes in educational practice were bolstered by the fact that, for most of the nineteenth century, the United States Congress was interested in college teaching only to the extent that it involved the sciences, especially those of immediate utility.

Notwithstanding these points, there are actually more persuasive counterarguments to the view that scientific subjects and curricular reform were substantially introduced into American colleges during the first half of the nineteenth century.[70] Outside of the educational institutions, scientific societies proliferated through the first half of the nineteenth century, and this activity culminated in

---

[69]Oliver B. Peirce, *Grammatical Instructor; or, Common School Grammar: A New and Practical System of English Grammar*, 3d ed. (Utica, N.Y.: William Williams, 1837), p. A1. See Broome (1903), pp. 40–46; Bronson (1914), pp. 204–316; Mary L. Smallwood, *An Historical Study of Examinations and Grading Systems in Early American Universities: A Critical Study of the Original Records of Harvard, William and Mary, Yale, Mount Holyoke, and Michigan from Their Founding to 1900* (Cambridge: Harvard University Press, 1935), pp. 15–18, 41–86; George N. Rainsford, *Congress and Higher Education in the Nineteenth Century* (Knoxville: University of Tennessee Press, 1972); Kelley (1974), pp. 167ff.

[70]Hofstadter and others have characterized this period as "the Great Retrogression" for American colleges due to "the pervasive national reaction against the Enlightenment" and to the founding of many new colleges by religious denominations after the second Awakening beyond the capacity of the country to support them. Richard Hofstadter and Walter P. Metzger, *The Development of Academic Freedom in the United States* (New York: Columbia University Press, 1955), pp. 209–222; Tewksbury (1932), pp. 62ff.; Miller (1976), pt. 3, chap. 10. Some have objected to this characterization of "retrogression," such as D. W. Moreo, "Higher Education in a New Nation: United States from 1800 to 1860," *PH* 11 (1971): 60–74. But Hofstadter reasoned qualitatively in terms of the advance of knowledge and production of leading scholars, while Moreo and others argue quantitatively that the increase in the number of colleges extended literacy, building the foundation for cultural development.

In an exhaustive study, Burke posits a much narrower definition of founding a college, concludes that a high ratio of the colleges succeeded, and consequently challenges Tewksbury's traditional interpretation of the high failure rate of colleges during the supposed "Great Retrogression." Moreover, Burke argues that since antebellum colleges had greater popular appeal than the traditional view gives them credit for and

the formation of the American Association for the Advancement of Science in 1848 and the National Academy of Sciences in 1862. Many scientific journals also appeared, anticipated by the founding, in 1818, of the *The American Journal of Science and Arts*. As in Europe, this activity suggests that learned societies, not the colleges, dominated the critical pursuit of knowledge.[71] Where educational institutions sought to incorporate some of this learning, the activity took place apart from the liberal arts faculties, that is, either in the medical schools or in the academies. These latter institutions were actually established to circumvent the unwillingness of grammar schools and colleges to change their curriculum, but even with this inspiration, the academies generally did not make innovations in the liberal arts. When applying the word "liberal" to education, they talked about "the liberal patronage of literature" or a school "provided for by the liberality of friends," and recommended that students "excell in studious industry, in refined manners, in an orderly and liberal subjection to [their] superiors."[72]

In the colleges, it was not long after the 1779 plan of William and Mary had been discredited and the 1784 plan for Columbia radically scaled down that the Princeton trustees eliminated the course of

---

since many of their graduates went on to secular and successful careers, then those colleges were not ideologically, pedagogically, or curricularly narrow, as the "traditional" historiography claims. This conclusion does not follow necessarily from the premises, the second of which the traditionalists did not deny anyway. Colin B. Burke, *American Collegiate Populations: A Test of the Traditional View* (New York: New York University Press, 1982).

[71]Bates (1965), chap. 2; Oleson (1976), pp. xx–xxiv; Greene (1976), pp. 1–20; Sally G. Kohlstedt, "Savants and Professionals: The American Association for the Advancement of Science, 1848–1860," in *The Pursuit of Knowledge in the Early American Republic: American Scientific and Learned Societies from Colonial Times to the Civil War*, ed. Alexandra Oleson and Sanborn C. Brown (Baltimore: Johns Hopkins University Press, 1976), pp. 299–325.

It has been argued that prominent American scientists from 1820 onward were members of college faculties, and this fact has been cited to demonstrate the responsiveness of colleges to science. Sloan (1971b), pp. 233; Daniels (1976), pp. 63–77. However, these professors usually belonged to the medical faculty, not the faculty of liberal arts. James H. Cassedy, "Medicine and the Learned Society in the United States, 1660–1850," in Oleson and Brown (1976), pp. 261–278. Moreover, a study of the associative nature of scientific societies demonstrates "the general line of differentiation between the educational institution and the learned societies," and indicates that the societies propagated themselves largely because of the reluctance of the colleges to take on scientific research and that "as the colleges developed a research capability, the society form of support gradually withdrew, to be taken over directly by the college." A. Hunter Dupree, "The National Pattern of American Learned Societies, 1769–1863," in Oleson and Brown (1976), pp. 28–29.

[72]Quotations are from Owen Biddle, *A Plan for a School on an Establishment Similar to That at Acksworth, in Yorkshire, Great-Britain, Varied to Suit the Circumstances of*

practical and scientific studies that President Smith had instituted near the turn of the century, even though graduates of that course had been granted merely a certificate and not the liberal arts degree. By 1812, Smith himself had been ousted because of his educational and theological eccentricities. Despite the Silliman-inspired appointment at Rutgers, the curriculum there was dominated by classical letters, with little room allowed for mathematics and metaphysics and only a modicum of natural philosophy. No different is the situation revealed by the statutes of Columbia, Brown, and Pennsylvania through 1830.[73] As for admission requirements, it should be noted that those in the classical subjects were raised along with, rather than being supplanted by, the additional requirements in mathematics, English, geometry, and history.

Regarding individual cases of reforming initiative, one must grant that Eliphalet Nott significantly affected both the range of studies available at Union College and the actual B.A. course, but other oft-cited reformers had a far less substantive influence on liberal education. At Vermont, James Marsh allowed for election of courses, yet students received the liberal arts degree only after completing the required classical letters. In Virginia, the report of the 1818 Commission was never actually instituted; and although students could choose their program of studies, by 1831 the University had adopted the conventional requirements for the liberal arts degree. Rensselaer never even claimed that its nontraditional subjects constituted a liberal education. When an attempt was made to incorporate nontraditional courses into liberal education, it is more often written of the reformer, as of Philip Lindsley at Nashville, that "his greatness did not lie in his achievements so much as it did in his dreams."[74] Similarly, Jacob Abbott's proposal to offer the B.A. course

the Youth within the Limits of the Yearly-meeting for Pennsylvania and New Jersey (Philadelphia: Joseph Crukshank, 1790), pp. 7, 12; David Tappan, Copy of an Address delivered to the Students of Phillips Academy in Andover (Exeter, N.H.: Stearns and Winslow, 1794), p. 7; Simeon Doggett, A Discourse on Education Delivered at the Dedication and Opening of Bristol Academy (Newbedford, Mass.: J. Spooner, 1797), p. 25. See E. W. Bagster-Collins, "History of Modern Language Teaching in the United States," in Studies in Modern Language Teaching (New York: Macmillan, 1930), p. 12; Middlekauf (1963), chap. 10; Theodore R. Sizer, ed., The Age of the Academies (New York: Bureau of Publications, Teachers College, Columbia University, 1964), pp. 2−7, 20, 28ff.

[73]Snow (1907), pp. 102−109, 122−123, 129−142; Wertenbaker (1946), chap. 5; Sloan (1971a), chaps. 4, 5; Miller (1976), pp. 280−284.

[74]Quotation is from Frederick Rudolph, The American College and University: A History (New York: Random House, 1962), p. 117. Rudolph (1977), pp. 63, 79−84; Russell Thomas, The Search for a Common Learning, 1800−1960 (New York: McGraw-Hill, 1962), pp. 11−15; Sloan (1971b), p. 234; Guralnick (1975), p. 28.

without classical languages was never realized at Amherst—founded in 1821 "for the Classical Education of indigent young men of piety and talent, for the Christian ministry." Even at Harvard—always somewhat outside the mainstream of American colleges from the time it launched Unitarianism early in the nineteenth century—the German model of free research, individual study, and pursuit of knowledge had relatively little effect on liberal education in this era. The 1825 reform at Harvard was an emaciated version of the reformers' ideal, and the faculty successfully resisted the skeletal core. Many in Cambridge concurred with the Yale *Reports* of 1828.[75]

These *Reports* consist of three essays written in response to proposals that Yale should change its curriculum and drop the classical languages. The first, by President Jeremiah Day, described and justified the existing curriculum; the second, by Classics Professor J.L. Kingsley, inquired into and defended the teaching of Greek and Latin letters; the third, by Connecticut Governor Gideon Tomlinson, adopted the preceding views on behalf of the Yale Corporation. The substance of the *Reports* differed little from statements issued by other colleges of the day. However, in 1828 Yale had perhaps the highest enrollment and largest number of living alumni spread over the widest geographical area of any college in the country. This influence, plus the fact that more college presidents appointed over the next few decades were graduated from Yale than any other place, made the *Reports* especially significant, and their fundamental message was that classical letters were the indispensable basis of "liberal education."[76]

Kingsley argued this first by appealing to common opinion, since if Yale granted the B.A. degree for completion of a course of modern subjects, "it would be to declare *that* to be a liberal education, which the world will not acknowledge to deserve the name."

---

[75]On Amherst, see Noah Porter, *The American Colleges and the American Public* (New Haven, Conn.: Charles Chatfield, 1870), pp. 9–10; Thomas H. LeDuc, *Piety and Intellect at Amherst College, 1865–1912* (New York: Columbia University Press, 1946), p. 2. On Harvard, see Morison (1936b), pp. 233–235; Daniel W. Howe, *The Unitarian Conscience: Harvard Moral Philosophy, 1805–1861* (Cambridge: Harvard University Press, 1970), chap. 1.

[76]Historians past and present have interpreted the influence of these *Reports* to be conservative. Zimmer (1938), pp. 34–35; George P. Schmidt, *The Liberal Arts College: A Chapter in American Cultural History* (New Brunswick, N.J.: Rutgers University Press, 1957), pp. 56–58; Willis Rudy, *The Evolving Liberal Arts Curriculum: A Historical Review of Basic Themes* (New York: Bureau of Publications, Teachers College, Columbia University, 1960), chap. 1; Melvin I. Urofsky, "Reforms and Response: The Yale Report of 1828," *HEQ* 5 (1965): 53–68; Kelley (1974), pp. 157–165;

Furthermore, not only would the world not recognize a degree in modern subjects as "liberal education", but "those who shall receive degrees in this way, will soon find, [the liberal education] is not what it is called." This would result because nothing else except the classics can provide (1) the appropriate development of "taste and fancy" for the liberal citizen and (2) the proper exercise of mental faculties. Therefore, even if Yale did change, it would make no difference. "A liberal education, whatever course the college should adopt, would without doubt continue to be, what it long has been."[77]

Those two rationales were repeated by Jeremiah Day. The first demonstrates the fundamental commitment to the oratorical tradition, as shown by Day's conviction that the classical letters mold gentlemen "of large and liberal views, of those solid and elegant attainments which will raise them to a higher distinction, than the mere possession of property."[78] The second rationale, however, provides evidence for an accommodation of the oratorical tradition in liberal education by introducing the popular nineteenth-century concept of mental discipline. This belief that learning in a certain subject trains faculties of the mind to learn in other areas is conveyed by Day's oft-quoted view that liberal education ought to contribute to "the *discipline* and *furniture* of the mind: expanding its powers and storing it with knowledge," a notion occurring no less prominently in the 1850s reports at Oxford and Cambridge than in those at Yale in 1828.[79]

The faculty psychology underlying this theory of mental disci-

---

Rudolph (1977), p. 279. Against this long-standing view have arisen counterinterpretations regarding the *Reports* as "comprehensive, open-minded and liberal" and "reasonably modern." Guralnick (1975), p. 30; Sloan (1971b), p. 246. I believe these reinterpretations overemphasize the apologetics included in the *Reports* (pp. 5, 44) because the *Reports* are conservative in two important respects. First, their conservatism appears not so much in the goals of liberal education that they do state, but in the ones they do not, such as the pursuit of knowledge. Secondly, while there is little conflict between the goals actually described by Day and Kingsley and some of those of the reformers of education, there is great disagreement over the studies recommended to achieve those ends. Ironically, revisionists who are working to assert the progressive tendencies of Yale in the late nineteenth century, when the college was still a conservative institution according to conventional historiography, assume the traditional view of the 1828 *Reports* in order to demonstrate the "progress" of Yale, contrary to the traditional interpretation of the later period. Louise L. Stevenson, "Between the Old-Time College and the Modern University: Noah Porter and the New Haven Scholars," *History of Higher Education Annual* 3 (1983): 39–57.

[77]*Reports* . . . *Yale* (1828), p. 41.
[78]*Reports* . . . *Yale* (1828), p. 29.
[79]*Reports* . . . *Yale* (1828), p. 7; Rothblatt (1976), pp. 130ff.

pline rested fundamentally on the Common Sense philosophy of Scotsman Thomas Reid, who had countered empiricist skepticism by arguing that one's mind at birth is not a *tabula rasa*. Rather, Reid felt it perfectly obvious that inherent structures of the mind must provide certain essential truths with which everyone agrees. "Such original and natural judgments are, therefore, a part of that furniture which Nature hath given to the human understanding. . . . They make up what is called *the common sense of mankind*; and, what is manifestly contrary to any of those first principles, is what we call *absurd*."[80] With this a priori belief in "furniture," Reid attempted to rebut Hume's absurd skepticism and Yale attempted to defend the classical liberal arts. Reid's reply supplied the basic epistemology of Yale's response to its liberal-free critics, who called for replacing the classics with modern subjects. Alarmed by the growing status of the new sciences, the proponents of the traditional liberal arts sought to preempt an encounter by annexing the battleground of intellect.

The rise of mental discipline theory, therefore, indicates that American advocates of teaching the humanist classics—long rationalized by means of characteristics of the *artes liberales* ideal—were beginning to accommodate their justification of the classics to the liberal-free ideal. On the one hand, this accommodation appeared in the emphasis placed on training the intellect rather than cultivating noble virtues, as the purpose for studying letters, a shift in purpose that occurred also in eighteenth-century England. On the other hand, this *artes liberales* accommodation can be seen in the defending of classical letters for their enhancement of "Freedom and Equality." Certainly, this approach had appeared much earlier in *Cato's Letters*, Richard Peters's *Sermon* on the Philadelphia Academy, and the essays of Samuel Knox and Samuel H. Smith. But the formulation was perhaps declared orthodox only with the pronouncement of Governor Tomlinson and the Yale Corporation that "the models of ancient literature, which are put into the hands of the young student, can hardly fail to imbue his mind with the principles of liberty"; and the failure "to appreciate justly the character of the ancients . . . these pristine exemplars of freedom" would result in having "the general standard of intellectual and moral worth lowered; and our civil and religious liberty jeoparded [sic], by ulti-

---

[80]Thomas Reid, "Inquiry into the Human Mind," in *The Works of Thomas Reid,* ed. William Hamilton (Edinburgh: MacLachlan and Stewart, 1858), chap. 7, sect. 4, p. 209. Paradoxically, Scottish empiricism offered a similar rationale for including empirical sciences in the curriculum, namely, that they provided verifiable certitude. Miller (1976), pp. 181–182.

mately disqualifying our citizens for the exercise of the right and privilege of self-government."[81]

The influence of the German universities contributed to the accommodation of the *artes liberales* to the liberal-free ideal, because those institutions had transformed their own classical scholarship, turning away from uncreative imitation of classical models toward historical and philological study of ancient texts, especially those from ancient Greece. This critical method effected a gradual metamorphosis of classical studies at English universities in the first half of the nineteenth century.[82] Thus, as the ancient philosophical tradition was being elevated, classical studies began to endorse the canons of specialized research, another way in which the *artes liberales* accommodation became manifest.

This evidence of transformation and discontinuity provides a harbinger of later developments. It does not offer proof of the establishment of experimental science in the liberal arts curriculum or the espousal of characteristics of the liberal-free ideal on behalf of institutionalized liberal education. And this situation changed very little until after the Civil War. As suggested earlier, this view of antebellum liberal education is easier to defend than if it were expanded to include all the academic activities and pursuits sponsored by the colleges. However, the judgment need not be confined to the narrower case. The modern subjects—experimental sciences, advanced mathematics, vernacular languages—were relatively inconsequential or even deprecated in antebellum colleges.[83] The old ways stood strong.

As in Europe during the Renaissance and the scientific revolution, new institutions were formed in antebellum America to address subjects not being taught in the colleges. Through the first half of the nineteenth century, scientific societies, academies, lyceums,

---

[81]*Reports . . . Yale* (1828), pp. 51–52; Rothblatt (1976), chap. 10. Number 71 of *Cato's Letters* (p. 189) stated:

This prodigious Progress of the *Romans* in [Greek] Learning had no other Cause than the Freedom and Equality of their Government. . . . Nothing is too hard for Liberty; that Liberty which made the *Greeks* and *Romans* Masters of the World, made them Masters of all the Learning in it: And, when their Liberties perished, so did their Learning. (Number 71, Saturday, March 31, 1722, "Polite Arts and Learning naturally produced in Free States and marred by such as are not free.")

Richard Peters quoted John 8:32, "And ye shall know the Truth and the truth shall make you free," and argued that "joining knowledge and liberty so closely together in the words of my text" testifies to the value of studying the classical "liberal arts and sciences" in order to promote freedom. Peters (1751), p. 1.

[82]Clarke (1959), chap. 8; Garland (1980), chaps. 1, 7. See chap. 5 n. 66 above.

[83]See Appendix 1.

and student literary societies flourished because they nurtured interests that found no outlet in the formal curriculum. At the same time, the reluctance of the colleges to enshrine new subjects and thinking is revealed by the general disaffection among the public. In some parts of the country, the number of students attending college stagnated or gradually decreased during the second quarter of the nineteenth century. Concurrently, state governments exhibited unwillingness to fund colleges, because of their neglect of practical, scientific subjects.[84]

Individual testimony also abounds. At Harvard, the most unorthodox college theologically if not educationally, complaints about the classical letters and recitations between 1825 and 1860 were virtually incessant. A future president of Columbia, F.A.P. Barnard, asserted in 1856 that the introduction of subjects like modern languages and sciences were "uncalled-for and unnecessary" because they could not discipline the intellect as well as could classical letters. Meanwhile, John Maclean, Jr., upon ascending to the presidency of Princeton, announced, "We shall not aim at innovation. . . . No chimerical experiments in education have ever had the least countenance here."[85] In the smaller institutions of the South and West, adherence to tradition is shown by the courses of study described for Randolph-Macon in 1842, Davidson in 1848, Mercer in 1850, and Oberlin in 1864. Meanwhile, the sixty or so Catholic colleges sought to maintain the *ratio studiorum*, claiming, at least in the Notre Dame catalog of 1863, to be satisfied if students learned merely "to converse and behave with the dignity and propriety of gentelmen [sic]."[86]

---

[84]Sizer (1964), pp. 1, 40–46; David F. Allmendinger, Jr., "New England Students and the Revolution in Higher Education, 1800–1900," *HEQ* 11 (1971): 381–389; James McLachlan, "The *Choice of Hercules*: American Student Societies in the Early 19th Century," in *The University in Society*, ed. Lawrence Stone (Princeton, N.J.: Princeton University Press, 1974), pp. 449–494; John S. Whitehead, *The Separation of College and State: Columbia, Dartmouth, Harvard, and Yale, 1776–1876* (New Haven, Conn.: Yale University Press, 1973), chap. 3; Leah G. Stambler, "The Lyceum Movement in American Education, 1826–1845," *PH* 21 (1981): 157–185. The traditional interpretation that student enrollments declined and that antebellum colleges were under attack or not held in high esteem is countered by David B. Potts, "Curriculum and Enrollments: Some Thoughts in Assessing the Popularity of Antebellum Colleges," *History of Higher Education Annual* 1 (1981): 88–109, and Burke (1982).

[85]Frederick A. Barnard, *Improvements Practicable in American Colleges* (Hartford, Conn.: Brownell, 1856), pp. 12ff.; John Maclean, *History of the College of New Jersey from Its Origins in 1746 to the Commencement of 1854.* (Philadelphia: J.B. Lippincott 1877), vol. 2, pp. 421, 427; Morison (1936b), p. 260.

[86]Sophia Jex Blake, *A Visit to Some American Schools and Colleges* (London: Macmillan, 1867), pp. 47–64; Richardson (1932), vol. 2, p. 234; Albea Godbold, *The Church*

The following year, in a sermon at the Dartmouth College commencement, S.C. Bartlett of the Chicago Theological Seminary remarked that the modern subjects—vernacular languages, natural sciences, and other innovations—were "too often pushed as substitutes for the means of liberal education." Course catalogs from the early 1850s at Dartmouth, one of the three largest colleges in the country at the time, indicate that its faculty substantially agreed with Bartlett.[87] Greek and Latin letters made up at least one-quarter of the curriculum, rhetoric and belles lettres in English another quarter. About one-quarter was devoted to history, moral philosophy, and divinity, and a final quarter to mathematics, physics, astronomy, and anatomy. The pedagogy consisted primarily of recitations, declamations, and disputations. The modicum of instruction in modern languages was relegated to the vacation term.

Such treatment of foreign languages is illustrative. When admitted to the curriculum of antebellum colleges, they were usually offered on an optional basis or in some way consigned to a secondary position. If incorporated as a fractional element in the B.A. course, the grading system was skewed so as to give this fraction less than proportional weight relative to the traditional subjects. When modern languages replaced classical languages in a course of study, the program was regarded as inferior, and the liberal arts degree was not conferred upon its graduates. Even professors of modern language, such as H.I. Schmidt at Pennsylvania in the 1840s, defended the "ancient classical languages" as the "indispensable" base of the curriculum.[88]

Similar strictures were applied to sciences entering antebellum

---

College of the Old South (Durham, N.C.: Duke University Press, 1944), p. 81, app. 1; Philip Gleason, "American Catholic Higher Education: A Historical Perspective," in The Shape of Catholic Higher Education, ed. Robert Hassenger (Chicago: University of Chicago Press, 1967), pp. 33–35. Notre Dame catalog quoted in Handlin and Handlin (1970), p. 24.

[87]Samuel C. Bartlett, Duties of Educated Men (Boston: Marvin, 1865), pp. 10–12; Catalogue of the Officers and Students of Dartmouth College for the Academical Year (1852–53) (Hanover, N.H.: Dartmouth College, 1852), pp. xxv–xxvii; Catalogue of the Officers and Students of Dartmouth College for the Academical Year (1854–55) (Hanover, N.H.: Dartmouth College, 1854), pp. xxvii–xxx. Bartlett became president of Dartmouth in 1877 and was brought to "trial" by the college community in 1881, partly due to the attitude expressed in this commencement address. This development at Dartmouth from the early 1850s to 1881, which is perfectly consonant with the traditional interpretation of the history of American colleges (even though the author wishes to distinguish herself from the traditional view), is ably told by Marilyn Tobias, Old Dartmouth on Trial: The Transformation of the Academic Community in Nineteenth-Century America (New York: New York University Press, 1982).

[88]Henry I. Schmidt, Education (New York: Harper and Brothers, 1842), pp. 249–250; Bagster-Collins (1930), pp. 49–62; Smallwood (1935), chap. 5.

liberal education. When scientific subjects were introduced into the B.A. program, the grading system was skewed against them. When they constituted any significant fraction of a program in which the classics were sacrificed, the graduates did not receive the liberal arts degree and their education was regarded as inferior. This had been the case at Rensselaer and Hobart in 1824 and Wesleyan in 1838. It continued when scientific degree courses were introduced at Brown and Harvard in 1851, at Yale and Dartmouth in 1852, at Michigan in 1853, and at Rochester in 1854.[89] Colleges were beginning to offer students some opportunity to enter a laboratory, but only in programs deemed less prestigious and less rigorous than their properly liberal counterpart.

If modern languages and science were thus scarcely accepted or respected in liberal education, by the Civil War these liberal-free subjects were at least teetering on the edge; and the existence of the accommodated *artes liberales* argument testifies to their proximity. One group pushing for acceptance were those advocating utility and technology. Proponents of the land-grant movement, for example, saw the traditional curriculum as their nemesis, and the passage of the Morrill Land Grant Act in 1862 testified to their influence.[90] Another stimulus for accommodating the *artes liberales* ideal and promoting the liberal-free ideal was the publication of *On the Origin of Species by Means of Natural Selection* by Charles Darwin in 1859. Indeed, during the previous year, the Reverend Thomas Hill had argued before the Phi Beta Kappa Society at Harvard for parity between the study of classical letters and sciences in order to convey "culture . . . liberal and broad for any people of any age," a liberal education nevertheless congenial with "the highest Christian theology and Christian morality."[91]

---

[89]In mathematics at Dartmouth, the four-year, liberal arts students completed plane geometry in their first year and went on to calculus in their second. The students in the three-year course of the "scientific school" finished plane geometry at the end of their second year and never went further. *Catalogue . . . (1854–55),* pp. xxvii–xxxix. See Blake (1867), pp. 50–54, 144–151; Broome (1903), p. 77; Milton H. Turk, " 'Without Classical Studies': The Hobart 'English Course' of 1824," *JHE* 4 (1933): 339–346; Smallwood (1935), chap. 5; Dutcher (1948), pp. 12–15; Rudolph (1962), chap. 11.

[90]Edward D. Eddy, Jr., *Colleges for Our Land and Time: The Land-Grant Idea in American Education* (New York: Harper and Brothers, 1957), chap. 1; Thomas (1962), chap. 2.

[91]Hill would serve as President of Harvard from 1862 to 1868. Thomas Hill, *Liberal Education: An Address Delivered before the Phi Beta Kappa Society of Harvard College* (Cambridge, Mass.: John Bartlett, 1858), pp. 20–21; G. Brown Goode, "The Origin of the National Scientific and Educational Institutions of the United States," *Papers of the American Historical Association,* 4, pt. 2 (New York: G. P. Putnam's Sons, 1890), pp. 151–153.

VI

Confrontation in America of the Oratorical and Philosophical Traditions

*A*S NEARLY AS I CAN DETERMINE, *the liberal arts were originally not arts at all as we understand the term; neither in the present sense of the word were they liberal. . . . [T]hey were liberal in that they constituted the education of the free man or gentleman in contrast to the vulgar craftsmanship developed by the slave. . . . We have come instead to emphasize another quality not originally intended but always easy to read into this word "liberal." The liberal arts, we say, are the liberalizing arts, the studies that liberate the mind and send it questing on strange and alluring adventures.*

ALFRED H. UPHAM*

*"The Liberal Arts" (1930).

IN A 1944 FORUM in *The American Scholar*, John Dewey noted, "Nothing is more striking in recent discussions of liberal education than the widespread and seemingly spontaneous use of *liberating* as a synonym for *liberal*"[1]—an observation depicting in cameo the general nature of the change in the definition of liberal education that occurred between the Civil War and World War II. Much earlier, of course, the founders of the Republic had argued that the cultivation of liberty and freedom was dependent on the proper education of the citizenry and leaders of society. And in the first half of the nineteenth century, proposals incorporating characteristics of the liberal-free ideal had been made for American higher education. But these did not lay any widespread claim to be called "liberal education." It was only after the Civil War that connotations of "liberating" and "freeing" gained widespread currency, as seen in Charles W. Eliot's promotion of "Liberty in Education" through the elective system at Harvard and James McCosh's strident objection from Princeton, "O Liberty! What crimes and cruelties have been perpetrated in thy name!"[2] Then, blown by the winds of pragmatism and progressivism through and beyond World War I, the liberating connotations of "liberal" education spread far and wide.

A few examples of the phenomenon may be read in a study comparing twenty-seven statements made on "liberal education" or "liberal culture" between 1842 and 1876 with forty such statements made between 1909 and 1920. The latter group was found to be moving toward the meaning "that the mind is 'deepened and broadened' until it is 'liberalized.' " Similarly, Louis Snow's 1907 history of the liberal arts held that "the *liberalizing* and *equalizing* of studies in the curriculum since 1870 is too well known to require extended comment." In 1926, Hansen applauded the advance of "liberation" in education in *Liberalism and American Education in the*

---

[1] John Dewey, "The Problem of the Liberal Arts College," *The American Scholar* 13 (1944a): 391.

[2] Charles W. Eliot, "Liberty in Education," in *Educational Reform: Essays and Addresses* (New York: Century, 1898), pp. 124–148; James McCosh, *The New Departure in College Education, Being a Reply to President Eliot's Defense of It in New York* (New York: Charles Scribner's Sons, 1885), p. 5. In the following discussion, I draw from Laurence R. Veysey, *The Emergence of the American University* (Chicago: University of Chicago Press, 1965), chaps. 2, 3; Hugh Hawkins, *Between Harvard and America: The Educational Leadership of Charles W. Eliot* (New York: Oxford University Press, 1972), chaps. 2, 3, 9; Hawkins, "University Identity: The Teaching and Research Functions," in *The Organization of Knowledge in Modern America, 1860–1920*, ed. Alexandra Oleson and John Voss (Baltimore: Johns Hopkins University Press, 1979), pp. 285–312.

Eighteenth Century, and in 1931, a Teachers College research study asked accusingly "whether the spirit of the institutional life in the liberal-arts college is fundamentally liberalized or liberalizing."[3] The following year, the president of Rollins College wrote on "Liberalizing a Liberal Education" in the *Yearbook of the National Society for the Study of Education* (NSSE), and Harvard President Conant held forth in similar terms later in the 1930s, a decade, according to Jacques Barzun, when "ten thousand Commencement speakers annually explained that the liberal arts were the liberating arts." By the time of Dewey's statement in 1944, the *Journal of Higher Education* was editorializing presumptively, "Does Liberal Education Liberalize?"[4]

Such educators were by and large not among those promoting the classical letters. But even this latter group, which included figures such as Irving Babbitt and Robert Hutchins, was not immune to the widespread tendency to talk about liberal education as "freeing," "liberating," or "liberalizing." These advocates of reading classical texts, however, extolled the freedom in liberal education that "begins with discipline and leads to self-discipline"—as was maintained by the president of the University of Louisville in 1939 and the president of Southwestern at Memphis in 1941. The common usage of language extolling the importance of freedom, liberty, and liberation, therefore, did not imply a growing consensus, but increasing ambiguity. By 1945, both "liberals" and "conservatives" were employing this language about liberal education, and the Eighth American Scientific Congress was admonished, "There must be some confusion here, if only in the use of our terms."[5]

---

[3]Louis F. Snow, *The College Curriculum in the United States* (New York: Bureau of Publications, Teachers College, Columbia University, 1907), p. 173; Leonard V. Koos and C. C. Crawford, "College Aims, Past and Present," *School and Society* 14, no. 362 (1921): 499–509; Allen O. Hansen, *Liberalism and American Education in the Eighteenth Century* (New York: Macmillan, 1926), pp. 61, 153; Margaret Kiely, *Comparisons of Students of Teachers Colleges and Students of Liberal-Arts Colleges* (New York: Bureau of Publications, Teachers College, Columbia University, 1931), p. 146.

[4]Hamilton Holt, "Liberalizing a Liberal Education," in *Changes and Experiments in Liberal-Arts Education: The Thirty-first Yearbook of the National Society for the Study of Education, Part II*, ed. Guy M. Whipple (Bloomington, Ill.: Public School Publishing, 1932), pp. 221–228; James B. Conant, "The American College," *AACB* 23 (1937): 44; R. H. Eckelberry, "Does Liberal Education Liberalize?" *JHE* 15 (1944): 224–225; Jacques Barzun, "Humanities, Pieties, Practicalities, Universities," *SR* 1 (November 14, 1973): 8.

[5]Henry W. Holmes, "What is a Liberal Education?" *Proceedings: Eighth American Scientific Congress Held in Washington May 10–18, 1940* (Washington, D.C.: U.S. De-

That confusion extended also to etymology, an issue raised in 1930 by the president of Miami University who objected to the liberal-free connotations accreting to "liberal" education:

> As nearly as I can determine, the liberal arts were originally not arts at all as we understand the term; neither in the present sense of the word were they liberal. . . . [T]hey were liberal in that they constituted the education of the free man or gentleman in contrast to the vulgar craftsmanship developed by the slave. . . . We have come instead to emphasize another quality not originally intended but always easy to read into this word "liberal." The liberal arts, we say, are the liberalizing arts, the studies that liberate the mind and send it questing on strange and alluring adventures.[6]

Others who also held generally to the oratorical tradition, such as Charles Diehl or Irving Babbitt's disciple, Norman Foerster, offered the same view of the root meaning of "liberal": education for "free men." In contrast, those espousing characteristics of the liberal-free ideal, such as Paul Schilpp or Thomas Briggs, "attempted to define liberal education . . . by the root meaning of *liberal*: education is to free an individual from something or for something."[7] Such skirmishes over etymological interpretations anticipated the larger battle over the prestige that had accrued to the term "liberal education" through history. As the Director of Education Programs for the National Youth Administration grumbled in 1940, "Does not everyone desire to share in liberal education? Does anyone venture to render an adverse judgment against anything that is liberal? With the verbal advantage that comes from the description of the traditional curriculum as made up of liberal subjects, the traditionalists lay claim to all the territory."[8]

---

partment of State, 1945), vol. 12, p. 147; R. A. Kent, "The College in a Democracy: Safeguarding the American College Against Regimentation and Indoctrination," *JHE* 10 (1939): 417–420; Charles E. Diehl, "Postwar Liberal Arts Education," *AACB* 29 (1943): 196–201.

[6]Alfred H. Upham, "The Liberal Arts," *AACB* 16 (1930): 332–333.

[7]Paul A. Schilpp, "An 'Apology' for Philosophy: The Place of Philosophy in the Liberal-Arts Curriculum," *JHE* 6 (1935): 233; Norman Foerster, *The Future of the Liberal College* (New York: Appleton-Century, 1938), chap. 1; Foerster, "United States," in *The Meaning of Liberal Education in the Twentieth Century: Yearbook of the International Institute of Teachers College,* ed. Isaac L. Kandel (New York: Bureau of Publications, Teachers College, Columbia University, 1939), p. 337; Thomas H. Briggs, "United States," in Kandel (1939), p. 317; Diehl (1943), pp. 196–201.

[8]Charles H. Judd, "The Organization of a Program of General Education in Secondary Schools and Colleges," *AACB* 26 (1940): 303.

These developments between 1860 and 1945 make it tempting to treat the liberal-free ideal as an outrigger of the larger political and social movement of "liberalism": as liberalism challenged "conservative" influences in society, so did the liberal-free ideal confront the *artes liberales* ideal in education. However, the relations between the artifical construct that I have called the liberal-free ideal and the phenomenon of liberalism are so equivocal and indirect that such an analogy is rather misleading.[9] Accordingly, having noted the increasing use of language about "freedom," "liberation," and "liberalism" in conjunction with "liberal education" and the resulting ambiguity that culminated in the 1930s and 1940s, let us return to events following upon the close of the Civil War.

Currently, to talk about the 1860s and 1870s as the beginning of the "Age of the University" or the "Dawning of a New Era" is to invite criticism for denigrating the antebellum colleges or, more generally, for relying on the dated and simplistic generalizations of traditional historiography. Nevertheless, however much one muddies the waters, the course of the stream remains clear. Profound changes did take place in American higher education over the last half of the nineteenth century. Obviously, the transformation can be exaggerated, and some will hurry to qualify Edward Shils's recent statement, "The establishment of Johns Hopkins was perhaps the single, most decisive event in the history of learning in the Western hemisphere."[10] But even setting aside the examples of Yale, which granted the first earned, American Ph.D. in 1861; or Cornell, founded as a nonsectarian university under A. D. White in 1868; or Harvard, which inaugurated C. W. Eliot as its president and so a commitment to the elective system in 1869; or Michigan, newly dedicated to graduate research under J. B. Angell in 1871; it is true that Shils may have overstated the case. Not only did some American universities antedate the founding of Johns Hopkins under D. C. Gilman in 1876, but others were begun soon afterward: Clark under G. S. Hall in 1889, Catholic under Bishop J. J. Keane in 1889, Stanford under D. S. Jordan in 1891, and Chicago under W. R. Harper in 1892.

Important stimuli for the development of universities in the United States existed in Germany. Visiting American graduate students and professors returned from German universities enamored of the specialized scholarship, the commitment to speculative research, and, above all, the atmosphere of freedom they had seen in

---

[9]See Appendix 2.

their host institutions. Particularly the latter aspect—*Lehrfreiheit* (freedom to teach what one wishes) and *Lernfreiheit* (freedom to study what one wishes)—impressed the Americans. It was seen "to follow from the searching function, from the presumption that knowledge was not fixed or final," a presumption underlying all aspects of the idealized German university that the Americans took to be "dedicated to a search to widen the bounds of knowledge rather than merely to preserve the store of knowledge undiminished."[11] Naturally, it took time before Yankee institutions could even begin to approach that research ideal; and it has been argued that early university leaders, such as C. W. Eliot, did not appreciate or encourage research and original scholarship, though they did argue for a questioning attitude in education. Over time, however, the growth of scientific disciplines, emergence of specializations, and establishment of well-defined and fortified academic departments to defend the specializations became a pattern in the United States, following that in Germany.[12]

Research, G. S. Hall once said, is "the very highest vocation of man," and although Clark University was particularly devoted to that calling, every university acknowledged its appeal and adopted its methods. Instruction through lectures, seminars, and laboratory practice—the innovations of the German universities—gradually displaced the recitation, and undergraduates began to utilize the library far more than the two or three hours per week commonly permitted theretofore. Concurrently, amateurs yielded the vocation of research to professionals teaching and studying in the universi-

---

[10]Edward Shils, "The Order of Learning in the United States: The Ascendancy of the University," in Oleson and Voss (1979), p. 28. Cf. Frederick Rudolph, *The American College and University: A History* (New York: Random House, 1962), chap. 11; James Axtell, "The Death of the Liberal Arts College," *HEQ* 11 (1971): 339–352.

[11]Quotations are from Paul Farmer, "Nineteenth-Century Ideas of the University: Continental Europe," in *The Modern University*, ed. Margaret Clapp (Ithaca, N.Y.: Cornell University Press, 1950), p. 15; Richard Hofstadter and Walter P. Metzger, *The Development of Academic Freedom in the United States* (New York: Columbia University Press, 1955), pp. 386–387. See George E. Peterson, *The New England College in the Age of the University* (Amherst, Mass.: Amherst College Press, 1964), chap. 1; Jurgen Herbst, *The German Historical School in American Scholarship: A Study in the Transfer of Culture* (Ithaca, N.Y.: Cornell University Press, 1965), chaps. 1, 2. Others have recently challenged the extent of German influence in this regard. Carl Diehl, "Innocents Abroad: American Students in German Universities, 1810–1870," *HEQ* 16 (1976): 321–341; Diehl, *Americans and German Scholarship, 1770–1870* (New Haven, Conn.: Yale University Press, 1978), chaps. 4–6; Charles E. McClelland, *State, Society, and University in Germany, 1700–1914* (Cambridge: Cambridge University Press, 1980), pp. 151–189.

[12]Joseph Ben-David, "The Universities and the Growth of Science in Germany and the United States," *Minerva* 7 (1968): 1–35; Shils (1979), pp. 19–47. For distinc-

ties.[13] These changes were encouraged by the Yankee ethic of utility, inasmuch as the research ideal promised greater material return for study than did the imitation of tradition. Yet even greater inspiration came from commitment to "science," a word whose use markedly increased in every field of scholarship over the last half of the nineteenth century. As a result, the meaning of "science" vacillated sharply, usually signifying either a predominantly deductive enterprise or one based on induction from empirical data and, hence, supposedly free of a priori assumptions. The late nineteenth-century search for "a science of education" demonstrates these trends exactly.[14]

The pursuit of scientific research also prompted a devotion to specialization outstripping even that of the German universities. Becoming the key characteristic of American scientific societies between 1866 and 1918, specialization inspired the development of the undergraduate "major" and "minor," in line with the departmentalization of graduate faculties according to fields of specialized scholarship. Yale had had eight departments in 1840, the college at Michigan five, and Illinois five. By 1905, the number of their departments were twenty-two, thirty-two, and twelve, respectively. Meanwhile, as early as 1880, Columbia's School of Political Science initiated the emergence of "super-departments," or schools, within the universities. Out of these specialized departments marched increasing numbers of Ph.D.'s. Before 1870, the total number of nonmedical doctorates granted in the United States amounted to 16. In 1880 alone, 54 were awarded; in 1890, 149; in 1900, 382.[15]

While all these developments in academic values, methodol-

tions between the American and German pattern, see Fritz K. Ringer, "The German Academic Community," in Oleson and Voss (1979), pp. 409–429; and the comparative essays in Konrad H. Jarausch, ed., *The Transformation of Higher Learning, 1860–1930: Expansion, Diversification, Social Opening, and Professionalization in England, Germany, Russia, and the United States* (Chicago: University of Chicago Press, 1983).

[13]G. Stanley Hall, *Life and Confessions of a Psychologist* (New York: D. Appleton, 1923), p. 338; Elliot R. Downing, "Methods in Science Teaching: Summary of Investigations of the Demonstration Method versus the Laboratory Method," *JHE* 2 (1931): 316–319; Herbst (1965), pp. 34ff.; Arthur T. Hamlin, *The University Library in the United States, Its Origins and Development* (Philadelphia: University of Pennsylvania Press, 1981), chaps. 2, 3, 9.

[14]J. P. Powell, "Some Nineteenth-Century Views on the University Curriculum," *HEQ* 5 (1965): 102–105; Paul Buck, ed., "Introduction," in *Social Sciences at Harvard, 1860–1920: From Inculcation to the Open Mind* (Cambridge: Harvard University Press, 1965), pp. 1–17; James R. Robarts, "The Quest for a Science of Education in the Nineteenth Century," *HEQ* 8 (1968): 431–446.

[15]George P. Schmidt, *The Liberal Arts College: A Chapter in American Cultural History* (New Brunswick, N.J.: Rutgers University Press, 1957), pp. 288–289; Earl J.

ogy, and organization—changes that had scarcely been seen since the medieval *studia*—were constitutive for the university on both sides of the Atlantic, they were highly perplexing for the American liberal arts college. As wrote one scholar, who came from study in Germany to teach at Amherst College only to be forced out after introducing the foreign teaching methods, "I confess that I am unable to divine what is to be ultimately the position of the Colleges which cannot become Universities and which will not be Gymnasia. I cannot see what reason they will have to exist."[16] Here was a question of institutional structure that the colleges had to address in order to respond to the changes in American higher education. Traditionalists, such as Noah Porter at Yale, tended to equate the German gymnasium and American college in order to exclude the new pedagogy and curricula from undergraduate education. But the gymnasium approach could also be used, as at Clark and Johns Hopkins, to demote the college to secondary education. Thus, it was unattractive to independent colleges not associated with a university.

Harvard eventually went the opposite direction and absorbed the college into the graduate faculty, while Stanford and Chicago tried splitting the college into two years of gymnasium and two years of university education. Meanwhile, the four-year colleges held to a conception of themselves as preserves of "liberal education" and thus distinct from either secondary or graduate training. The research advocates, from D. C. Gilman at Johns Hopkins to A. F. West at Princeton, did not dispute that this had been their traditional role. However, many of the university builders, such as W. R. Harper at Chicago, warned that this conception of a four-year, independent undergraduate education would gradually be superseded and expire. Thus, the debate over institutional structure inevitably concerned the colleges' view of the relationship between free research and liberal education.

McGrath, *The Graduate School and the Decline of Liberal Education* (New York: Bureau of Publications, Teachers College, Columbia University, 1959), p. 10; Philip W. Payton, "Origins of the Terms 'Major' and 'Minor' in American Higher Education," *HEQ* 1 (June 1961): 57–62; Ralph S. Bates, *Scientific Societies in the United States*, 3d ed. (Cambridge: MIT Press, 1965), chap. 3; John Higham, "The Matrix of Specialization," in Oleson and Voss (1979), pp. 3–8.

[16]Quoted in Herbst (1965), pp. 49–50; Thomas H. LeDuc, *Piety and Intellect at Amherst College, 1865–1912* (New York: Columbia University Press, 1946), p. 15. For the following discussion about the four-year college, see Noah Porter, *The American Colleges and the American Public* (New Haven, Conn.: Charles Chatfield, 1870), chaps. 1, 15; Daniel C. Gilman, "Is It Worth While to Uphold Any Longer the Idea of Liberal Education?" *Educational Review* 3 (1892): 109; William R. Harper, *The Prospects of the Small College* (Chicago: University of Chicago Press, 1900); Andrew F. West, *Short*

In *De oratore*, Cicero remarked that the great orator avoids the narrow specialization that follows inevitably upon speculative philosophy, and English education for Renaissance gentlemen, as Ruth Kelso notes, emphasized "breadth but not depth," in line with the humanist tradition. It was natural, therefore, that in the American liberal arts college the oratorical tradition of civic and polite learning militated against the specialized research of the university, as also, and no less importantly, did the commitment to piety. In particular, New England sectarian colleges, such as Amherst, along with their large, mid-western progeny, fought the tendency to place academic research ahead of religious faith. But neither of these commitments alone nor the combination of the two in the ideal of the Christian gentleman could long withstand the pressures of urbanization and industrialization, the decline of evangelism, the advance of Darwinism, and the general success of the university model. By 1900, even the small Christian colleges began to devote themselves to the transmission of specialized learning.[17]

Somewhat typical was Dartmouth, where the arrival of W. J. Tucker as president in 1893 inaugurated an upgrading and expansion of the faculty and curriculum, with the greatest number of additions coming in physics, chemistry, biology, economics, and German.[18] Similarly, a study of course catalogs of eleven liberal arts colleges between 1883 and 1933 indicates that the proportion of faculty members holding the Ph.D. rose from 17 to 49 percent, while there was a significant decline in the number of teachers in classical languages, mathematics, and astronomy, a group of subjects perhaps more than coincidentally analogous to the *septem artes liberales*. Other national studies of colleges and universities by the

---

Papers on Liberal Education (New York: Charles Scribner's Sons, 1907), pp. 65, 90ff.; Jurgen Herbst, "Liberal Education and the Graduate Schools: An Historical View of College Reform," *HEQ* 2 (1962): 244–258. Recently, it has been argued that McCosh of Princeton and Porter of Yale were both moderates and tried to reconcile "the Old-time College and the Modern University." J. David Hoeveler, Jr., *James McCosh and the Scottish Intellectual Tradition: From Glasgow to Princeton* (Princeton, N.J.: Princeton University Press, 1981), chap. 7; Louise L. Stevenson, "Between the Old-Time College and the Modern University: Noah Porter and the New Haven Scholars," *History of Higher Education Annual* 3 (1983): 39–57.

[17]Cicero, *De oratore* 3. 132–140; Ruth Kelso, *The Doctrine of the English Gentleman in the Sixteenth Century* (Urbana: University of Illinois Press, 1929), pp. 125–127; LeDuc (1946), chaps. 2–3; McGrath (1959), pt. 1; Peterson (1964).

[18]Robert F. Leavens and Arthur H. Lord, *Dr. Tucker's Dartmouth* (Hanover, N.H.: Dartmouth College, 1965), chaps. 3–4, pp. 152–156; Marilyn Tobias, *Old Dartmouth on Trial: The Transformation of the Academic Community in Nineteenth-Century America* (New York: New York University Press, 1982), pp. 127–143.

Modern Language Association reveal a steady decline in classical language requirements for the bachelor's degree between 1884 and 1906. Conversely, there was an increase in modern language requirements.[19]

This increase is all the more significant because it contravened the simultaneous movement of undergraduate programs away from prescription and toward election of courses. Over the last half of the nineteenth century, more and more freedom to choose courses was granted to undergraduates, whose average age at graduation rose to twenty-two years. The justification for this expanding freedom, beyond the increased maturity of the students, lay in the implicit equality of subjects posited by the university builders, who welcomed all subjects of study—an outlook typified by Ezra Cornell's famous statement, "I would found an institution in which any person can find instruction in any study." Harvard President C. W. Eliot in particular combined this equality of studies with the doctrine of mental discipline, so popular throughout the nineteenth century, and with a psychology admitting profound differences among individuals. He consequently inferred that (1) practically any study could discipline the mind and (2) individuals ought to be free to choose the subjects most congenial to their own psyches for this discipline.

Prominent critics of this "System of Freedom" included the presidents of Yale and Princeton, who argued for the special virtues of the classics and for limits, standards, and values. Others rose to counterattack, such as C. F. Adams, Jr. in 1883. But it was Eliot at Harvard who came to be perceived as the chief spokesman for student election of courses. He answered the opposition in the same way that John Locke had argued that a person should be allowed to choose among religions: "Free choice implies that there are no studies which are recognized as of supreme merit. . . . [T]he accumulated wisdom of the race cannot prescribe with certainty the studies which will best develop the human mind in general between the ages of eighteen and twenty-two." As suggested there, Eliot even-

---

[19]E. W. Bagster-Collins, "History of Modern Language Teaching in the United States," in *Studies in Modern Language Teaching* (New York: Macmillan, 1930), pp. 68–72; Merle Kuder, *Trends of Professional Opportunities in the Liberal Arts Colleges* (New York: Bureau of Publications, Teachers College, Columbia University, 1937), pp. 124–126, 129. The 1921 *Report of the Commission on the College Curriculum* of the Association of American Colleges found that especially during World War I, the election of "modern" subjects increased, while "Greek, Latin, mathematics, and astronomy decline"—again, perhaps a more-than-coincidental analogue to the *septem artes liberales*. F. C. Ferry, "Tables of Student Hours of Instruction of 18 Colleges and Universities for the College Years 1911–12, 1915–16, and 1919–20," *AACB* 8 (1922): 18–26.

tually translated "mental discipline" into a kind of intellectual stimulation and so encouraged wholly liberal-free interpretations of his
position by later progressivist historians. Whether or not he actually went that far, it may be said that from 1867, when a Harvard
committee held it to be characteristic of a university, until the re-
trenchment early in the twentieth century, the elective system accompanied the growth of free research.[20]

If one now steps back to survey the general trend toward "liberating" language, university building, pursuit of truth through scientific research, and free choice of courses by individual students,
it is clear that characteristics of the liberal-free ideal can be abstracted from the discussion about liberal education. This is not to
say that the situation was uniform or unambiguous. But speaking
in general, one can discern liberal-free characteristics wound into
Tappan's 1852 inaugural discourse; White's letter of 1862 calling for
"a true liberal university" accessible to women and blacks; the motto
of Johns Hopkins, *Veritas vos Liberabit*; and Eliot's definition that
"Liberal studies . . . are those 'which are pursued in the scientific
spirit for truth's sake.' " The ideal of speculative research, however
much qualified in one institution or another, promoted "the liberation of intellect for its own sake," in Veysey's words, and undermined "the classical notion of a liberal education . . . in which truth
was looked upon as uniform, fixed, and eternal," according to
Butts.[21] These opinions are verified by the breakdown of the required senior-year course in moral philosophy traditionally taught
by the president of the nineteenth-century college, a course that was

---

[20]Eliot (1898), pp. 140–141; Charles F. Adams, Jr., *A College Fetich: An Address
Delivered before the Harvard Chapter of the Phi Beta Kappa Society, June 28, 1883* (Boston: Lee and Shepard, 1883). For views of the presidents, see Porter (1870), pp. 39–91;
McCosh (1885). For the tenor of later debate, see Gilman (1892), p. 106; West (1907),
pp. 112–113. The Harvard elective system grew to be anomalous in that seniors were
freed from all requirements in 1872, partial election for freshmen was introduced in
1884, and in 1899 nearly all courses were made elective. Because no one else followed
it precisely, this system has rather disingenuously been called "the least significant"
in the country. W. H. Cowley, "College and University Teaching, 1858–1958," *Educational Record* 39 (1958): 314–316. Most colleges adhered to a "group elective system"
in which student chose courses from selected groups within which there was a prescribed regimen. George W. Pierson, "American Universities in the Nineteenth Century: The Formative Period," in Clap (1950), pp. 85–87.

[21]Robert F. Butts, *The College Charts Its Course: Historical Conceptions and Current
Proposals* (New York: McGraw-Hill, 1939), p. 163; Veysey (1965), p. 142. Other refer-
ences are drawn from Henry P. Tappan, *A Discourse Delivered by Henry P. Tappan,
D.D., at Ann Arbor, Mich., on the Occasion of his Inauguration as Chancellor of the Uni-
versity of Michigan, December 21st, 1852* (Detroit: Advertiser Power Presses, 1852); Hugh
Hawkins "The University-Builders Observe the Colleges," *HEQ* 11 (1971): 353–354;

founded upon the commitments to a unified, prescribed curriculum, to absolute virtues and conventions learned from canonical texts, and to preparation of the student for citizenship. Beginning in the 1880s, due to the "scientific" emphasis on value-free research and to the advance of pragmatism in ethical theory, the senior-year course eroded away.[22]

The rise of pragmatism, with its epistemological antagonism toward absolutes, was integrally related to the development of Darwinism and progressivism in the United States, all of which encouraged educators to incorporate characteristics of the liberal-free ideal into theories of education. Somewhat paradoxically, however, the influence of Darwinism initially ran counter to this trend. This was due, on the one hand, to the initial belief that by clearing the mind of a priori assumptions and making inductions from an enormous pile of empirical data, as Darwin had seemed to do, one could achieve certainty. Only toward the end of the nineteenth century was that belief undermined by the multitude of different answers proffered by the social scientists who employed the inductive method. On the other hand, the very tenets of evolutionary theory were dogmatized in the "Social Darwinism" or "Conservative Darwinism" of Herbert Spencer and William Graham Sumner, who justified the status quo by employing the metaphors "struggle for existence" and "survival of the fittest." Not until the 1890s was the social interpretation of Darwinism transformed by those who argued for a psychology and philosophy of "evolutionary meliorism" in the belief that there is freedom to change the environment, that the individual can effect this change that the possibility is "equalitarian," and that evolution itself is "progressive" and changing rather than an absolute law.[23]

Hawkins (1972), p. 105. Charles Wegener's interpretation perfectly supports the judgment made here. After describing the historical context of the American university with attention to Dewey's ideas, he describes the goal of "liberal education" to be "*that persons may become freely functioning participants in intellectual activity and autonomous members of the intellectual community*" (*Liberal Education and the Modern University* [Chicago: University of Chicago Press, 1978], p. 95).

[22]Douglas Sloan, "The Teaching of Ethics in the American Undergraduate Curriculum, 1876–1976," in *Ethics Teaching in Higher Education*, ed. Daniel Callahan and Sissela Bok (New York: Plenum, 1980), pp. 2–19. Note, too, the change from Richard Peters's 1751 sermon at Philadelphia to the Johns Hopkins's motto. Both had relied on John 8:32: *Et cognoscetis veritatem, et veritas liberabit vos.* But Johns Hopkins eliminated the first clause. Richard Peters, *A Sermon on Education, Wherein Some Account is Given of the Academy Established in the City of Philadelphia* (Philadelphia: Franklin and Hall, 1751), p. 1; Wegener (1978), p. 34.

[23]Richard Hofstadter, *Social Darwinism in American Thought*, rev. ed. (Boston: Beacon, 1955a), chaps. 1, 5, 9; Lawrence A. Cremin, *The Transformation of the School:*

The revised outlook stemmed directly from pragmatism. Though adopting many Darwinian concepts, the pragmatists did not regard the environment as a static given, but emphasized the organism's ability to transform the environment. Pragmatism or "experimentalism," as it came to be popularized at Teachers College, rested centrally on the works of George H. Mead, Charles S. Peirce, and William James. But insofar as it constituted the philosophical foundation of educational progressivism, its formulation derived from John Dewey.[24] Refined at the University of Chicago between 1894 and 1904, Dewey's thought was oriented against affirming the certitude of any absolute standards and values and toward appreciation of the individuality of each human being and reliance on a free experimental approach to every new situation encountered in life.[25] While this philosophy, so congenial to the liberal-free ideal, was being developed in the 1890s, the Populist party revived the Jacksonian cry, "Equal rights for all, special privileges for none." Then, between 1900 and the First World War, progressivism emerged as a broad movement of criticism and change devoted to social, political, and educational reform. As progressivism suffused educational discussion, so did those characteristics it shared with the liberal-free ideal, even though progressivist educators were reluctant to empha-

---

Progressivism in American Education, 1876–1957 (New York: Alfred A. Knopf, 1961), chap. 4; Buck (1965), pp. 1–17.

[24]Hofstadter (1955a), chaps. 7, 8. On "experimentalism" in Dewey's thought and as a euphemism for pragmatism, see Katerine C. Mayhew and Anna C. Edwards, *The Dewey School: The Laboratory School of the University of Chicago, 1896–1903* (New York: Appleton-Century, 1936), chap. 15; John L. Childs, "Experimentalism and American Education," *Teachers College Record* 44 (1943): 539–543; Abraham F. Citron, "Experimentalism and the Classicism of President Hutchins," *Teachers College Record* 44 (1943): 544–553; Hal G. Lewis, "Meiklejohn and Experimentalism," *Teachers College Record* 44 (1943): 563–571.

[25]Arthur G. Wirth believes Dewey's thought to have been essentially framed between 1894 and 1904 when, in Wirth's words, Dewey concluded, "The kind of person who should emerge from a truly liberalized education would be one prepared to learn throughout life." "John Dewey's Design for American Education: An Analysis of Aspects of his Work at the University of Chicago, 1894–1904," *HEQ* 4 (1964): 86. Dewey's opposition to dogmatism is clearly expounded in *The Quest for Certainty* (New York: Minton, Balch, 1929), especially chap. 2, "Philosophy's Search for the Immutable." Following from this opposition is, first, rejection of commitment to standards and rules of behavior that are seen to exist abstractly and absolutely and, second, emphasis upon evaluating each existential situation on its own merit and according to its consequences. John Dewey, *Human Nature and Conduct: An Introduction to Social Psychology* (New York: Henry Holt, 1922), chap. 7. This emphasis necessarily implies both great respect for individualism and an "experimental" view of truth, a position outlined perhaps more clearly by William James in *Pragmatism; a New Name for Some Old Ways of Thinking: Popular Lectures on Philosophy* (New York: Longmans, 1907), chap. 6. This "experimental" approach to each new situation suggests an ev-

size the intellect or to distinguish "liberal education" from second-ary or graduate education.[26]

In the post–Civil War decades, therefore, characteristics of the liberal-free ideal that would gradually surface in pragmatism and progressivism entered the mainstream of American definitions of liberal education, challenging both the *artes liberales* ideal and its accommodation and provoking intense discussion. In but four na-tional magazines over the last third of the nineteenth century—*At-lantic, Harper's, North American Review, Scribner's*—there appeared some one hundred articles devoted largely to discussing the status of scientific and modern subjects, the elective system, and the hu-manities in liberal education.[27] Stimulating this discourse, both di-rectly and indirectly, were the debates over "liberal education" taking place in England, where universities had experienced pres-sures similar to those in the United States.

Oxford and Cambridge carried over from the Georgian period to Victorian liberal education the study of classical languages, "the belief that all wisdom is received and that innovation is primarily a restatement of what is already known," and a commitment to "character formation" leading to the graduation of a gentleman. But after midcentury, while not as enthusiastically as the Yankees, Cambridge and Oxford moved toward the German model of free scholarship and academic research. Out of this movement

> a new centre was found and a new justification for liberal edu-cation. . . . It appeared first in Victorian times. It was the result of

---

olutionary outlook on experience and knowledge: "Our net conclusion is that life is development and that developing, growing, is life." John Dewey, *Democracy and Ed-ucation: An Introduction to the Philosophy of Education* (New York: Macmillan, 1916), p. 49. Dewey thus opposed prescription of a required regimen for undergraduate edu-cation because such an approach will never achieve "education for freedom or a 'lib-eral education.' " John Dewey, "Challenge to Liberal Thought," *Fortune* 30 (August 1944b): 154–157. Also implicit in this outlook is the close interrelationship between knowledge and freedom. Although Dewey resolutely opposed isolating and elevating intellect above other faculties of the human being, he emphasized that empirical knowledge of the consequences of action is a prerequisite for freedom. Dewey (1922), pp. 163–256, 278–286.

[26]David Snedden, "What of Liberal Education?" *The Atlantic Monthly* 109, no. 1 (1912): 111–117; William H. Kilpatrick, "The Proper Work of the Liberal Arts Col-lege," *AACB* 29 (1943): 37–44; Richard Hofstadter, *The Age of Reform: From Bryan to F.D.R.* (New York: Alfred A. Knopf, 1955b), chaps. 2, 5; Cremin (1961), pp. 88–89; Cremin, "Curriculum-Making in the United States," *Teachers College Record* 73 (1971): 207–211.

[27]John C. Hepler, "The Developing Theory of Liberal Arts, 1850–1900," *AACB* 31 (1945): 543–546.

the knowledge revolution, of the research ideal, of a belief in the power of the intellect, of specialism and professionalism, of the breakdown of the teleological universe and even the positivist universe, and of the disintegration of a traditional confidence in the strength of education to produce a reliable social type. The new meaning of a liberal education that superseded all the others was the search for truth—not abiding truth, but contingent truth, based on facts and sources. [28]

That this change was neither uniform nor continuous can easily be seen in the 1868 *Essays on a Liberal Education*, solicited from fellows of Cambridge and Oxford because "the principles and methods of Liberal Education are at the present time undergoing considerable discussion." [29] The most noted expression of contention, however, came from an exchange between English writers Thomas H. Huxley and Matthew Arnold. Their opinions were widely quoted in America and demonstrate perfectly the reemergence of direct conflict between the philosophical and oratorical traditions of liberal education in the late nineteenth century.

In 1880, Huxley delivered a public address entitled "Science and Culture," in which he attacked Arnold's well-known view of humanist culture. Huxley argued that "liberal education" should be dedicated to increasing human knowledge and founded upon "an unhesitating faith that the free employment of reason, in accordance with scientific method, is the sole method of reaching truth." Appropriately—especially for someone who had crusaded on behalf of Darwin's *Origin of Species* and extolled Joseph Priestley as one who

[28]Quotations are from Sheldon Rothblatt, *Tradition and Change in English Liberal Education: An Essay in History and Culture* (London: Faber and Faber, 1976), pp. 159–160, 173. See Hugh F. Kearney, *Scholars and Gentlemen: Universities and Society in Pre-Industrial Britain, 1500–1700* (London: Faber and Faber, 1970), pp. 174–180; Martha McMackin Garland, *Cambridge before Darwin: The Ideal of a Liberal Education, 1800–1860* (Cambridge: Cambridge University Press, 1980), chap. 7. The professionalization of the academicians at Oxford and Cambridge accompanied this development. Sheldon Rothblatt, *The Revolution of the Dons: Cambridge and Society in Victorian England* (New York: Basic Books, 1968), pp. 89–93, 258ff.; Arthur J. Engel, *From Clergyman to Don: The Rise of the Academic Profession in Nineteenth-Century Oxford* (Oxford: Clarendon, 1983).

[29]Frederic W. Farrar, ed., *Essays on a Liberal Education* (London: Macmillan, 1868), p. v. Reflecting in 1877 about the changes in English universities, one historian wrote: "No one who has any experience of the working and life of Cambridge can be ignorant how completely we have been removed from Cambridge of half a century ago, or that we have lost almost the last glimpse of what our University, even forty years since, was like." Christopher Wordsworth, *Scholae Academae: Some Account of Studies at the English Universities in the Eighteenth Century* (1877; reprint, London: Frank Cass, 1968), p. v, chap. 1.

"set a much higher value upon the advancement of knowledge and the promotion of that freedom of thought which is at once the cause and consequence of intellectual progress"—Huxley maintained that the study of natural sciences should be prominently included in liberal education. During a lecture tour of the United States in 1883, Arnold responded in "Literature and Science." He staunchly defended his proposition that teaching *"the best which has been thought and said in the world,"* derived from a body of classical texts, conveys the proper standards for the formation of culture, the human personality, and, consequently, liberal education.[30] In this exchange, the disagreement between Huxley and Arnold can be understood as an instance of the longstanding conflict between the perspectives of the liberal-free and *artes liberales* ideals. This understanding is confirmed by observing two ways in which they misunderstood each other.

Regarding curriculum, both pursued the unhelpful tactic of erecting and cutting down strawmen. Huxley attacked Arnold by assaulting those who, he said, totally rejected the natural sciences and relied solely on classical letters for "liberal education." However, Arnold had acknowledged great value in the study of natural sciences, holding simply for an emphasis upon the classics. On the other hand, Arnold responded by opposing those, like Huxley, who, he said, wished to subordinate the classics to the natural sciences in liberal education—even though Huxley had expressed great admiration and respect for the classics as part of liberal education. Their disagreement over literary texts and scientific *artes* was thus really a matter of emphasis and intention, and they were actually closer together than their words sometimes suggested.

The second misunderstanding resides in their mistaken belief that they concurred that the object of liberal education is "criticism of life." Each of them employed this phrase, but neither seemed to realize that the other used it quite differently. For Arnold, "criticism of life . . . which constitutes culture" meant criticism according to recognized conventions and values based on *"the best which has been thought and said in the world."* This had nothing to do with the critical, scientific method that, in principle, regards all truths as tentative hypotheses. In Arnold's interpretation, science was "the

---

[30]Thomas H. Huxley, *Science and Education* (New York: D. Appleton, 1898), pp. 97–110, 134–135, 152; Matthew Arnold, *Discourses in America* (London: Macmillan, 1885), pp. 79–101. A more extended discussion of this debate may be found in my article, "Matthew Arnold, Thomas Huxley, and Liberal Education: A Centennial Retrospective," *Teachers College Record* 86 (Spring 1985): 475–487.

habit of dealing with facts" and "an excellent discipline" derived from accumulating little bits of knowledge into a systematized whole, a view reminiscent of Cicero's misappreciation of Plato. In Huxley's mind, "criticism of life" denoted the critical rationality that rejects absolute conventions derived from tradition, and he assailed classical letters for the dogmatic way in which they were taught and their irrelevance to the exercise of the scientific method in pursuit of truth.[31] Ultimately, Arnold and Huxley disagreed, but they never really disputed each other. Their arguments missed because they argued from fundamentally different ideals of liberal education.

Huxley had delivered the main address at the opening of Johns Hopkins University, and though his view was popular among Americans, Arnold received no little sympathy in the United States for his address "Literature and Science," particularly at the many small colleges that clung to the oratorical tradition. In the 1890s, historian W. H. Woodward considered Renaissance humanism still to be the paragon of liberal education; and in 1900 there were merely 5,668 graduate students in the country compared to 237,592 candidates for the bachelor's degree. At the same time, a group of academic humanists in the universities began to argue loudly and caustically that gentlemanly culture, rather than specialized research, ought to be the focus of higher education. Consequently, although commitment to the *artes liberales* ideal had significantly weakened, there occurred by the turn of the century a reaffirmation of "New Humanism" or "liberal culture" or "collegiate concerns."[32] Bolstering this movement were the resilience of classical letters at

---

[31]Arnold (1885), pp. 82, 87–88, 97–100, 124; Huxley (1898), pp. 100ff., 142–149. The contradiction between Arnold's and Huxley's views of criticism and science extends as well, and appropriately, to their mutual esteem for Socrates. For Huxley, the Athenian philosopher was the first agnostic whose words expressed most keenly the "antidogmatic principle" of agnosticism. In fact, not unlike Socrates in the *Apology* (29a–31b), Huxley rebuts the charge that an inquiring outlook is a destructive or mischievous force in society. Thomas H. Huxley, "Agnosticism," in *Collected Essays* (London: Macmillan, 1893–94), vol. 5, p. 245; James G. Paradis, *T. H. Huxley: Man's Place in Nature* (Lincoln: University of Nebraska Press, 1978), p. 177. In contrast, Arnold maintained: "In my opinion, the speech most proper, at present for a man of culture to make . . . is Socrates': *Know thyself!*" Matthew Arnold, *Culture and Anarchy: An Essay in Political and Social Criticism* (London: Smith, Elder, 1869), pp. 3–4. That Socratic dictum appears frequently in Arnold's writings; and in "Literature and Science" (pp. 105–112), he interprets the speech of Diotima at the end of the *Symposium* (203e–212b) as a statement about relating knowledge to beauty and moral goodness, rather than as an explanation of the distinction between *sophia* and *philosophia* in praise of the endless search for truth.

[32]For this point and the following discussion on "liberal culture" and the *artes liberales* accommodation, I draw from Rudolph (1962), chap. 21; Sherman B. Barnes, "The Entry of Science and History in the College Curriculum, 1865–1914," *HEQ* 4

women's colleges[33] and the continuing influence of collegiate pietism, the latter evidenced in a book by the president of Western Reserve University entitled *A Liberal Education and a Liberal Faith* (1903). No less supportive of the "New Humanism" were the Catholic institutions, especially those operated by the Jesuits, who severely criticized the new *moderni* and "relied on a modified version of the literary-rhetorical program of studies that had been adapted by the Renaissance humanists from Quintilian and Isocrates."[34]

The chief herald of the "liberal culture" movement—a scholar the Catholics read with special, sympathetic interest—was Irving Babbitt, who warned against taking a romantic interest in individuality and experimentalism. Opposing election of courses, premature specialization, and the research ideal, Babbitt linked the latter to technological development and so failed to appreciate the open-ended search for truth, just as Arnold had. His writings, such as *Literature and the American College* (1908) and *Rousseau and Romanticism* (1919), do include phrases suggesting that social and educational standards cannot be permanently established and must be continually reevaluated. However, at the same time, he criticized James and Dewey for their individualistic relativism and, with other advocates of liberal culture, talked as if enduring standards could be located in a body of classical literature.[35]

In fact, it was the presumption of certitude in extolling these "actual standards of past civilization" that led to Walter Lippmann's

---

(1964): 45, 53–58; Veysey (1965), pp. 79ff., 269, chap. 4; Veysey, "The Plural Organized Worlds of the Humanities," in Oleson and Voss (1979), pp. 51–92; Hawkins (1972), chap. 9; Hawkins (1979), pp. 353–360; Higham (1979), pp. 6, 12–18; McGrath (1959), pt. 2. I disagree with Herbst's rejoinder to McGrath's positing of an antithesis between "advanced graduate study" and liberal education. Herbst (1962), pp. 244–246.

[33]Mabel L. Robinson, *The Curriculum of the Women's College*, U.S. Bureau of Education Bulletin No. 6 (Washington, D.C.: Government Printing Office, 1918). A recent, well-researched effort to revise this judgment about women's colleges only succeeds in emphasizing the barriers to change prior to 1885. Patricia Palmieri, "*Incipit Vita Nuova*: Founding Ideals of the Wellesley College Community," *History of Higher Education Annual* 3 (1983): 59–78.

[34]Philip Gleason, "American Catholic Higher Education: A Historical Perspective," in *The Shape of Catholic Higher Education*, ed. Robert Hassenger (Chicago: University of Chicago Press, 1967), pp. 45–46. Charles F. Thwing dedicated his book to "the purpose of making education more nobly religious, religion more wise, and both more liberal." Charles F. Thwing, *A Liberal Education and a Liberal Faith* (New York: Baker and Taylor, 1903), p. iii. See Willis Rudy, *The Evolving Liberal Arts Curriculum: A Historical Review of Basic Themes* (New York: Bureau of Publications, Teachers College, Columbia University, 1960), chap. 9.

[35]Irving Babbitt, *Literature and the American College: Essays in Defense of the Humanities* (Boston: Houghton Mifflin, 1908), pp. 49–51, 57–60; Babbitt, *Rousseau and Romanticism* (Boston: Houghton Mifflin, 1919), pp. 5–9.

attack on Babbitt in "Humanism as Dogma" in *The Saturday Review of Literature*. But without such commitment to standards, the humanists knew it would be impossible to educate the orators, "men of character who were needed to assume positions in business, government and the professions . . . men of quality . . . men adhering to standards." Babbitt's disciple Norman Foerster carried forward the oratorical notion of liberal education for an elite by quoting from Vergerio, "We call those studies *liberal* which are worthy of a free man." Significantly, Foerster interpreted the eighteenth century as the period in which governing educational ideals moved from "humanistic and religious" to "scientific."[36] He eventually became the most vociferous of the New Humanists: the allies and students of Babbitt who were to carry forth the *artes liberales* ideal in subsequent decades.

Actually, this "New Humanism" is wrongly named because the movement truly belongs to the tradition of Roman and Renaissance humanism, which never was extinguished. The term "New Humanism," or "Neo-humanism," applies more appropriately to the accommodation of the *artes liberales* ideal, which appeared prominently in discussion about liberal education during the early twentieth century. As was noted concerning the 1828 Yale *Reports*, the accommodation of the oratorical ideal had its roots in the effort to preserve traditional liberal letters in the face of a competing ideal. That effort relied heavily upon Common Sense philosophy, faculty psychology, and mental discipline theory, which enjoyed widespread popularity in the nineteenth century. However, while saving appearances, the rationale of training the mind amounted to a first step toward the intellectual search for truth characteristic of the liberal-free ideal. Indeed, the nascent *artes liberales* accommodation became so prevalent that, in a bit of short-sighted historicizing, the 1939 *Yearbook of the International Institute of Teachers College* noted how "the traditional concept of a liberal education . . . led to over-intellectualization . . . [I]t cultivated intelligence, but did not develop emotional attitudes."[37]

---

[36]Walter Lippmann, "Humanism as Dogma," *The Saturday Review of Literature* 7 (15 March 1930): 817–819; Foerster (1938), pp. 5–6; Foerster (1939), pp. 333–343. The quotations are from Michael R. Harris, *Five Counterrevolutionists in Higher Education: Irving Babbit, Albert Jay Nock, Abraham Flexner, Robert Maynard Hutchins, Alexander Meiklejohn* (Corvallis: Oregon State University Press, 1970), pp. 67–68.

[37]Kandel (1939), pp. xii, xix. For the following, I draw from Martin L. Clarke, *Classical Education in Britain, 1500–1900* (Cambridge: Cambridge University Press, 1959), pp. 113–120, 170–174; Herbst (1965), chap. 3; Rothblatt (1976), pp. 164–173; Diehl (1978), chap. 1; McClelland (1980), pp. 99–131; Garland (1980), chap. 7.

Leaning ever further in that direction over the course of the nineteenth century, the oratorical rationale for classical letters could not withstand the influence of *Geisteswissenschaft* (humanistic science) and *Altertumswissenschaft* (science of antiquity). Beginning in the late eighteenth century, German scholars had applied the methodology of empirical science to texts and artifacts of classical civilizations and developed the historicocritical method of evaluating such materials. Brought to the United States as another product of the scientific movement, this *Neuhumanismus* began to transform the meaning of classical study in liberal education, both here and in England, for two reasons. First, it incorporated the methodology of specialized research, and second, the new classical scholarship especially revived Greek sources and hence the roots of the philosophical tradition. The *Republic* and other Platonic dialogues consequently received increasing emphasis in the honors examinations in classics at Oxford and Cambridge.

The challenge to the oratorical liberal education thus proceeded not only through frontal assaults on the tenets of the *artes liberales* ideal and the curriculum of humanist letters, but also through the reinterpretation of what was meant by classics and how they should be studied. In fact, the reinterpretation extended to the teaching faculty as well as to the curriculum. By the 1890s, a second camp of academic humanists had emerged in America (in addition to those advocating "liberal culture"), and this new contingent advocated specialized research in the classics along the lines of the German historicocritical school. As early as 1868, the Governing Board of the Sheffield Scientific School at Yale had warned that classical disciplines would become specialized and narrow, but the departmentalization and specialization in humanities scholarship was not fully realized until late in the nineteenth century.

At that point, the *artes liberales* accommodation, with its foundation in the Neo-humanist movement, attained mature expression among advocates of classical letters who had moved beyond the mental discipline theory. They did this not in the manner of U.S. Commissioner of Education W. T. Harris, who earlier invoked "Darwinism" while justifying the study of "culture from Greece and Rome" as part of "liberal education" because "the embryology of modern civilization is to be found in the literature and institutions of those wonderful people." Rather, their advocacy lay in promoting the study of classical texts as a means to enhance critical intellect. This latter rationale provides the key distinction between pure liberal culture advocates, whose ideas can be associated with the *artes liberales* ideal, and those educators who offered what Veysey calls an "intellectualized" approach to liberal culture.[38] The latter group endorsed the *artes liberales* accommodation in that they prescribed the reading of classical texts with the primary aim of training the critical and self-reliant intellect, not of disciplining future citizens according to inherited values of civility.

For example, although President A. L. Lowell of Harvard talked about the "well-rounded man," he was fundamentally "an intellectual aristocrat" and concentrated on raising academic standards at Harvard and enforcing them. Convinced that "our universities . . . do not strive enough in the impressionable years of early manhood to stimulate intellectual appetite and ambition; nor do they foster productive scholarship enough," Lowell introduced, as the best type of liberal education, a system of concentration and distribution that aimed "at producing men who know a little of everything and something well." This involved rolling back Eliot's electivism, which had cut into the study of classical letters, and reestablishing a prescribed foundation of culture such as a liberally educated person should be expected to know. The fundamental justification for this system of concentration and distribution, which Lowell continued to reiterate, from his 1909 inaugural address to his 1934 *At War with Academic Traditions in America*, lay in developing a critical intellect of "strength" and "elasticity." That this rationale leaned toward the research ideal rather than conservation of tradition and character formation is shown by Samuel E. Morison's approbation for the fruit of Lowell's efforts at Harvard, represented by "the increasing number of undergraduates who undertake additional study in order to obtain honors at graduation."[39]

Alexander Meiklejohn also adopted the Neo-humanist approach. From 1912 to 1938, at Amherst College, the Experimental College of the University of Wisconsin, and the School for Social

---

[38]Veysey (1965), chap. 4; William T. Harris, "Equivalents in a Liberal Course of Study," *The Addresses and Journal of Proceedings of the National Education Association* (Salem, Ohio: National Education Association, 1880), pp. 173–174. Harris served as U.S. Commissioner of Education from 1889 to 1906. His thought demonstrates well this "transitional" period of intermingling rationales for "liberal education." Lawrence A. Cremin, *Traditions of American Education* (New York: Basic Books, 1977), pp. 15–16; Higham (1979), pp. 6–7.

[39]Abbott L. Lowell, *At War with Academic Traditions in America* (Cambridge: Harvard University Press, 1934), p. 5; Samuel E. Morison, *Three Centuries at Harvard, 1636–1936* (Cambridge, Mass.: Belknap, 1936), pp. 441, 448; George H. Chase, "Real Education is Self-Education: The Academic Principles Realized by Mr. Lowell during his Presidency at Harvard," *JHE* 4 (1933): 281–285. See also W. H. Cowley, "Intelli-

Studies, San Francisco, he promoted "liberal education" as a process of "making minds" and a "liberal college" as "fundamentally a place of the mind, a time for thinking, an opportunity for knowing." In this respect, some of his words seem to invoke the theory of mental discipline. And his rejection of electivism and his prescription of reading a sequence of Great Books along with his desire to advance certain standards of conduct and character—as reflected in his occasional discussion about liberal education for "making men"—point to the *artes liberales* ideal. However, his discussion always returned to "making minds," and he specifically contradicted Dewey's allegation that he recommended the Great Books in order to establish "the acceptance of the standards of the past as superior to our own." Rather, looking back in 1944, Meiklejohn said the classics are read primarily "to cultivate, in the minds of teachers and pupils, the processes of critical intelligence."[40]

The tensions and countervailing tendencies in this accommodated *artes liberales* position demonstrate that it is not wholly systematic, which is simply to say that it amounts to an effort at rapprochement between two ideals. It is a "synthetic reinterpretation" of the two traditions of liberal education, to borrow a phrase from David Sidorsky,[41] and as such incorporates the inherent conflicts between them. Another such tension in Meiklejohn's position was the conflict between intellectualism and egalitarianism. That Meiklejohn emphasized a fundamentally intellectual liberal education is not disputed; and that, based on a commitment to democracy, he wanted universal liberal education—"the same for all the members of a society, and all alike must have it"—is attested by his

---

gence is Not Enough: Holoism—the Development of the Whole Man—the Philosophy of the Liberal Arts College," *JHE* 9 (1938): 474; David Riesman, "Educational Reform at Harvard College: Meritocracy and Its Adversaries," in *Education and Politics at Harvard,* ed. Seymour M. Lipset and David Riesman (New York: McGraw-Hill, 1975), pp. 293–303. This interpretation might also apply to A. F. West, who, while acknowledging that "the old-fashioned course is gone," does make clear his view that liberal education should include reading classical texts in order to hone the intellect; and he elsewhere links liberal education to the philosophical tradition of Plato and Aristotle rather than the oratorical tradition. West (1907), pp. 77, 97, 113; West, *Alcuin and the Rise of the Christian Schools* (New York: Charles Scribner's Sons, 1901), chap. 1. Confirmation for this interpretation is found in testimony that West "was concerned primarily with high academic standards of a broadly designed graduate curriculum for an aristocracy of scholars." Herbst (1962), p. 251.

[40]Alexander Meiklejohn, *The Liberal College* (Boston: Marshall Jones, 1920), pp. 4, 23, pt. 4; Meiklejohn, "A Reply to John Dewey," *Fortune* 31 (1945): 207–219; Lewis (1943), pp. 565–569; Leduc (1946), pp. 149–152.

[41]David Sidorsky, "Varieties of Liberalism and Liberal Education," *SR* 5 (1977): 222.

own words. But he made such statements without questioning whether every citizen is capable of such an intellectual education, that is, whether such a liberal education belongs inevitably to an elite. Reflecting partly the progressivist ambivalence over the need for experts, Meiklejohn could talk in terms of liberally educating the leaders of a democracy where all are "free and equal," but he apparently preferred to de-emphasize the tension between the desire for intellectual leadership and for equality.[42]

This conflict also belonged to the Neo-humanist, *artes liberales* accommodation of Robert M. Hutchins, although with him the tension developed somewhat differently. Hutchins has commonly been taken as one of the "radical conservatives for liberal education," a view that places him at the opposite pole from Dewey, pragmatism, and progressivism, as he himself suggested.[43] Along these lines, he advanced a prescribed course comprising "the greatest books of the western world" accompanied by a set of contemporary disciplines precisely analogous to and drawn from the *septem artes liberales*. Critics attributed this prescription to his belief that freedom "consists in allowing men the opportunity to develop good moral, spiritual and intellectual habits"—a belief that, in turn, rested fundamentally on "a presupposition of . . . a static world" underlying the existence of certain "metaphysical principles." As Hutchins wrote: "Education implies teaching. Teaching implies knowledge. Knowledge is truth. The truth is everywhere the same. Hence education should be everywhere the same."[44]

These assertions correspond to characteristics of the *artes liberales* ideal, as does Hutchins's frank desire to identify an elite for

---

[42]Alexander Meiklejohn, "Required Education for Freedom," *The American Scholar* 13 (1944): 393; Richard Hofstadter, *Anti-Intellectualism in American Life* (New York: Alfred A. Knopf, 1963), chap. 8; Harris (1970), pp. 166–171.

[43]Many of the group whom I call Neo-humanists and align with the *artes liberales* accommodation are termed "radical conservatives for liberal education" by Amy A. Kass, "Radical Conservatives for Liberal Education" (Ph.D. diss., Johns Hopkins University, 1973). For analyses and criticisms of Hutchins (some incorporating wrongfully invidious comparisons with John Dewey on "liberal education") see Henry S. Canby, "A Review of *The Higher Learning in America*," *The Saturday Review of Literature* 14(24 Oct. 1936): 10–11; Robert Freeman Butts, "A Liberal Education and the Prescribed Curriculum in the American College," *Educational Record* 18 (1937): 548–564; Porter Sargent, "What's Ahead in Higher Education? Universities Are Unready for Present Crises," *JHE* 12 (1941): 321; Benjamin Fine, *Democratic Education* (New York: Thomas Y. Crowell, 1945); Schmidt (1957), chap. 10.

[44]Robert M. Hutchins, *The Higher Learning in America* (New Haven, Conn.: Yale University Press, 1936), pp. 66, 85. For critics' statements, see Citron (1943), pp. 544–547; Harris (1970), p. 141.

higher education, although the latter point is just where such analysis begins to break down. For, while Hutchins sought to skim off an elite for graduate study, he maintained that every person in a democracy should be liberally educated. Indeed, "why should he not be?" The question was asked rhetorically, yet the same contradiction found in Meiklejohn arises here if it is noted that Hutchins's liberal education is primarily devoted to nurturing the analytical and critical faculties of the intellect, a goal attested by his own words, by his reliance on the Neo-Aristotelianism of Mortimer Adler, and by his numerous references to Aristotle, Thomas Aquinas, and John Henry Newman in *The Higher Learning in America*.[45]

Many of Hutchins's critics did not appreciate this point, for they believed that his liberal training of the intellect was neither critical nor open-ended but aimed toward inculcating certain metaphysical principles and truths about living a good life. The fundamental question of where precisely Hutchins stood, a question that bears directly on the nature of the *artes liberales* accommodation, is answered finally by observing that Hutchins had no "precise" position. He never explicitly identified his "metaphysical principles." Again and again, he called for truth and for unity around the absolute, and because of this call the experimentalists, progressivists, and pragmatists decried him. But his recommendations halted at "metaphysics, the science of first principles" or "the cultivation of intellectual powers" capable of discovering metaphysical principles. He never finally presented a system, despite his sometime furtive endorsement of Neo-Aristotelianism, other than that everyone ought to be liberally educated in the Great Tradition so as to become smart enough to find first principles. As he commented at his inauguration to the presidency of the University of Chicago in 1931: "Our income tax goes now in part to keep our neighbors alive. It may have to go in part to make our neighbors intelligent." So, with Meiklejohn, Hutchins left it a matter of speculation whether or not these neighbors could even become so or what conclusions they would ultimately draw if they did.[46]

---

[45]Hutchins (1936), pp. 61, 80, 118; Mortimer J. Adler, *How to Read a Book: The Art of Getting a Liberal Education* (New York: Simon and Schuster, 1940), chap. 17.

[46]Robert M. Hutchins, "The Higher Learning in America: How May the American University Make Provision for the Superior Student?" *JHE* 4 (1933): 2; Hutchins (1936), pp. 63, 105–106. My discussion here is informed by conversations with James Luther Adams and Bernard M. Loomer, both of whom were at Chicago during the Hutchins era, and by Harry D. Gideonse, *The Higher Learning in a Democracy: A Reply to President Hutchins' Critique of the American University* (New York: Farrar & Rine-

The eclectic language of these schoolmen, who sometimes borrowed from writers on liberal education with whom they were not, for the large part, in sympathy, demonstrates the blurring of arguments arising from the confrontation between the *artes liberales* and liberal-free ideals, a tendency that illustrates precisely the "accommodation" phenomenon. In another respect, however, their borrowing signifies a forming of alliances against common foes, particularly that of utility. In this context, "utility" denotes the rationale behind a broad range of phenomena that reshaped the configuration of American higher education between the Civil War and World War I. Utility stood behind the Morrill Land Grant Acts of 1862 and 1890. These acts and subsequent legislation in the first fifteen years of the twentieth century supported postsecondary institutions for teaching "agriculture and the mechanic arts" and then introduced more practical, technical, and vocational subjects into the rest of higher education.[47] Utility was cited also by university builders, especially in the Midwest, where the establishment of new institutions could be coordinated with the land-grant effort to develop the country. In the final decades of the nineteenth century, as the United States became increasingly industrialized and urbanized, the changing patterns of American life and collegiate culture also were defended on grounds of utility.

Those changes accompanied the growth of the middle class and the social ideal of "money-making," which advocates of the humanist tradition increasingly criticized toward the end of the nineteenth century. These economic and social changes therefore stimulated the revival of "liberal culture" and "collegiate concerns" as much as did the rise of the liberal-free ideal. Moreover, industrialization and urbanization were symptoms of advancing technol-

---

hart, 1947), pp. 1–4. Moreover, the understanding of Hutchins's view as an "accommodation" is suggested by the "remarkable parallelism" noted between Hutchins and the twelfth-century transitional figure, John of Salisbury. Daniel D. McGarry, "Educational Theory in the *Metalogican* of John of Salisbury," *Speculum* 23 (1948): 665. Similarly, Richard McKeon is said to have chided progressivist relativism and skepticism while failing to proclaim first or final principles of his own—except for an Aristotelianism that was attributed to him but that he did not expressly endorse. See Wayne C. Booth, "Between Two Generations: The Heritage of the Chicago School," in *Profession 82*, ed. Phyllis P. Franklin and Richard I. Brod (New York: Modern Language Association of America, 1982), p. 19; Richard McKeon, "Criticism and the Liberal Arts: The Chicago School of Criticism," in Franklin and Brod (1982), p. 17.

[47]Edward D. Eddy, Jr., *Colleges for Our Land and Times: The Land-Grant Idea in American Education* (New York: Harper and Brothers, 1957), p. 1, chaps. 2, 6; Henry S. Brunner, *Land-Grant Colleges and Universities, 1862–1962*, U.S. Bureau of Education Bulletin No. 13 (Washington, D.C.: Government Printing Office, 1962), p. 104.

ogy, the utilitarian expression of the scientific research that liberal-free idealists promoted. With all this in mind, advocates of the *artes liberales* ideal attacked utility both because of its essential compromising of idealism and pure virtue and because of its association with scientific, liberal-free research. This distinction, however, often escaped essayists such as Irving Babbitt and Norman Foerster due to their misappreciation of the notion of free research.[48]

The distinction was made, however, by many free-research advocates, such as President D. C. Gilman of Johns Hopkins and Dean A. F. West of Princeton, who stood together during the last decade of the nineteenth century in defining as "liberal" those studies that were not "technical" or were "pursued without regard to their marketable value." Subsequently, Thorstein Veblen championed pure research by way of attacking the pressures of utility introduced by those who administered universities: "the schoolmasters and utilitarians" and "the captains of erudition" whose "corrupting effect on the scientists and scholars . . . induces in them also something of the same bias toward 'practical' results in their work."[49] Although Veblen's position in *The Higher Learning in America* (1918) may have been "extreme," many professors harbored some notion that administrative organization and an ethic of efficiency undermined the pursuit of pure research and so the highest purpose of the university. As a faculty member of Louisiana State University argued, philosophy was declining relative to commercial subjects because *"educational business men"* rather than *"educators"* were running the show.[50]

Although Gilman, Veblen, and others made this distinction between ostensibly useful research and pure, free research, those aligned with the *artes liberales* ideal may have had good reason to confuse the arguments, insofar as the progressivists tended to blur the distinction. This is because the progressivists, while embracing many characteristics of the liberal-free ideal, did not regard scholarly research and the pursuit of knowledge as ends in themselves in-

[48]Foerster (1938), chap. 1; Peterson (1964), p. 4; Veysey (1965), p. 181; Oscar Handlin and Mary F. Handlin, *The American College and American Culture: Socialization as a Function of Higher Education* (New York: McGraw-Hill, 1970), chap. 4; Hawkins (1972), pp. 263ff.

[49]Gilman (1892), p. 109; West (1907), pp. 97–100; Thorstein Veblen, *The Higher Learning in America: A Memorandum on the Conduct of Universities by Business Men* (New York: B. W. Huebsch, 1918), pp. 31, 32, 89; Veysey (1965), pp. 121, 346–356.

[50]Peter A. Carmichael, "The Role of Philosophy and the Classics," *AACB* 23 (1942): 559. See also Arthur G. Wirth, *Education in the Technological Society: The Vocational-Liberal Studies Controversy in the Early Twentieth Century* (Scranton, Pa.: Intext Educational Pub., 1972), pp. 141–223.

asmuch as they did not acknowledge any final ends. And since they regarded all knowledge as a means to some further end, they began to call for including vocational and useful education in liberal education. Into the second quarter of the twentieth century, the calls mounted—from Middlebury, from Lafayette, from Western Reserve, from Columbia, from the Church Divinity School of the Pacific, from Dewey.[51] By that time, too, the progressivist impulse had been reinforced by the elevation of the service ideal in American higher education during World War I. In response, protests against vocationalism and utility were voiced during the 1920s by every manner of liberal education advocate in the Association of American Colleges (AAC), and a 1933 study of thirty-five Methodist colleges echoed this sentiment. In 1939, "non-professional education" served as the defining criterion to identify "liberal arts colleges" for a national survey by the National Society for the Study of Education (NSSE).[52]

The opposition to utility occasionally allied proponents of the *artes liberales* and liberal-free ideals, when they properly understood each other, but it was not a happy alliance, indeed, scarcely an alliance at all. Testimony to the acrimonious dissension over the rationales for the liberal college—sometimes thought to be a more recent phenomenon—can be found throughout the first four decades of the twentieth century. As early as 1907, the president of Cornell University repeated the substance of West's 1903 address to the National Education Association: "The college is without clear-cut notions of what a liberal arts education is and how it is to be se-

---

[51]David Snedden, "Toward Free and Efficient Liberal Colleges: What Really Functional Educations Can Liberal Colleges Provide?" *JHE* 6 (1935): 307–313; Harold Chidsey, "Culture in Education: The Cultural and Practical in the Curriculum of the Small College," *JHE* 8 (1937): 175–184; William S. Lee, "Curriculum and Career: A Description of the Pre-Vocational Work of Middlebury College," *JHE* 8 (1937): 191–193; J. Hugh Jackson, "The Professional School: The Relationship of the Liberal-Arts College to the Professional School," *JHE* 8 (1937): 129–135; Briggs (1939), p. 315; C. C. Arbuthnot, "The Liberal Arts College and Vocational Education," *AACB* 25 (1939): 299–304; Kandel (1939), p. xix; Arnold S. Nash, "The Liberal Arts College and Professional Education," *The American Scholar* 13 (1944): 398–401; Kenneth C. Sills, "The Useful and Liberal Arts and Sciences," *The American Scholar* 13 (1944): 400–402; Ernest Earnest, "Even A.B.'s Must Eat," *The American Scholar* 13 (1944): 402–405; Dewey (1944a), pp. 391–393.

[52]Robert L. Kelly, "Report of the Commission on the Organization of College Curriculum," *AACB* 9 (1923): 70–79; Frank W. Chandler, "The Function of the Liberal Arts Colleges in a University," *AACB* 10 (1924): 156; Floyd W. Reeves et al., *The Liberal Arts College: Based Upon Surveys of Thirty-five Colleges Related to the Methodist Episcopal Church* (Chicago: University of Chicago Press, 1932), chap. 21; John D. Russell, "General Education in the Liberal Arts Colleges," in *General Education in the*

cured . . . and the pity of it is that this is not a local or special disability, but a paralysis affecting every college of arts in America."[53]

Such chaos was particulary threatening to the *artes liberales* ideal, and advocates of the liberal-free ideal initially welcomed "the spirit of experimentation" in the liberal arts colleges. But soon, across the spectrum, from liberal culture advocates to progressivist educators, the lack of agreement and consensus over both the content and the purpose of liberal education prompted great concern. Such was the import of a survey of periodical literature immediately following World War I, a 1921 essay by the director of the American Council on Education (ACE), a 1922 supplement in *The New Republic*, a 1923 report by the Commission on the Organization of the College Curriculum, a 1925 Commonwealth Fund study of forty colleges and universities, and a 1932 study of "one hundred twenty-eight outstanding changes and experiments" in liberal arts education.[54]

Efforts to combat this recognized disunity assumed many forms, one of the most popular being an early twentieth-century innovation: the survey course. Originating in Columbia University's War Aims Course, and evolving slowly in the 1920s, "survey" or "integration" or "orientation" courses multiplied in the 1930s.[55] Throughout the nation, from Reed College to the University of Iowa to Syracuse to Guilford to Grinnell, some type of unifying course was introduced in nearly every discipline: classics, humanities, political science, social studies, and natural science. By 1942, a poll of 350 colleges and universities revealed that over half had instituted gen-

---

American College, The Thirty-Eighth Yearbook of the National Society for the Study of Education, ed. Guy M. Whipple (Bloomington, Ill: Public School Publishing Co., 1939), p. 171; Merle Curti, "The American Scholar in Three Wars," *JHI* 3 (1942): 241–264.

[53]Quoted in Abraham Flexner, *The American College: A Criticism* (New York: Century, 1908), p. 7; West (1907), pp. 74–77. Leon B. Richardson, *A Study of the Liberal College* (Hanover, N.H.: Dartmouth College, 1924), pp. 29ff.; Frederick J. Kelly, *The American Arts College: A Limited Survey* (New York: Macmillan, 1925), p. vii; Irving Maurer, "The Liberal Arts Education in the Light of Present Difficulties," *AACB* 19 (1933): 15–21; James L. McConaughy, "Is the Liberal-Arts College Doomed?—Certain Precautions Necessary to Save the Liberal Arts for All Students of Collegiate Level," *JHE* 9 (1938): 59–67; Kent (1939), p. 417; Donald J. Cowling, "The Work and Future of Liberal Arts Colleges," *AACB* 30 (1944): 95.

[54]Samuel P. Capen, "The Dilemma of the College of Arts and Sciences," *Educational Review* 61 (1921): 277–285; Koos and Crawford (1921), pp. 499–509; "The American College and Its Curriculum," *The New Republic* 32, no. 412 (25 October 1922) pt. 2, pp. 1–15; Kelly (1923), p. 71; Kelly (1925), pp. 17ff.; Kathryn McHale, "Introduction," in Whipple (1932), p. 1; Frances V. Speek, "One Hundred Twenty-eight Outstanding Changes and Experiments," in Whipple (1932), pp. 143–156.

[55]Capen (1921), pp. 283–284; "Unity in the Curriculum," *AACB* 10 (1924): 220–237; John J. Coss, "A Survey Course: The Columbia College Two-Year Survey Course in the Social Studies," *JHE* 2 (1931): 118; Byron L. Johnson, ed., *What About Survey*

eral survey or orientation courses.[56] Even so, this innovation had its detractors, who charged that such courses were superficial, as did a University of Notre Dame professor who proposed instead that a course in philosophy unify the curriculum.[57]

That proposal came to be another popular way of trying to combat disunity in the liberal arts curriculum, and it is telling that such a proposal should come from a Catholic university. Although incorporating some degree of electivism and change by the early 1900s, Catholic and other sectarian institutions had begun to receive acclaim as "the only fixed points in the whole unstable world of higher liberal education" because of their relatively traditional curriculum and, more importantly, their commitment to a particular faith or creed that served as the foundation of their liberal education. In Meiklejohn's words of 1923, "The chief trouble with our teaching . . . today is that we haven't anything to teach . . . we haven't got a gospel, a philosophy, we haven't in the proper sense of the term a religion to give them."[58]

Whether one spoke this way about "religion," as did professors

---

Courses? (New York: Henry Holt, 1937); J. M. Hughes, "Curriculum Organization and Integration: Principles to Guide in Realizing Integration at Collegiate Levels," *JHE* 10 (1939): 268–272; Jerome B. Cohen, "On Survey Courses," *JHE* 10 (1939): 465–469; Louis T. Bénézet, *General Education in the Progressive College* (New York: Bureau of Publications, Teachers College, Columbia University, 1943), pp. 37–41; Robert L. Belknap and Richard Kuhns, *Tradition and Innovation: General Education and the Reintegration of the University, A Columbia Report* (New York: Columbia University Press, 1977), pp. 45ff.

[56]The poll is found in W. W. Charters, "General Survey Courses," *JHE* 13 (1942): 1–4. The cited examples can be found in Homer C. Sampson, "A Program for General Botany: The Use of the Problem-Discussion Method in Teaching a Course in General Botany," *JHE* 2 (1931): 127–132; H. H. Newman, "An Orientation Course: The Nature of the World and of Man," *JHE* 2 (1931): 121–126; "Some Progressive College Projects: Curriculum Reorganization, Orientation, and Survey Courses," *AACB* 17 (1931): 313–316; A. Gordon Dewey, "The General Course in Political Science," *JHE* 6 (1933): 9–14; E. W. McDowell, "A General Humanities Course," *JHE* 7 (1936): 16–22; Byron L. Johnson, "General Education Changes the College," *AACB* 24 (1938): 229–234; B. L. Ullman, "Classical Culture in the College Curriculum Either Through Language Courses, General-Survey Courses, or Courses in Ancient Civilization," *JHE* 11 (1940): 189–192.

[57]William F. Cunningham, "A Challenge to Survey Courses," *AACB* 22 (1936): 580. See also Herbert G. Espy, "The Curriculum of the Liberal Arts College, with Particular Reference to the Aims and Curriculum Organization in the Independent College" (Ed.D. diss., Harvard Graduate School of Education, 1929), p. xx; George Sherburn, "Discussion of Professor Jones's Paper," in *General Education: Its Nature, Scope, Essential Elements,* ed. William S. Gray (Chicago: University of Chicago Press, 1934), pp. 55–58; George A. Works, "Summary of the Conference," in Gray (1934), pp. 180–184; Schiller Scroggs, "Generality in the General Course," *AACB* 24 (1938): 482–486.

[58]Quotations are from Capen (1921), p. 278; Alexander Meiklejohn, "Report of the Commission on the Organization of the College Curriculum," *AACB* 9 (1923): 88–89.

of Springfield College and the University of Pennsylvania, about "theology," as did a professor of Union Theological Seminary, about "philosophy," as did the president of Dickinson College, or about all three together, in the fashion of W. E. Hocking, this approach to unifying and giving coherence to undergraduate liberal education was much acclaimed.[59] But simply to call for a "sound or consistent philosophy, thesis or principle," in the manner of Abraham Flexner, was easy and left the difficult task undone. As Harry D. Gideonse responded to Robert M. Hutchins, "To write volumes in support of the thesis that there should be a unifying philosophy, without specific indication of the type of unity or of philosophy, is to miss the essential problem underlying the modern dilemma."[60]

The wistful hope "that there should be a unifying philosophy" had some effect, however, as did also the pressures of standardization and utility that were applied by "the captains of erudition," no matter how strongly idealists opposed them. The *artes liberales* accommodation had begun to emerge in the nineteenth century when advocates of the *artes liberales* ideal adapted their arguments, consciously and unconsciously, to the arising liberal-free ideal. Now the reverse happened when the liberal-free ideal was influenced by the pressures for conceptual uniformity, institutional standardization, and curricular utility and was therefore accommodated to the *artes liberales* ideal. The liberal-free accommodation, of course, did not spring forth *ex nihilo* but had distant precursors, just as the *artes liberales* accommodation had looked back to the teaching of Aristotle during the high tide of medieval scholasticism. The liberal-free accommodation also had immediate antecedents, as the *artes liberales* accommodation had had in the nineteenth-century argument of teaching classics for mental discipline.

See Gleason (1967), pp. 39–46; Frederick Rudolph, *Curriculum: A History of the American Undergraduate Course of Study Since 1636* (San Francisco: Jossey-Bass, 1977), pp. 16, 171.

[59]William E. Hocking, "Philosophy and Religion in Undergraduate Education," *AACB* 23 (1937): 45–54; William A. Brown, *The Case for Theology in the University* (Chicago: University of Chicago Press, 1938); Fred P. Corson, "A Philosophy for the Liberal-Arts College," *AACB* 24 (1938): 224–225; C. C. McCracken, "The Unique Function of the Christian Liberal Arts College in American Life," in *The William Rainey Harper Memorial Conference, Held in Connection with the Centennial of Muskingum College*, ed. Robert N. Montgomery (Chicago: University of Chicago Press, 1938), pp. 66–81; Thornton W. Merriam, "Religion in Higher Education Through the Past Twenty-Five Years," in *Liberal Learning and Religion*, ed. Amos N. Wilder (New York: Harper and Brothers, 1951), pp. 3–23.

[60]Gideonse (1947), p. 3; Abraham Flexner, *Universities—American, English, German*, 2d ed. (New York: Oxford University Press, 1930), p. 213. See also the repre-

One precursor of the liberal-free accommodation lay in the eighteenth-century English justification for the New Science, that the study of it, like the study of Greek and Latin, leads to moral and social refinement. Chemistry, for example, was said to accomplish "precisely the same ends of liberal instruction as classical languages"; and Hume himself argued that scientific study "softens and humanizes the temper, and cherishes those fine emotions, in which true virtue and honour consists." The president of the Massachusetts Institute of Technology reasoned similarly in 1891. Scientific and technical studies, he said, provide "almost the perfection of education for young men" because, on the one hand, these studies "rise in the higher grades into original investigation and research," and on the other, they develop "the manhood and the citizenship for the country" by inculcating values that are "no less noble and fine" than those learned by studying classical subjects.[61]

The appeal to character formation, however, was somewhat anomalous. The liberal-free ideal more typically was accommodated in other ways during its emergence and confrontation with the *artes liberales* ideal in American liberal education. The intellectual positivism of the post-Darwinian era infected many American academicians, who often traveled to German universities expecting the new scientific methodology to lead to absolute truth. This certitude, evident in books such as W. J. McCallister's *The Growth of Freedom in Education* (1932), importantly characterized the liberal-free accommodation. The positivism led, in turn, to prescribing the natural sciences and "modern" subjects as the fundamental content of a liberal education, that is, the necessary information for an educated person. The collegiate commitment to teaching, long allied with the *artes liberales* ideal because of its devotion to the transmission of traditional culture, also contributed to this transformation of the scientific pursuit of knowledge into the handing down of scientific credenda. Beyond specifically required courses, a striking example of this approach can be found in the 1930s Oberlin plan, which took as the "Basic Philosophy" and unifying principle of the liberal arts

sentative exchange in the following articles: Boyd H. Bode, "Aims in College Teaching: To Assist Every Student to Develop an Independent Philosophy of Life," *JHE* 3 (1932): 475–480; Bode, "The Answer: Another Word on Aims in College Teaching," *JHE* 4 (1933): 168–170; Homer P. Rainey, "Aims in College Teaching: A Question," *JHE* 4 (1933): 165–168.

[61]Quotations and discussion of this point are drawn from Francis A. Walker, "The Place of Schools of Technology in American Education," *Educational Review* 2 (1891): 209–219; David Hume, *Essays, Moral, Political, and Literary* ed. T. H. Greene and T. H. Grose (London: Thames, 1912) vol. 1, p. 315; Rothblatt (1976), pp. 43–44.

curriculum the concept of evolution and organized the curriculum according to an evolutionary scheme of knowledge.[62]

At the same time, the constraints brought on by the institution-alization of the research model and the professionalization of the faculty in universities reinforced the accommodation of the liberal-free ideal.[63] Even though characteristics of the liberal-free ideal might be straightforwardly delineated by an academic dean at the University of Minnesota in *The Liberal College in Changing Society*, the formalizing of requirements, guidelines, and standards led to the establishment of hierarchies among institutions. By the turn of the century, admission requirements, grading standards, and degree requirements were raised; and within faculties and departments, quality rankings and extensive institutionalized hierarchies emerged. The Ph.D. became the mark of scholarly competence in all fields, leading to the founding of meritocracy and intensification of elitism.[64]

The accommodation of the liberal-free ideal via a commitment to elitism has a history since it was the social and political elites that promoted the Enlightenment in Scotland, university reform in Germany, and Jeffersonianism in America. Allegiance to their social class confounded the supposed egalitarian commitments of such groups, as has been observed about Locke and the Levellers. Similarly, the young American Philosophical Society recruited primarily "gentlemen . . . whom Providence hath blessed with affluence, and whose

---

[62]Ernest H. Wilkins, "The Revision at Oberlin College: An Interpretation of the Seven-fold Plan as the Basic Philosophy of the New System," *JHE* 2 (1931): 66–68; Harvey A. Wooster, "To Unify the Liberal-Arts Curriculum: The Principle of Evolution as a Unifying Concept for the College Curriculum," *JHE* 3 (1932): 373–380. The history of liberal education was favorably interpreted as an accelerating progression toward student freedom by W. J. McCallister, *The Growth of Freedom in Education, A Critical Interpretation of Some Historical Views* (New York: Richard R. Smith, 1931). On this transformation, see Farmer (1950), pp. 16–19; Buck (1965), pp. 1–17; Hofstadter (1955a), chaps. 5, 9; Herbst (1965), chap. 3.

[63]Hawkins (1979), p. 302; Veysey (1965), p. 240; Burton J. Bledstein, *The Culture of Professionalism: The Middle Class and the Development of Higher Education in America* (New York: W. W. Norton, 1969), chap. 8.

[64]John B. Johnston, *The Liberal College in Changing Society* (New York: Century, 1930), p. 242; Mary L. Smallwood, *An Historical Study of Examinations and Grading Systems in Early American Universities: A Critical Study of the Original Records of Harvard, William and Mary, Yale, Mount Holyoke, and Michigan from Their Founding to 1900* (Cambridge: Harvard University Press, 1935), pp. 78ff.; Harold S. Wechsler, *The Qualified Student: A History of Selective College Admission in America* (New York: John Wiley, 1977), chap. 10; Veysey (1979), pp. 63ff.; David S. Webster, "Academic Quality Rankings: Why They Developed in the United States and Not Europe," *History of Higher Education Annual* 2 (1982): 102–127.

understanding is improved by a liberal education."[65] However, even more fundamental to this history was the intrinsic elitism of the intellectual who, like Anthony Collins in *A Discourse of Free-Thinking* (1713), disdained the orthodox and uneducated, regarding them as a weight on society. This attitude was transmitted to the new American universities, where the scientist and researcher often viewed popular acclaim for their work with skepticism, and the latent elitism in the liberal-free perspective was eventually institutionalized with the establishment of quality-rankings and hierarchies. Meanwhile, the historical association of leisure with speculative philosophy (with its lineage traceable through Aristotle, Boethius, Locke, and C. W. Eliot, each of whom recognized the necessity of liberal means and time for research to be productive) provided another point of liberal-free accommodation to the *artes liberales* ideal.[66]

In the ideas of Abraham Flexner one finds an example of the liberal-free accommodation that clearly demonstrates the ambiguity and tension inherent in this kind of approach.[67] Like Meiklejohn and Hutchins, Flexner was distressed by the plurality and uncertainty of purposes prevalent in early twentieth-century liberal education. However, he rejected the notion of prescribing a program of classical texts for undergraduate education, recommending instead the incorporation of college and graduate faculties and studies because, he felt, higher education should be devoted to advancing knowl-

---

[65]Quoted in John C. Greene, "Science, Learning, and Utility: Patterns of Organization in the Early American Republic," in *The Pursuit of Knowledge in the Early American Republic: American Scientific and Learned Societies from Colonial Times to the Civil War*, ed. Alexandra Oleson and Sanborn C. Brown (Baltimore: Johns Hopkins University Press, 1976), p. 3. Nicolas T. Phillipson, "Culture and Society in the 18th Century Province: The Case of Edinburgh and the Scottish Enlightenment," in *The University in Society*, ed. Lawrence Stone (Princeton, N.J.: Princeton University Press, 1974), vol. 2, pp. 407–448; Charles E. McClelland, "The Aristocracy and University Reform in Eighteenth Century Germany," in *Schooling and Society: Studies in the History of Education*, ed. Lawrence Stone (Baltimore: Johns Hopkins University Press, 1976), pp. 146–176; Edmund Leites, "Conscience, Leisure, and Learning: Locke and the Levellers," *Sociological Analysis* 39 (1978): 39–45.

[66]Anthony Collins, *A Discourse of Free-Thinking, Occasion'd by the Rise and Growth of a Sect Call'd Free Thinkers* (London: n. p., 1713), pp. 118–123; Aristotle *Nicomachean Ethics* 1177a11–1179a33; Charles W. Eliot, "Inaugural Address as President of Harvard College," in *Educational Reform: Essays and Addresses* (New York: Century, 1898), pp. 27ff.; Veysey (1965), pp. 122, 318–323; Leites (1978), pp. 54–61.

[67]For the following, I rely upon Flexner (1908), pp. 6–9, 18–22, chap. 4; Flexner (1930), pts. 1, 2; William H. Kilpatrick, "Universities: American, English, and German," *JHE* 2 (1931): 357, 361; Harris (1970), pp. 107–129, 146–147; David Riesman, "Introduction" in *The Higher Learning in America: A Memorandum on the Conduct of Universities by Business Men*, Thorstein Veblen (1918; reprint, Stanford, Calif.: Academic Reprints, 1954), p. xiii.

edge through specialized research. While this view recalls the liberal-free ideal, it was a position that critics asserted to be rigid and dogmatic. And, in fact, Flexner was ambivalent about individual freedom of choice, in that undergraduates were to be allowed to choose among different programs of study within which all courses were prescribed. In addition, Flexner's *Universities—American, English, German* (1930), like his *Report on Medical Education in the United States and Canada* (1910), promoted the goal of intellectual research through a commitment to clear standards by which graduates and institutions could be evaluated and ranked. These ambiguities bespeak an accommodation of the liberal-free ideal, a judgment confirmed by Flexner's leadership at Princeton's Institute for Advanced Study from its opening in 1930 until 1939. In contrast to his recommendations for "college education" or "liberal education," Flexner's institute, which approximated Veblen's ideal, manifested characteristics of the liberal-free ideal without any contingencies or accommodations. Flexner sought to encourage the pursuit of truth via free research in any field, to treat scholars as equal members of an academic community, and to eschew rules and regulations, thereby maximizing freedom and tolerance for individual projects of study. But this was an institute for senior scholars, not a liberal arts college.

No less than Flexner, Frank Aydelotte, president of Swarthmore from 1921 to 1940, cited characteristics of the liberal-free ideal: that liberal education is nonvocational and nontechnical, that "each person is unique," that the "ideals of liberal education" include "freedom and individualism," and that "the very foundation of our democracy is our conception of liberal education and the freedom of the mind which that implies." Aydelotte also rejected prescription of a classical course for liberal education. Yet, indicative of the liberal-free accommodation, he acknowledged a certain elitism. "It requires courage in a democracy like ours, which considers each man as good as his neighbor, if not a little better, to put into operation what seems to many an aristocratic method of education. But we must learn to see the error in that superficial interpretation of democracy which assumes that all men are equal in intellectual ability."[68]

Believing elitism to follow necessarily from intellectualism in liberal education, Aydelotte committed Swarthmore to rigorous ac-

---

[68]Frank Aydelotte, *Breaking the Academic Lock Step: The Development of Honors Work in American Colleges and Universities* (New York: Harper and Brothers, 1944), pp. 1, 6, 9, 11, 13.

ademic standards instituted through an honors program, open scholarships, more selective admissions, and competitive final exams. This is not to say that he ignored moral and spiritual concerns, but in the last chapter of *Breaking the Academic Lock Step* (1944), he measures success in liberal education and "freedom of the mind" by "citing accomplishment in the graduate school as a yardstick." Furthermore, in his final presidential report, he found fit to repeat from his inaugural address "the conviction . . . only deepened by nineteen years of practical experience" that "perhaps the most fundamentally wasteful feature of our educational institutions is the lack of a higher standard of intellectual attainment."[69] Inspired by this conviction, other colleges—Wells, Franklin and Marshall, Colgate, Reed, Southwestern at Memphis—followed the example of Swarthmore in instituting honors courses, tutorials, seminars, and comprehensive or general examinations.[70]

The appearance of such examinations and courses demonstrates that the liberal-free accommodation arose in concert with efforts to find a unifying principle or technique for college education, in other words, a limit to the freedom of institutions and individuals to define liberal education. These attempts occurred more often as time passed. The editor of the 1932 NSSE yearbook, *Changes and Experiments in Liberal Arts Education*, noted that there had been more such efforts "in the past five years than in the previous twenty-five years."[71] This concern contributed directly to the founding or reor-

---

[69]Frank Aydelotte, "The American College of the Twentieth Century," *AACB* 12 (1926): 7–18; Aydelotte (1944), chaps. 3–7, 13; Aydelotte, "Excerpts from the Final Presidential Report of Frank Aydelotte," *AACB* 26 (1940): 310; Burton R. Clark, *The Distinctive College: Antioch, Reed, and Swarthmore* (Chicago: Aldine, 1970), chap. 8.

[70]"Some Progressive College Projects: Curriculum Reorganization, Orientation, and Survey Courses," *AACB* 17 (1931): 317–319; "Some Progressive College Projects II: Academic Tenure and Promotion," *AACB* 17 (1931): 485.

[71]McHale (1932), p. 2. Compare the accounts of the following foundings and reorganizations in Malcolm S. Maclean, Winston L. Little, and George A. Works, "The General Colleges," in *General Education in the American College*, ed. Guy M. Whipple (Bloomington, Ill.: Public School Publishing Co., 1938), pp. 135–170; Robert L. Leigh, "The Bennington College Program: A Proposed New Venture in Progressive Education for Women," *JHE* 1 (1930): 520–524; J. Anthony Humphreys, "General Education and Specialization: A Study Based upon Students' Choices of Courses under the Chicago College Plan," *JHE* 7 (1936): 296–300; Walter J. Matherly, "Comprehensive Courses: The Program of Courses in the General College of the University of Florida," *JHE* 7 (1936): 124–133; Alvin C. Eurich and Palmer O. Johnson, *The Effective General College Curriculum as Revealed by Examinations* (Minneapolis: University of Minnesota Press, 1937); A. Curtis Wilgus, "From St. John's to Mark Hopkins: A Vital Problem in Present-Day Education," *JHE* 10 (1939): 24–29; R. H. Eliassen, "Survey of 'New' College Plans: A Review of Programs and Procedures," *JHE* 10 (1939): 256–262.

ganization at about this time of Sarah Lawrence, Bennington, Black Mountain, Bard, St. John's, and general or experimental colleges at the universities of Wisconsin, Chicago, Minnesota, and Florida, among others. Few of these cared about offering a universal model for liberal education, but they were all perceived as seeking a particular organizing principle for their own curriculum. Thus emerged the paradox that the more such organizing or unifying principles were sought, the less uniformity or continuity there seemed to be in the large picture of American college education. Another complicating factor was the increasing number of students graduating from high school and seeking to enter college, as well as the greater diversity in this population compared to what colleges had seen previously. In this context, many academicians took up the phrase "general education," a phrase that was not coined in the 1920s as Louis Bénézet suggested, but has appeared frequently in history and may well have a greater claim to ancestry in *enkuklios paideia* than has "liberal education."

Though shortsighted on etymology, Bénézet was correct in his assessment that "There is throughout the literature a persistent mushiness in the distinctions between general education and liberal education."[72] Perhaps the only (occasionally) firm distinction stemmed from A. L. Lowell's plan for a college education to consist of a component of breadth and distribution plus a component of depth and concentration. This approach, which attracted many adherents over the 1920s and 1930s, resulted in a tendency to call the broad, distributive studies "general education" and to make them a subset of the four-year program of "liberal education."[73] The growth of the junior college movement reflected, in part, the popularity of this distinction.[74] In effect, Lowell's scheme was a concession to the

---

[72]Bénézet (1943), pp. 20—27, 177. Here and below, I draw from Alvin C. Eurich, "A Renewed Emphasis Upon General Education," in Whipple (1939), pp. 3, 7; Donald P. Cottrell, "General Education in Experimental Liberal Arts Colleges," in Whipple (1939), pp. 193—218; Homer P. Rainey, "Social Factors Affecting General Education," in Whipple (1939), pp. 15—19; Russell (1939), pp. 171—178; Ivol Spafford, *Building a Curriculum for General Education: A Description of the General College Program* (Minneapolis: University of Minnesota Press, 1943), chaps. 1, 2; Russell Thomas, *The Search for a Common Learning, 1800—1960* (New York: McGraw-Hill, 1962), pp. 40—41, 49—63, 68—91.

[73]Richardson (1924), pt. 3; C. S. Boucher, "Current Changes and Experiments in Liberal-Arts Colleges," in Whipple (1932), p. 17; Rudy (1960), p. 43, chap. 4.

[74]A study of catalogs of 100 colleges through the 1920s found a widening split between the first two years of college devoted to general or distributive education and the last two years tending toward specialized university scholarship. The split prompted and reflected a widespread growth in the number of junior colleges, which

fact that academicians no longer agreed on the content or meaning of liberal education, except that it ought to include a "major" field of study. To say that general education meant broad distributive studies was a way of stating positively the negative and operational definition that general education meant that part of liberal education that was not in the major. And since the major was the late nineteenth-century manifestation in undergraduate education of the ideal of specialized research, to say that general education meant broad distributive studies was to say that general education meant that part of liberal education that was not preparation for specialized research. General education, conceived of in Lowell's terms, could thus not escape the problem that no one agreed on the meaning or content of that part of liberal education not devoted to preparation for specialized research.

On the other hand, many educators, such as H. M. Wriston at Lawrence College and U. E. Fehlau at the University of Cincinnati, equated "general" and "liberal" studies.[75] In 1939, an NSSE study of thirty-five "liberal arts colleges" with highly publicized programs of general education found that most of those colleges did not distinguish between the two terms and concluded that there seemed to be "no useful service" in doing so. The 1944 report of the ACE Committee on a Design for General Education agreed, and this

---

had begun to attract many of the increasing number of new high school students who could not handle or did not want the more advanced studies of the four-year colleges. Floyd W. Reeves, "The Liberal-Arts College: The Fate of the Independent Arts College if the Cleavage Between the Freshman-Sophomore and Junior-Senior Years Persists," *JHE* 1 (1930): 373–380; Jay C. Knode, "Implications of the General College: Some Generalizations Regarding this College of Recent Growth (at the University of New Mexico)," *JHE* 7 (1936): 403–410; George B. Cutten, "The Future of the American Liberal-Arts College," *JHE* 10 (1939): 50–61. While some disagreed with this interpretation (Homer P. Rainey, "The Future of the Arts College, *JHE* 1 [1930]: 381), many expressed dismay either that liberal education was being fragmented or that the four-year college institution was splitting into two two-year segments. William F. Cunningham, "The Liberal College: The Structure of the College Curriculum in Relation to Its Function," *JHE* 6 (1935): 253–260; Donald J. Cowling, "Liberal Arts in the Postwar World," *AACB* 31 (1945): 384–395. A proposal by the University of Chicago to grant the B.A. after four years of general education, beginning in the third year of secondary school and lasting until the normal sophomore year, was seen in this context to encourage junior colleges to grant the B.A. and so to undermine the role and stature of the four-year college. The proposal attracted protest from many quarters. Richard M. Gummere, "The Bisected A.B.," *The Southern Association Quarterly* 6 (1942): 211–222; Walter C. Eells, "The Bachelor's Degree," *AACB* 28 (1942): 587–601.

[75]Andrew F. West, *American General Education: A Short Study of Its Present Condition and Needs* (Princeton, N.J.: Princeton University Press, 1932), p. v; Henry M. Wriston, "Nature, Scope, and Essential Elements in General Education," in *General Education: Its Nature, Scope, and Essential Elements*, ed. William S. Gray (Chicago:

equating of terms both reflected and exacerbated the blurring of distinctions in liberal education.[76]

"Every program of general education designed to date stresses the *need for integration* . . . the constant emphasis upon it signalize[s] a *quest* for some sort of *unity* now lacking in educational matters," wrote the chairman of the 1939 NSSE Yearbook Committee on General Education in the American College. Beyond this vague characteristic, although there was some disputed consensus about holding general education to exclude vocational or technical education, no more specific agreement on the kind of integration or unity ever was attained.[77] Still, most interpretations of general education, though variegated, were oriented with respect to three axes that intersected at one widely recognized ambiguity: that the term "general education" seemed to imply either education for an individual's life in general or education for all people in general.

In other words, general education implied, on one axis, that individual students would be prepared for life in general according to their particular needs and desires. Influential here was the emphasis upon the individual that characterized progressivism and the liberal-free ideal. The General College of the University of Minnesota, for example, emphasized this approach through its first decade. However, such institutions commonly found a difficulty in maintaining this emphasis relative to the second axis of general education: that all people in general would receive the same education. Observers with this sort of "common denominator" orientation, such as the director of the American Youth Commission in 1939, talked about "general education" for "intelligent participation in the experiences of life shared by all persons"; and in 1940, a former chairman of the education department at the University of Chicago contrasted "general," meaning egalitarian, with the "liberal" tradition, which he associated with high social standing.[78] If that axis

---

University of Chicago Press, 1934), p. 1; Wriston, *The Nature of a Liberal College* (Appleton, Wis.: Lawrence College Press, 1937); Butts (1939), pp. 15–16; Uhland E. Fehlau, "What About Liberal Arts?" *AACB* 26 (1940): 275–278.

[76]Russell (1939), pp. 171–192; Thomas R. McConnell et al., *A Design for General Education for Members of the Armed Forces* (Washington, D.C.: American Council on Education, 1944), pp. 4–5, 7.

[77]Quotation is from Eurich (1939), p. 7. Whipple (1939), chaps. 11, 12. The 1934 conference of the Institute for Administrative Officers of Higher Institutions concluded by resignedly changing its original theme title because no agreement could be reached on "A New Definition of General Education." Works (1934), p. 180; Louis Wirth, "Nature, Scope, and Essential Elements in General Education," in Gray (1934), p. 26.

[78]Rainey (1939), p. 22; Judd (1940), pp. 303–304; Spafford (1943), pp. 1, 24ff.

constituted the "lowest common denominator," the third axis relied on an understanding of "general" more congenial to the *artes liberales* ideal. This might be termed the "highest common denominator," or the common education to which everyone in general should aspire—*culture générale* as opposed to *culture généralisée* in the words of H. I. Marrou—and this view recalled the expectation of "universal knowledge" in a liberally educated English gentleman of the mid-nineteenth century.[79]

These three axes of "general education"—individualism, egalitarianism, culture—cut through the historical ideals of liberal education, and so the ways in which people talked about liberal education. The consequent blurring of historical distinctions led to a simultaneous phenomenon in both liberal and general education: the defining of either term as a basket of many diverse educational goods without providing a systematic rationale. For example, the wartime report of the ACE Committee on a Design for General Education listed these "Objectives of General Education": aesthetic, physical, emotional, intellectual, and moral development of the individual, plus social, ethical, familial, and vocational training.[80]

With respect to liberal education, the piling together of many different goods was not without precedent, as can be found in the nineteenth-century writings of John Henry Newman.[81] But it was only after the first World War that the "basket" approach became a prominent gambit in American discussions of liberal education. During the 1930s, this kind of definition was included in statements issued by the nationwide radio program seeking financial help for "The Liberal Arts College," by the executive director of the AAC, by the president of the American Association of University Women, and

[79]Wriston (1934), p. 1; Wriston, "A Critical Appraisal of Experiments in General Education," in Whipple (1939), pp. 320–321. Coleman R. Griffith, "A Comment on General Education: The Necessary Items in a Formula for General Education," *JHE* 10 (1939): 291–295; Paul L. Dressel and Lewis B. Mayhew, *General Education, Explorations in Evaluation: The Final Report of the Cooperative Study of Evaluation in General Education of the American Council on Education* (Washington, D.C.: American Council on Education, 1954), pp. 4–6; Henri Marrou, "les arts libéraux dans l'antiquité classique," in *Actes* (1969), p. 16; Rothblatt (1976), pp. 178–183.

[80]McConnell (1944).

[81]John Henry Newman's *The Idea of a University, Defined and Illustrated*, 3d ed. (1873: reprint, Notre Dame: University of Notre Dame Press, 1982) has probably been the most widely read essay on higher education in English. However, despite its notoriety or, perhaps, contributing to it, the *Idea* is somewhat eclectic and unsystematic. In terms of presentation, Newman's "prose and the meandering character of his method of arguing . . . and the distance, literally and figuratively, between essential positions of his thinking . . . cause difficulty and give rise to conflicting interpretations." Moreover, the logic of Newman's argument occasionally breaks down

by the Southern Association of Colleges and Secondary Schools. As in speeches from the presidents of Knox College and Drury College, these descriptions of liberal education affirmed diversity but called for unity; offered breadth and eschewed superficiality; extolled freedom and called for discipline; proclaimed democratic equality while demanding standards; honored individuality beside social responsibility; hailed intellectual along with spiritual, emotional, and physical development; promised "a foundation on which to base . . . occupational activities" but not vocational education; and recognized that no idea of liberal education is final but expected their students to find a firm philosophy of life. No surprise was it that the director of the Progressive Education Association's eight-year study on schools and colleges sighed in 1942: "Liberal arts college faculties seldom state clearly what they mean by liberal or general education. Perhaps they do not know."[82]

Nevertheless, the historical distinctions were not completely obliterated in the "liberal college," a term used interchangeably with "liberal arts college" by the seven hundred or so institutions claiming the name.[83] The four general types of historical argument about liberal education persisted into the 1940s.

Expressions of the *artes liberales* ideal, for example, can be found in statements by historian E. K. Rand in 1928 and by Ruth Kelso, who in 1929 defended the integrity of the Renaissance gentlemanly tradition and "a liberal or aristocratic education." Norman Foerster repeated the same argument many times during the 1930s. In 1941, just as a few decades earlier philosophical idealists had allied themselves with the liberal culture movement, T. M. Greene maintained that, in the argument for the study of humanities to inculcate val-

---

as well, while "a number of crucial issues become entangled." Powell (1965), p. 104; Sheldon Rothblatt, "Newman's Idea: John Henry Newman, The Idea of a University," *HEQ* 17 (1977): 327; Daniel G. Mulcahy, "The Role of the Disciplines in Cardinal Newman's Theory of A Liberal Education," *The Journal of Educational Thought* 6 (1972): 49–58. Appropriately, Henry Tristam would seem to have Newman be all things to all students. *The Idea of a Liberal Education: A Selection from the Works of Newman* (London: Harrap, 1952).

[82]Bénézet (1943), p. 43. See Robert L. Kelly, "The Future of the Liberal Arts College," *AACB* 16 (1930): 443–452; Kelly, "The Liberal College and Human Values," *AACB* 16 (1930): 340–346; Archie M. Palmer, "The Liberal Arts College on the Air," *AACB* 17 (1931): 421–430; Meta Glass, "The Contribution of the Humanities," *AACB* 23 (1937): 55–63; Carter Davidson, "The Liberal Arts of Maturity," *AACB* 25 (1939): 213–220; James F. Findlay, "The Liberal Arts College and the Whole Student," *AACB* 27 (1941): 286–295; "Some Aims and Objectives of Liberal Arts Education of the Southern Association of Colleges and Secondary Schools," *AACB* 18 (1942): 486.

[83]Whipple (1932), pt. 1; Walter J. Greenleaf, "Colleges in 1935: Reclassification, Accrediting, Mergers, and Reorganizations of Colleges and Universities," *JHE* 6 (1935): 130.

ues, "the fundamental premise is this: that in some sense aesthetic, moral, and religious values have an objective character."[84] Meanwhile, presidents of some liberal colleges aimed to educate the versatile and refined good citizen for society. W. M. Lewis of Lafayette wrote on "The College and Leisure" while upholding a gentlemanly standard for undergraduates, and W. H. Cowley of Hamilton advanced "holoism [sic] . . . the development of the whole man." A national study of fifteen selective colleges and universities concluded in 1945 (1) that "the primary objective of liberal education is the analysis and discrimination of values," (2) that "the humanities constitute the group of disciplines most vital to such analysis and discrimination," and (3) that their decline was due to the growth of "science and the scientific method." At the same time, statements defending the reliance on classical letters were heard, ironically enough, from professors of English—the most recent *antiqui*—at such institutions as Vanderbilt University and Goucher College.[85]

The defending of humanist classics testifies as well to the continuing support for the *artes liberales* accommodation, since traditionalists were being forced to call for the study of classical texts at least in translation, if in no other way. Moreover, the rejection of teaching about "artists in rhetoric" in favor of Socratic philosophers appeared in statements such as a 1945 address by the president of the New School for Social Research. He declared, "Liberal education, so far as I know, began with Socrates . . . . Socrates was the first who undertook to liberate man from fear, by way of reason." Two years earlier, Mark Van Doren had elaborated a similar view in *Liberal Education*. Appealing repeatedly to Socrates, Plato, and Aristotle while mentioning Cicero only once and Isocrates and Quintilian not at all, Van Doren argued for prescribed reading in a program of Great Books and adopted the framework of the *septem artes liberales* for his proposed curriculum. He was able, as he saw it, to acknowl-

---

[84]Edward K. Rand, *Founders of the Middle Ages* (Cambridge: Harvard University Press, 1928), pp. 218–232; Kelso (1929), p. 146; Foerster (1938); Foerster (1939), pp. 333–343; Theodore M. Greene, "The Realities of Our Common Life: The Contribution of the Humanities to the National Welfare," *JHE* 13 (1942): 344; Veysey (1965), pp. 191ff.

[85]William M. Lewis, "The College and Leisure," *AACB* 17 (1931): 222–227; Cowley (1938), pp. 469–477; Fred B. Millett, *The Rebirth of Liberal Education* (New York: Harcourt, Brace, 1945), p. v, chaps. 1, 5. The English professors are Edwin Mims, "The War and Higher Education," *AACB* 28 (1942): 542–548; Annette B. Hopkins, "Eclipse of Liberal Education," *AACB* 29 (1943): 223–225. As intimated earlier, the idea of the "education of the whole man" belongs historically more to the oratorical tradition, as a facet of preparing the Orator and Gentleman to be a versatile leader or Governor for society.

edge the importance of moral education while holding with the medieval schoolmen that "the conscious business of education is with the intellect," since intellectualism ultimately coincides with virtue.[86]

In 1943, Thomistic philosopher Jacques Maritain advanced a similar view at Yale. While prescribing a traditional curriculum that recalled the *trivium* and *quadrivium*, he asserted that "the chief aspirations of a person are aspirations to freedom" and "the task of the teacher is above all one of liberation." But such "liberation" involved this proviso: "The freedom of which we are speaking is not a mere unfolding of potentialities without any object to be grasped" because "the highest aim of liberal education is to make youth possess the fountains of wisdom." Having moved from "liberation" to "wisdom" and thereby demonstrating the ambiguity in the *artes liberales* accommodation, Maritain finally insisted that a liberal education in the traditional texts serves "not to shape the will and directly to develop moral virtues in the youth, but to enlighten and strengthen reason."[87]

The fact that Maritain had to take account of an interpretation of "freedom" as the "unfolding of potentialities" demonstrates the popularity of rationales that rode the waves of pragmatism and progressivism and approximated the liberal-free ideal.[88] Citing Peirce, James, Mead, and Dewey and attacking figures like Meiklejohn and Hutchins, the arguments continued to come forth that "a liberal education is simply that which increases the number and variety and intensity of one's interests," as held the writer of a 1929 Harvard dissertation on "The Curriculum of the Liberal Arts College" and subsequent proponents from Teachers College at Columbia University. Again and again, rising academic leaders, such as the future

---

[86]Alvin Johnson, *Liberal Education Fact and Fiction* (New York: New School for Social Research, 1945), p. 3; Mark Van Doren, *Liberal Education* (New York: Henry Holt, 1943), pp. 60–64, chap. 6; Sherman P. Young, "The Classics in Translation: Making Available to the College Student the Treasures of Greek and Roman Culture as Interpreted by Great Scholars," *JHE* 8 (1937): 241–244.

[87]Jacques Maritain, *Education at the Crossroads* (New Haven, Conn.: Yale University Press, 1943), pp. 10–11, 27, 39, 43, 56–57, 71. On the parallelism between Van Doren, Maritain, and Thomism, see George E. Ganss, *Saint Ignatius' Idea of a Jesuit University: A Study in the History of Catholic Education, Including Part IV of the Constitutions of the Society of Jesus* (Milwaukee: Marquette University Press, 1954), pp. 167–169, 269; William F. Cunningham, *General Education and the Liberal College* (St. Louis: B. Herder, 1953), pp. 17–18, 53.

[88]Given that Lawrence Cremin calls 1917–1957 "the Progressive Era in American Education," it is perhaps indicative of the culminating influence of the progressive movement that the 1957 Annual History of Education Lecture delivered at the Uni-

president of Brooklyn College, derided "the claim to have isolated immutable ideas and indubitable first principles" and affirmed the belief that "truth to finite man is never single, complete, and static . . . rather [it is] multiple, fractional, and evolving." This belief was thought to be consonant with, just as the liberal arts were based upon, "the observational-hypothetical-deductive-observationist procedure" of experimental science.[89] While various scientists, from an Oberlin chemistry professor to the dean of medical sciences at the University of Minnesota, also advanced this interpretation of liberal or general education,[90] certain philosophy professors likewise held absolute or immutable world views to be incompatible with the "mental, moral or spiritual liberation" of liberal education. "The liberal arts curriculum is to liberate the student for the freedom of independent thinking," one professor wrote. "It is the task of philosophy to develop the skeptical attitude in the student."[91]

If some proponents of liberal education talked in terms of the characteristics of the liberal-free ideal, which was rooted in the philosophical tradition, that general type was at the same time being compromised and accommodated both to the progressivists' interest in utility and "holoism" and to the constraints of institutionalizing the commitment to research. Over the 1930s, such groups as

---

versity of Michigan suggested that "liberal education" could be a synonym for "Progressivist American Education." Louis Filler, "Main Currents in Progressivist American Education," *History of Education Journal* 8 (1957): 33n. After concentrating on social and poltiical reform from 1876 to 1917, progressivism moved centrally into the educational arena with the stimulus of those who "in creative self-expression . . . found the quintessential meaning of the progressive education movement." The movement was institutionalized with the 1919 founding of the Progressive Education Association, whose aim was "the freest and fullest development of the individual, based upon the scientific study of his mental, physical, spiritual and social characteristics and needs." Cremin (1961), pp. 183, 240–241; Patricia A. Graham, *Progressive Education: From Arcady to Academe, A History of the Progressive Education Association, 1919–1955* (New York: Teachers College Press, 1967), chaps. 1–2. Anticipated in the "Wisconsin Idea" under Charles R. Van Hise, the "progressive college" came to emphasize attention to the individual needs of students, greater student freedom in planning their courses, and an experimental approach to the entire program, as seen in varying degrees at Sarah Lawrence, Bennington, and Rollins. Ernest H. Wilkins, "What Constitutes a Progressive College?" *AACB* 19 (1933): 108–109; Bénézet (1943), pp. 13ff., 46ff.

[89]Espy (1929), p. 7; Gideonse (1947), pp. 6–7, 28, 32. For testimony from Teachers College, see Thomas H. Briggs, "Interests as Liberal Education," *Teachers College Record* 29 (1928): 667–674; Briggs (1939), pp. 315–329; Childs (1943), pp. 539–543; Citron (1943), pp. 544–553; Lewis (1943), pp. 563–571.

[90]Richard E. Scammon, "The Relation of the Natural Sciences to General Education," in Gray (1934), p. 64; Harry N. Holmes, "The Contribution of the Physical Sciences," *AACB* 23 (1937): 67–72.

[91]Schilpp (1935), pp. 234–235, 239.

the American Council of Learned Societies, the Social Science Research Council, the American Council on Education, and the American Association of University Professors sponsored studies that concluded that good teaching is rarely found apart from good research. This finding contributed to placing greater emphasis upon independent study and honors work in the colleges over the second quarter of the twentieth century.[92] As a result, the liberal-free accommodation could be heard from academic leaders who had to adapt their ideal both to the organizational strictures that seemed useful to researchers and to the lingering characteristics of the *artes liberales* ideal.

H. M. Wriston, president of Lawrence College and, later, Brown University, stated, on the one hand, that liberal or general education "must be something which gives the mind freedom" and that prescription of courses is incompatible both with that freedom and with appreciating the individual differences of students. On the other hand, he affirmed, education must have "universal validity" and "a quality of permanence" because "a liberal education consists in the acquisition and the refinement of standards of values." This acquisition and refinement is accomplished, Wriston held, through the discipline of "reflective synthesis," which is derived from "the validity of the intellectual experience itself." Consequently, the "standards of values" depend upon intellectual criteria by which an elite is to be identified. This conclusion led Wriston to apologize, "The 'aristocracy' of intellectualism is of a character wholly in harmony with both the theory and practice of democracy." Nevertheless, he was criticized for incorporating into liberal education a critical and open-ended viewpoint and an emphasis upon freedom and individuality while also identifying an "aristocracy" according to standards of intellectual performance that were designed "to fit [his] preconceived purpose of the liberal education concept."[93]

The liberal-free accommodation naturally held a special attraction for academicians in the natural sciences, such as Hans Zinsser of Harvard Medical School. Rejecting the view, which he attributed

---

[92]Butts (1937), pp. 548–564; Butts (1939), pp. 1–16; Dwayne Orton, "Liberal Education and the Modern World: Neither the Classics nor the Sciences Are All of Education," *JHE* 10 (1939): 237–242; Walter E. Bundy and Harold Zink, "A Summary of Facts and Opinions: Research and Creative Work in a Liberal-Arts College," *JHE* 10 (1939): 30–36; Rudy (1960), chap. 4.

[93]Wriston (1937), pp. 1–4, 9, 14; Wriston (1939), pp. 307, 320; Wriston, "Liberal Learning," *AACB* 25 (1939): 365–369. For criticism, see R. A. Kent, "An Excellent Production: *The Nature of a Liberal College* by Henry M. Wriston," *JHE* 8 (1937): 502.

to R. M. Hutchins, that the scientific methodology leads to "confusion," Zinsser pointed out "the value of scientific discipline for liberal education." The value of such discipline arises from observing the "orderliness both in physical and organic nature which, to the sensitive scholar, is a sort of religious experience." In this way, Zinsser held, the sciences amount to "a New Humanism," a new classical tradition for liberal education that "only a small percentage of individuals either desire or are capable of acquiring."[94] This is the liberal-free accommodation par excellence.

Although the colleges had not fully enlisted in the war effort until the final three months of the First World War, higher education began mobilizing behind the government immediately after Pearl Harbor, as editorials in professional journals and statements issued by conferences and institutes attest.[95] Divisiveness and criticism over "liberal education" were stifled, while liberal study itself was, by almost anyone's definition, acknowledged to be of marginal necessity when compared to the initial increase in technical training required to meet wartime needs. Little time passed, however, before the calls came from Carleton College, from the University of the South, and from the University of Illinois, to name a few, asserting that if liberal education were sacrificed during the war nothing would be won.[96] And even the academicians who were inclined to see the war won first—from colleges and universities such as Swarthmore, Rutgers, Wisconsin, and Southwestern at Memphis—commenced to clamor that liberal education had to be reinstated immediately after the conflict.[97] But no sooner did the topic arise than confusion erupted once more. Those inclined toward the liberal-free ideal feared that free thought and individualism would

[94]Hans Zinsser, "What Is a Liberal Education?" *School and Society* 45, no. 1172 (1937): 803–806. See E. E. Reinke, "Liberal Values in Premedical Education," *AACB* 22 (1936): 602.

[95]Mary A. Molloy, "The Post-War Curriculum," *AACB* 6, no. 2 (1920): 125–129; John H. MacCracken, "The Liberal Arts College of the Future," *AACB* 26 (1940): 482; W. W. Charters, "The War and the Colleges," *JHE* 13 (1942): 51–52; W. G. Reeder, "College Standards and the War," *JHE* 13 (1942): 111–112; Meta Glass, "How Shall the College Curriculum Be Adjusted to Wartime Conditions and Needs?" *AACB* 28 (1942): 549; Carol S. Gruber, *Mars and Minerva: World War I and the Uses of the Higher Learning in America* (Baton Rouge: Louisiana State University, 1975), chap. 6.

[96]Alexander Guerry, "Liberal Arts Education," *AACB* 28 (1942): 483–485; Max Black and Arthur E. Murphy, "Liberal Arts in Wartime," *JHE* 14 (1943): 121–125; Donald J. Cowling, "The Preservation of Liberal Education in Time of War," *AACB* 29 (1943): 187–191.

[97]Diehl (1943), pp. 196–201; Aydelotte (1944), p. 5; Robert C. Clothier, "The Ed-

be eroded by totalitarianism, and those oriented toward the *artes liberales* ideal feared the loss of the "Great Tradition" of western civilization.

In 1944, Sidney Hook loosed "Thirteen Arrows Against Progressive Liberal Education," while President A. D. Henderson of Antioch defined liberal education as "an education that tends to produce the liberal individual—the person who . . . helps to facilitate needed change in the world."[98] In the same year, a gathering of philosophy and religion professors at Williams College agreed, despite other disputes, that their disciplines are necessary to liberal education; and five months later a group of scientists meeting at Princeton did the same. Meanwhile, a history professor from Smith College defended his discipline in "History: Its Place in a Liberal Education," and a professor from Coe College argued similarly for economics.[99] At the same time, the teaching of "humanities" was being studied by the Phi Beta Kappa Society, the Modern Language Association of America, and the Classical Association of the Middle West and South, among others.

For every demand that the postwar liberal education should draw its subject matter from modern social issues, there was a rebuttal prescribing "the monuments of Western civilization." For every rejection of "a return to the classic disciplines," there was a reply that classics would be "essential" after the war.[100] Some, including a dean from the University of Minnesota, saw professional training being accepted into the "liberal arts college"; but others, like the dean of St. John's College, Annapolis, rushed to oppose utility. Meanwhile, the "mushiness" of the basket approach could be found in books by S. G. Cole of Kalamazoo College or D. L. Evans of Ohio

ucation of the Free Man," *AACB* 30 (1944): 504–506; C. J. DuCasse, "Liberal Education and the College Curriculum: Through the Discipline of Formal Thinking, Empirical Investigation, and Hypothesis, to Appreciation," *JHE* 15 (1944): 1–10; Walter R. Agard, "Liberal Education after the War," *JHE* 16 (1945): 57–62.

[98]Algo D. Henderson, *Vitalizing Liberal Education: A Study of the Liberal Arts Program* (New York: Harper and Brothers, 1944), p. 15; Sidney Hook, "Thirteen Arrows Against Progressive Liberal Education," *The Humanist* 4 (Spring 1944): 1–10; Hook, "A Challenge to the Liberal-Arts College," *JHE* 10 (1939): 14–23.

[99]Hans Kohn, "History: Its Place in a Liberal Education," *AACB* 30 (1944): 250–263; C. Ward Macy, "Economics in the Liberal Arts Curriculum," *AACB* 30 (1944): 264–273; James P. Baxter III, "Report of the Commission on Liberal Education," *AACB* 31 (1945): 153.

[100]Seba Eldridge, "The Liberal-Arts College: A Diagnosis of Its Shortcomings," *JHE* 14 (1943): 343–347; Cyril F. Richards, "The Function of Liberal Arts in Reconstruction: Can the Liberal Arts Use Current Problems in Place of Classical Studies?" *JHE* 15 (1944): 65–70; Herbert Weisinger, "The Rôle of the Liberal-Arts College," *JHE* 15 (1944): 249; Herbert N. Couch, "The Classics in the Liberal-Arts College," *JHE* 16 (1945): 227.

State University.[101] The discussion over "general education" differed little, and by 1944, a University of Chicago professor of education proclaimed, "A furious controversy rages over the future of liberal education."[102] The same year, *The American Scholar* sponsored a forum on this topic, and in 1945 a survey of "two-score typical liberal arts colleges in the East" revealed that nearly every one had formed a committee to assess the status of postwar "liberal education." In the meantime, a partial bibliography of writings on liberal education for 1943–44 containing 289 entries was compiled by the AAC Commission on Liberal Education.[103]

The story of the Commission and its confederates depicts rather well the nature of discussion about liberal education at the conclusion of the war. Established in 1942 with fourteen members, the Commission met for the third time early in 1943, while a committee appointed in 1939 by the American Council of Learned Societies was completing its report, *Liberal Education Re-examined*.[104] The president of Knox College stated that this reexamination might "become the 'Bible' of liberal-arts educators in America."[105] But canonization had scarcely begun before the Commission on Liberal Education decided there was a need for another statement on liberal education and appointed its own Committee on the Re-Statement of the Nature and Aims of Liberal Education.

Shortly thereafter, this Committee issued "The Nature and Purpose of Liberal Education." On the side of "Nature," they included

---

[101]Stewart G. Cole, *Liberal Education in a Democracy: A Charter for the American College* (New York: Harper and Brothers, 1940), chap. 3; D. Luther Evans, *Essentials of Liberal Education* (Boston: Ginn, 1942), pp. 7–8; Scott Buchanan, "Liberal Education and Politics," *The American Scholar* 13 (1944): 396–398; Thomas R. McConnell, "The Revival of General Education," in *On General and Liberal Education: A Symposium*, Joseph P. Blickensderfer, chairman (Washington, D.C.: Association for General and Liberal Education, 1945), p. 34.

[102]Ralph W. Tyler, "Foreword," in Henderson (1944), p. ix. On general education, see the complaints in Earl J. McGrath, "Factors Influencing the Development of General Education," *AACB* 31 (1945): 566; Max Black, "What is General Education?" *JHE* 15 (1944): 117–121; Marvin T. Herrick, "A Revival of General Education: An Experiment at the University of Illinois," *JHE* 15 (1944): 243–247.

[103]"The American Scholar Forum: The Function of the Liberal Arts College in a Democratic Society," *The American Scholar* 13 (1944): 391–407; Commission on Liberal Education, *Liberal Education: Ends and Means, Partial Bibliography, 1943–44* (New York: Association of American Colleges, 1944); Benjamin Fine, "Liberal Arts to Remain," in Blickensderfer (1945), p. 10.

[104]Theodore M. Greene, "Liberal Education and Democracy," *AACB* 27 (1941): 45–52; Theodore M. Greene et al., *Liberal Education Re-examined; Its Role in a Democracy, by a Committee Appointed by the American Council of Learned Societies* (New York: Harper and Brothers, 1943).

[105]Carter Davidson, "A Meaningful Pattern," *JHE* 14 (1943): 55.

physical, intellectual, aesthetic, spiritual, and moral training through a curriculum of social and natural sciences, arts, classics, philosophy, language, and literature, all of which together had the "Purpose" of promoting individual freedom and fulfillment as well as social responsibility along with the "skills and abilities . . . to use intelligently and with a sense of workmanship some of the principal tools and techniques of the arts and sciences." Adopted by the Commission in 1943, this report was capsuled in a news release sent to 1,894 newspapers; summarized in a booklet distributed to 7,000 educational organizations, journals, elected officials, and heads of schools, colleges, and universities; and sold in unabridged form to 6,000 institutions of higher education, most of which were revising their curricula.[106]

Despite all this effort, and despite the "enthusiasm" with which many educational leaders, including the president of Bennington College, greeted the report, members of the Commission themselves, such as the president of the College of the Holy Cross, were soon advancing their own plans for liberal education and talking as though nothing had been resolved.[107] Small wonder, then, that others continued to disagree. The chairman of the New York City Board of Higher Education observed in 1944, "There are almost as many characterizations of the meaning of the liberal arts as there have been writers upon the theme."[108] In the same year, despite the two preceding reports, a Conference of University Administrators on General and Liberal Education was called at Chicago to discuss the

> age-old questions which continue to defy satisfactory answers, such as: What is the definition of liberal education? What is the relationship between the cultural and the utilitarian in liberal-arts study? How may one distinguish between liberal education and general education? What are the objectives of liberal and of general education?[109]

---

[106]"The Post-War Responsibilities of Liberal Education: Report of the Committee on the Re-Statement of the Nature and Aims of Liberal Education," *AACB* 29 (1943): 275–299; James P. Baxter III, "Commission on Liberal Education Report," *AACB* 29 (1943): 269–274.

[107]Lewis W. Jones, "The Reconstruction of Liberal Education," *AACB* 30 (1944): 320; Joseph R. Maxwell, "Reconstruction of Liberal Education," *AACB* 30 (1944): 78–82; James P. Baxter III, "Reconstruction of Liberal Education," *AACB* 30 (1944): 76–77.

[108]Ordway Tead, "Why Liberal Colleges Tomorrow?" *AACB* 30 (1944): 308.

[109]J. Hillis Miller, "Agreement Needed," review of *Report of Proceedings of the Conference of University Administrators on General and Liberal Education, JHE* 16 (1945): 278; Joseph P. Blickensderfer, ed., *Report of Proceedings of the Conference of University Administrators on General and Liberal Education* (Norman: University of Oklahoma Press, 1944).

VII
A Typology
of
Contemporary
Discussion

*I*N RECENT WEEKS *I have tried, in a dozen different ways, to frame those propositions that might enter into a distinctly American view of liberal education. I am now ready to pronounce unqualifiedly that the effort has been a failure. I suspect, indeed, there is no such thing as the American theory of liberal education.*

THOMAS F. GREEN*

*Liberalism and Liberal Education: The Good Life and the Making of the Good Man," *SR* 5 (1976): 27.

IN PREPARATION FOR SKETCHING a simple typology of the historical rationales for liberal education current in contemporary America, it may be helpful to review briefly the argument up to this point. Origins of the education or arts called "liberal" lie in the *artes liberales*, a curriculum known to the Middle Ages as the normative program that an educated person would have studied. The formation of this normative program can best be attributed to Latin antiquity, despite the popular modern appeal to ancient Athens, because in Greek antiquity there existed a variety of approaches out of which relative consensus was achieved only in Roman times. Although etymological, curricular, and theoretical antecedents of the *artes liberales* existed in Athens, the normative program appeared only in the later period; and its rationale in Rome owed more to orators like Cicero than to philosophers like Socrates. In fact, even if the argument about Latin versus Greek consensus is denied, the lineage of the normative approach toward *artes liberales* can better be traced to Isocrates than to Plato and Aristotle, as is often done by the schoolmen of the modern academy.

While abstracting certain characteristics of the orators' rationale for liberal arts into a general type labeled the *"artes liberales* ideal," I have said that the liberal education which began as oratorical deteriorated to the merely sophistic from the time of Quintilian in the first century c.e. to that of Martianus Capella in the fifth century. In the course of this deterioration, the pagan liberal arts were gradually adopted and reinforced with standards and values for molding the good citizen by Christian educators, who embraced the oratorical tradition and its curricular tendencies. The *septem artes liberales* were studied to enhance the understanding of and preaching from scriptural texts. The study of language and letters were therefore emphasized, and the art of grammar, which incorporated literature, history, and moral instruction, and the art of rhetoric were made preeminent. Logic was treated as an adjunct to rhetoric, and music was studied in its practical and sonorous dimension. The mathematical and scientific disciplines were regarded as bodies of facts providing technical information useful for exegesis. Specialization and advanced study were not encouraged or were even discouraged as self-indulgent, and the term *philosophia* was often ambiguously applied to the entire program.

The Christian accommodation of the *artes liberales* ideal was codified and transmitted by Cassiodorus, Isidore, and the Carolingian schools, despite the speculative inquiries of Boethius and Johannes Scotus Erigena. Eventually, in the twelfth and thirteenth centuries, it was challenged by the scholastics, whose incisive appreciation for critical and speculative thought derived from the newly received works of Greek, Jewish, and Islamic philosophy and science. In the aborning universities, the orators and philosophers clashed again over the rationale for the liberal arts, with the theoretical and curricular orientation of the *moderni* coming to dominate. Logic emerged supreme as a refined analytic tool and mathematics and music increasingly addressed *quantitas abstracta* rather than technical or practical matters. Rhetoric practically dropped from sight or was transformed into a highly formal, even formulaic, *ars*, while grammar was transmuted into linguistic analysis and stripped of its association with the literary tradition. Overall, the liberal disciplines became narrow and relatively brief *scientiae speculativae* intended to prepare the student for advanced and specialized study, and *philosophia* was distinguished from and elevated above them.

The provocative scholastic disputations gradually deteriorated to sophistry during the fourteenth and fifteenth centuries, while the characteristics of the *artes liberales* ideal were being reinvigorated by the *antiqui* of the Italian Renaissance. The humanism of the *antiqui*, derived from Cicero and Quintilian, was transmitted to the rest of Western Europe during the fifteenth and sixteenth centuries. It was this outlook, amplified by notions of "courtesy" and Christian ethics, that was eventually transmitted to the American colonies in the archetype of the Christian gentleman. Meanwhile, ideas that would come to be associated with a different type of liberal education surfaced prominently in discussions among leaders of the seventeenth-century scientific revolution and eighteenth-century Enlightenment, who looked back reverently to the Socratic and Pythagorean philosophical tradition. Those characteristics, which I have abstracted in a second general type and labeled the "liberal-free ideal," began to appear in American discussion about liberal education in the late eighteenth and early nineteenth centuries.

Confrontation between these two educational types inevitably resulted, as in the late nineteenth-century debate between Matthew Arnold and Thomas Huxley in which they fundamentally rehearsed the long-standing dispute between orators and philosophers. Out of the frequent confrontations occurring in the course of this dispute emerged two kinds of accommodation between the two different perspectives. Over the course of the nineteenth century, certain educators, whose views were congenial to the *artes liberales* ideal and who prescribed the reading of classical texts, adapted their arguments consciously and unconsciously to the "modern" one, arriving at a position here denoted by the *artes liberales* accommodation." Conversely, as characteristics of the liberal-free ideal entered the mainstream of definitions for liberal education in the new research universities of the late nineteenth and early twentieth centuries, certain advocates of that general type, enamored of pure scientific research and yet constrained by the strictures of organizing institutions to pursue it and to make it useful, adapted their arguments consciously and unconsciously, producing finally the "liberal-free accommodation." Nevertheless, after all this posturing through the first half of the twentieth century, dissension and confusion did not diminish in the decades following the Second World War.

Reporting in 1946 on discussion among the 590 members of the Association of American Colleges, the AAC Commission on Liberal Education declared, "the hubbub has been immense." Clinging hopefully to the term "liberal education," even if its meaning were not at all clear, the Association changed the name of its journal in 1959 to *Liberal Education* "because it is the most concise and widely accepted expression of the end to which members of the Association are dedicated." In 1963, the Commission on Liberal Education decided once again "the time is appropriate for a thorough review and restatement of the aims of liberal education,"[1] and the AAC annual meetings of 1964, 1969, 1972, 1976, and 1978 sought to analyze, define, justify, and explain liberal education amid the turmoil of a rapidly changing society.

Meanwhile, after spinning off a Special Committee on Liberal Studies, the Commission on Liberal Education in 1973 joined with the American Association of University Professors, the American Association of State Colleges and Universities, and other national associations in "A Project to Create Institutional Change by Developing and Implementing Alternative Curriculum Models for Undergraduate Liberal Education." Efforts by other groups along these lines included the founding of *The Forum on Liberal Education* in 1977, Project QUILL: Quality in Liberal Learning in 1978, and National Project IV: Liberal Education Varieties and Their Assessment in 1979. Surveying all this hubbub, a professor of the College of William and Mary observed that "the twentieth century curricular landscape is

---

[1]Gordon K. Chalmers, "Report on a Work in Progress: Education, The Redefinition of Liberal Education," *AACB* 32 (1946a): 60; "Editorial Notes," *Liberal Education* 45 (1959): 175; Byron K. Trippett, "Commission on Liberal Education,"*Liberal Education* 49 (1963): 105.

strewn with attempts to reinvigorate the liberal learning," and "the failure of most attempts to revitalize the liberal tradition is difficult to refute."[2]

Whether or not "failure" is the right word, certainly conflict and confusion have continued to reign. Thomas Woody's appraisal of the situation in 1951 was quoted and confirmed by Saul Sack in 1962: "We need a liberal education for today. Equally beyond cavil is the fact that, as in Aristotle's time, there is little agreement as to what liberal education should be. Both theory and practice are confused and contradictory." Theodore Greene acknowledged this, as well, and Caroline Bird scoffed at the fact in a 1975 parody, "The Liberal Arts Religion," while academicians echoed a professor from St. Peters College who inquired, "What are the Liberal Arts?"[3] By the 1980s, not only did everyone recognize the fact that individuals defined liberal education however they pleased, but the dean of faculty at Buena Vista College affirmed it as an entitlement: "In the course of educational events, one thing is certain above all others: that the liberal arts will be defined *ad infinitum*. Like history, the liberal arts must be defined by the individual according to the season and the reason of the day. . . . Each age demands its own interpretation; indeed, it has a right to create one."[4]

Having noted the character of the situation, I do not intend to discuss chronological steps of development in the American discussion about liberal education and liberal arts between 1945 and the present. The length of time is so short and perspective so lacking that such observations would be largely gratuitous. I mean this in the sense that, in terms of historical appeals about liberal education and the typologies theorized here, I do not find new arguments emerg-

---

[2]Clifton E. Conrad, *The Undergraduate Curriculum: A Guide to Innovation and Reform* (Boulder, Colo.: Westview, 1978), p. 53. For reports on the various efforts, see Edward J. Shoben, "Commision on Liberal Learning," *Liberal Education* 60 (1974): 54; Joel Read, "Commission on Liberal Learning," *Liberal Education* 61 (1975): 39; "A Report of Project QUILL," issue of *The Forum for Liberal Education* 2 (December 1979): 1−16; Richard Hendrix, "Liberal Education Varieties: Background to National Project IV," *The Forum for Liberal Education* 2 (March 1980): 1−3.

[3]Thomas Woody, *Liberal Education for Free Men* (Philadelphia: University of Pennsylvania Press, 1951), p. 1; Saul Sack, "Liberal Education: What Was It? What Is It?" *HEQ* 2 (1962): 210; Theodore M. Greene, *Liberal Education Reconsidered* (Cambridge: Harvard University Press, 1953), p. 1; Caroline Bird, *The Case Against College*, ed. Helene Mandelbaum (New York: David McKay, 1975), chap. 6; John P. Hughes, "What Are the Liberal Arts?" *AACB* 41 (1955): 614−625.

[4]Fred D. Brown, "Toward a Better Definition of Liberal Education: Seven Perspectives," *Liberal Education* 65 (1979): 383.

ing out of those discussions. Yes, the degree of influence enjoyed by various arguments changes from decade to decade, but their essential nature does not.

The call continues for liberal education dedicated to a "unifying conviction," as the Commission on Liberal Education declared in 1952, "to a faith which will do away with both cynicism and bigotry, serve to undercut the present manifold disagreements in belief and provide the colleges with a basis for a rejuvenated sense of mission." In fact, this sentiment was bolstered soon after the war by the perception of a Communist threat. Addresses from the presidents of Kenyon College and Princeton University about "Education for Liberalism" and "Education for Freedom" right after the war gave way to such speeches as "To Teach Wisdom" in the early 1950s.[5] Naturally, the shift in terminology was not wholly indicative of a change in thinking, for, as in earlier times of national crisis, statements about "free men" and claims that "liberal education . . . is the antithesis of everything which totalitarian education undertakes" could be advanced from both a liberal-free and an *artes liberales* perspective.[6] In 1959, E. J. McGrath reiterated the call for unity and bemoaned the rise of academic specializations and fragmentation of liberal education, concluding, *"The liberal arts college must, however, regain and affirm a clear, feasible, and independent mission."* This view was echoed at Brown University in 1961, and a decade later, Russell Kirk offered the pragmatic argument that "commitment to principle brings success as a by-product" for the institution. Thus, "a reinvigoration of truly liberal learning" based on "the restoration or establishment of a college with principle" is not only sound theory but also an effective strategy for appealing to philanthropists.[7]

Another postwar argument reminiscent of earlier discussion is the call from religion departments and sectarian colleges for a creedal or theological perspective to anchor the curriculum. From McPherson College in 1946, Southwestern University in 1950, and

---

[5]Nathan Pusey, "Report of Commission on Liberal Education," *AACB* 38 (1952): 110. For the presidents' statements, see Gordon K. Chalmers, "The Break in Liberalism" *AACB* 32 (1946b): 378–386; Chalmers, "Report of Commission on Liberal Education," *AACB* 37 (1951): 135–140; Harold W. Dodds, "Education for Freedom," *AACB* 33 (1947): 453–463; Dodds, "To Teach Wisdom," *AACB* 38 (1952): 385–388.

[6]For the quotations and examples, see George F. Kennan, "The Liberal Arts in Contemporary American Society," *AACB* 39 (1953): 416–423; Francis E. Corkery, "Education for Freedom or Slavery?" *AACB* 39 (1953): 37; Franc L. McCluer, "Liberal Education: The Years Ahead," *AACB* 42 (1956): 110–111.

[7]Earl J. McGrath, *The Graduate School and the Decline of Liberal Education* (New York: Bureau of Publications, Teachers College, Columbia University, 1959), pp. 8–9;

Juniata College in 1955 came addresses and essays proclaiming the Bible is "The Classic of Classics" and that, since "*veritas liberat*—the truth sets free," "Christian liberal arts education" is indeed "education for free men."[8] By 1957, the National Council of Religion in Higher Education and *The Christian Scholar* had also declaimed on the issue, but it was Catholics who seemed able to hold the line most effectively. As Bernard Rattigan observed, "The contrast between the confusion that prevails in secular institutions and the unanimity of thought in Catholic colleges has often been noted."[9] This contrast encouraged appeals from Southern Illinois University in 1959, from the University of Michigan a decade later, and from Augustana College in 1973 to the effect that the "Church-related college" has a "special mission" to respond to the lack of direction and purpose in "modern liberal arts education" and that it ought not become "a value-free institution." More recently, the evangelical Protestant colleges have championed this point of view.[10] Nevertheless, the strength of the modern academic creed—which undermines all efforts to build a widespread commitment to a set of virtues—has not diminished since the dean of the Divinity School at the University of Chicago observed in 1951: "The god of the university professor is specialized competence. His whole intellectual life is defined in terms of it and all the rest of his life is dependent upon it."[11]

Sympathetic to the religionists' desire for unity are the inheritors of the prewar appeal to philosophy to accomplish the same end.

George W. Morgan, "Liberal Education: An Assessment of Afflictions and Suggestions for Reform," *Liberal Education* 47 (1961): 376–395; Russell Kirk, "The Revitalized College: A Model," in *Education in a Free Society*, ed. Anne H. Burleigh (Indianapolis: Liberty Fund, 1973), pp. 88–89.

[8] W. W. Peters, "The Christian College Looks Ahead," *AACB* 32 (1946): 387–396; John Osman, "The Classic of Classics," *AACB* 36 (1950): 460–463; Calvert N. Ellis, "The Church-Related Liberal Arts College," *AACB* 41 (1955): 365–372.

[9] Bernard T. Rattigan, *A Critical Study of the General Education Movement* (Washington, D. C.: Catholic University of America Press, 1951), p. 167; Victor L. Butterfield, "Liberal Learning and Religion in the American College," in *Liberal Learning and Religion*, ed. Amos N. Wilder, for the National Council in Religion and Higher Education (New York: Harper & Brothers, 1951), pp. 145–146; J. Edward Dirks, "The Future of the Education of Free Men in the Christian Colleges," *AACB* 43 (1957): 63–77.

[10] E. Earle Stibitz, "A Religious Point of View in Teaching the Liberal Arts," *Liberal Education* 45 (1959): 249–262; Stephen J. Tonsor, "The Church-Related College: Special Mission or Educational Anachronism," *Liberal Education* 56 (1970): 403–411; William R. Matthews, "What Should a Church College Be For? Or Should It Be At All?" *Liberal Education* 59 (1973): 417; William C. Ringenberg, *The Christian College: A History of Protestant Higher Education in America* (Grand Rapids, Mich.: Wm. B. Eerdmans, 1984), chaps. 5, 6.

[11] Bernard M. Loomer, "Religion and the Mind of the University," in Wilder (1951), p. 155.

From Princeton in 1964, W. J. Oates argued for "having liberal education give to philosophy the central position which is its due." But this appeal, as discussed in the previous chapter, could imply one of two very different things. Philosophy could mean a system of true propositions or realizable values, as it did for a philosophy professor at Morgan State who put at the center of liberal education "philosophy in the great tradition . . . as the source of rationally founded judgment."[12] On the other hand, philosophy could mean not so much "what a certain number of chosen philosophers think" or "some particular concepts" but rather "the continuing process of reflective thought," as it did to a dean at Jacksonville University in 1960. "Philosophy is criticism. . . . The philosophy class is . . . a laboratory of critical and creative thinking," wrote another philosophy professor in 1969. "Philosophy as a habit of critical reflection is the most practical thing one can carry away from a liberal arts education."[13]

One other argument continuing after World War II is the recommending of general education. As these recommendations gained strength after the war, there emerged more and more clearly a standard plan of undergraduate studies resembling that of Columbia University: general education in the three areas of humanities, social sciences, and natural sciences in the first two years, and a major or concentration in the last two years. The college of the University of Chicago was also influential through its brief abstention from prescribing a major, a reluctance based on "the notion that a liberal education should constitute a single whole."[14] Nor was Columbia insensitive to this outlook, viewing its Contemporary Civilization and Humanities Course as the unifying aspect of its undergraduate program. By 1960, a selective nationwide study found only St. John's College in Annapolis rejecting the distribution and concentration format.[15]

---

[12]Richard I. McKinney, "Some Aspects of the Teaching of Philosophy," *Liberal Education* 46 (1960): 366; Whitney J. Oates, "Philosophy as the Center of Liberal Education," *Liberal Education* 50 (1964): 213. See Brand Blanshard, "Values: The Polestar of Education," in *The Goals of Higher Education*, ed. Willis D. Weatherford, Jr. (Cambridge: Harvard University Press, 1960), p. 80.

[13]Richard K. Morton, "Philosophy and the College Student," *Liberal Education* 46 (1960): 255; Robert H. Miekle, "The Role of Philosophy," *Liberal Education* 55 (1969): 581, 583–584.

[14]F. Champion Ward, "Principles and Particulars in Liberal Education," in *Humanistic Education and Western Civilization: Essays for Robert M. Hutchins*, ed. Arthur A. Cohen (New York: Holt, Rinehart and Winston, 1964), p. 123.

[15]Russell Thomas, *The Search for a Common Learning, 1800–1960* (New York: McGraw-Hill, 1962), pp. 18, 110, 231–232, 299; Daniel Bell, *The Reforming of General*

If the curricular structure has become relatively firm, the rationale for general education remains the object of much disagreement. The 1952 NSSE yearbook noted that "wide disagreement appears" once one moves beyond the assertion that general education has something to do with general purposes, and subsequent studies concurred in that judgment.[16] The lack of agreement did not prevent the emergence in the 1970s of a reemphasis on establishing core curricula for the sake of "unifying general education." Various "integrating" or "organizing" principles, from "selected competencies" to "social problems," were tried.[17] By 1978, when the Harvard faculty voted in a new core curriculum and Yale altered its distribution requirement, such programs were already under way across the country. Yet the relationship between liberal education and general education is held to be just as uncertain in the 1980s as it was in the 1920s.[18]

Still another argument continuing from before World War II concerns the widespread use of language about "liberation," "liberalism," and "freeing" in connection with liberal education. As noted previously, this kind of talk—that "a liberal education is a liberating education" which "begins and ends with liberal people"—is extremely ambiguous. But still it comes forth, from Hollins College in 1951, the University of Delaware in 1963, Lake Forest Col-

---

Education: The Columbia College Experience in Its National Setting (New York: Columbia University Press, 1966), chap. 5; Robert L. Belknap and Richard Kuhns, *Tradition and Innovation, General Education and the Reintegration of the University: A Columbia Report* (New York: Columbia University Press, 1977), chaps. 8–9.

[16]Thomas R. McConnell, "General Education: An Analysis," in *The Fifty-First Yearbook of the National Society for the Study of Education, Part I*, ed. Nelson B. Henry (Chicago: University of Chicago Press, 1952), pp. 3–5, 11–13; Paul L. Dressel and Lewis B. Mayhew, *General Education, Explorations in Evaluation: The Final Report of the Cooperative Study of Evaluation in General Education of the American Council on Education* (Washington, D.C.: American Council on Education, 1954), pp. 268–282; Thomas (1962), p. 277.

[17]William Kramer, "Unifying General Education," *Liberal Education* 58 (1972): 533–539; "Core Curriculum," issue of *The Forum for Liberal Education* 1 (October 1977): 1–10; Conrad (1978), pp. 48, 56–77; Milton Kornfeld, "A New Opportunity for General Education," *Alternative Higher Education* 3 (1979): 254–259.

[18]Daniel Catlin, Jr., *Liberal Education at Yale: The Yale College Course of Study, 1945–1978* (Washington, D.C.: University Press of America, 1981), chap. 8; "Report on the Core Curriculum," rev. ed. (Cambridge: Harvard University, Faculty of Arts and Sciences, 3 April 1978); M. Elizabeth LeBlanc, "The Concept of General Education in Colleges and Universities, 1945–1979" (Ph.D. diss., Rutgers University, 1980); Ernest L. Boyer and Arthur Levine, *A Quest for Common Learning, the Aims of Liberal Education* (Princeton, N.J.: Princeton University Press, 1981); Jerry G. Gaff, *General Education Today: A Critical Analysis of Controversies, Practices and Reforms* (San Francisco: Jossey-Bass, 1983).

lege in 1969, and Claremont Graduate School in 1981.[19] And the ambiguity of language is not lessened by appeals to etymology or historical usage.

In *Educating Liberally*, H. H. Hudson of Stanford University acknowledged two possible derivations for *liberalis*, of which he preferred education "that frees the mind" from a priori judgments to education for "the free man." Endorsing this preference, many proponents of "the liberation arts," the "liberal university," or "libertarian education" in the 1970s and 1980s link these terms to the questioning of all norms, customs, and conventions.[20] On the other hand, William Cunningham affirmed a point in 1953 that Theodore deBary put in these words two decades later: "Liberal education, most people would agree, aims to liberate the powers of the individual by disciplining them."[21] In support of this view, Cunningham quoted from Epictetus (55–135 C.E.), "Rulers may say that only free men should be educated, but we believe that only educated men are free." Now Cunningham employed the quotation correctly, because Epictetus believed that "education for freedom was to learn the right and how to do it."[22] But Alexander Meiklejohn had earlier cited the same words of Epictetus on behalf of a notion of freeing the critical intellect to pursue truth.[23] Quoted sources, Latin and Greek roots, and English definitions, therefore, seem to do lit-

---

[19]John R. Everett, "The Liberal Arts—What Good Are They?" *AACB* 37 (1951): 246; Bruce Dearing, "The Liberation of Liberal Education," *Liberal Education* 49 (1963): 384–390; Forest Hansen, "On the Liberating Arts," *Liberal Education* 55 (1969): 441–445; Christopher C. Harmon, "Liberal Education Should Do More than Just Liberate," *The Chronicle of Higher Education*, 23, no. 7 (1981): 24.

[20]Hoyt H. Hudson, *Educating Liberally* (Stanford: Stanford University Press, 1945), p. 7; Immanuel Wallerstein and Paul Starr, eds., *The University Crisis Reader*, 2 vols. (New York: Random House, 1971); Joel Spring, *A Primer of Libertarian Education* (Montreal: Black Rose, 1975); Paul Kurtz, "Education for the Future: The Liberating Arts," in *The Philosophy of the Curriculum: The Need for General Education*, ed. Sidney Hook et al. (Buffalo, N.Y.: Prometheus, 1975), pp. 197–204. See David Riesman's discussion in the "Afterword," in *Liberating Education*, Zelda F. Gamson and Associates (San Francisco: Jossey-Bass, 1984), pp. 217–242.

[21]William F. Cunningham, *General Education and the Liberal College* (St. Louis: B. Herder, 1953), pp. 17–18, 77, 153; W. Theodore deBary, "General Education and the Humanities," *SR* 1 (October 22, 1973): 1. See also Theodore M. Distler, "The Liberating Arts in a Puzzled World," *AACB* 40 (1954): 412–422; William C. DeVane, *The American University in the Twentieth Century* (Baton Rouge: Louisiana State University, 1957), pp. 38–57.

[22]Benjamin L. Hijmans, Jr., "ΑΣΚΗΣΙΣ: Notes on Epictetus' Educational System (Assen, Neth.: Von Gorcum, 1959), pp. 16–19, 35–37, 81–83. See Cunningham (1953), p. 17; Epictetus, *Discourses* 2.1.25.

[23]Alexander Meiklejohn, "Required Education for Freedom," *The American Scholar* 13 (1944): 392.

tle to clarify the relationship of liberation and freedom to liberal education.

Discussion since 1945 about liberal education continues to abound with mercurial terminology about liberation, with clamorings for general education, and with concern about the evident pervasiveness of disagreement and uncertainty. Nevertheless, amid the contemporary debate, the two historical ideals and their two accommodations can be discerned as well. The *artes liberales* ideal can be abstracted from the 1950 essay "An Ideal for Liberal Arts Education," in which the author, a Washington College professor, recalled the *"uomo universale* of the Renaissance," the *"litterae humaniores,"* and "Cicero's concept of *humanitas."* While placing himself in the oratorical tradition of seeking standards and virtures from great texts by which to educate and measure a civic elite, he maintained that liberal education is "not for the masses" but for "developing students of exceptional caliber for positions of leadership in the modern world." Although others opposed the "invidious connotation of obsolete aristocracy" clinging to the tradition,[24] classics professor Gilbert Highet of Columbia University also argued for commitment by "the liberal educator" to "good qualities" because "the young learn much by the power of example." A. Whitney Griswold, president of Yale, was partial to this view as well.[25]

In 1977, the necessity of passing on the civic virtues enshrined in classical texts was reaffirmed by Waldemar Zagars. Adhering to what he called the "correct definition and description of Liberal Arts in the original, classical sense of that term," Zagars recommended a liberal arts education dedicated to "the education of a citizen" according to society's "highest ideals." Such education cultivates "aristocratic sentiment" which identifies the "first among equals" according to "the present day significance of ancient wisdom."[26] A congenial but less rigid view had been offered a few years earlier by J. L. Adams, a professor at Harvard Divinity School, who has been called a scion of Irving Babbitt. Citing the words of Matthew Arnold that "the educated man wants to know the best that has been

---

[24]R. C. Simonini, Jr., "An Ideal for Liberal Arts Education," *AACB* 36 (1950): 428–433; Richard Hofstadter and C. DeWitt Hardy, *The Development and Scope of Higher Education in the United States* (New York: Columbia University Press, 1952), p. 210.

[25]A. Whitney Griswold, *Liberal Education and the Democratic Ideal and Other Essays* (New Haven, Conn.: Yale University Press, 1959), pp. 1–6; Gilbert Highet, "The Liberal Educator," *AACB* 41 (1955): 105.

[26]Waldemar Zagars, *The Liberal Arts Education: A Popular Myth* (Gettysburg, Pa.: Baltic, 1977), pp. 21ff., 221–235.

thought and said," Adams challenged both the "utilitarian" view of the "Dewey Pragmatist" that science has no "terminal ends" and the view that "the purpose of a liberal arts education . . . is the development of the ability to think," to criticize. Instead, he maintained, "a liberal education is oriented primarily to terminal values."[27]

Adams's testimony against pragmatism corroborates the opinion of philosopher P. H. Hirst that the kind of argument about liberal education here framed in the *artes liberales* ideal has traditionally looked askance at the unconditional, open-ended search for truth. It also helps to explain why the *artes liberales* ideal is frequently heard in theological circles and from sectarian colleges, which are occasionally held up for praise in the contemporary era because of their belief that some truth is known. "A religious point of view," asserted a professor at Southern Illinois University in 1959, meets "the two valid criticisms of modern liberal arts education . . . that it fails to provide the student with a unified view of its varied subject matter and that it fails to develop in him a sense of values."[28] From this perspective, the president of Emory University wrote in 1946 about "The Liberal Arts Ideal and the Christian College" and the president of Manhattanville College of the Sacred Heart spoke in 1955 on "Liberating the Liberal Arts Student" from the uncertainty, chaos, and confusion of the postwar era. Subsequently, philosopher Elton Trueblood of Earlham College—one of the most academically competitive of the colleges promoting "Christian liberal education"—incorporated characteristics of the *artes liberales* ideal in *The Idea of a College.*[29]

Proceeding from the historical appeals to Ciceronian *humanitas* and Renaissance humanism, from the association with Arnold and Babbitt, from the criticism of Dewey and pragmatism, from the prescription of "highest ideals" and "terminal values" for "the educa-

---

[27]James L. Adams, "The Purpose of a Liberal Arts Education," *Journal of the Liberal Ministry* 9 (Spring 1969): 3–8; Michael R. Harris, *Five Counterrevolutionists in Higher Education: Irving Babbitt, Albert Jay Nock, Abraham Flexner, Robert Maynard Hutchins, Alexander Meiklejohn* (Corvallis: Oregon State University Press, 1970), p. 49.

[28]Paul Hirst, "Liberal Education and the Nature of Knowledge," in *Philosophical Analysis and Education*, ed. Reginald D. Archambault (New York: Humanities Press, 1965), pp. 113–116; Morris T. Keeton, *Models and Mavericks: A Profile of Private Liberal Arts Colleges* (New York: McGraw-Hill, 1971), pp. 14–18.

[29]Goodrich C. White, "The Liberal Arts Ideal and the Christian College," *AACB* 32 (1946): 29–33; Eleanor M. O'Byrne, "Liberating the Liberal Arts Student," *AACB* 41 (1955): 98–104; D. Elton Trueblood, *The Idea of a College* (New York: Harper & Brothers, 1959), chaps. 1–3, 6, 9, 12. See the illuminating introduction by Mark A. Noll in Ringenberg (1984), pp. 1–36.

tion of a citizen," one also hears contemporary discussion of "liberal education" that incorporates characteristics of the liberal-free ideal. This discussion gives no weight to statements about a "correct definition and description of Liberal Arts in the original, classical sense of the term." In fact, such an appeal would be suspect because, as Paul Hazard notes, freethinkers have always distrusted arguments from history. Instead, their emphasis is on process and progress, as in the 1964 argument of a University of Maine philosophy professor that "the threefold cycle of liberal education" involves unendingly "the process of analysis, evaluation and commitment . . . the general philosophical background of this view is of course explicit in the writings of A. N. Whitehead; it is confirmed by the central doctrines of John Dewey."[30] Others spoke of Dewey's "Socratic spirit of unremitting critical inquiry," and Willis Rudy talked about a "pragmatist-progressivist" concept of liberal arts that he associated with Dewey, who "wished such subjects to be taught in a liberating manner—in other words, to liberate students in their thinking."[31]

Although a concern for citizenship is not left unmentioned by these academicians, they primarily attend to the desires and aspirations of the individual. Their public pronouncements and curricular programs aim "at contributing to the student's appreciation of the liberal arts ideal—an idea whose basic presupposition is that each individual must be free to realize his full potential."[32] The studies they see as best suited to achieving this goal are, in a general sense, any disciplines dedicated to pursuing truth through critical rationality. But for historical and methodological reasons, mathematics and the natural and technical sciences are especially associated with the characteristics of the liberal-free ideal. Assigned to speak on "Liberalism, Engineering and Liberal Education" at the 1977 Columbia Seminar on General Education in the Humanities, an engineering professor remarked that "the juxtaposition of the words

---

[30]Charles F. Virtue, "The Threefold Cycle of Liberal Education," *Liberal Education* 50 (1964): 482; Paul Hazard, *The European Mind, 1680–1715*, trans. J. Lewis May (New Haven, Conn.: Yale University Press, 1952), pp. 53–55.

[31]Greene (1953), p. 3; Willis Rudy, *The Evolving Liberal Arts Curriculum: A Historical Review of Basic Themes* (New York: Bureau of Publications, Teachers College, Columbia University, 1960), p. 131.

[32]Quoted from Garry D. Hays and Robert C. Haywood, "Liberal Education at Southwestern: An Interdisciplinary Approach," *Liberal Education* 53 (1967): 529. See Harold Taylor, "Individualism and the Liberal Tradition," in Weatherford (1960), pp. 9–25; Sack (1962), p. 222; Morris T. Keeton, "Alternative Pathways to Liberal Education," in *Prospect for Renewal: The Future of the Liberal Arts College*, ed. Earl J. McGrath (San Francisco: Jossey-Bass, 1972), pp. 84–85.

'liberalism,' 'engineering,' and 'liberal education' might seem incongruous to many people." However, after hearing another speaker connect liberal education to "the habit of encouraging and reward-ing the systematic critique of first principles," the engineer said he had decided that the juxtaposition was not incongruous because "all of this sounds very much like an engineering mentality."[33]

The rising status of the liberal-free ideal is implied in Laurence Veysey's belief that although "few new ideas have been advanced on the purpose of higher education since 1900, . . . one might be a redefinition of the liberal arts curriculum away from the genteel tra-dition toward identification with critical intellect and creativity."[34] Rather ironically, the same point was made at the 1977 AAC annual meeting by the keynote speaker, who quoted Henry Adams's *Education*:

> "Harvard College . . . taught little, but it left the mind open, free from bias, ignorant of facts, but docile. The graduate had few strong prejudices. He knew little, but his mind remained supple, ready to receive knowledge." Adams doubtlessly intended that to be a harsh judgment. But he has, quite unintentionally, I sup-pose, left us a tolerable definition of what a first-class liberal ed-ucation can do for young men and women.[35]

This shift in intention demonstrates the emergence of a new viewpoint and suggests the existence of accommodations, which will be considered shortly. First, however, the integrity of the two edu-cational ideals must be reemphasized: each is systematic, and their individual characteristics are integrally part of a whole. In the *artes liberales* ideal, a presumption of certitude underlies the identifica-tion of virtues and standards reposited in classical texts; and com-mitment is thereby demanded, identifying an elite who embrace the virtues and preserve them as leaders of society. The foundation of the curriculum lies in the study of language and letters, required in order for the student to fathom the texts and then to express their lessons in public forums as advocates, statesmen, preachers, or

---

[33]Peter Likins, "Liberalism, Engineering and Liberal Education," *SR* 5 (1977): 156–157.

[34]Laurence R. Veysey, *The Emergence of the American University* (Chicago: Uni-versity of Chicago Press, 1965), p. 338.

[35]Elie Abel, "Liberal Learning: A Tradition with a Future," *Liberal Education* 64 (1978): 115. See Henry Adams, *The Education of Henry Adams: An Autobiography* (Bos-ton: Massachusetts Historical Society, 1918), chap. 4.

professors. In the liberal-free ideal, skeptical doubt undermines all certainty, casting individuals entirely upon their own intellect for judgments that can never finally be proven true. Consequently, the views of others must be tolerated and respected equally, while all beliefs must change and develop over time. Logic and mathematics, which hone the intellect, and experimental science, which teaches the honed intellect to turn old truths into new hypotheses for further testing, form the core of the curriculum designed to graduate the scientist and researcher who loves knowledge and therefore pursues it without end.

Each of these abstracted types for "liberal education" stands on its own, is an ideal in that sense, and therefore is something of a caricature of reality. Accordingly, one must not expect to find many arguments about liberal education that can be circumscribed by either type. Neither is it surprising that the *artes liberales* and liberal-free interpretations are caricatured by opponents or qualified by proponents. Nor is it startling that, because the ideals are "pure" and the contemporary era is especially agonized, relatively fewer arguments about liberal education can be associated with either ideal. More popular are the accommodations, a fact that, while perfectly understandable, is also highly problematic. Since the accommodations attempt, in a sense, to bridge the ideals, they are more comprehensive definitions of "liberal education." However, they sacrifice integrity—internal consistency—and so inevitably incorporate contradictions and conflicts of which the purer, and hence more confining, types are innocent.

The *artes liberales* accommodation amounts, in a phrase, to prescribing the reading of classical texts primarily in order to develop critical intellect. In the previous chapter, Meiklejohn and Hutchins were identified with this view, and it follows naturally that such an outlook might persist at institutions identified with them. For example, the committee reconsidering Amherst's Liberal Studies Program in 1978 asked how it lived up to the vision of Meiklejohn, who "constantly stressed the central place of intellectual understanding" above training other "powers of body, mind and soul." Concerning the "general" or "liberal" education at the University of Chicago, Daniel Bell outlined the "completely prescribed curriculum" with its emphasis on "Aristotelianism . . . the effort to find controlling principles of 'classification' "; and the Dean of the College in 1964 characterized the purpose of the curriculum as "to teach students 'how to think,' " to educate them progressively up three levels of investigation: "acquaintance, analysis, and criticism."[36]

Such an appeal was influential also at St. John's College, which had been founded at Annapolis in 1789 full of the post-Revolutionary enthusiasm for "the Republican tradition that came down . . . from Rome and Greece." For the next seventy years, St. John's remained a small, staid, antebellum college, enlivening the curriculum after the Civil War with "more and better Greek and Latin." Hence, through the beginning of the twentieth century, the college "clung much longer to the old ideas" than did places like Eliot-led Harvard. In 1937, several individuals who came from the University of Chicago reorganized the curriculum of St. John's around a prescribed program of reading great texts.[37] Two decades later, Dean Jacob Klein cited Plato and Aristotle while maintaining that whenever "a formal discipline, a subject matter . . . is being studied for its own sake, whenever the metastrophic way of questioning is upheld, whenever genuine wonderment is present, liberal education is taking place." Predictably, "the overwhelming presence" of Plato was still attributed to St. John's in 1978,[38] the same year that the dean of Bethel College was espousing the view that "liberal arts education is an effort to move the student up the Platonic value scale" to a stage where the individual is ruled by reason, "the highest element of the soul," a movement achieved by stimulating critical intellect.[39]

---

[36]Ward (1964), p. 129; Bell (1966), p. 33; Lawrence Babb et al., *Education at Amherst Reconsidered: The Liberal Studies Program* (Amherst, Mass.: Amherst College Press, 1978), p. vii.

[37]Tench F. Tilghman, *The Early History of St. John's College in Annapolis* (Annapolis, Md.: St. John's College Press, 1984), pp. xii, 86–88, 119, 136–137. See also Thomas (1962), pp. 230–243; Bell (1966), pp. 26–27n. The parallelism suggested here between St. John's and the situation at Chicago (see chap. 6, n. 46) is supported by the story of the relationship of Mortimer Adler, Richard McKeon, and the first dean of St. John's, Scott Buchanan. During the 1920s and 1930s, these three encouraged each other in castigating the rest of American academe for its lack of intellectual unity and coherence and for commensurately neglecting the seven liberal arts and Aristotle. When finally brought together by Hutchins at the University of Chicago in 1935 to form the Committee on the Liberal Arts, whose purpose was "to think, talk and write about the liberal arts," they discovered that they themselves were not in agreement or unified on what they meant by the seven liberal arts or Aristotle; and so "the enterprise blew up" after the first meeting of the Committee, and the members went off to other things. J. Winfree Smith, *A Search for the Liberal College: The Beginning of the St. John's Program* (Annapolis, Md.: St. John's College Press, 1983), pp. 13–21.

[38]Jacob Klein, "The Idea of Liberal Education," in Weatherford (1960), pp. 35–36; Gerald Grant and David Riesman, *The Perpetual Dream: Reform and Experiment in the American College* (Chicago: University of Chicago Press, 1978), p. 42.

[39]Marion Deckert, "Liberal Arts: A Platonic View," *Liberal Education* 62 (1976): 40–47.

The appeal to Plato and Aristotle typifies "The Neo-Classical Revival," in the phrase of Grant and Riesman;[40] and in a sense perhaps unintended by them, I would put the emphasis on "neo." Far removed from the views of Zagars, Babbitt, and Arnold, this *artes liberales* education is not of the orators, but an accommodation to the philosophers. It is not classical but "new-classical," although a decent argument could be made that this outlook for liberal education descended from the Academy and Lyceum through Boethius and Johannes Scotus Erigena to the twelfth- and thirteenth-century schoolmen and then appeared in the *Neuhumanismus* of the German universities and finally the American research universities. In fact, the reduction of so much of modern Anglo-American philosophy to epistemological analysis of logic and language can be compared to the scholastic pursuits in *grammatica speculativa* and nominalism— and to their subsequent deterioration.[41] However, the fact that many proponents seemingly ignore this lineage indicates to my mind the novelty of the *artes liberales* accommodation. Hence, I see it emerging only in the nineteenth century, commensurate with the changing orientation of classical study.

From this standpoint, Hutchins's and Meiklejohn's approach to liberal education is scarcely less modern than the progressivist program they condemned. Likewise, Jacob Klein's appeal to "the Greeks" in the 1958 Cooper Lectures at Swarthmore is hardly more traditional than the appeal of Harold Taylor, in the same lectures, to the origins of liberalism in the seventeenth and eighteenth centuries. Of course, this interpretation of the "neo-classical revival" un-

---

[40]Grant and Riesman (1978), chap. 3. J. Winfree Smith, without citing Grant and Riesman, objects to their phrase and the interpretation adopted here insofar as either implies that St. John's puts particular emphasis upon the ideas and texts of Plato or Aristotle, or ancient texts in general, as opposed to other and modern "great texts" which are also included in the curriculum. But Smith does also say that "the Platonic dialogue" provides a model for the pedagogy of St. John's and that, beyond all other learnings, "the habit of reflective inquiry" is the sine qua non of a St. John's education. Smith (1983), pp. 2–5.

[41]See Richard Rorty, *Philosophy and the Mirror of Nature* (Princeton, N.J.: Princeton University Press, 1980); Desmond P. Henry, *That Most Subtle Question: The Metaphysical Bearing of Medieval and Contemporary Linguistic Disciplines* (Dover, N.H.: Manchester University Press, 1984). A closely related phenomenon is the tendency of modern medievalists to prefer to treat the seven liberal arts in their function as epistemic or heuristic categories for the scholastics, rather than as arts of an encyclopedic curriculum. See William E. Carlo, "The Medieval Battle of the Liberal Arts: A Key to Contemporary Philosophy," in *Actes* (1969), pp. 745–750; Louis M. Regis, "L'être du langage et l'humanisme médiéval et contemporain," in *Actes* (1969), pp. 281–294; David L. Wagner, *The Seven Liberal Arts in the Middle Ages* (Bloomington: Indiana University Press, 1983).

dermines its integrity and thus its attractiveness. The lure of the *artes liberales* accommodation resides in its combining a seeming venerability with a very *modernus* allegiance to unrestrained critical intellect. To those who say that they do not know what studies to prescribe for liberal education, the accommodation holds aloft a venerable tradition, and to those who say that this amounts to dogmatic prescription, the accommodation cites as its purpose the training in a method of critical inquiry that is the antithesis of dogmatism. This is not to deny that Meiklejohn and Hutchins called for commitment to "a religion" and "metaphysical principles." But their own unwillingness to articulate such a program—to tie the bell on the cat—forced them into accommodation.

The *artes liberales* accommodation, then, accounts for one of the conflicting interpretations of the historical origins of liberal education, as described in chapter 1. To this accommodation must be attributed the widespread tendency to assert that "the notion of a liberal education was introduced by the Greeks," meaning Socrates, Plato, and Aristotle. I have argued in chapter 2 that this contention is difficult to defend; it has little or no historical basis. It stems rather from the circular reasoning of its advocates, who begin with the presumption that liberal education ought to mean, most fundamentally, training in analytical and critical thinking. Since the origins of such training can rightfully be attributed to Greek philosophers, it is inferred that these philosophers introduced liberal education. But what such statements actually mean is that a kind of training introduced by Greek philosophers was introduced by Greek philosophers. Or, the statements tell about the origins of what some people think liberal education *ought* to be. In either case, they do not necessarily give information about the origins of liberal education because the question of what liberal education might have been or meant is not considered.

Conversely, one cannot credit this related opinion: "The notion that a liberal education should consist entirely of literary studies, especially classical literary studies, is a relatively modern corruption of Aristotle's view."[42] To the contrary, it makes more sense to say that the appeal to Aristotle's view is a relatively modern corruption of liberal education in classical literary studies. How else to explain why the bibliographic references of that same source and others that

---

[42]Paul Hirst, "Liberal Education," in *The Encyclopedia of Education*, ed. Lee C. Deighton (New York: Macmillan, 1971), vol. 5, p. 507. See chap. 1, nn. 8, 9, and chap. 2, n. 5 herein.

share this view leap from the fourth century B.C.E. to nineteenth- and twentieth-century America? Only when one jumps twenty-one centuries does the historical appeal to Athenian philosophers appear compelling.

This question of historical lineage is important because it points to a central conflict within the *artes liberales* accommodation. Those who prescribe the reading of Plato to develop a critical intellect can offer, I believe, no convincing response to the critical intellect that turns to speculate on why it should study Plato rather than, say, Marx or mathematics or engineering—unless they appeal to an a priori standard that can in turn be criticized. In other words, this rationale offers no reason why the student must read the *Republic*. Indeed, Plato himself maintained that one can not learn philosophy by reading his or others' works. Philosophy is something one engages in, not something one reads about.[43] The reliance on sanctified classics fundamentally conflicts with the liberal-free mind, and the *artes liberales* accommodation, in attempting to bridge the two ideals, incorporates within itself the source of its own negation.

A second tension in this accommodation was perceptively analyzed in 1965 by Leo Strauss, whose own arguments are couched in terms of this approach. Acknowledging that "liberal education" in the American colonies entailed an aristocratic notion of gentlemanly education, Strauss maintains that the hope to build a democratic society arose in the United States, where "democracy in a word is meant to be an aristocracy which has broadened into a universal aristocracy." However, when the rise of modern science and philosophy undercut the norms and virtues traditionally prescribed for the gentleman, notions of excellence were vitiated, and the early conception of democracy as a "universal aristocracy" degenerated to a "mass democracy" of the lowest common denominator.[44] Strauss's interpretation accounts for the egalitarianism earlier attributed to Meiklejohn and Hutchins, since their notion of liberal education for all is clearly derived from the concept of "universal aristocracy" rather than "mass democracy." Yet, egalitarian motives cannot allay the dialectical tension, the contradiction even, in the former concept. In attempting to bridge the two ideals, the accommodation

---

[43]Plato, Letter 7, in *Plato: The Collected Dialogues including the Letters*, ed. Edith Hamilton and Huntington Cairns (Princeton, N.J.: Princeton University Press, 1961), 341c–d.

[44]Leo Strauss, "Liberal Education and Mass Democracy," in *Higher Education and Modern Democracy: The Crisis of the Few and the Many*, ed. Robert A. Goldwin (Chicago: Rand McNally, 1967), p. 75.

again sacrifices systematic integrity for the sake of comprehensiveness.

The tension of "universal aristocracy" appears as well in the liberal-free accommodation, although there it has somewhat different implications and developed in the opposite way from the above mentioned challenge to a preexisting elitism. After World War II, higher educational institutions were inundated with applications, particularly from returning veterans. While most colleges and universities began to expand, some also chose to become more exclusive, as the "faculty pressure for strictly meritocratic selection" based on intellectual criteria rose markedly.[45] This pressure overturned the oratorical commitment to forming good citizens (the special interest colleges for Catholics, women, and blacks being the last holdouts), while it commensurately strengthened specialization in undergraduate education. By 1960, a national study found that *many of the liberal arts faculty members equated liberal arts education to a major in one of the liberal arts* and that they regarded "as liberal any discipline which offers a student an opportunity to prove his intellectual ability by becoming competent in a narrow discipline."[46] This accommodation of the liberal-free ideal was catalyzed by the launching of Sputnik, which markedly affected

> the character of the crisis of liberal education in this country. . . .
> The easygoing era dominated by the notions of individual "self-fulfillment" and academic egalitarianism was past. Standards had to be set and the raw talent mined from the earliest high school years. The result was the establishment of great rewards, moral and material, for excellence, particularly in the sciences.[47]

Indeed, as Sputnik soared in 1957, the liberal-free accommodation could be heard from the president of Franklin and Marshall College, who employed the proper scientific metaphors. "The real

[45]Christopher Jencks and David Riesman, *The Academic Revolution* (Garden City, N.Y.: Doubleday, 1968), pp. 25, 104, 480.

[46]Paul L. Dressel and Margaret F. Lorimer, *Attitudes of Liberal Arts Faculty Members toward Liberal and Professional Education* (New York: Bureau of Publications, Teachers College, Columbia University, 1960), pp. 37, 51; Donald H. kenson and Lawrence F. Stevens, *The Changing Uses of the Liberal Arts College: An Essay in Recent Educational History* (New York: Pageant Press for Harvard College, 1969), p. 111; Frederick Rudolph, *Curriculum: A History of the American Undergraduate Course of Study since 1636* (San Francisco: Jossey-Bass, 1977), pp. 11–12, chap. 7.

[47]Allan Bloom, "The Crisis of Liberal Education," in *Higher Education and Modern Democracy: The Crisis of the Few and the Many*, ed. Robert A. Goldwin (Chicago: Rand McNally, 1967), p. 121.

purpose of the great variety of subjects in our liberal arts curriculum is . . . to provide a safe laboratory for a sequence of intellectual and emotional experiments," he said, since the "training of the intellect is the prime task of our liberal arts colleges" in order to produce "a small coterie of specially qualified men and women" to lead society. Successively, the accommodation could be heard from the president of the California Institute of Technology in 1964 and the president of Worcester Polytechnic Institute in 1971 in assertions that the sciences form the core of the liberal arts because they constitute the foundational knowledge necessary for an educated person. In 1980 a Michigan State physicist went so far as to claim that "physics is the most important liberal art—the fundamental one in our attempts to answer first questions about our universe and ourselves."[48] Explicit in these statements is the commitment to knowing scientific subject matter and especially to employing the experimental method in the pursuit of truth through advanced research, a commitment transferred to other disciplines and thus adopted as the standard of excellence throughout academe.

Here is where the tension between "democracy" and "aristocracy" enters the liberal-free accommodation. In 1948, the dean of Furman University warned against "aristocratic specialization" compromising "democratic procedure" in higher education; and in 1965 at Hendrix College, E. J. McGrath opposed "The Rising Academic Elitocracy" in "the liberal arts college." These warnings were repeated and expanded upon in the following turbulent years by groups that regarded "elitocratic" education as other than liberating or liberal.[49] Nevertheless, the allegiance to meritocracy reasserted itself, a fact evident in a series of articles on American higher education appearing in *Daedalus* in 1974 and 1975. Again and again, "intellectual aristocracy" and "the cultivation of excellence" are contrasted with the "new egalitarianism," the writers' language implying that true democracy is something akin to Strauss's "universal aristocracy."[50] The instability of the concept, however, is made manifest by the continuing disagreement.

[48]Frederick D. Bolman, Jr., "The Educated Free Mind," *AACB* 43 (1957): 423, 426–427; Lee A. DuBridge, "Science and a Liberal Education," *Liberal Education* 50 (1964): 263–272; George W. Hazzard, "Engineering as a Liberal Education," *Liberal Education* 57 (1971): 463–467; Richard Schlegel, "Physics: The Most Important of the Liberal Arts," *The Key Reporter* 45 (Spring 1980): 4.

[49]A. E. Tibbs, "How Can We Preserve Democratic Procedure in Aristocratic Specialization?" *AACB* 34 (1948): 493–499; Earl J. McGrath, *The Liberal Arts College and the Emergent Caste System* (New York: Teachers College Press, 1966), chap. 3.

[50]See Adam B. Ulam, "Where Do We Go from Here?" *Daedalus* 103 (Fall 1974):

If the combining of "excellence" and "mass education" gained comprehensiveness and sacrificed systematic integrity for the liberal-free accommodation, it also pointed to a more central conflict: that this accommodation extolls the absoluteness of a critical rational method while presuming nothing to be absolute. The paradox is not at all semantic. As Theodore deBary stated in 1973: "With few conventional molds left to break out of, the liberal convention of mold-breaking has only itself to be emancipated from. Thus 'liberation' has almost come full circle." DeBary's criticism was aimed at the radicalism of the 1960s, but it pertains as well to the methodology of the "knowledge elites." The "liberal convention of mold-breaking" is merely a reflection of the challenging of hypotheses in the academician's never-ending pursuit of truth, leading to ever-narrowing specialization. The narrowness leads to great reliance on expertise on the one hand, and the relativizing of opinion on the other—the two "mindless" effects that Belknap and Kuhns described. "The first effect emerges in the students who dare not make any statement at all on a given subject because they are not experts on it. Such people are the destined victims of the false experts. The second effect emerges in those students who believe that anything that they say sincerely is true."[51]

There lies the paradox inherent in sanctifying the liberal-free search for truth, in applauding the fact, criticized by Robert Bellah, that "the pursuit of truth for its own sake can become, and has become, a kind of supreme rationality."[52] The more one knows and becomes expert on a particular subject, the less one is willing to discuss authoritatively and the fewer are those who can verify or challenge one's opinion. The "liberal convention of mold-breaking" comes full circle. A liberal education dedicated to identifying and stimulating an intellectual elite for the liberal-free search for truth cannot excise these contradictions.

The four historical types of arguments about liberal education therefore persist in the contemporary era, although one must never forget the danger involved in abstracting general types of argu-

---

80–84; Gordon A. Craig, "Green Stamp or Structured Undergraduate Education?" *Daedalus* 103 (Fall 1974): 143–147; Morton W. Bloomfield, "Elitism in the Humanities," *Daedalus* 103 (Fall 1974): 128–137; Kenneth E. Boulding, "Quality Versus Equality: The Dilemma of the University," *Daedalus* 104 (Winter 1975): 298–303; Martin Meyerson, "After a Decade of the Levelers in Higher Education: Reinforcing Quality While Maintaining Mass Education," *Daedalus* 104 (Winter 1975): 304–321.

[51]Belknap and Kuhns (1977), pp. 39–40; deBary (1973), p. 3; Martin E. Marty, "Knowledge Elites and Counter-Elites," *Daedalus* 103 (Fall 1974): 104–109.

[52]Robert N. Bellah, "The New Religious Consciousness and the Secular University," *Daedalus* 103 (Fall 1974): 110.

ments. Such generalizations cannot account for all the particularities of individual statements about liberal education. But they do provide a useful frame to comprehend the contours of the debate, and it may be helpful to depict the four historical types of arguments that underlie contemporary American definitions of liberal education as shown in the schema on page 228.

What the schema does not portray are the ahistorical and arbitrary approaches to liberal education that also circulate in the contemporary era. These, however, arise solely from the minds of their proponents and might as well be called "alpha education" as anything else. For example, S. M. Cahn treats "liberal education" as good education or quality education, and finally employs the term interchangeably with "education."[53] Slightly more refined is the "basket" definition, which amounts simply to listing all the things that the writer believes will make for "good" education. The relationships between the items listed are generally not explored, and often there is little attention to or understanding of the traditions involved in liberal education. This approach attracted criticism, both before and after the war, from those who have observed that "it is easy to define the mission of the liberal arts college" if one assumes "education can do everything" and "no conflicting purposes" are acknowledged. The weakness results from listing desiderata "as if ambiguities do not exist," as if trade-offs and tensions do not arise while inculcating a priori values, individualism, social conscience, aesthetic refinement, scientific knowledge, critical intellect, respect for freedom, and so on.[54] Nevertheless, that the basket approach continues to be seductive can be seen in the 1952 description of the "liberally educated man" from the Blackmer Committee—subsequently quoted by the education editor of the *Saturday Review* in 1968 and the Four-School Study Committee in 1970—as well as in more recent writings.[55]

---

[53]Steven M. Cahn, *Education and the Democratic Ideal* (Chicago: Nelson-Hall, 1979), chap. 2.

[54]Criticism and quotations are drawn from Robert M. Hutchins, "Report of the President's Commission on Higher Education, *Educational Record* 29 (1948): 112–114; Joseph J. Schwab, "On Reviving Liberal Education—In the Seventies," in *The Philosophy of the Curriculum: The Need for General Education*, ed. Sidney Hook et al. (Buffalo, N.Y.: Prometheus, 1975), p. 37; Sheldon Rothblatt, *Tradition and Change in English Liberal Education: An Essay in History and Culture* (London: Faber and Faber, 1976), p. 193.

[55]Alan R. Blackmer et al., *General Education in School and College: A Committee Report by Members of the Faculties of Andover, Exeter, Lawrenceville, Harvard, Princeton, and Yale* (Cambridge: Harvard University Press, 1952), pp. 19–20; Paul Woodring, *The Higher Learning in America: A Reassessment* (New York: McGraw-Hill, 1968), pp. 202–203; The Four-School Study Committee, 16–20: *The Liberal Education of an Age*

Seven *artes liberales* characteristics:

(1) Training citizen-orators to lead society (2) requires identifying true virtues, (3) the commitment to which (4) will elevate the student and (5) the source for which is great texts, whose authority lies in (6) the dogmatic premise that they relate the true virtues, (7) which are embraced for their own sake.

MERITOCRATIC
RESEARCH
SPECIALIZATIONS

Appeal to mathematics, sciences, and "modern" subjects

liberal-free accommodation

artes liberales ideal

ORATORS

liberal-free ideal

PHILOSOPHERS

artes liberales accommodation

Appeal to classical letters and texts

NEO-HUMANISM

Seven liberal-free characteristics:

(1) Epistemological skepticism underlies (2) the free and (3) intellectual search for truth, which is forever elusive, and so all possible views must be (4) tolerated and given (5) equal hearing (6) with the final decision left to each individual, (7) who pursues truth for its own sake.

The operational definition of "liberal education" also circulates in contemporary American discussion. A typical instance can be found in a 1962 study maintaining that since "the term 'liberal arts' has been emptied of much of its meaning," the "liberal arts colleges" can be investigated by looking for institutions that use this name. A decade later, two researchers conducting a study of *Efficiency in Liberal Education* followed the same strategy.[56] A more recent example, National Project IV: Liberal Education Varieties and Their Assessment, sponsored by the federal Fund for the Improvement of Postsecondary Education and administered through the University of Michigan, demonstrates how the operational definition eventually meets the "basket" approach and thus how all these relativistic definitions are arbitrary in the long run. When planning National Project IV, FIPSE cited a full bushel's worth of the "premises of liberal education," and apparently any institution employing a rationale of "liberal education" included in this collection could apply to participate in National Project IV—and many did.[57]

These uses of the term "liberal education" or "liberal learning" cannot be called wrong, simply arbitrary. Likewise, one cannot attach great historical significance to contemporary debate over whether vocational/practical/experiential education is "liberal,"[58] although it has been stated that the writings of "Dewey, Whitehead, Veblen, Cardinal Newman, Van Doren, [and] Aristotle" demonstrate that "the tension between what is 'liberal' and what is 'useful' is one of the oldest and most persistent problems in education." Clearly, the cited authorities do not justify the conclusion, given the

---

Group (New York: College Entrance Examination Board, 1970), pp. 11–13. See also Martin Meyerson, "Civilizing Education: Uniting Liberal and Professional Learning," *Daedalus* 103 (Fall 1974): 173–179; Paul L. Dressel, "Liberal Education: Developing the Characteristics of a Liberally Educated Person," *Liberal Education* 65 (1979): 314.

[56]T. H. Hamilton, "Preface," p. vi, in Lewis B. Mayhew, *The Smaller Liberal Arts College* (Washington, D.C.: Center for Applied Research in Education, 1962); Peter E. Siegle, "Liberal Education for Adults," *AACB* 43 (1957): 485–490; Howard R. Bowen and Gordon K. Douglass, *Efficiency in Liberal Education: A Study of Comparative Instructional Costs for Different Ways of Organizing Teaching-Learning in a Liberal Arts College* (New York: McGraw-Hill, 1971).

[57]Zelda F. Gamson, "Liberal Education Varieties and Their Assessment (LEVA)," *The Forum for Liberal Education* 2 (March 1980): 3–6. "The premises of liberal education" for National Project IV are found in Hendrix (1980), p. 2. The arbitrariness of the definition is, perhaps, shown by the later report of National Project IV, which begins with the normative, rather than the historical, question "What Should Liberal Education Mean?" Gamson (1984), pp. 1–28.

[58]The development of the "pro" argument can be read in Algo D. Henderson and Dorothy Hall, *Antioch College: Its Design for Liberal Education* (New York: Harper & Brothers, 1946), p. 18; David A. Shepard, *Liberal Education in an Industrial Society* (New

gap of twenty-one centuries between Aristotle and the rest. Yet this sort of jump from modernity back to Greek philosophers is evident in other examples of scholarly and popular discourse about liberal arts and vocational/practical/experiential education.[59]

The long gap in time between the authorities cited for this judgment is significant because it confirms that "utility" became an important matter of contention only when the oratorical consensus about liberal education began to break down in the eighteenth century. An outcry had been raised during the genesis and growth of medieval scholasticism, especially at the school of Chartres, against the narrow "pre-professionalism" developing in the liberal arts. And warnings had always been voiced against studying the *artes liberales* primarily for advancing one's career. But until the eighteenth century, the usefulness—indeed, the necessity—of knowing classical languages and writings for studying the professions was so self-evident as not to require extended comment. It was therefore assumed that the liberal arts were useful while it was also agreed that they provided something more. Subsequently, the utility of classical study was eroded as the professions became increasingly independent of classical sources and as the longstanding *artes liberales* ideal was undermined, leading to accommodations and confusion. By the end of the nineteenth century, D. C. Gilman and A. F. West surveyed the chaos and could find no other universally accepted characteristic of "liberal education" than its being defined, in con-

---

York: Public Affairs Committee, 1957); DuBridge (1964), p. 265; Martin Meyerson, "Play for Mortal Stakes: Vocation and the Liberal Learning," *Liberal Education* 55 (1969): 86–94; Maxwell H. Goldberg, "Vocational Training, Career Orientation, and Liberal Education," *Liberal Education* 61 (1975): 309–318; H. Bradley Sagen, "Careers, Competencies, and Liberal Education," *Liberal Education* 65 (1979): 150–166. The opposition has included John Wendon, "Liberal Education in the Service of Individualism," *AACB* 42 (1956): 457–461; Earl J. McGrath with the assistance of Charles H. Russell, *Are Liberal Arts Colleges Becoming Professional Schools?* (New York: Bureau of Publications, Teachers College, Columbia University, 1958), pp. 1–3; Samuel Eilenberg, "A Mathematician Looks at Liberal Education," *SR* 5 (1977): 172–174; Willard F. Entemann, "When Does Liberal Education Become Vocational Training?" *Liberal Education* 65 (1979): 167–171; *A Report of Project QUILL* (1979). In the 1980s, declarations that a liberal education *is* preparation for work are stimulated by the rising cost of education and the desire for a concrete, immediate return on the investment in college education. Robert G. O'Neal and Wayne E. Wallace, "A Liberal Education *IS* Preparation for Work," *Journal of College Placement* 40 (Summer 1980): 61–67.

[59]Quotation is from Earl F. Cheit, *The Useful Arts and the Liberal Tradition* (New York: McGraw-Hill, 1975), pp. 2–3. See Ormond H. Smythe, "Practical Experience and Liberal Education: A Philosophical Analysis" (Ed.D. diss., Harvard Graduate School of Education, 1978), pp. 130ff.; Smythe, "Practical Experience and the Liberal Arts: A Philosophical Perspective," in *Enriching the Liberal Arts Through Experiential Learning,* ed. Stevens E. Brooks and James A. Althof (San Francisco: Jossey-Bass, 1979), pp. 1–12.

trast to technical or professional education, as non-useful, pursued for its own sake.[60] Transmitted to the twentieth century, this demarcation became the battle line on which many liberal educators took their stand, with some even arguing that only a "useless" education can be called "liberal."[61]

The fact that the strict dichotomy between useful and liberal is a modern development is further confirmed by the misguided appeal to Aristotle and, sometimes, Plato, who are cited as originators and defenders of the distinction between "useful" and "liberal." This interpretation, however, does not do them justice.[62] Like the orators, neither Plato nor Aristotle was committed to the exclusionary rationale that studies that are useful in one's work, career, or profession are *ipso facto* illiberal. (This is what the American argument degenerated to.) Rather, for the philosophers, the crucial question was, what else do the studies accomplish? Do they prepare the mind for further reflection, for contemplation of higher truth?

Their asking this question does not mean that Aristotle and Plato did not regard studies that are useful in one's work, career, or profession as tending to contravene the inspiration of the mind to higher speculation. On the contrary, they stated it to be so, for if one is studying something useful, then one's mind tends to be "degraded" in the sense that one tends to focus on the end-in-view rather than urging the mind onward to transcendent ends. This point explains the significance of the root meaning of *liberalis* and *eleutherios*: of a free person, of a person with leisure. The value of leisure resides in affording time free from labor. But even more importantly, leisure means by definition that one has no end in view. Hence, at the same time that one has free time, one also has the mental disposition to transcend one's ordinary ends-in-view and

---

[60]Daniel C. Gilman, "Is It Worth While to Uphold Any Longer the Idea of Liberal Education?" *Educational Review* 3 (1892): 109; Andrew F. West, *Short Papers on Liberal Education* (New York: Charles Scribner's Sons, 1907), pp. 97ff.

[61]Robert L. Kelly, "Report of the Commission on the Organization of College Curriculum, *AACB* 9 (1923): 70–79; Frank W. Chandler, "The Function of the Liberal Arts Colleges in a University," *AACB* 10 (1924): 156; Floyd W. Reeves et al., *The Liberal Arts College: Based upon Surveys of Thirty-five Colleges Related to the Methodist Episcopal Church* (Chicago: University of Chicago Press, 1932), chap. 21; Mark Van Doren, *Liberal Education* (New York: Henry Holt, 1943), pp. 166–167; Arthur G. Wirth, *Education in the Technological Society: The Vocational-Liberal Studies Controversy in the Early Twentieth Century* (Scranton, Pa.: Intext Educational Pub., 1972), pp. 141–223; Brand Blanshard, *The Uses of a Liberal Education and Other Talks to Students*, ed. Eugene Freeman (London: Alcove, 1973), chap. 3.

[62]For the following, see Plato, *Republic* 522, 528–531; Aristotle, *Politics* 1337b–1338a.

contemplate unseen ends. The necessity of this disposition explains why the philosophers held that studies that particularly involve the senses or are pursued out of coercion will also tend to be "degraded" and illiberal. On the other hand, because contemplation is an end in itself, certain liberal studies will have no usefulness for work, career, or profession.

Therefore, the relationship is not dichotomous. Some useful studies can be liberal, and vice versa—it all depends on the intentions involved, as Aristotle noted quite clearly. Historically speaking, then, the burden on modern advocates for vocational/practical/experiential education is not to show that liberal studies have been useful; centuries of tradition attest to this. Rather, they must demonstrate that the vocational/practical/experiential studies accomplish the "somelthign more" that liberal education accomplishes. The orators and philosophers agreed on this point, which is why utility—except as the accommodating influence noted earlier—does not serve as a differentiating characteristic among historical types of liberal education.

Returning to those characteristics that do make a difference, one must bear in mind that the four abstracted types do not circumscribe all the ideas of any particular writer on "liberal education." Rather, the types indicate sets of points held in common by a range of educators, more or less. The difficulty in "typing" specific arguments or historical claims is shown, for example, by the fact that the writings of Plato and Aristotle are both classical texts and philosophical works. Consequently, as Richard McKeon has observed:

> [I]n modern universities . . . two Platos and two Aristotles exist and flourish, one pair in classics departments, the other in philosophy departments. The one pair has Greek texts to be construed but no philosophy to be discussed; the other has philosophies closely akin to the modern philosophies in the languages into which they were translated but not always easily retranslated into idiomatic Greek.[63]

Nevertheless, a typology can be helpful in discerning a primary orientation in contemporary statements about "liberal education," while

---

[63]Richard McKeon, "Criticism and the Liberal Arts: The Chicago School of Criticism," in *Profession 82*, ed. Phyllis P. Franklin and Richard I. Brod (New York: Modern Language Association of America, 1982), p. 3.

departures from that orientation may be noted and historical claims evaluated. Among prominent examples of such statements, one might first consider the 1945 Harvard report, *General Education in a Free Society*, while granting for purposes of argument its declaration that "general and liberal education have identical goals."[64]

Called the "now famous Harvard report" by 1946, its philosophical bent was labeled eclectic by commentators in subsequent decades.[65] Nevertheless, though written as if by a committee, the report was more than simply a "basket" into which were piled random educational goods. Its desiderata had a systematic pattern that frankly incorporated various dialectical tensions and conflicts. Ascribing to "liberal" the common double-edged etymology—for the free person and for freeing the person—the report sought to respect conviction while admitting tentativeness of conclusions, to honor heritage and lessons of the past while recognizing a modern emphasis on process and change, to advance "unity conditioned by difference," to promote "tolerance not from absence of standards but through possession of them," to find "Jeffersonianism and Jacksonianism" complementary. Although this program appears to amount to "a synthetic reinterpretation" of the two historical ideals of liberal education,[66] one primary orientation does dominate the report—for the Harvard Committee did not actually seek conviction, heritage, and unity; it only said it did. This can be shown in three ways.

First, its greatest admirers praised it precisely for this ambivalence. The chairman of the AAC Commission on Liberal Education extolled the report for expressing a "faith" or a "credo" that was "something close to religion" but not "religious"—a "humanistic faith" that was not "a denial of religion." One is reminded again of the call of Meiklejohn for "a religion" and Hutchins for "metaphysical principles" and the reply of Gideonse: "To write volumes in

[64]Here and below, I refer to Paul H. Buck et al., *General Education in a Free Society: Report of the Harvard Committee* (Cambridge: Harvard University Press, 1945), pp. 27–35, 42–53, 66, 76–78, 92ff.

[65]Chalmers (1946a) pp. 63; George E. Ganss, *Saint Ignatius' Idea of a Jesuit University: A Study in the History of Catholic Education, including Part IV of the Constitutions of the Society of Jesus* (Milwaukee: Marquette University Press, 1954), p. 269; Hirst (1965), pp. 116–121; John S. Brubacher and Willis Rudy, *Higher Education in Transition: A History of American Colleges and Universities, 1636–1976*, 3d ed. (New York: Harper & Row, 1976), p. 303.

[66]David Sidorsky, "Varieties of Liberalism and Liberal Education," *SR* 5 (1977): 221–222. Efforts toward such a synthesis and their failings have been discussed by Marvin Bressler, "The Liberal Synthesis in American Higher Education," in *The An-*

support of the thesis that there should be a unifying philosophy without specific indication of the type of unity or of philosophy, is to miss the essential problem underlying the modern dilemma."[67] Secondly, the Committee did not understand the "heritage" of which it spoke. Liberally sprinkled throughout the report are the attributions "in Plato's charming words," "according to Socrates," and "as Aristotle says." But there is merely one reference to Cicero and none whatever to Isocrates or Quintilian, even in the report's hasty discussion of rhetoric. The orators were sacrificed for the sake of the philosophers. Finally, Harvard itself did not take seriously the professed allegiance to conviction, heritage, and unity. By 1949, when the Committee's program of general education was made compulsory, significant alterations had been adopted in the direction of more freedom of choice for students and greater departmental orientation for course offerings.[68] What the report fundamentally respected and effected, therefore, is commitment to the liberal-free pursuit of truth through its classical roots in the Socratic philosophical tradition, an accommodation of the *artes liberales* ideal congenial to a research-oriented university.

If the Harvard report looks something like the *artes liberales* accommodation in its primary orientation, despite a certain eclecticism, Daniel Bell's *The Reforming of General Education* (1966) is of quite a different type. Bell rejects even the appearance of prescribing studies in order to preserve conviction, heritage, and unity. Instead, he dedicates general or liberal education to initiating the student into understanding the principles of inquiry at increasingly sophisticated levels, and concludes, "All knowledge, thus, is liberal (that is, it enlarges and liberates the mind) when it is committed to continuing inquiry."[69] In this fashion, he is clearly verging on the liberal-free ideal; and various commentators, whether they praise his ideas or not, acknowledge that "the concept of liberal learning to be inferred from the 'Bell thesis' does not presume any particular doc-

---

nals of the American Academy of Political and Social Science, ed. Marvin Bressler (Philadelphia: The American Academy of Political and Social Science, 1972), pp. 183, 189–193.

[67]Chalmers (1946a), pp. 63–65; Harry D. Gideonse, *The Higher Learning in a Democracy: A Reply to President Hutchins' Critique of the American University* (New York: Farrar & Rinehart, 1947), p. 3.

[68]Paul M. Doty et al., "Report of the Special Committee to Review the Present Status and Problems of the General Education Program" (Cambridge: Harvard University, Faculty of Arts and Sciences, May 1964), pp. 6–9.

[69]Bell (1966), pp. 8, 152, 274.

trine of man, any particular scheme of social organization, or any goal of professional or vocational training."[70]

This lack of presumption, however, is precisely the presumption that Bell's critics point out. They assert that his commitment to "continuing inquiry" and rejection of the possibility of deriving "permanent truths" from great texts regarding the supreme questions of life is in itself a priori. Thus, "Mr. Bell's framework . . . gives an appearance of openness but is actually grounded on very narrow and dogmatic premises."[71] Bell's response, demonstrated perfectly by his explanation for choosing "Reforming" instead of "Reform" for the title of his book, is that, of course, the principle of continuing inquiry is itself the object of continuing, or endless "reforming."[72] However, this response, too, is subject to the criticism that Bell presupposes the centrality of inquiring method because he denies that classical texts could lead to "permanent truths."

The explicit conflict between the philosophical and oratorical traditions remains with us, therefore. It stands graphically recapitulated in presentations made by Charles Frankel and Paul O. Kristeller at the Columbia University seminar on "Liberalism and Liberal Education." Frankel identifies seven different kinds of "liberalism," which incorporate characteristics of the liberal-free ideal. When he turns to address "liberal education," his definition also approximates that general type, for he says such education "is to protect the liberal emphasis on critical method and a pluralistic, competitive society." Indeed, he goes on to say: "In education, if a principle is adopted as a basic guiding principle, it also becomes a goal in itself. Thus, I view toleration as an end-value and not simply a means. Toleration expresses a certain belief in the value of every individual." And then, "to come back to liberal education, I do not understand what we do in universities if it is said that our primary objective is anything but the criticism of inherited ideas, institutions, and cultures—and the pursuit of truth in the broad sense." Consistent with positing an ideal, Frankel also warns against falling into accommodation:

---

[70]C. Douglas Nicoll, "Liberal Learning, History, and the 'Bell Thesis,' " *Liberal Education* 58 (1972): 318. See George E. Arnstein, "Books—*The Reforming of General Education: The Columbia College Experience in Its National Setting* by Daniel Bell," *Liberal Education* 52 (1966): 347–351.

[71]Bloom (1967), pp. 133–134; Henry D. Aiken, *Predicament of the University* (Bloomington: Indiana University Press, 1971), pp. 150–154.

[72]Bell (1966), p. 274; Bell, "The Reform of General Education," in Goldwin (1967), pp. 97–119.

Today, however, liberal culture is in a relatively new condition. It has always been an adversary culture, existing in a context in which traditionalism and religious or moral orthodoxy have been the order of the day. But what happens when the regnant orthodoxy becomes the orthodoxy of individualism and eccentricity? . . . When liberal culture becomes the dominant culture, the problem it faces is to look at its own self-parody, its own rigidifications, and to return to its contextual method of criticism.[73]

Frankel's view is then countered by the presentation of Kristeller, upon whom I have relied for his interpretation of Renaissance humanism with its emphasis upon the classical orators. He states:

The title of our series might suggest that liberalism and liberal education are related or interdependent. In my opinion, this is not the case. Liberal education in a broad sense existed for many centuries before political liberalism was even heard of. Liberal education did not produce liberalism, but flourished under many different political systems that were not at all liberal. Conversely, liberal education is not a necessary product of liberalism, and it may actually decline and disappear in a politically liberal society.[74]

Kristeller proceeds to criticize "the current outcry against elitism" and "the seeds of a cultural revolution in which the present will be cut loose from all ties with our past and tradition and thrown back on its own resources—which I frankly consider to be intellectually, culturally and morally inadequate." Rather, he is "convinced of the intrinsic value of classical studies" which "still provide us with valid standards of excellence." Then, in a vein reminiscent of the "criticism of life" of Matthew Arnold, he concludes, "The student who develops critical judgment does not lose his freedom when he submits to what is true and valid."[75]

---

[73]Charles Frankel, "Intellectual Foundations of Liberalism," *SR* 5 (1976): 4–6, 11–14.

[74]Paul O. Kristeller, "Liberal Education and Western Humanism," *SR* 5 (1976): 15.

[75]Kristeller (1976), pp. 21–22. More recently, Professor Kristeller has commented on "our acute problem and its theoretical basis":

After 1968, most colleges abolished requirements in foreign languages, as well as literature, history and philosophy prior to this century. This is the root of the crisis of the humanities, and the crisis (also the professional crisis for Ph.D.'s) cannot be overcome without restoring some of these requirements. As a scholar, I am a

That stand-off between Frankel and Kristeller demonstrates the difficulty today, as ever, in carrying on debate between those subscribing to the opposing ideals of liberal education. These ideals are sui generis, consistent within themselves and immune to challenge, except at the level of their epistemological assumptions, and each ideal offers tremendous advantages. Those of the philosophical view and liberal-free ideal—academic freedom, scholarly autonomy, specialized research, and so on—scarcely need to be repeated because they are preeminent today and constitute the bill of rights of contemporary academe. Their codification resulted from the revitalization of the *universitas*, the professional guild of the *moderni*, over the last 150 years. On the other hand, the oratorical mind and *artes liberales* ideal emphasize the investigation of the best of tradition and the public expression of what is good and true, rather than the discovery of new knowledge. The fact that the investigation and expression are no less important and creative than the discovery is not appreciated today. What has been emphasized instead in the twentieth century is that the oratorical concern with expression and tradition—with language and texts—tempts dogmatic conservation in education and culture, tending in the long run toward authoritarianism. The liberation from such dogmatism and oppression is what the university builders and then the progressivists celebrated in the late nineteenth and early twentieth centuries.

Conversely, what is also not appreciated is that the individualism and free pursuit of truth of the philosophical mind and liberal-free ideal hazard self-indulgent and nihilistic education and culture, which can lead finally to anarchy. The chaotic liberal education of the late twentieth century stands, in fact, at the opposite pole from the dogmatic liberal arts of the early nineteenth century. This connection between value-free research and chaotic amoralism has often been noted, and many individuals, including prominent scientists, have recently raised questions about the social implications of unbridled research—questions on topics ranging, ironically, from modern weaponry to life-support medicine. These questions and others about the "limits to growth" of technology it-

---

product of rational philosophy, and of rigid philology and history, not of rhetoric or literary criticism . . . the school which I attended did not teach philosophy, but it treated Plato in Greek (not Isocrates), it taught foreign languages (French), mathematics and physics, and it applied modern philology to the classical texts we read. I prefer this to the humanist school of the Renaissance. (Personal correspondence of 26 July 1983)

self suggest a groping for moral guidelines that the orators, at their best, have always claimed to find in the noble tradition of great writings and discourse. In this regard, what is rarely understood is the underlying lesson of the *Antidosis* and *De oratore*: that searching for truth without giving commensurate attention to the importance of public expression inevitably leads the individual to isolation and self-indulgence and the republic to amoralism and chaos.

Surely this point can be appreciated by academicians in all fields, who so often declare that American undergraduates are illiterate, that they are indulged and undisciplined, and that liberal education is anarchic. The orators have always maintained that these results proceed inevitably from a liberal education that is taught by individuals who enshrine the Socratic pursuit of truth and the advance of knowledge as their cardinal virtues. The sole remedy, the orators contend, is the introduction of teachers who discipline themselves. This contention may seem redundant because specialized research, after all, demands its own kind of stringent discipline. But the oratorical discipline requires that teachers submit themselves, just as they expect their students to submit, to the highest kinds of expression, to the tradition of great texts. Their point is not that truth lies explicitly in the texts, but rather that it emerges through the disciplined effort to understand and express the meaning of the texts.

Another exercise of discipline required by the oratorical view is the submission of autonomous scholars to the consensus of their colleagues. Here, too, a philosophical kind of discipline already exists, for the canons of specialized research require the submission of research findings to the members of the speciality for criticism. But the submission demanded by the oratorical liberal education involves the surrendering of one's personal view for the sake of consensus within the community of academicians. Recent attempts to formulate core curricula have shown that this kind of discipline, or surrender, is not happening. These curricula, however much they may be draped with rationales of breadth and depth, are largely products of balancing the political interests of entrenched departments and programs. The reason that such curricula are bundles of the disciplines' courses rather than the courses of disciplined reading and expression that the oratorical ideal recommends is that the latter would require the professional scholar to submit to the curriculum, rather than vice versa, and thus to relinquish the freedom and autonomy of the philosophical ideal—a freedom and autonomy so painstakingly earned a century ago and now so lavishly enjoyed.

The contemporary problem, then, of liberal education lies in the paradox that the strengths of its ideal are also the source of its greatest liabilities. In this book, I have tried to demonstrate that, speaking historically and systematically, the situation could not be otherwise. One cannot eliminate the liabilities of the ideal without sacrificing its strengths. The same paradox would arise if the humanistic and gentle education of the *artes liberales* ideal were paramount, except that the particular strengths and liabilities would differ. The efforts by many academicians to deny the paradox and to recover the strengths of either ideal without the attendant liabilities contribute to the confusion in current discussion about liberal education.

Saying this does not mean that improvement cannot take place. Everyone agrees that major problems exist in contemporary liberal education, and the historical interpretation advanced here would suggest that analogous problems have arisen whenever one ideal of liberal education has become preeminent and the dialectical balance between the two ideals has been lost. The balance is to be preserved because it lies in the nature of things, so to speak—it arises from the distinction between reason and speech, between *ratio* and *oratio*. These two capacities, combined together in the Greek word *logos*, have been considered since the time of Isocrates and Plato the defining characteristics of human nature—of what, in the Western view, separates human beings from animals.[76] The balance between the two ideals is difficult to maintain because the distinction between reason and speech, though apparently sharp and clear, becomes obscure when analyzed closely, as shown by the fact that for the Greeks both capacities were denoted by the term *logos*. What, after all, really is the relationship between the thought and the word?

From this perspective, it may be said that the long debate about liberal education is also a debate about the fundamental characteristics of human nature. However, it is a debate, not about any and every characteristic of being human, but about two particular characteristics—about whether reason or speech, each a pole of *logos*, is preeminent. I am arguing, in fine, that this interpretation of the

---

[76]The most widely cited and powerful testimony of the power of *logos* is from Isocrates, *Antidosis* 253ff. and *Nicocles* 5ff.:

> For in our other faculties we do not excell the animals. Many of them are fleeter or stronger or otherwise better than we. But because we were endowed with the power of persuading one another and explaining [ourselves], we were not only released from bestial ways of living, but came together and founded states and established laws and invented arts. It was speech *(logos)* which enabled us to perfect almost everything we have achieved in the way of civilization. For it was

history of liberal education is empirically demonstrable while it is also theoretically compelling, in the sense that the two ideals are perfectly complementary even as they are, by themselves, internally systematic. To endorse this interpretation, however, requires that a good deal of the twentieth-century American historiography about liberal education be reinterpreted or discarded.

As for addressing the contemporary problems of liberal education, which inhere in the philosophical ideal, this interpretation would suggest a restoring of the balance between the two ideals and, therefore, between *ratio* and *oratio*, the two poles of *logos*. But this is far easier said than done. The oratorical view recommends that those most secure, most invested, and with the most to lose—the senior scholars at the premier research institutions—discipline themselves by submitting to their corporate wisdom and to a curriculum with the study of expression and rhetoric elevated from a freshman requirement to a centerpiece. One often hears admonitions about the former kind of submission—"To restore integrity to the bachelor's degree, there must be a renewal of the faculty's corporate responsibility for the curriculum"[77]—but there is rarely a recognition that the means to accomplish the resuscitation of the community of learning lie in elevating and emphasizing the study of expression, rhetoric, and the textual tradition of the community. Yet the means are self-evident. A community is, after all, a group of people who talk to each other and do it well.

This view of community was dear to Socrates, no less than to Cicero. However, the notion may still appear nonsensical or dangerous to modern Socratic scholars because the study of expression leads inexorably to frivolous display and the dulling of critical faculties, as Plato so greatly feared. Consequently, one can harbor no expectation that there will emerge any change from within the higher

---

speech which laid down the standards of right and wrong, nobility and baseness, without which we should be unable to live together. It is through speech that we convict bad men and praise good ones. By its aid we educate the foolish and test the wise. . . . With the help of speech we dispute over doubtful matters and investigate the unknown. . . . If we sum up the character of this power, we shall find that no reasonable thing is done anywhere without the power of logos, that logos is the leader of all actions and thoughts and that those who make most use of it are the wisest of mankind. Therefore those who despise education and culture must be hated just as we hate those who blaspheme against the gods. (Translation taken from Werner Jaeger, *Paideia: The Ideals of Greek Culture*, trans. Gilbert Highet, 2d ed. (Oxford: Basil Blackwell, 1944), vol. 3, pp. 89–90.)

[77]Mark H. Curtis et al., *Integrity of the College Curriculum; A Report to the Academic Community by the Project on Redefining the Meaning and Purpose of Baccalaureate Degrees* (Washington, D.C.: Association of American Colleges, 1985).

learning in America, as it is presently constituted. The alternative exists, however, because the Ciceronian and Socratic conceptions of liberal education continue to stand in tension, as they have since antiquity, like the two foci of an ellipse whose locus includes the varying approaches to liberal education of any particular time. And the points on the ellipse are defined by their relation to Isocrates and Plato, Isidore and Boethius, Orléans and Paris, Arnold and Huxley, that is, to the orators and the philosophers.

Appendix I

In *THE ACADEMIC REVOLUTION*, Christopher Jencks and David Riesman observed that "historians are always torn between looking for watersheds and looking for continuities." To this might be added the corollary that if established scholars have discovered watersheds, then the rising generation tends to find continuities, and vice versa. This being so, it is not surprising that in the past two decades some historians have begun "a concerted attack" on the "standard account of the history of higher education in America." Their attack has involved, among other things, uncovering more appreciation in colonial and antebellum colleges for modernity, experimental science, progressivism, and the like than "the familiar historiography" gives them credit for.[1] Clearly, this revisionism could have important implications for an analysis of liberal education in light of the two general types theorized in this volume.

Actually, "revisionism" is a poor term—and not only because of its prejudicial connotations. On the one hand, the term has been used in regard to efforts to rewrite the history of American higher education according to the ideological perspective contravening "Whig history," as well as by employing the methodology of "social history."[2] On the other hand, "revisionism" is a poor term be-

---

[1]Quotations are drawn from Jurgen Herbst, "Essay Review III, American College History: Re-examination Underway," *HEQ* 14 (1974): 259–267; Christopher Jencks and David Riesman, *The Academic Revolution* (Garden City, N.Y.: Doubleday, 1968), p. 9. See Douglas Sloan, "Harmony, Chaos, and Consensus: The American College Curriculum," *Teachers College Record* 73 (1971b), pp. 223ff.; James Axtell, "The Death of the Liberal Arts," *HEQ* 11 (1971): 339–352. Especially helpful is James McLachlan, "The American College in the Nineteenth Century: Towards a Reappraisal," *Teachers College Record* 80 (1978): 287–306.

[2]Bernard Bailyn, *Education in the Forming of American Society: Needs and Opportunities for Study* (Chapel Hill: University of North Carolina Press, 1960). On the

cause the "standard account of the history of higher education in America" is not so uniform as critics sometimes take it to be. Samuel Morison's volumes on Harvard are well known for their "modernist" outlook, and according to Lawrence Cremin, *The College Charts Its Course* (1939) by R. F. Butts "dominated the outlook of the 1940s [and] tended to view the pre-Civil War period largely as an age of reform in higher education." Theodore Hörnberger's *Scientific Thought in the American Colleges, 1638–1800* (1945) was also congenial to a modernist view; and even Richard Hofstadter, whose term "the Great Retrogression" is so often taken to exemplify the views of those who regard the colonial and the antebellum college as parochial and conservative, maintained that "the greater part of the history of the colleges in the eighteenth century is one of progressive liberalization, at least in academic theory and curricular content if not in formal academic practices."[3]

Therefore, the argument that colonial and antebellum colleges were sympathetic to new studies and pedagogy is not a new one, though it has lately become more popular, and it can be termed a "modernist" view of the colleges. Under this term are included arguments about various sorts of subjects—foreign languages, practical studies, English—but the following discussion will address only arguments about the introduction of natural science into colonial and antebellum colleges. This is because natural science is the subject most centrally linked to the modernist argument, and through its association with the New Philosophy can most readily be taken as a tentative proxy for the liberal-free ideal. Particularly, I will have in mind works by Hornberger (1945), Hangartner (1955), Sloan (1971, 1972), Warch (1973), Guralnick (1975, 1976), and Humphrey (1976).[4]

---

many aspects of revisionism, see Floyd M. Hammack, "Rethinking Revisionism," *HEQ* 16 (1976): 53–61; William W. Brickman, "Revisionism and the Study of the History of Education," *HEQ* 4 (1964): 209–223; Brickman, "Theoretical and Critical Perspectives on Educational History," *PH* 18 (1978): 42–83; Sol Cohen, "The History of the History of American Education, 1900–1976: The Uses of the Past," *Harvard Educational Review* 46 (1976): 298–330; Diane Ravitch, *The Revisionists Revised: A Critique of the Radical Attack on the Schools* (New York: Basic Books, 1978); Jennings L. Wagoner, Jr., "Essay Review IV: Historical Revisionism, Educational Theory, and an American *Paideia*," *HEQ* 18 (1978): 201–210; and the essays in John H. Best, ed., *Historical Inquiry in Education: A Research Agenda* (Washington, D.C.: American Educational Research Association, 1983).

[3]Richard Hofstadter and Walter P. Metzger, *The Development of Academic Freedom in the United States* (New York: Columbia University Press, 1955), p. 159; L. A. Cremin, "Preface," in *The Colleges and the Public, 1782–1862*, ed. Theodore R. Crane (New York: Bureau of Publications, Teachers College, Columbia University, 1963), p. v; Herbst (1974), pp. 259–260. See also Richard J. Storr, *The Beginnings of Graduate Education in America* (Chicago: University of Chicago Press, 1953).

[4]Herbst (1974) cites most of the works mentioned here, though he does not use

At one point in a discussion of these historiographical issues, Jurgen Herbst appears to divide historians between those who have "uncritically accepted" and those who have begun "a concerted attack" on the traditional interpretation of colonial and antebellum colleges. This division epitomizes the hard-and-fast dichotomy often found in the modernist literature, where there is no place for those who "critically accept" the traditional view. (For example, Douglas Sloan criticizes Frederick Rudolph for even qualifiedly and partially adhering to the standard interpretation.) This dichotomous approach amounts to setting up a strawman, which is what Stanley Guralnick does when he announces his opposition to the view that the colleges "confine[d] their program of study, as is usually held, to the classical languages," or when he rejects "the usual form of the argument that we hear today—namely, that the study of Latin and Greek kept science out of the [curricular] program."[5]

The first problem with this approach is that it ignores the question of identifying a proper standard of comparison. Yes, a student of 1642 might find much change in the curriculum of 1764; but this does not necessarily mean, as Rudolph would have us believe, that L. F. Snow was wrong to consider the programs of 1642 and 1764

the term "modernist." Hangartner's thesis has been called "the best general consideration of curriculum and pedagogy" by Lawrence A. Cremin, *American Education: The Colonial Experience, 1607–1783* (New York: Harper & Row, 1970), p. 662; Carl A. Hangartner, "Movements to Change American College Teaching, 1700–1830"(Ph.D. diss., Yale University, 1955). Many others have relied on these works for their own "modernist" interpretations, such as M. St. Mel Kennedy, "The Changing Academic Characteristics of the Nineteenth-Century American College Teacher," *PH* 5 (1965): 360–371. Sloan defends the argument better than others do, while Guralnick's work is obviously significant although marred by its small and skewed sample of colleges, among other things. Despite Guralnick's assertion that his sample is "adequate for the presentation of a well-balanced and representative picture," he relies primarily on 15 of the 182 antebellum colleges. Moreover, of those 15, all are located in the northeast, 12 were founded before 1800, and all are among the oldest, largest, and wealthiest. That these colleges are the ones most likely to exhibit scientific influence is shown by studies demonstrating that, for example, scientific activity in the southeast lagged far behind that in the rest of the country until 1860. Guralnick includes no colleges from this area among his 15. Stanley M. Guralnick, "Preface," in *Science and the Ante-Bellum American College* (Philadelphia: American Philosophical Society, 1975); Ralph S. Bates, *Scientific Societies in the United States*, 3d ed. (Cambridge: MIT Press, 1965), pp. 45–51; Joseph Ewan, "The Growth of Learned and Scientific Societies in the Southeastern United States to 1860," in *The Pursuit of Knowledge in the Early American Republic: American Scientific and Learned Societies from Colonial Times to the Civil War*, ed. Alexandra Oleson and Sanborn C. Brown (Baltimore: Johns Hopkins University Press, 1976), pp. 208–218.

[5]Herbst (1974), pp. 259–260; Guralnick (1975), pp. 152, 157; Stanley M. Guralnick, "Sources of Misconceptions on the Role of Science in the Nineteenth-Century American College," in *Science in America since 1820*, ed. Nathan Reingold (New York: Science History Publications, 1976), pp. 48–52; Sloan (1971b), p. 227. Sloan's views

relatively similar when he looked back at them from the year 1907.[6] Obviously, one may well formulate different opinions about science in the curriculum of 1764 depending on whether one compares it to the scientific knowledge of 1642, 1764, or 1907. The contextual standard influences historical judgment, and inattention to this issue produces the sorts of contradictory statements and non sequiturs that can freqently be found in modernist writings. For example, Hornberger and Guralnick argue that the colonial colleges of 1740 did not attend to science, that the colleges included more science in the curriculum in ensuing decades, but that somehow the science in colleges of 1800 was still insignificant.[7]

Even within the same period, problems of contextual standard arise, as when Hornberger asserts, "The earliest generous recognition of the sciences in America came at William and Mary," and then describes the unproductive activities of the first two professors of mathematics and natural philosophy. Similarly, Guralnick lauds the science of colleges of the 1860s at the beginning of his book, and then retreats from this view to the point of contradicting himself—or changing his standard—at the end. In the same vein, Warch equates the education at "Harvard, Oxford, Cambridge, Edinburgh, and the various English Dissenting academies" and considers them to be giving "a substantial and broad education" early in the eighteenth century.[8] Many historians would disagree, even compared to the standard of the time.

The second problem with the treatment of the traditional historiography by modernist interpreters is that it cannot account for ambiguity in historical evidence. A dichotomous treatment cannot

---

on Rudolph's 1962 history are significant because Rudolph's 1977 *Curriculum* reveals his sensitivity to the new historiography in that he appears more critical of the traditional view, as in his comments on L. F. Snow, and he talks more about the discontinuity in the curriculum than he did in his earlier work. Frederick Rudolph, *The American College and University: A History* (New York: Random House, 1962), pp. 25–26, 227; Rudolph, *Curriculum: A History of the American Undergraduate Course of Study since 1636* (San Francisco: Jossey-Bass, 1977), pp. 1–24, 53ff. The effort to strike a balance between the views that colleges were either enemies or friends of science is made by Theodore R. Crane, ed.; *The Colleges and the Public, 1782–1862* (New York: Bureau of Publications, Teachers College, Columbia University, 1963), pp. 1–36.

[6]Rudolph (1977), p. 53.

[7]Theodore Hornberger, *Scientific Thought in the American Colleges, 1638–1800* (Austin: University of Texas Press, 1945), pp. 35, 192; Guralnick (1975), pp. 9–15.

[8]Hornberger (1945), pp. 25–26; Richard Warch, *School of the Prophets: Yale College, 1701–1740* (New Haven, Conn.: Yale University Press, 1973), p. 243; Guralnick (1975), pp. vii, 128–137.

comprehend the fact of Benjamin Silliman's appointment at Yale, or the 1827 reform at Amherst, having been cited both as evidence for the appreciation of science by antebellum colleges and as evidence against it.[9] The opinion depends on the presupposed standard. Still another problem in the modernist view is the use of prejudicial language, of which one less important but still meaningful aspect is the crusading or defensive rhetoric of modernist writings. Morison's work has been noted for this sort of language, and it continues to be a special problem for those who write about their own institutions, such as Warch and Humphrey. Reading them, one is reminded of the historian of Wake Forest College who, seeking at a much later date for evidence with which to defend his institution's early modernity, lamely wrote, "The Board of trustees from the first were awake to the importance of scientific instruction and sought to make provision for it, but were at a loss what to do."[10]

Warch interlards discussion of the early Yale curriculum with such comments as: "This same impulse toward modernity seems to have been at work in the development of the Yale curriculum. Because Yale wanted to be up-to-date, it was not afraid to revise and change its courses." And when something makes Yale look less than progressive, he is quick to say, "This fact, however, does not convict Yale of backwardness." Alongside this crusading language runs a theme of putative competition with Harvard in the race toward modernity, as when he declares in describing mathematical studies, "Yale had forged ahead of Harvard in this one area"; or when his discussion on the curriculum triumphantly concludes, "By 1738, it was at least possible for Yale to be seen as a model for Harvard."[11]

---

[9]Cf. Russell Thomas, *The Search for a Common Learning, 1800–1960* (New York: McGraw-Hill, 1962), pp. 13ff. with Melvin I. Urofsky, "Reforms and Response: The Yale Report of 1828," *HEQ* 5 (1965): 54–55. Cf. Richard P. McCormick, *Rutgers: A Bicentennial History* (New Brunswick, N.J.: Rutgers University Press, 1966), p. 45 and Douglas Sloan, *The Scottish Enlightenment and the American College Ideal* (New York: Teachers College Press, 1971a), p. 236, with Rudolph (1962), p. 223, and Brooks M. Kelley, *Yale: A History* (New Haven, Conn.: Yale University Press, 1974), pp. 135ff.

[10]Winthrop S. Hudson, "The Morison Myth Concerning the Founding of Harvard College," *Church History* 8 (1939): 148–159; G. W. Paschal, *History of Wake Forest College* (Winston-Salem, N.C.: Wake Forest College, 1935), p. 135. Similarly, Burke argues against the "traditional view" and maintains that antebellum colleges were largely "flexible and receptive to science," but ends up offering an apology that confirms the traditional point of view: "They would have offered more science in their schools, but the high costs of teaching the subject, the lack of student demand, and the scarcity of adequately trained instructors hindered many of the institutions." Colin B. Burke, *American Collegiate Populations: A Test of the Traditional View* (New York: New York University Press, 1982), p. 39.

[11]Warch (1973), pp. 220, 238, 247, 249.

Given Yale's foundation as a defender of Calvinist orthodoxy against Harvard's latitudinarianism, one wonders whether it was really so eager to outstrip the Cambridge school in this fashion, especially in its first forty years.

Humphrey's description of "progressive," "up-to-date" influences on Samuel Johnson's early curriculum at Columbia (1754–1763) is also clearly an apologetic intended to demonstrate that Johnson "instituted an educational program that fell little short of the curricula at other American colleges in its fidelity to the New Learning." While this view may have some truth, the standard of "other American colleges" is hardly rigorous, and it does not take into account that most learning was done by recitation, that is, memorization and repetition. By the time Humphrey writes that "if Johnson did not turn his back on Newton in designing the King's College curriculum, neither did he reject other progressive currents" and that if he had only found well-qualified students "his curriculum might have been more progressive than it was," one believes one has found in Johnson an eighteenth-century John Dewey.

All this is buttressed by the proof that "Johnson realized that science appealed to the undergraduates and that without an emphasis on natural philosophy his college could never compete for students." The exaggeration in this statement is shown by the continued success of the college after Johnson was succeeded by Myles Cooper, who, in Humphrey's own words, "prescribed an almost overwhelming dose of the classics" while "the official program ignored natural philosophy and mathematics." Of course, Johnson was not so much of a progressivist to begin with, so the continued success under Cooper is not surprising. In fact, Johnson's late-in-life rejection of Newtonianism and his revivial of religious orthodoxy are quite disconcerting for Humphrey's interpretation of the early Johnson, and Humphrey does not dispute the terms "that historian Theodore Hornberger uses to assess Johnson's mind a decade later, as 'sadly lacking in perspective and warped by a determination that science must be subservient to orthodoxy, whatever the cost.' " To this, Humphrey can offer only the observation that Johnson's mind changed a good deal late in life.[12]

Guralnick, too, provides an example of crusading rhetoric when he attributes the traditional interpretation of antebellum colleges to "the undocumented platitudes of liberal academics" who have been

[12]David C. Humphrey, *From King's College to Columbia, 1746–1800* (New York: Columbia University Press, 1976), pp. 173–176.

"dismissing the subtle problems of religion, ideology, education, and science which cry for recognition."[13] Paradoxically, a more significant aspect of the problem of language in modernist writings is also revealed by Guralnick's work. Sensitive to the general issue, he attributes much of the error in the traditional historiography to "semantic distortions," meaning that scholars have misinterpreted colonial and antebellum "natural philosophy" to mean abstract philosophical speculation. Thus, he criticizes Howard Mumford Jones for writing "that the 'natural philosophy' course of the period 'unlike most modern science courses was really philosophical.' " In this way, Guralnick is concerned to identify properly the content of subjects taught in colonial and antebellum colleges, so as not to be misled by the older terms.[14] Certainly, this is a contribution and to the better. But it is only a beginning and, left by itself, superficial, because Guralnick completely misses the deeper sense in which Jones's words are quite perceptive, that "the 'natural philosophy' course of the period" *was* rooted in the scholastic three philosophies, not the New Science, and thus "was really philosophical."

The evidence presented for modernist interpretations can also be challenged, especially when these histories assert the presence of science teaching and "experimental lectures" in antebellum colleges on the basis of books prescribed for courses. Hangartner is a good example. In a study of college teaching and curricula from 1700 to 1830, he argues for the influence of works by Descartes, Newton, and Locke on American colleges by first showing how textbooks by John Desaguliers, Benjamin Martin, William J. Gravesande, and William Enfield relied on those works. After demonstrating briefly that these textbooks were used at Harvard and Yale, he speaks about "the widespread use of these books" and links the College of William and Mary and King's College to "experimental lectures" in Scotland. Without considering how much of the curriculum was devoted to these textbooks, and while acknowledging that little, or no, or even contradicting, evidence exists as to whether experimental demonstrations were performed in class, Hangartner proceeds to describe in relatively great detail the contents of the textbooks, inferring from them the nature of the classroom experience.[15]

Aside from the fact that "the widespread use of these books" is not demonstrated and that these lectures and texts played a very

[13]Guralnick (1975), p. 150; Guralnick (1976), p. 48.
[14]Guralnick (1975), p. 60; Guralnick (1976), p. 50.
[15]Hangartner (1955), pp. 40–53, chap. 3.

minor role in the curricula in which they were included, the argument based on books raises the important question of pedagogy. Hangartner himself acknowledges that recitation was the standard method of college teaching through the eighteenth century and "many years" beyond. Indeed, the recitation method was considered by reformers to be the "root" problem in liberal education right through the Civil War.[16] Recitation required memorization of texts by individual students who then recited them in class and possibly responded to questions. Even the latter was a rote operation, however.[17]

Classroom progress under this system was measured by the amount of material memorized in a given time, and the standard applied to Locke's *Essay Concerning Human Understanding* as well as to Cicero's *De oratore* and to readings in natural philosophy. Continuing the practice from colonial times, Benjamin Silliman employed it at Yale; and Denison Olmsted's *An Introduction to Natural Philosophy* (1844), a text popular around midcentury, was sytematized to avoid the need for explanation so that the professor could simply require that the text be repeated aloud. When lecturing began to be introduced at the colleges, it meant the professor merely read from the textbook and commented upon it. And even this kind of lecturing was kept to a modicum. The 1854–55 Dartmouth course catalog contained three-and-a-half pages listing subjects and authors with their books to be recited. Next, as an afterthought, almost as a footnote, it cited "courses of lectures" in nine lines.[18]

This pedagogy does not mean that the colleges did not see value in scientific equipment. Quite the reverse is true. Many were the proud announcements about scientific "apparatus" obtained, and modernist historians echo this theme, such as Hornberger about colonial colleges. However, the implication that this equipment was

---

[16]Hangartner (1955), p. 65; Hofstadter and Metzger (1955), pp. 228–232; John S. Brubacher and Willis Rudy, *Higher Education in Transition: A History of American Colleges and Universities, 1636–1976*, 3d ed. (New York: Harper & Row, 1976), pp. 84–90.

[17]For testimony on the persistence of the recitation method, see Louis F. Snow, *The College Curriculum in the United States* (New York: Bureau of Publications, Teachers College, Columbia University, 1907), pp. 86–114, 142; Samuel E. Morison, *Three Centuries of Harvard, 1636–1936* (Cambridge, Mass.: Belknap, 1936), pp. 228–236, 260–263; Albea Godbold, *The Church College of the Old South* (Durham, N.C.: Duke University Press, 1944), app. 1; Edward D. Eddy, Jr., *Colleges for Our Land and Time: The Land-Grant Idea in American Education* (New York: Harper & Brothers, 1957), p. 4; Kelley (1974), pp. 157–161.

[18]*Catalogue of the Officers and Students of Dartmouth College for the Academical Year (1854–55)* (Hanover, N.H.: Dartmouth College, 1854), p. xxx; Denison Olmsted, *An*

used to introduce "observation and experiment" into the classroom is rarely proven. For example, Humphrey cites instances of Columbia professors using equipment in their rooms and then concludes without further proof that they must have used it in the classroom as well. Yet if this conclusion is generally warranted, why would Henry Thoreau, graduating from Harvard in 1836, not even realize that he had studied "navigation," though Harvard certainly had navigation equipment among its natural philosophy "apparatus"?[19]

It appears that colleges acquired such equipment in order to gain prestige and yet kept it away from students for the professors to tinker with. At turn-of-the-century Yale, for example, experiments were "performed separately from the actual lecture" in a curtained room that consequently "took on an aura of mystery." Even when such equipment was brought into the classroom for "experimental lectures," the students merely observed, and did not participate in, the demonstrations. Benjamin Silliman, a pioneer in the experimental lecture even though he relied most heavily on recitations, "much preferred that [his students] would refrain from meddling with his apparatus in any way." Only in 1835 was a college chemistry laboratory opened for student instruction, and only in 1868, a physics laboratory. This distance between the students and the scientific "apparatus" was later confirmed in the reflections of Charles W. Eliot, an 1853 graduate of Harvard. "To the best of my knowledge and belief I was the only undergraduate in Harvard College who had the privilege of studying a science by the laboratory method."[20] Indeed, students were not even allowed in the libraries of antebellum colleges for more than a few hours per week.[21] Why should they be permitted at all in the laboratories?

Introduction to Natural Philosophy: Designed as a Textbook for the Use of Students in Yale College, Compiled from Various Authorities, 1st ed. 1931, stereotype ed. (New York: Collins, 1844).

[19]Henry D. Thoreau, Walden; or, Life in the Woods (Boston: Ticknor and Fields, 1854), p. 37; Humphrey (1976), pp. 175–181.

[20]Quotations are drawn from Hangartner (1955), pp. 169–170; Charles W. Eliot, A Late Harvest: Miscellaneous Papers Written between Eighty and Ninety (Boston: Atlantic Monthly Press, 1924), p. 10. See Elliot R. Downing, "Methods in Science Teaching: Summary of Investigations of the Demonstration Method versus the Laboratory Method," JHE 2 (1931): 316–319; Kelley (1974), pp. 157ff. In the field of botany, for example, American scientists were solely "taxonomic" until the 1870s when the "laboratory method" began to be introduced. Charles E. Ford, "Botany Texts: A Survey of their Development in American Higher Education, 1643–1906," HEQ 4 (1964): 59–71.

[21]Arthur T. Hamlin, The University Library in the United States: Its Origins and Development (Philadelphia: University of Pennsylvania Press, 1981), chaps. 1, 2, 9.

Finally, one must consider the meaning of "experimental," a word often used by modernists and by antebellum educators. The latter applied it perhaps most commonly to "experimental lectures" given in courses of natural philosophy, and this usage was carried into the statutes and laws of the antebellum colleges. The modernists addressed here generally take the term at face value without much discussion. Hornberger does not attend to it when he tries to compute the percentage of colonial curricula given over to "science." Warch and Humphrey straightforwardly infer from it the testing of hypotheses. Even Guralnick, who claims to be sensitive to "semantic distortions," easily equates natural philosophy courses with "modern science" and does not ask what it meant to be "experimental" in the antebellum period.[22] However, contrary to more modern usage, "experimental" seems to have incorporated two meanings through at least the first half of the nineteenth century. While it did, on the one hand, denote "ascertained by experiment . . . trial," it also meant "relating to experience." Warch himself throws light on this alternative possibility when he clarifies the meaning of an eighteenth-century clergyman's reference to "experimental knowledge of God" by substituting "experiential" for "experimental." The same denotation of "experiential" could be heard from Gilbert Tennent during the Great Awakening, and it was also employed a century later when Emerson talked about looking through a telescope as an "experimental" lesson in science. In this way, one can see that the term "experimental" when applied to lectures did not necessarily imply the consideration of tentative hypotheses, but rather the discussion of empirical phenomena.[23]

In fact, Schmidt believes that experimental lectures involved simply "demonstrations" of known truths, and a 1931 study found only four colleges in 1872 that were teaching anything by the "laboratory method," as opposed to the "demonstration method."[24]

---

[22]Hornberger (1945), pp. 23, 29; Hangartner (1955): pp. 124–128; Warch (1973), p. 216; Guralnick (1975), chap. 1; Humphrey (1976), p. 180.

[23]*The Oxford English Dictionary*, s. v. "experimental"; H. G. Good, "Emerson: An Educational Liberal," *History of Education Journal* 1, no. 1 (1949): 12–13; Gilbert Tennent, *The Danger of an Unconverted Ministry* (Philadelphia: B. Franklin, 1740), p. 10; Warch (1973), pp. 287–288. The difference between antebellum and twentieth-century ideas of experimental and scientific method is well described in Sloan (1971a), pp. 159–160, 214–217; George H. Daniels, *American Science in the Age of Jackson* (New York: Columbia University Press, 1968), chaps. 3, 4, 5, 6.

[24]Downing (1931), pp. 316–319; George P. Schmidt, *Princeton and Rutgers: The Two Colonial Colleges of New Jersey* (Princeton, N.J.: D. Van Nostrand, 1964), pp. 32–35. It is interesting to note that the orrery was the favorite item of college scientific "apparatus." Hornberger (1945), p. 67. It *demonstrated* the true picture of the universe and still was not directly empirical.

Among the modernists, Hangartner displays the most insight about this point by setting "experimental lecture" in the context of the antebellum recitation method:

> A century and more of American college students were apparently taught that the proper method for teachers to follow was to proceed from the general principles of a science to its more detailed applications, although they were assured that the way to grow in knowledge of a science was to proceed from particular facts to general principles.[25]

Thus, it may well be that "the Colonies . . . took Newton and Locke to heart," as Cremin has written, but it is another thing to show that they took them to mind. That this approach was not seriously altered after the colonial period can be seen in the 1826 statement of Thomas Clemson (later a pioneer of the land-grant college movement) that he studied in Europe since "there is not a single scientific institution on this continent where a proper scientific education can be obtained."[26] This opinion indicates that "the experimental lecture . . . was still a considerable step away from the laboratory method itself," for "at best students were only able to witness scientific demonstrations performed by the professor himself in the lecture room." Examinations in science courses during the first half of the nineteenth century also reveal this continued orientation to seek illustrations for given truths.[27] From this perspective, the colonial and antebellum colleges appear to be farther from science than from that "humanism" defined by Giustiniani as "solicitude for handed down knowledge (in contrast to experimental research)."[28]

Eddy has written: "As late as 1850 not a single college had a laboratory, or anything like a laboratory, in its physical plant. . . . This would smack of the experimental, and experiments were intolerable to the prevailing educational thought."[29] Such words are perhaps extreme and may well exemplify the sort of expression of the

---

[25]Hangartner (1955), pp. 237−239.

[26]Quoted from Eddy (1957), p. 6; Cremin (1970), p. 256.

[27]Brubacher and Rudy (1976), p. 90. See Sherman B. Barnes, "The Entry of Science and History in the College Curriculum, 1865−1914," *HEQ* 4 (1964): 45−48; Laurence R. Veysey, *The Emergence of the American University* (Chicago: University of Chicago Press, 1965), pp. 133−142; Guralnick (1975), apps. 2, 3, 4.

[28]His parenthesis. Vito R. Giustiniani, "Umanesimo: La parola e la cosa," in *Studia Humanitatis, Ernesto Grassi zum 70. Geburtstag,* ed. Eginhard Hora and Eckhard Kessler (Munich: Wilhelm Fink, 1973), p. 25.

[29]Eddy (1957), p. 4−5.

traditional historiography that the modernists seek to counteract. To do so is justifiable and helpful; however, it will do only harm to overreact. Here it has been contended that the material that modernist historians regard as science constituted a relatively small fraction of the colonial and antebellum college curriculum; that most of this science was taught by rote recitations; that when colleges obtained "scientific apparatus," the students did not always see it in the classroom; and that if they did, they rarely ever touched it. Finally, it has been argued that the "experimental" lectures—a fraction of a fraction—were probably meant to be demonstrations of known truths. Upon searching through Morison, Hornberger, Hangartner, Sloan, Warch, Humphrey, and Guralnick, one will find scarcely a single example of college students being asked to make observations about a natural phenomenon, to theorize a hypothesis, and then to devise a test for it and carry out the test.[30] Granting that statements like that of Eddy go too far, can one yet say that science—in the modern and experimental sense of the word—was being taught in the colonial or antebellum colleges? I think not.

---

[30]I believe these points about science in antebellum college curricula hold also against the comments of James Findlay, " 'Western Colleges,' 1830–1870: Educational Institutions in Transition," *History of Higher Education Annual* 2 (1982): 33–63. For further discussion about the historiography of the American college, see my "Essay Review: *History of Higher Education Annual*, vols. 1–4, 1981–1984," forthcoming in *Minerva*.

Appendix II

"In the period between the Reformation and the French Revolution . . . a new philosophy was evolved. . . . This new philosophy was liberalism," wrote H. J. Laski in his well known *Rise of Liberalism.* While there are supporters for this view, it is highly problematic regarding both the origins and the definition of this "new philosophy." One can easily find testimony that "the liberal tradition is woefully incoherent," leading many to hold with W. D. Grampp that " 'Liberalism' has so many meanings—is such a rich source of controversy and inconclusion—that it has become nearly an un-word or an antiword, one that means nothing or even less."[1]

In recent times, the ambiguity and elusiveness in meaning have certainly not abated and may even have worsened such that the phenomenon of liberalism "is often regarded with suspicion by the Right and with contempt by the doctrinaire Left." Prominent political scientists—from T. J. Lowi at the University of Chicago to H. C. Mansfield at Harvard—have joined the chorus that "liberal leaders" lack "the resoluteness of men certain of the legitimacy of their positions, the integrity of their institutions, or the justness of the programs they serve."[2] Bearing this critique in mind, I wish to examine very briefly whether this liberalism, which emerged triumphant in

---

[1]Harold J. Laski, *The Rise of Liberalism: The Philosophy of a Business Civilization* (New York: Harper & Brothers, 1936), pp. 1–2; William D. Grampp, *Economic Liberalism* (New York: Random House, 1965), vol. 1, p. vii. See David J. Manning's rejection of three standard approaches to reconciling discontinuity in the liberal tradition in *Liberalism* (New York: St. Martin's Press, 1976), pp. 139ff.

[2]Theodore J. Lowi, *The End of Liberalism: Ideology, Policy, and the Crisis of Public Authority* (New York: W. W. Norton, 1969), p. 288. See Harry K. Girvetz, *The Evolution of Liberalism*, rev. ed. (New York: Collier, 1963), p. 154; Robert P. Wolff, *The Poverty of Liberalism* (Boston: Beacon, 1968), chap. 1; Clarence J. Karier, "Liberalism and the Quest for Orderly Change," *HEQ* 12 (1972): 57–80; Harvey C. Mansfield, Jr., *The Spirit of Liberalism* (Cambridge: Harvard University Press, 1978).

the second half of the nineteenth century, is in any significant way parallel to the liberal-free ideal, which could then be considered an outrigger of the larger political and social movement of liberalism. A. O. Hansen is not alone in describing liberal education as "liberation" and facilely linking both to "liberalism."[3]

The first possible parallelism concerns the time of the formation of liberalism and the identity of thinkers often associated with it: Hobbes, Locke, and Priestley in seventeenth- and eighteenth-century England; Descartes, Spinoza, and Rousseau in seventeenth- and eighteenth-century France. A second parallelism might lie in the congeries of characteristics usually attributed to "liberalism." Whether in a classic work by Guido de Ruggiero or a popular introduction by J. S. Schapiro, there is often reference to respect for equality, progress, critical skepticism, rationalism, individualism, and freedom.[4] These last three points in particular, amounting to what L. T. Hobhouse called the "self-directing power of personality," are repeatedly mentioned. Indeed, in "the classical expression of English Liberal thought," *On Liberty* (1859), John Stuart Mill defends "liberty of thought and feeling, absolute freedom of opinion and sentiment on all subjects, practical or speculative, scientific, moral or theological."[5] Another possible parallel to the liberal-free ideal lies in the attention "liberals" have frequently paid to education. A fourth may be inferred from the connections often drawn between science and "the new philosophy" of liberalism. This last inference follows, on the one hand, from attributing to early mod-

---

[3]Allen O. Hansen, *Liberalism and American Education in the Eighteenth Century* (New York: Macmillan, 1926), pp. xiv, 61–62, 153; Elbert V. Wills, *The Growth of American Higher Education: Liberal, Professional, and Technical* (Philadelphia: Dorrance, 1936), pp. 180ff. I am reserving from consideration here contemporary discussion, such as the 1976–77 seminar at Columbia University's General Education program, which explicitly attempts to link "liberalism and liberal education." "Liberalism and Liberal Education," issue of *SR* 5, nos. 1–2 (Fall 1976).

[4]Guido de Ruggiero, *The History of European Liberalism,* trans. R. G. Collingwood (London: Oxford University Press, 1927), pp. 1–90, 347–363; Laski (1936), chaps. 1–3; J. Salwyn Schapiro, *Liberalism: Its Meaning and History* (New York: Van Nostrand Reinhold, 1958), chaps. 1–2; Caroline Robbins, *The Eighteenth-Century Commonwealthman: Studies in the Transmission, Development, and Circumstance of English Liberal Thought from the Restoration of Charles II until the War with the Thirteen Colonies* (Cambridge: Harvard University Press, 1959), chap. 1; Alan L. Bullock and Maurice Shock, eds., *The Liberal Tradition from Fox to Keynes* (New York: New York University Press, 1957), p. xx–xxv; David G. Smith, "Liberalism," in *International Encyclopedia of the Social Sciences,* ed. David L. Sills (New York: Macmillan, 1968), vol. 9, pp. 276–282.

[5]John S. Mill, *On Liberty,* ed. Alburey Castell (1859; reprint, New York: Appleton-Century-Crofts, 1947), chap. 1, lines 446–448; Leonard T. Hobhouse, *Liberalism*

ern science and Newtonian cosmology great influence upon the "New Philosophy" of liberalism and, on the other hand, from attributing to late nineteenth-century social science great influence in changing the liberal outlook during the last half of that century.[6]

That very phenomenon of change in the liberal outlook, however, calls into question the plausibility of interpreting the liberal-free ideal as an extension of the movement of "liberalism." In contrast to the social and political movement, the liberal-free is an artificial construct that, though abstracted from various thinkers and factions over time, maintains its own systematic coherence and integrity. It remains essentially consistent and cannot properly be aligned with the discontinuous phenomenon of liberalism.

The discontinuity is exemplified by the middle and late nineteenth-century shift from "classical liberalism" to "modern liberalism," or "democratic liberalism," which then became the dominant American ideology of the era. This shift is often explained as a movement from the ideal of "negative" liberty, of freedom from state authority, to the ideal of "positive" liberty, of the freedom of the individual to accomplish personal goals. The impetus for the change was provided, in part, by Mill's implicit elevation of the principle of utility above the authority of individual judgment.[7] Such a manner of accounting for the change in liberal ideology is often heard; but the discontinuity has also been explained by positing two preexisting kinds of liberalism, a political-academic version in Britain and a rationalistic version on the Continent, that are thought to have merged in the nineteenth century.[8] Under this interpretation, Continental liberalism has definite similarities to the liberal-free ideal; and it would be tempting to align the two, except that there is little

(New York: H. Holt, 1911), pp. 123ff.; Bullock and Shock (1957), p. xxxv. The notes and essays of Lord Acton's preparations for his never-begun *The History of Liberty* reveal similar views on freedom of thought and individualism. William H. McNeill, ed., *Lord Acton: Essays in the Liberal Interpretation of History, Selected Papers* (Chicago: University of Chicago Press, 1967), pp. xii–xx.

[6]A. Duncan Yocum, "Dr. Dewey's 'Liberalism' in Government and in Public Education," *School and Society* 44, no. 1123 (1936): 1–5; Girvetz (1963), pp. 23–47, 162, chap. 7; Smith (1968), pp. 280–282; Werner E. Mosse, *Liberal Europe: The Age of Bourgeois Realism, 1848–1875* (London: Thames and Hudson, 1974), pp. 9ff.; Manning (1976), pp. 14–31.

[7]Mill, *On Liberty*, chap. 3; Schapiro (1958), p. 45, chap. 3; Girvetz (1963), pp. 23–26; Mosse (1967), p. 7; Bullock and Shock (1957), pp. xli–liii; Wolff (1968), chap. 1; Isaiah Berlin, *Four Essays on Liberty* (London: Oxford University Press, 1969).

[8]Ruggiero (1927); Friedrich A. Hayek, *New Studies in Philosophy, Politics, Economics, and the History of Ideas* (London: Routledge & Kegan Paul, 1978), pp. 119–132.

convincing evidence for the necessary corollary that British liberalism was less receptive to the liberal-free ideal during its formative
period.

Such discontinuity points to a second difference between liberalism and the liberal-free ideal, because the nineteenth-century
shift from classical to modern liberalism centrally concerned the belief that people are by nature equal. While this characteristic is constitutive of the educational ideal, early liberalism tended to oppose
liberty to equality, or, as with Mill and Lord Acton, to treat equality
as contravening social progress, which was attributed to the exercise of individual talent. Only with the "New Liberalism" of Hobhouse and his colleagues was the essential equality of human beings
posited as a tenet of liberal thought.[9] Thus, the shift on this particular issue distinguishes liberal ideology from the liberal-free ideal.

A third and more important difference, however, relates to the
epistemological skepticism, which is a foundational characteristic of
the liberal-free ideal and does not appear in the movement of liberalism. In the liberal-free ideal, the characteristics of freedom, tolerance, equality, individualism, and intellectualism are
systematically related by the refusal to affirm any absolute truths. In
contrast, some have viewed liberalism as evidencing a clear dogmatism; and while many do not agree with this view, neither do they
see skepticism as constitutive of liberalism.[10] Rather, the movement
is consistently associated with certain political and economic poli-
cies. For example, Laski wrote, "The idea of liberalism, in short, is
historically connected, in an inescapable way, with the ownership
of property"; and Louis Hartz considered it primarily a political tradition in America, where the absence of a feudal tradition contributed, in his words, to a "natural liberalism", as opposed to that in
Europe.[11] Confirmation lies in the fact that attempts to find early

---

[9]Hobhouse (1911), pp. 231ff.; Laski (1936), pp. 7–8; Kingsley Martin, *French Liberal Thought in the Eighteenth Century: A Study of Political Ideas from Bayle to Condorcet*, ed. J. P. Mayer, 2d ed. (London: Phoenix, 1962), pp. 9–11, 221–223; Hayek (1978),
pp. 141–142. But see David L. Jacobson, ed., *The English Libertarian Heritage from the
Writings of John Trenchard and Thomas Gordon in "The Independent Whig" and "Cato's
Letters"* (New York: Bobbs-Merrill, 1965), pp. xxxvi–xxxvii.

[10]Manning (1976), p. 119. But see Schapiro (1958), chaps. 1–2; Robbins (1959), pp.
7–12; Smith (1968).

[11]Louis Hartz, *The Liberal Tradition in America: An Interpretation of American Political Thought since the Revolution* (New York: Harcourt, Brace, 1955), p. 5; Laski (1936),
p. 9; John M. Robertson, *The Meaning of Liberalism* (London: Methuen, 1912), pp.
10–44; Girvetz (1963), chaps. 1–7; Grampp (1965), vol. 2, pp. 94–101; Lionel Trilling,
The Liberal Imagination: Essays on Literature and Society (New York: Viking, 1950), p.
viii.

roots of liberalism in Greek and Roman antiquity led F. A. Hayek and W. D. Grampp back to the politicial doctrines of Cicero and the Stoics, not the Socratics. Furthermore, the advocacy for science expressed by liberals has often had little to do with respect for the scientific method, which treats its conclusions like new hypotheses and is enshrined in the liberal-free ideal. Instead, the link between science and liberalism has more often involved respect for technological progress,[12] and that certainly implies a distinction between liberalism and the liberal-free ideal.

---

[12]Chaim Wirszubski, Libertas *as a Political Ideal at Rome during the Late Republic and Early Principate* (Cambridge: Cambridge University Press, 1950); Schapiro (1958), p. 16; Grampp (1965), vol. 1, chap. 1; Smith (1968), pp. 277–279; Hayek (1978), pp. 119–123. On the other hand, the "liberal" tradition in ancient Greek thought—an evolutionary, egalitarian, progressive, pragmatic view of the world—has been linked to the sophists, in contrast to Socrates and Plato. Eric A. Havelock, *The Liberal Temper in Greek Politics* (New Haven, Conn.: Yale University Press, 1957), pp. 30, 80–81; Frederick A. Beck, *Greek Education, 450–350 B.C.* (London: Methuen, 1964), pp. 149–150.

Author Index

Abel, Elie, 218n
Abelson, Paul, 6n, 23n, 30n
Acton, Lord John, 256n–257n, 258
Adams, Charles F., Jr., 166, 167n
Adams, Henry, 218, 218n
Adams, James Luther, 180n, 215–216, 216n
Adams, Jeremy Y. DuQuesnay, 54n
Adamson, John W., 131n
Adler, Mortimer J., 180, 180n
Aeschines, 18, 20, 20n
Agard, Walter R., 201n–202n
Ahrbeck, Hans, 90n, 93n
Aiken, Henry D., 235n
Ailred of Rievaulx, 65n
Akenson, Donald H., 224n
Alain de Lille, 71, 71n, 76
Alcuin, 50–53, 52n, 53n, 54n, 55–56, 70, 78, 88
Allard, Guy-H., 42n
Allen, P., 124n
Allmendinger, David F., Jr., 154n
Antweiler, Anton, 101n
Aquinas, Thomas, 7, 43, 65–67, 66n, 76, 90–91, 180, 198
Arbuthnot, C. C., 183n
Arcoleo, Santo, 71n
Aristotle, 5, 7, 9–10, 15, 17, 17n, 19–21, 19n, 20n, 24nn, 25–26, 26nn, 28–29, 29n, 31, 34–35, 42, 45–48, 52, 58–59, 61, 64–67, 72–73, 86, 95, 98, 111, 125, 132, 180, 186, 189, 189n, 197, 206, 209, 219–223, 229–232, 231n, 234
Arnaldi, Girolamo, 115n
Arnhart, Larry, 26n

Arnold, Matthew, 171–174, 172n, 173n, 207, 215–217, 221, 236, 241
Arnstein, George E., 235n
Arrowood, Charles F., 79n
Ascham, Roger, 100, 100n, 109
Ashworth, E. J., 70n–71n
Audet, Louis-Phillippe, 104n, 107n, 111n
Augustine, 7, 13, 30, 41–42, 41nn, 42nn, 44–45, 50, 58, 65–67, 69, 90–91
Axon, William E., 132n
Axtell, James, 162n, 243n
Aydelotte, Frank, 3, 190–191, 190n, 191n, 201n

Babb, Lawrence, 220n
Babbitt, Irving, 120n–121n, 159–160, 174–175, 174n, 182, 215–217, 221
Bacon, Francis, 111, 111n, 125–126
Bagster-Collins, E. W., 149n, 155n 166n
Bailyn, Bernard, 6n, 103n, 113n, 243n
Bainton, Roland H., 91n
Baker, Peter H., 42n
Baldwin, Charles S., 18n, 26n, 33n, 52n
Baldwin, John W., 53n
Baldwin, Thomas W., 100n
Banker, James R., 69n, 80n
Barnard, Frederick A., 154, 154n
Barnard, Howard C., 94n, 96n, 98n, 108n
Barnes, Sherman B., 173n–174n, 253n
Baron, Hans, 117n
Baron, Roger, 59n
Bartlett, Samuel C., 155, 155n
Barzun, Jacques, 4n, 159, 159n
Bates, Ralph S., 136n–137n, 148n, 163n–164n, 245n

Baxter, James P., III, 202n, 204nn
Beales, Arthur C., 99n, 100n
Bean, J. M., 64n
Beaujouan, Guy, 68n
Beck, Frederick A., 14n, 16n, 25n, 33n, 116n, 259n
Belknap, Robert L., 184n–185n, 212n–213n, 226, 226n
Bell, Daniel, 212n–213n, 219, 220nn, 234–235, 234n, 235n
Bellah, Robert N., 226, 226n
Bellincioni, Maria, 30n
Bellomo, Manlio, 70n
Belok, Michael V., 109n, 142n
Ben-David, Joseph, 162n
Bénézet, Louis T., 4, 4n, 184n–185n, 192, 192n, 196n, 198n, 199n
Benrath, Gustav A., 93n
Benson, Robert L., 57n
Berlin, Isaiah, 257n
Best, John H., 243n–244n
Biddle, Owen, 148n–149n
Biechler, James E., 77n–78n
Billanovich, Giuseppe, 70n, 77n
Bird, Caroline, 209, 209n
Black, Max, 201n, 203n
Blackmer, Alan R., 227n
Blake, Sophia Jex, 154n, 156n
Blanshard, Brand, 212n, 231n
Bledstein, Burton J., 188n
Blickensderfer, Joseph P., 203nn, 204n
Bloom, Allan, 224n, 235n
Bloomfield, Morton W., 225n–226n
Bode, Boyd H., 186n–187n
Boehm, Laetitia, 81n–82n
Boethius, 42, 47–48, 47n, 48nn, 51, 54n, 55–59, 189, 206, 221, 241
Bolgar, Robert R., 22n, 25n, 38n, 49n–50n, 52n, 79n, 95n, 96n
Bolman, Frederick, D., Jr., 225n
Bonaventure, Brother, 65, 66, 75n
Bonner, Stanley F., 20n, 25n, 28n, 31n, 32n, 34n, 51n
Booth, Wayne C., 180n–181n
Born, Lester K., 87n
Boskoff, Priscilla S., 58n
Boucher, C. S., 192n
Boulding, Kenneth E., 225n–226n
Bouwsma, William, J., 77n, 91n
Bowen, Howard R., 229n

Bower, Calvin, 48n
Bowman, Merle, 145n
Boyancé, Pierre, 34n
Boyer, Ernest, L., 213n
Brann, Eva T. H., 142n–143n
Brauer, George C., Jr., 109n, 110n, 111n–112n
Bressler, Marvin, 233n–234n
Brickman, William W., 243n–244n
Briggs, Thomas H., 160, 160n, 183n, 199n
Brockliss, Laurence B., 98n, 128n
Bronson, Walter C., 140n, 147n
Broome, Edwin C., 104n, 144n, 147n, 156n
Brown, Fred D., 209n
Brown, Harcourt, 118n
Brown, John H., 100n
Brown, Peter R., 40n–41n
Brown, William A., 186n
Brubacher, John S., 233n, 250n, 253n
Bruce, Gustav M., 93n
Brunner, Henry S., 181n
Buchanan, Scott, 203n
Buck, Paul H., 163n, 168n–169n, 188n, 233n
Bullock, Alan L., 256n–257nn
Bullough, Vern L., 73n, 130n
Bultot, Robert, 45n
Bundy, Walter E., 200n
Burckhardt, Jakob, 77, 77n
Burke, Colin B., 147n–148n, 154n, 247n
Burtt, Edwin A., 118n
Butterfield, Herbert, 117n, 123n
Butterfield, Victor L., 211n
Butts, Robert Freeman, 6n, 8, 134n, 141n, 145, 146n, 167, 167n, 179n, 193n–194n, 200n, 244

Cady, Edwin H., 107n, 109n, 111n–112n, 142n
Cahn, Steven M., 227, 227n
Calhoun, Daniel H., 138, 138n
Callus, Daniel A., 66n, 68
Canby, Henry S., 179n
Capella, Martianus. See Martianus Capella
Capen, Samuel P., 2n, 184nn, 185n
Caplan, Harry, 69n
Carlo, William E., 221n

Carmichael, Peter A., 182n
Carrell, William D., 137n
Caspari, Fritz, 89n, 107n, 108n, 109nn, 111n–112n, 131n
Cassedy, James H., 148n
Cassiodorus, 13, 22–23, 23n, 42, 44–47, 44nn, 46nn, 49–50, 54n, 55, 61, 64, 90, 206
Cassirer, Ernst, 77n–78n, 120n–121n, 123n, 128n
Castiglione, Baldassare, 89n, 107–108, 108n
Catlin, Daniel, Jr., 213n
Chadwick, Henry, 47nn
Chailley, Jacques, 45n
Chalmers, Gordon K., 208n, 210n, 233n, 234n
Chandler, Frank W., 183n, 231n
Channing, William Ellery, 143n
Charlton, Kenneth, 75n, 99n, 101n
Charters, W. W., 185n, 201n
Chase, George H., 177n
Chaucer, Geoffrey, 107n
Cheit, Earl F., 230n
Cheyney, Edward P., 135n, 139n, 140n, 141n
Chidsey, Harold, 183n
Childs, John L., 169n, 199n
Cicero, 2, 5, 7–8, 11–13, 13n, 20, 24–25, 24nn, 25n, 27–34, 27n, 28n, 29n, 30n, 32n, 33nn, 36–42, 36nn, 37n, 38n, 42n, 45, 52–53, 70, 76–78, 78n, 84, 88, 92–96, 99–103, 108–109, 111, 116–117, 126, 132, 165, 165n, 172–173, 197, 206–207, 215–216, 234, 240–241, 250, 258–259
Citron, Abraham F., 169n, 179n, 199n
Clapp, Margaret, 162n
Clark, Burton R., 191n
Clark, Donald L., 18n, 33n, 100n
Clarke, Martin L., 30n, 32n, 86n, 87n, 100n–101n, 128n, 129n, 130n, 133n, 153n, 175n
Clothier, Robert C., 201n–202n
Cobban, Alan B., 62n, 63nn, 81n, 86n, 107n
Cohen, Jerome B., 184n–185n
Cohen, Sol, 243n–244n
Cole, Stewart G., 202–203, 203n
Colish, Marcia L., 70n

Collins, Anthony, 120n, 189, 189n
Commager, Henry S., 141n–142n
Conant, James B., 159, 159n
Conrad Clifton E., 209n, 213n
Constable, Giles, 57n
Contreni, John J., 55n
Copleston, Frederick C., 38n, 129n–130n
Corkery, Francis E., 210n
Corson, Fred P., 186n
Corte, Francesco della, 24n, 27n, 28n, 29n, 30n, 32n, 38n
Coss, John J., 184n
Costello, William T., 101n
Cottrell, Donald P., 192n
Couch, Herbert N., 202n
Courcelle, Pierre P., 47n, 48nn, 56n
Cowley, Elizabeth B., 145n
Cowley, W. H., 167n, 177n–178n, 197, 197n
Cowling, Donald J., 184n, 192n–193n, 201n
Cragg, Gerald R., 128n, 129n
Craig, Gordon A., 225n–226n
Crane, Theodore R., 245n–246n
Crawford, C. C., 159n, 184n
Cremin, Lawrence A., 103n, 108n, 110, 110n, 141n, 142, 142n, 168n–169n, 170n, 175n, 198n–199n, 244, 244n–245n, 253, 253n
Cressy, David, 75n, 100n, 102n
Crombie, Alastair C., 117n
Crowe, Michael B., 67n
Cunningham, William F., 4, 4n, 185n, 192n–193n, 198n, 214, 214nn
Curti, Merle, 183n–184n
Curtis, Mark H., 109n, 113n, 240n
Curtius, Ernst R., 53n
Cutten, George B., 192n–193n

Daniels, George H., 145n, 148n, 252n
Davidson, Carter, 196n, 203n
Davis, Charles T., 67n, 80n
Day, Jeremiah, 150n–151n
Dearing, Bruce, 214n
deBary, W. Theodore, 4, 4n, 214, 214n, 226, 226n
Debus, Allen G., 128n
de Chelminska, H., 93n
Deckert, Marion, 220n
Dehnert, Edmund J., 42n, 48n

de Jonge, Henk, 92n
Delbanco, Andrew, 143n
Delhaye, Philippe, 58n, 65n, 66n–67n
DeMolen, Richard L., 75n
Dermience, Alice, 34n
Descartes, René, 118–120, 120n, 125–126,
    125n, 126n, 128–129, 134, 249, 256
DeVane, William C., 214n
Dewey, A. Gordon, 185n
Dewey, John, 5, 158–159, 158n, 169,
    169n–170n, 174, 179, 183, 183n, 198,
    215–217, 229, 248
Dexter, Franklin B., 107n
Díaz, Manuel C. Díaz y, 50n, 52n, 54n
Diehl, Carl, 133n, 146nn, 162n, 175n
Diehl, Charles E., 159n–160nn, 160, 201n
Diogenes Laertius, 22n, 24n
Dirks, J. Edward, 211n
Distler, Theodore M., 214n
Dobson, John F., 13n, 23n, 30n
Dodds, Harold W., 210n
Doggett, Simeon, 148n–149n
Donne, John, 118, 118n
Doty, Paul M., 234n
Douglass, Gordon K., 229n
Downing, Elliot R., 163n, 251n, 252n
Dresden, Sem, 78n, 85n
Dressel, Paul L., 6n, 13n, 195n, 213n,
    224n, 227n–229n
DuBridge, Lee A., 225n, 229n–230n
DuCasse, C. J., 201n–202n
Duckett, Eleanor S., 51n
Dupree, A. Hunter, 148n
Dutcher, George M., 146n, 156n

Earnest, Ernest, 183n
Eby, Frederick, 79n
Eckelberry, R. H., 159n
Eddy, Edward D., Jr., 156n, 181n, 250n,
    253–254, 253nn
Edwards, Anna C., 169n
Eells, Walter C., 192n–193n
Eilenberg, Samuel, 229n–230n
Eldridge, Seba, 202n
Eliassen, R. H., 191n
Eliot, Charles W., 158, 158n, 160–161,
    166–167, 167n, 177, 189, 189n, 220,
    251, 251n
Ellis, Calvert N., 211n
Ellspermann, Gerard L., 40n–41n

Elyot, Sir Thomas, 108, 108n, 109
Engel, Arthur J., 171n
Entemann, Willard F., 229n–230n
Epictetus, 214, 214n
Erasmus, Desiderius, 8, 84, 87–90, 87n,
    89n, 90n, 93, 95, 98–100, 107–109,
    112
Erbse, Hartmut, 18n
Erigena, Johannes Scotus, 55, 55n, 206,
    221
Espy, Herbert G., 185n, 199n
Eurich, Alvin C., 191n, 192n, 194n
Evans, D. Luther, 202–203, 203n
Evans, G. R., 57n, 73n
Evans, J. D. G., 26n
Evans, R. J., 127n
Everett, John R., 214n
Ewan, Joseph, 244n–245n
Ewing, Alfred C., 123n
Exner, Hellmuth, 87n

Falardeau, Jean-Charles, 28n, 32n, 33n
Farmer, Paul, 162n, 188n
Farrar, Frederic A., 171n
Farrell, Allan P., 95n, 96n, 98n
Faulhaber, Charles B., 70n
Federici, Graziella, 68n
Fehlau, Uhland E., 193n–194n
Fellerer, Karl G., 28n, 46n, 48n, 52n,
    60n, 68n
Ferguson, James P., 125n
Ferguson, Wallace K., 77n
Ferry, F. C., 166n
Filler, Louis, 198n–199n
Findlay, James, 254n
Findlay, James F., 196n
Fine, Benjamin, 179n, 203n
Finkelstein, Martin, 145n
Fiore, Silvestro, 44n
Fletcher, John M., 73n, 75n, 100n–101n
Flexner, Abraham, 2, 2n, 184n, 186,
    186n, 189–190, 189n
Foerster, Norman, 7, 8n, 160, 160n, 175,
    175n, 182, 182n, 196, 197n
Fontaine, Jacques, 28n, 46nn
Ford, Charles E., 251n
Fortescue, John, 110n
France, Peter, 126n
Franceschini, Adriano, 80n
Frankel, Charles, 235–237, 236n

Frankena, William K., 15n, 123n
Franklin, Benjamin, 5, 135, 135n, 136,
    140–141, 140n–141n
Fránquiz, José A., 45n
Frick, George F., 136n–137n
Fumagelli, Mariateresa B., 67n

Gabriel, Astrik L., 63n, 65n, 75n–76n,
    81n, 85n, 96n
Gadol, Joan, 117n
Gaff, Jerry G., 213n
Gagné, Jean, 68n
Gamson, Zelda F., 214n, 229n
Ganss, George E., 95n, 96n, 198n, 233n
Garin, Eugenio, 3, 79n, 80nn, 109n,
    115n, 116n
Garland, Martha McMackin, 133n, 153n,
    171n, 175n
Gay, Peter, 116n, 117n, 119n, 120n–121nn,
    129n–130n
Gellius, Aulus, 38n–39n, 78, 78n
Ghellinck, Joseph de, 57n
Giacon, Carlo, 75n–76n
Gibson, Margaret T., 54n, 55n, 56n
Gideonse, Harry D., 180n–181n, 186,
    186n, 199n, 233–234, 234n
Gilman, Daniel C., 161, 164, 164n, 167n,
    182, 182n, 230–231, 231n
Gilmore, Myron P., 87n
Gilson, Etienne, 41–42, 42n, 45n
Giraud, Jean, 80n
Girvetz, Harry K., 255n, 257, 257nn,
    258n
Giustiniani, Vito R., 38n, 77n, 78n,
    115n, 253n
Glass, Meta, 196n, 201n
Gleason, Philip, 154n–155n, 174n,
    185n–186n
Glorieux, Palémon, 66n–67n
Gneo, Fernando, 66n
Godbold, Albea, 154n–155n, 250n
Goldberg, Maxwell H., 229n–230n
Goldwin, Robert A., 224n
Good, H. G., 252n
Goode, G. Brown, 156n
Gössmann, Elisabeth, 60n
Grafton, Anthony, 85n–86n, 98n
Graham, Patricia A., 198n–199n
Grampp, William D., 255, 255n,
    258–259, 258n, 259n

Grant, Gerald, 220n, 221n
Grassi, Ernesto, 36n
Gray, William S., 185n
Greaves, Richard L., 101n, 113n,
    130n–131n
Green, Vivian H., 129n–130nn, 131n
Greene, John C., 136n–137n, 148n, 189n
Greene, Theodore M., 196–197, 197n,
    203n, 209, 209n, 217n
Greenleaf, Walter J., 196n
Gregory of Tours, 44, 44n
Griffith, Coleman R., 195n
Grimaldi, William M., 26n, 35n
Griswold, A. Whitney, 215, 215n
Grossmann, Maria, 84n
Gruber, Carol S., 201n
Guerry, Alexander, 201n
Gummere, Richard M., 138nn, 140n,
    192n–193n
Guralnick, Stanley M., 139n, 145n, 149n,
    151n, 244–246, 244n–245nn, 246nn,
    248–249, 249nn, 252, 252n, 253n,
    254
Gwynn, Aubrey, 19n, 32n, 33n, 35n

Haarhoff, T. J., 28n, 33n, 48n
Hackett, G. B., 62n, 63n
Hall, A. R., 118n, 121n, 127n, 128n
Hall, Dorothy, 229n
Hall, G. Stanley, 161–162, 163n
Hall, Maria Boas, 117n, 127n
Halley, Edmund, 118n
Hamilton, T. H., 229n
Hamlin, Arthur T., 163n, 251n
Hammack, Floyd M., 243n–244n
Hammerstein, Notker, 127n
Hampshire, Stuart, 128n
Handlin, Mary F., 108n, 110n, 145n,
    154n–155n, 182n
Handlin, Oscar, 108n, 110n, 145n,
    154n–155n, 182n
Hangartner, Carl A., 134nn, 135n–136n,
    139n, 145n, 244, 244n–245n, 249,
    249n, 250n, 251n, 252n, 253, 253n,
    254
Hans, Nicholas, 124n, 128n, 130n, 131n
Hansen, Allen O., 8, 8n, 136n–137n,
    144n, 158–159, 159n, 256, 256n
Hansen, Forest, 214n
Harbison, E. Harris, 91n

Hardy, B. Carmon, 40n–41n
Hardy, C. DeWitt, 215n
Haring, Nicholas M., 65n
Harmon, Christopher C., 215n
Harper, William R., 161, 164, 164n
Harriman, Philip L., 8n
Harris, Michael R., 175n, 179nn, 189n, 216n
Harris, William T., 176–177, 177n
Hartmann, Wilfried, 60n
Hartz, Louis, 258, 258n
Havelock, Eric A., 116n, 259n
Hawkins, Hugh, 158n, 167n–168n, 173n–174n, 182n, 188n
Hay, Denys, 77n, 86n, 95n, 96n, 99n .
Hayek, Friedrich A., 120n, 257n, 258–259, 258n, 259n
Hays, Garry D., 217n
Haywood, Robert C., 217n
Hazard Paul, 116n, 120n, 121n, 217, 217n
Hazzard, George W., 225n
Heilbrunn, Gunther, 25n, 34n
Heimert, Alan, 143n
Henderson, Algo D., 202, 202n, 229n
Hendley, Brian P., 61n
Hendrix, Richard, 209n, 229n
Henri d'Andeli, 43, 72–73, 72n–73n
Henry, Desmond P., 221n
Hepler, John C., 170n
Herbst, Jurgen, 96n, 104n, 162n, 163n, 164n–165n, 173n–174n, 175n, 177n–178n, 188n, 243n, 244nn–245n, 245
Herrick, Marvin T., 203n
Hexter, Jack H., 107n, 109n 112n
Higham, John, 163n–164n, 173n–174n, 177n
Highet, Gilbert, 215, 215n
Hijmans, Benjamin L., Jr., 214n
Hill, Thomas, 156, 156n
Hindle, Brooke, 145n
Hirst, Paul H., 5n, 8, 8n, 10n, 216, 216n, 222n, 233n
Hobbes, Thomas, 119, 122, 122n, 125–126, 125n, 129, 256
Hobhouse, Leonard T., 256, 256n–257n, 258, 258n
Hocking, William E., 185–186, 186n
Hödl, Ludwig, 57n, 60n
Hoepffner, E., 94n, 117n

Hoeveler, J. David, Jr., 129n–130nn, 164n–165n
Hofstadter, Richard, 147n, 162n, 168n, 169n, 170n, 179n, 188n, 215n, 244, 244n, 250n
Holmes, Harry N., 199n
Holmes, Henry W., 159n–160n
Holt, Hamilton, 159n
Hook, Sidney, 202, 202n
Hopkins, Annette B., 197n
Horn, Francis H., 1, 6n
Hornberger, Theodore, 134n, 137n, 139n, 141n, 244, 246, 246nn, 248, 250, 252, 252nn, 254
Howe, Daniel W., 150n
Howell, Wilbur S., 52n, 99n, 101n, 126n, 128n
Hrubý, František, 94n
Hubbell, Harry M., 33n
Hudson, Hoyt H., 214, 214n
Hudson, Winthrop S., 247n
Hughes, Andrew, 68n
Hughes, J. M., 184n–185n
Hughes, John P., 209n
Hugh of St. Victor, 59–61, 59n, 60n
Huizinga, Johan, 87n
Hume, David, 121–122, 121n, 125–126, 126n, 129, 152, 187, 187n
Humphrey, David C., 134n–135nn, 140n, 244, 247–248, 248n, 251–252, 251n, 253n, 254
Humphreys, J. Anthony, 191n
Hunt, Everett L., 16n, 34n
Hutchins, Robert M., 3, 159, 179–180, 179n, 180nn–181n, 186, 189, 198, 200–201, 219, 221–224, 227n, 233–234
Huxley, Thomas H., 8, 171–173, 172n, 173n, 207, 241
Huygens, R. B., 59n
Hyma, Albert, 88n–89n

Ijsewijn, Jozef, 79n, 85n
Irsay, Stephen d', 23n, 96n, 98n, 127nn, 130n
Isidore, 13, 14, 42, 44, 44n, 46–47, 46nn, 49–50, 54, 54n, 58–61, 64, 66, 70, 78, 90, 241
Isocrates, 2, 5, 17–21, 17n, 18nn, 20n, 25, 27, 27nn, 28, 28n, 31, 33–36, 33n,

35nn, 36n, 41, 80, 87, 103, 108–109, 111, 174, 197, 206, 234, 239, 239n–240n, 241

Jackson, J. Hugh, 183n
Jacobson, David L., 143n, 258n
Jaeger, Werner, 2, 16n, 19, 19n, 24n, 31n, 240n
James, William, 169, 169n, 174, 198
Jarausch, Konrad H., 162n–163n
Jardine, Lisa, 81n
Jauss, H. R., 60n
Javelet, Robert, 59n
Jeauneau, Edouard, 61n
Jencks, Christopher, 224n, 243, 243n
Jerome, 40, 40n, 44–45
John of Garland, 71–72, 72n, 73
John of Salisbury, 60nn, 61, 61nn, 73, 180n–181n
Johnson, Alvin, 5n, 198n
Johnson, Byron L., 184n–185nn
Johnson, Palmer O., 191n
Johnson, Richard, 14n, 28n, 31nn, 39n, 40n, 52n, 55n
Johnson, Samuel, 112, 134, 137–139, 138n, 248
Johnson, W. R., 41n
Johnston, John B., 188n
Jones, Leslie W., 44n
Jones, Lewis W., 204n
Jones, Richard F., 128n
Judd, Charles H., 10n, 160n, 194n

Kaestle, Carl F., 141n–142n
Kagan, Richard L., 95n
Kaminsky, Howard, 75n–76n
Kandel, Isaac L., 8n, 160n, 175n, 183n
Kant, Immanuel, 116, 116nn, 119, 122–123, 123n
Karier, Clarence J., 255n
Kass, Amy A., 179n
Katzenellenbogen, Adolf, 59n
Kearney, Hugh F., 100n–101n, 102n, 107n, 109nn, 111n–112nn, 124n, 128nn, 130n, 131n, 171n
Keeton, Morris T., 216n, 217n
Kelley, Brooks M., 134n, 138n, 139n, 147n, 150n, 247n, 250n, 251n
Kelly, Frederick J., 184nn
Kelly, Robert L., 183n, 184n, 196n, 231n

Kelso, Ruth, 99n, 107n, 109n, 111n, 165, 165n, 196, 197n
Kennan, George F., 210n
Kennedy, George A., 16n, 18n, 20n, 26n, 28n, 33nn, 34n, 39n, 40n–41n
Kennedy, M. St. Mel, 146n, 244n–245n
Kent, R. A., 159n–160n, 184n, 200n
Kibre, Pearl, 54n, 62n, 68n–69n
Kiely, Margaret, 159n
Kiger, Joseph C., 136n–137n
Kilpatrick, William H., 104n, 170n, 189n
Kingsley, James L., 150n–151n
Kirk, Russell, 210, 210n–211n
Klassen, Frank, 136n–137n, 138n, 144n
Klein, Jacob, 15n, 220, 220n, 221
Klibansky, Raymond, 15n, 20n, 60n–61n, 133n
Klinkenberg, Hans M., 23n, 46n, 48nn, 52n
Knight, Edgar W., 103n, 104n, 106nn
Knode, Jay C., 192n–193n
Knoll, Paul W., 83n
Knowles, David, 57n
Knox, Samuel, 144, 144n, 152
Knox, Vicesimus, 114, 132, 132n
Koerner, James D., 9–10, 10n
Kohlstedt, Sally G., 148n
Kohn, Hans, 202n
Koller, Hermann, 21n
Kölmel, Wilhelm, 81n
Koos, Leonard V., 159n, 184n
Kornfield, Milton, 213n
Kramer, William, 213n
Kraus, Joe W., 135n–136n, 138n
Kretzmann, Norman, 67n
Kristeller, Paul O., 22n, 26n, 54n, 68n–69n, 77nn–78n, 79n, 81n, 91n, 118n, 235–237, 236nn–237n
Kuder, Merle, 166n
Kühnert, Friedmar, 13nn, 21n, 23n, 29n, 30n, 40n
Kuhns, Richard, 184n–185n, 212n–213n, 226, 226n
Kurbis, Brygida, 84n
Kuritz, Hyman, 141n–142n
Kurtz, Paul, 214n
Kuttner, Stephan, 57n

Laistner, Max L., 49n
Lamacchia, Ada, 70n

Laski, Harold J., 255, 255n, 256n, 258nn
Leavens, Robert F., 165n
LeBlanc, M. Elizabeth, 213n
LeClercq, Jean, 45n, 49n–50n, 51n
LeDuc, Thomas H., 150n, 164n, 165n, 178n
Lee, Gordon C., 141n–142nn
Lee, Jeanette A., 6n
Lee, Patricia-Ann, 109n, 131n
Lee, William S., 183n
Leff, Gordon, 62nn, 63n, 65n, 66n–67n, 75n–76n
Leff, Michael C., 47n, 67n
Le Goff, Jacques, 80n, 85n, 98n, 127n–128n
Lehmann, Paul, 52n
Leigh, Robert L., 191n
Leites, Edmund, 189nn
LeMoine, Fanny, 31n, 39n, 40n
Lésnodorski, Boguslaw, 127n
Levine, Arthur, 213n
Lewis, Hal G., 169n, 178n, 199n
Lewis, William M., 197, 197n
Lhotsky, Alphons, 83n
Liccaro, Enzo, 60n
Likins, Peter, 218n
Limbrick, Elaine, 116n
Lippman, Edward A., 28n, 46n, 52n
Lippmann, Walter, 174–175, 175n
Little, Winston L., 191n
Locke, John, 114, 119, 119n, 121–122, 121n, 122n–123n, 125–126, 125nn, 126n, 128–129, 132, 134, 137, 141, 166, 188–189, 249–250, 253, 256
Logan, George M., 77n–78n, 115n
Loomer, Bernard M., 180n, 211n
Looney, Jefferson, 102n
Lord, Arthur H., 165n
Lord, Carnes, 23n, 28n
Lorimer, Margaret F., 224n
Lowell, Abbott L., 177, 177n, 192
Lowi, Theodore J., 255, 255n
Lubac, Henri de, 57n
Lucki, Emil, 90n
Luria, Maxwell S., 60n
Luther, Martin, 74, 88, 91–94, 92nn–93n
Lutz, Cora E., 53n, 55n, 56nn, 90n

McCallister, W. J., 187, 188n
McCarthy, Joseph M., 23n, 66n

McClelland, Charles E., 127n, 133n, 146n, 162n, 175n, 189n
McCluer, Franc L., 210n
McConaughy, James L., 184n
McConnell, Thomas R., 194n, 195n, 203n, 213n
McCormick, Richard P., 134n, 146n, 247n
McCosh, James, 158, 158n, 167n
McCracken, C. C., 186n
MacCracken, John H., 201n
McDowell, E. W., 185n
McGarry, Daniel D., 61n, 180n–181n
McGrath, Earl J., 6n, 7, 7nn, 163n–164n, 165n, 174n, 203n, 210, 210n, 225, 225n, 229n–230n
McGrath, Fergal, 50n
McHale, Kathryn, 184n, 191n
McKeon, Richard, 26n, 54n, 66n, 78n, 180n–181n, 232, 232n
MacKinney, Loren C., 61n
McKinney, Richard I., 212n
McLachlan, Herbert, 124n, 130n
McLachlan, James, 154n, 243n
McLaughlin, Mary M., 57n
Maclean, John, Jr., 154, 154n
MacLean, Malcolm S., 191n
McNeill, William H., 256n–257n
Macy, C. Ward, 202n
Magoun, Francis P., Jr., 56n
Mahoney, John L., 131n
Mandelbaum, Helene, 209n
Manning, David J., 255n, 257n, 258n
Mansfield, Harvey C., Jr., 255, 255n
Marenbon, John, 55n
Maritain, Jacques, 4, 4n, 198, 198n
Marrou, Henri I., 2, 15n, 16n, 18–19, 19n, 20n, 21n, 23n, 25n, 28n, 29n, 30nn, 31n, 32n, 38n, 41n, 42nn, 195, 195n
Martianus Capella, 22–23, 23n, 30–32, 31n, 37–40, 40n, 44, 47–48, 52, 55–56, 58, 64, 76, 90, 206
Martin, Everett D., 7–8, 8n
Martin, Kingsley, 121n, 128n, 258n
Marty, Martin E., 226n
Masi, Michael, 55n
Mason, John E., 108n
Matherly, Walter J., 191n
Mathon, Gérard, 51n, 53n, 55n, 94n
Mattfeld, Jacquelyn A., 5n

Matthews, William R., 211n
Maurer, Irving, 184n
Maurer, Wilhelm, 91n, 93n
Maxwell, Joseph R., 204n
Mayer, Mary H., 67n
Mayhew, Katerine C., 169n
Mayhew, Lewis B., 195n, 213n, 229n
Meador, Prentice A., Jr., 36n
Meiklejohn, Alexander, 3, 177–180,
    178n, 179n, 185, 185n–186n, 189,
    198, 214, 214n, 219, 221–224, 233–234
Meister, Richard, 14n
Merello-Altea, Maria G., 56n, 70n
Meriwether, Colyer, 105n
Merriam, Thornton W., 186n
Mette, Hans J., 15n, 21n, 23n, 29n
Metzger, Walter P., 147n, 162n, 244n,
    250n
Meyerson, Martin, 225n–226n,
    227n–230n
Michaud-Quantin, Pierre, 62n, 67n
Michel, Alain, 33n
Middlekauf, Robert, 100n, 103n, 113n,
    138n, 144n, 149n
Miekle, Robert H., 212n
Miles, Edwin A., 138n, 142n
Mill, John Stuart, 256–258, 256n, 257n
Miller, Howard, 134n–135n, 145n, 147n,
    149n, 152n
Miller, J. Hillis, 204n
Miller, Samuel, 138n
Millett, Fred B., 197n
Mims, Edwin, 197n
Molloy, Mary A., 201n
Moore, Ernest C., 81n
Moreo, D. W., 147n
Morgan, George W., 210n–211n
Morison, Samuel E., 6n, 102n,
    104n–105nn, 106n, 107n, 111nn,
    112n, 135n–136n, 146n, 150n, 154n,
    177, 177n, 244, 247, 250n, 254
Morton, Richard K., 212n
Mosellanus, Petrus, 84–85, 85n, 95, 95n,
    112
Mosse, Werner E., 257nn
Mulcahy, Daniel G., 195n–196n
Mulcaster, Richard, 111, 111n
Müller, Kurt, 127n
Murdoch, John E., 68n
Murphy, Arthur E., 201n

Murphy, James J., 33n, 34n, 39n, 41n,
    46n, 52n, 58n, 61n, 69n
Murray, Alexander, 73n

Nash, Arnold S., 183n
Nash, Paul, 19n, 141n–142n
Neckham, Alexander, 69n
Newman, H. H., 185n
Newman, John Henry, 7–8, 180, 195,
    195n–196n
Nicoll, C. Douglas, 235n
Nicomachus of Gerasa, 47n
Noll, Mark A., 216n
Norton, Alfred O., 85n
Notestein, Wallace, 110n
Nuchelmans, Gabriel, 23n, 30n, 31n,
    53n, 58n

Oates, Whitney J., 212, 212n
Oberman, Heiko A., 77n, 79n, 91n
O'Byrne, Eleanor M., 216n
O'Donnell, James J., 44nn, 49n
O'Donnell, J. Reginald, 69n
Oleson, Alexandra, 136n–137n, 148n,
    158n
Olmsted, Denison, 250, 250n–251n
O'Neal, Robert G., 229n–230n
Ong, Walter J., 101n
Orme, Nicholas, 86n
Ornstein, Martha, 117n, 127n
Orton, Dwayne, 200n
Osman, John, 211n
Overfield, James H., 84n–85n

Paetow, Louis J., 66n–67n, 70nn, 81n
Palmer, Archie M., 196n
Palmieri, Patricia, 174n
Pantin, W. A., 86n, 90n, 124n
Paquet, Jacques, 53n
Paradis, James G., 173n
Parks, E. Patrick, 39n
Paschal, G. W., 247n
Patkaniowski, Michal, 85n
Paulston, Roland G., 146n
Payton, Philip W., 163n–164n
Pederson, Fritz E., 39n
Pederson, Olaf, 66n–67n, 117n
Peirce, Oliver B., 147n, 198
Peters, Richard, 135n, 140, 140n–141n,
    152, 153n, 168n

Peters, Richard S., 5n, 8, 8n
Peters, W. W., 211n
Peterson, George E., 162n, 165n, 182n
Phillipson, Nicolas T., 189n
Philostratus, 39n
Piccolomini, Enea Silvio de, 82–83, 83n
Pierson, George W., 167n
Plato, 2, 5, 7–9, 11, 14–29, 17nn, 18nn,
    19n, 20n, 23n, 24nn, 26nn, 27n,
    28nn, 29n, 31, 33–34, 35nn, 36, 40,
    42, 44, 47–48, 65, 68, 72–73, 77, 116,
    129, 172–173, 173n, 176, 197, 206,
    220–223, 223n, 231–232, 231n, 234,
    239–241
Porter, Noah, 150n, 164n, 167n
Post, Gaines, 62n, 63n
Potts, David B., 154n
Powell, J. P., 163n, 195n–196n
Prest, Wilfred R., 110n
Priestley, Joseph, 119, 125, 125n, 129n,
    143–144, 143n, 171–172, 256
Proussis, Costas M., 19n
Pryde, George S., 104n–105n, 106n, 111n
Pusey, Nathan, 210n

Quain, E. A., 59n
Quintilian, 5, 7, 12, 13, 22, 22n, 25,
    25nn, 27, 27nn, 28–29, 29n, 31–39,
    32nn, 33nn, 34nn, 35n, 36n, 37nn,
    38n, 52–53, 58, 61, 70, 76–77, 80,
    82–83, 87, 92–93, 96, 99–100,
    108–109, 111, 116, 174, 197, 206–207,
    234

Rackham, H., 38n
Rainey, Homer P., 186n–187n,
    192n–193n, 194n
Rainsford, George N., 147n
Rajna, Pio, 51n
Rand, Edward K., 23n, 47n, 105n, 196,
    197n
Randall, John H., Jr., 8, 8n
Rashdall, Hastings, 62n, 63n, 67n, 86n
Rattigan, Bernard T., 211, 211n
Ravitch, Diane, 243n–244n
Read, Joel, 209n
Reece, Benny R., 56n
Reeder, W. G., 201n
Reeves, Floyd W., 183n, 192n–193n,
    231n

Regis, Louis M., 70n, 221n
Reid, Thomas, 129, 151–152, 152n
Reinhold, Meyer, 142n–143n
Reinke, E. E., 201n
Renner, Richard R., 7n
Reynolds, Leighton D., 22n, 51n
Richards, Cyril F., 202n
Richardson, Leon B., 138n, 154n, 184n,
    192n
Riché, Pierre, 45n, 48n–50n, 52, 52n,
    53n, 54nn, 55n, 56nn
Riesman, David, 177n–178n, 189n, 214n,
    220n, 221n, 224n, 243, 243n
Rijk, Lambert de, 6n, 16n, 21n, 23n,
    51n, 56n
Ringenberg, William C., 211n, 216n
Ringer, Fritz K., 162n–163n
Robarts, James R., 163n
Robbins, Caroline, 256n, 258n
Robbins, Charles L., 93n
Robertson, John M., 258n
Robinson, Mabel L., 174n
Robson, David W., 144n
Roos, Heinrich, 66n–67n, 69n, 70n
Rorty, Richard, 221n
Roseman, Norman, 16n
Ross, James B., 81n–82n
Rothblatt, Sheldon, 9, 9n, 115n, 131nn,
    141n–142n, 151n, 153n, 171n, 175n,
    187n, 195n–196n, 227n
Rother, Wolfgang, 84n
Rott, J., 94n
Rouse, R. H., 50n, 58n, 69n
Rousseau, Jean-Jacques, 114, 116, 116n,
    119, 119n, 120, 120n–121n, 122,
    122n–123n, 126, 126n, 132, 141, 256
Rudolph, Frederick, 9n, 135n, 136, 136n,
    144n, 146n, 149n, 150n–151n, 156n,
    162n, 173n, 185n–186n, 224n,
    245–246, 245n–246nn, 247n
Rudy, Willis, 7, 7n, 8, 150n, 174n, 192n,
    200n, 217, 217n, 233n, 250n, 253n
Ruggiero, Guido de, 256, 256n, 257n
Russell, Charles H., 6n, 229n–230n
Russell, John D., 183n–184n, 192n, 194n
Ryan, Lawrence, 100n
Ryan, Mary B., 61n

Sachse, William L., 137n
Sack, Saul, 7n, 14n, 209, 209n, 217n

Sagen, H. Bradley, 229n–230n
Sampson, Homer C., 185n
Sargent, Porter, 179n
Sarton, George, 60n
Scammon, Richard E., 199n
Schalk, Fritz, 52n, 107n
Schapiro, J. Salwyn, 256, 256n, 257n,
    258n, 259n
Schilpp, Paul A., 160, 160n, 199n
Schindling, Anton, 96n
Schlegel, Richard, 225n
Schmidt, George P., 6, 6n, 134n, 150n,
    163n, 179n, 252, 252n
Schmidt, Henry I., 155, 155n
Schmitt, Charles B., 78n
Schoeck, R. J., 69n, 75n
Schubert, Ernst, 95n
Schwab, Joseph J., 227n
Scroggs, Schiller, 185n
Shepard, David A., 229n–230n
Sherburn, George, 185n
Shils, Edward, 161, 162nn
Shklar, Judith N., 122n
Shoben, Edward J., 209n
Shock, Maurice, 256–257nn
Shores, Louis, 106n
Sidorsky, David, 178, 178n, 233n
Siegle, Peter E., 229n
Sills, Kenneth C., 183n
Simon, Joan, 99n, 100n–101n, 107n,
    111n–112n
Simonini, R. C., Jr., 215n
Simons, William E., 6n
Sinz, William, 90n
Siraisi, Nancy G., 63n, 66n–67n,
    68n–69n, 70n
Sizer, Theodore R., 149n, 154n
Sjöstrand, Wilhelm, 141n–142n
Sloan, Douglas, 106n, 134n–135n, 137n,
    140n, 145n, 148n, 149nn, 151n, 168n,
    243n, 244–245, 245n–246n, 247n,
    252n, 254
Smail, William M., 19n, 32n
Smalley, Beryl, 48n
Smallwood, Mary L., 104n–105n, 147n,
    155n, 156n, 188n
Smith, David G., 256n, 257n, 258n, 259n
Smith, F. Joseph, 68n
Smith, J. Winfree, 5n, 220n, 221n
Smith, Preserved, 88n, 91n

Smith, Samuel H., 144, 144n, 152
Smith, Terry W., 135n, 141n
Smythe, Ormond H., 230n
Snedden, David, 170n, 183n
Snow, Louis F., 8, 8n, 105n, 107n, 135n,
    138n, 140n, 141n, 144n, 149n, 158,
    159n, 245–246, 250n
Sottili, Agostino, 83n
Southern, R. W., 61n
Spafford, Ivol, 192n, 194n
Speek, Frances V., 184n
Spitz, Lewis W., 81n, 83n, 84n, 92n
Sprengard, Karl A., 81n, 130n
Spring, Joel, 214n
Stahl, William H., 14n, 28n, 31nn, 39n,
    40n, 52n, 55n
Stambler, Leah G., 154n
Starobinski, Jean, 120n–121n
Starr, Paul, 214n
Steinmetz, M., 93n
Stelling-Michaud, Sven, 81n, 84n
Stevens, Lawrence F., 224n
Stevenson, Louise L., 151n, 164n–165n
Stibitz, E. Earle, 211n
Stone, Lawrence, 75n, 109n
Storr, Richard J., 146n, 244n
Strauss, Gerald, 93n
Strauss, Leo, 223–225, 223n
Stremooukhoff, D., 93n–94n
Suetonius, 32n, 34n
Sullivan, Thérèse, 41n
Swanson, Robert N., 80n

Talbot, Charles H., 49n, 65n
Tappan, David, 148n–149n
Tappan, Henry P., 167n
Taylor, Charles H., 63n, 69n
Taylor, Harold, 5, 5n, 8, 217n, 221
Tead, Ordway, 204n
Tennent, Gilbert, 252, 252n
Tewksbury, Donald G., 141n–142n, 147n
Thomas, Russell, 149n, 156n, 192n, 212n,
    213n, 220n, 247n
Thompson, Craig R., 100n–101n
Thomson, Robert P., 144n
Thoreau, Henry D., 251, 251n
Thorndike, Lynn, 63n, 65n, 67n, 70n,
    83n
Thwing, Charles F., 174n
Tibbs, A. E., 225n

Tilghman, Tench F., 220n
Tobias, Marilyn, 155n, 165n
Tobriner, Marian L., 86n, 90n, 113n
Toccafondi, Eugenio T., 52n, 67n
Tognolo, Antonio, 66n
Tompson, Richard S., 124n
Tonsor, Stephen J., 211n
Tracy, James D., 89n
Traina, Mariano, 67n
Trilling, Lionel, 258n
Trippett, Byron K., 208n
Tristam, Henry, 196n
Troeltsch, Ernst, 91n
Trueblood, D. Elton, 216, 216n
Turk, Milton H., 156n
Turner, R. Steven, 127n, 146n
Tyler, Ralph W., 203n

Ulam, Adam B., 225n–226n
Ullman, B. L., 185n
Upham, Alfred H., 157, 160n
Urofsky, Melvin I., 150n, 247n

Valgiglio, Ernesto, 34n
Van Doren, Mark, 197–198, 198n, 229, 231n
Vasoli, Cesare, 71n, 77n, 117n
Vassar, Rena, 106n
Veblen, Thorstein, 182–183, 182n, 189n, 229
Verbeke, Gérard, 67n
Verdenius, Willem J., 16n
Verdier, Philippe, 39n, 59n
Vergerio, Pier Paolo, 79, 79n, 175
Veysey, Laurence R., 158n, 167, 167n, 173n–174n, 176–177, 177n, 182nn, 188nn, 189n, 197n, 218, 218n, 253n
Viarre, Simone, 44n
Vine, Phyllis, 138n
Virtue, Charles F., 217n
Vitruvius, 22, 22n, 30, 30n
Vives, Juan Luis, 74, 86, 90, 90n, 92, 92n, 95, 100, 112
Vocht, Henri de, 95n, 99n
von Arnim, Hans, 2, 16n
Voss, John, 158n

Waddell, Helen, 45n
Wager, Willis J., 6n
Wagner, David L., 3n, 6n, 221n

Wagoner, Jennings L., Jr., 243n–244n
Walcott, Robert, 99n
Walker, Francis A., 187n
Wallace, Karl R., 126n
Wallace, Wayne E., 229n–230n
Wallach, Luitpold, 26n, 51n, 52n, 53n, 56n
Wallerstein, Immanuel, 214n
Walsh, James J., 135n–136n
Walsh, William H., 123n
Warch, Richard, 104n–105n, 107n, 134n, 139n, 244, 246–247, 246n, 247n, 252, 253nn, 254
Ward, F. Champion, 212n, 220n
Ward, John O., 52n, 60n, 61n
Watson, Foster, 100n, 108n, 113n
Webster, Charles, 131n
Webster, David S., 188n
Wechsler, Harold S., 188n
Wegener, Charles, 9, 9n, 167n–168n
Weisheipl, James A., 54n, 59n, 63n, 66n–67n, 68n, 73n, 75n, 81n
Weisinger, Herbert, 77n, 202n
Weiss, Roberto, 86n
Wendon, John, 229n–230n
Wertenbaker, Thomas J., 134n, 140n, 149n
West, Andrew F., 15n, 164, 164n–165n, 167n, 177n–178n, 182, 184n, 193n, 230–231, 231n
Whipple, Guy M., 159n, 183n–184n, 191n, 194n, 196n
Whitbread, Leslie G., 59n
White, F. C., 16n
White, Goodrich C., 216n
White, John S., 89n
Whitehead, John S., 154n
Wieruszowski, Helene, 63nn, 67n, 69n, 70n, 81n
Wilder, Amos N., 211n
Wilgus, A. Curtis, 191n
Wilkins, Ernest H., 188n, 198n–199n
Willard, H. M., 69n
Williams, John R., 56n
Wills, Elbert V., 256n
Wilson, N. G., 22n, 51n
Wirszubski, Chaim, 13n, 122n, 259n
Wirth, Arthur G., 169n, 182n, 231n
Wirth, Louis, 194n
Wise, John, 6n, 7, 8n

Wolff, Robert P., 255n, 257n
Wolter, Hans, 25n, 52n, 60n, 61n
Wood, Norman, 100n–101n
Woodring, Paul, 227n
Woodward, William H., 79nn, 80n, 83n, 86n, 87n, 96n, 109n, 173
Woody, Thomas, 7, 7n, 209, 209n
Woolsey, Theodore Dwight, 139, 139n
Wooster, Harvey A., 188n
Wordsworth, Christopher, 171n
Works, George A., 185n, 191n, 194n
Wright, C. Conrad, 143n
Wright, Louis B., 108n, 109n

Wriston, Henry M., 193, 193n–194n, 195n, 200, 200n
Wyczanski, Andrzej, 81n

Yates, Frances A., 54n
Yocum, A. Duncan, 257n
Young, Sherman P., 198n

Zagars, Waldemar, 5n, 215, 215n, 221
Zimmer, Agatho, 141n–142n, 150n
Zink, Harold, 200n
Zinsser, Hans, 200–201, 201n

Subject Index

Abbott, Jacob, 146, 149
Abelard, Peter, 57, 61, 70–71, 111
Academica (Cicero), 78
Academic Revolution, The (Jencks and Riesman, 243
Académie des Sciences, 127
Academies. *See also* Dissenting Academies
  as alternatives to universities, 124, 153
  in Enlightenment, 124
Acta Eruditorium, 127
Actes du quatrième Congrès international de philosophie médiévale: Arts libéraux et philosophie au moyen âge, 3
Acts of Supremacy, 99
Adagia (Erasmus), 87
Adams, John, 141
Adelard of Bath, 68
Aenas, 53–54
Against the Sophists (Isocrates), 17–18
Age of Reason, 120
Agricola, Rodolphus, 83, 85
Albert the Great, 65, 67
Alexander III, 18
American Academy of Arts and Sciences, 136, 137
American Academy of Fine Arts, 137
American Association for the Advancement of Science, 148
American Association of State Colleges and Universities, 208
American Association of University Professors, 200, 208
American Association of University Women, 195

American Council of Learned Societies, 200, 203
American Council on Education (ACE), 2, 184, 200
  Committee on a Design for General Education, 193
  Committee on a Design for Liberal Education, 195
American education
  antebellum, 153–156, 243–254
  artes liberales accommodation in, 219–223, 234
  artes liberales ideal in, 111–113, 156, 215–216, 230, 237, 240
  classical letters important in, 107, 133–141, 144, 152
  colonial, 103–107, 110–113, 133–141
  commercial subjects in, 182
  elective system in, 166–167, 177, 178
  Enlightenment's influence on, 141–153
  gentlemanly ideal in, 110–113
  German influence on, 146, 150, 153, 161–162, 176
  humanist influence on, 105, 107, 133, 207
  insulated from Enlightenment, 136
  intellectual positivism's influence on, 187
  liberal-free ideal subjects introduced into, 144–153, 155–156
  medieval education vs., 107
  modeled after British system, 103–107, 111, 133
  modern, 209–241
  New Science introduced into, 133–135, 153

American education (*continued*)
from 1900 to World War I, 201–204
post–Civil War, 158–170
post-revolutionary, 141–153
pragmatism and, 168–170
progressivism and, 168, 169–170
recitation used in, 250–253, 254
research in, 161–162, 165, 182–183, 193
scientific subjects introduced into, 145–153
Scottish universities' influence on, 105, 134, 135
service ideal in, 183
specialization in, 163–165, 210
survey courses introduced into, 184–185
utility in, 181–184, 202, 230
vocational training in, 181, 183, 235
World War I and, 201–204
American Journal of Science and Arts, 148
American Philosophical Society, 136, 137, 144
American Scholar, The, 158, 203
American Youth Commission, 194
Amherst College, 146, 164, 165, 177, 219, 246–247
Anaxagoras, 35
Angell, J. B., 161
Angers University, 63
Anglican church, 101
Anselm of Canterbury, 57, 70, 71
Antidosis (Isocrates), 17–18, 35, 238
Arezzo, University of, 63, 70
Aristophanes, 34
Arithmetic
in colonial American colleges, 105, 106, 138
in Greek education, 23
in medieval education, 14
in post-revolutionary American education, 144
in Renaissance education, 110
in Roman education, 36
Ars dictaminis, 69, 75
Artes liberales. *See also Septem artes liberales* (seven liberal arts)
career advancement and, 230, 231
curricular approaches to origins of, 15–16, 22–23, 206
discontinuity in character of, 14

earliest recorded use of, 13
as end in itself, 38
etymological approaches to origin of, 15, 20
humanist program for, 78–79, 115
logic as heart of, 67, 73
in medieval education, 64–73
men made free by, 115
normative program and, 24–25, 29, 36, 206
oratorical vs. Socratic goals for, 38, 206
in Roman education, 29–36, 206
Artes liberales accommodation
ambiguity in, 198
antecedents of, 186
aristocracy vs. egalitarianism and, 223–224
classical texts important to, 176–177, 197, 219–221, 223
critical intellect enhanced by, 176–177
Darwinism as stimulus for, 156
emergence of, 186, 207–208
freedom vs. wisdom and, 198
German influence on, 153
intellect vs. noble virtues in, 152
lure of, 222
origins of liberal education and, 222–223
pragmatism and, 170
precursors of, 186
progressivism and, 170
"New Humanism" and, 175, 176–180
Artes liberales ideal
in American Revolution, 142
characteristics of, 37–39, 53–55, 87–89, 111–113, 179, 228
Christian accommodation of, 206
Christian ethics and, 88–89, 206, 207
in colonial American colleges, 111–113
Erasmus's standards and, 87–89
as frame of reference, 36–37
in general education, 195, 196
humanism and, 78, 79, 87–89, 90, 173, 207
in liberal education, 175, 176, 177, 215–216
liberal-free ideal allied with, 183–184
liberal-free ideal congenial with, 156
liberal-free ideals vs., 143–144, 161

in medieval education, 52–55
in modern liberal education, 175, 176,
   215–216
pragmatism as challenge to, 170
presumption of certitude in, 218
progressivism as challenge to, 170
Protestant Reformation and, 91
in Roman education, 36–39
teaching of classics justified by, 152
utility opposed by, 182–184
weakening commitment to, 173
*Artes Liberales von der antiken Bildung
   zur Wissenschaft des Mittelalters*
   (Koch, ed.), 3
Association of American Colleges
   (AAC), 3, 183, 208, 218
   Commission on Liberal Education,
      203, 208, 233–234
   Committee on the Re-Statement of
      the Nature and Aims of Liberal
      Education, 203–204
Astrology, 28
Astronomy
   in antebellum American education,
      155
   in colonial American colleges, 105,
      106, 134
   decline in study of, 165
   in Greek education, 23, 24, 27–28
   in medieval education, 14
   in post–Civil War American
      education, 165
   in Renaissance education, 110
   in Roman education, 36
Atlantic, 170
*At War with Academic Traditions in
   America* (Lowell), 177
Augustana College, 211

Baccalarius, 63–64
Bacon, Roger, 65, 68
Bailey, Nathan, 132
Bard College, 192
Barlow, Thomas, 102
Barnard College, 5
Basel, University of, 83–84, 94
Bataille des VII ars, La (Henri d'Andeli),
   72
Beattie, James, 129
Bec monastic school, 56

Bennington College, 192, 204
Beranger of Tours, 57
Berkeley, George, 129
Bethel College, 220
Beza, Theodore, 94
Blackmer Committee, 4, 227
Black Mountain College, 192
Blair, James, 105
Board of Higher Education (New York
   City), 204
Bobbio monastery, 50, 56, 57
Boke Named the Gouernour, The (Elyot),
   108
Bologna, University of, 63, 67, 68,
   69–70, 73, 83
Boyle, Robert, 128
Breaking the Academic Lock Step
   (Aydelotte), 191
Brethren of the Common Life, 88, 93
Brooklyn College, 199
Brownell, Thomas C., 145–146
Brown University, 133, 146, 149, 156,
   200, 210
Bucknell University, 8
Buena Vista College, 209
Burr, Aaron, 140

California Institute of Technology, 225
Calvin, John, 92, 94, 96
Cambridge University, 63, 112, 151, 171
   curriculum of, 100–102, 104, 105,
      129–130, 132, 170, 246
   scholastic-humanist tradition of,
      127–128, 129, 131, 176
Campbell, George, 129
Carleton College, 201
Carolingian Renaissance, 51–52
Catholic Church, colleges established
   by, 94–95
Catholic University, 161
Cato's Letters, 143, 152
Celtis, Conradus, 82, 83
*Changes and Experiments in Liberal Arts
   Education,* 191
Chartres monastic school, 60, 61, 230
Chauncy, Charles, 104
Chicago, University of, 3, 161
   Divinity School at, 211
   faculty of, 180, 194, 203, 255
   liberal education at, 169, 212, 219–220

Chicago, University of (*continued*)
  organization of, 164, 192
Chicago Theological Seminary, 155
Christ Church College, Oxford
  University, 101
Christianity
  Aristotelian thought vs., 65
  artes liberales ideal and, 88–89, 206,
    207
  classical culture condemned by, 40,
    44–45
  corruption by liberal arts feared by,
    45
  formation of schools encouraged by,
    56
  humanism and, 88–89, 206, 207
  moral corruption of Roman
    civilization and, 40–41
  oratorical tradition embraced by, 206
  pagan arts compatible with, 42, 206
  pagan learning feared by, 50
  septem artes liberales adopted by, 41,
    44
Christian Scholar, 211
Chrysippus, 24
Church Divinity School of the Pacific,
  183
Cincinnati, University of, 193
Cistercians, 65
Clap, Thomas, 134, 138
Claremont Graduate School, 213–214
Clark College, 161, 162
Classical Association of the Middle
  West and South, 202
Cleland, James, 109
Clemson, Thomas, 253
Clermont, Collège de, 98
Clouds (Aristophanes), 34
Coe College, 202
Coimbra, University of, 63, 86
Colet, John, 99
Colgate University, 191
College Charts Its Course, The (Cremin),
  244
Colleges
  antebellum American, 243–254
  colonial American, 103–107, 110,
    243–254
  of English universities, 102
  in Enlightenment, 124

gymnasia vs., 164
liberal arts, 164, 165
liberal arts taught by, 97–98
post-revolutionary American, 144–153
sectarian, 210–211, 216
"Collegiate concerns." *See* "New
  Humanism"
Cologne, University of, 75–76, 83
Columbia Seminar on General
  Education in the Humanities,
  217–218
Columbia University, 3, 235, 251
  educational innovations and, 133,
    134–135, 145, 148, 163, 183, 184,
    248, 249
  faculty of, 112, 137, 139, 154, 215
  traditional studies at, 139, 154, 215
Commission on Liberal Education, 208,
  210
Commission on the Organization of the
  College Curriculum, 184
*Common School Grammar: A New and
  Practical System of English Grammar*
  (Peirce), 147
Common Sense philosophy, 129, 152,
  175
Commonwealth Fund, 184
Conference of University
  Administrators on General and
  Liberal Education, 204
Confessiones (Augustine), 42
Constitutions of the Society [of Jesus],
  95
Convivio, Il (Dante), 76
Cooper, Myles, 139, 248
Copernicus, Nicolaus, 118
Coram, Robert, 142
Cornell, Ezra, 166
Cornell University, 161, 183
Corpus Christi College, 100–101
Cortegiano, Il (Castiglione), 107–108
Council of Trent, 94
Course in Experimental Philosophy, A
  (Greenwood), 134

Daedalus, 225
Dante Alighieri, 76
Dartmouth College, 133, 138, 155, 156,
  165, 250

Darwin, Charles, 117, 156, 171
Darwinism, 168, 176
Davidson College, 154
Day, Jeremiah, 150, 151
De artibus liberalibus (Grosseteste), 66
De artibus liberalibus (Melanchthon), 96
De civitate Dei (Augustine), 41
Declamatio de pueris statim ac liberaliter
    instituendis (Erasmus), 87, 89
De consolatione Philosophiae (Boethius),
    48, 55–56
De differentiis topicis (Boethius), 47
De doctrina christiana (Augustine), 41, 69
De ingenuis moribus et liberalibus
    adolescentiae studiis (Vergerio), 79
De intitutione arithmetica (Boethius), 47
Delaware, University of, 213–214
De linguae latinae elegentia (Valla), 80
Demosthenes, 18, 21
De nuptiis Philologiae et Mercurii
    (Martianus), 30–31, 39–40, 55
De oratore (Cicero), 33, 37, 76, 165, 238,
    250
De ordine (Augustine), 42
De ratione studii (Erasmus), 87, 89
Desaguliers, John, 249
De tradendis disciplinis (Vives), 90
Dialectic
    applied to theology, 75–76
    in Greek education, 24, 26–27
    in medieval education, 45, 46, 52
    origins of, 24
    philosophers' vs. orators' views of,
        18–19, 26–27
    in Renaissance grammar schools, 97
    scholastics' use of, 57
Dialecticae disputationes contra
    aristotelicos (Valla), 80
Dialogus super auctores (Conrad of
    Hirsau), 58–59
Dickinson College, 137–138, 186
Diderot, Denis, 120
Directions for a Student in the Universitie
    (Merryweather), 102
Directions for Younger Scholars (Barlow),
    131
Discours de la méthode (Descartes), 120,
    126
Discourse of Free-Thinking, A (Collins),
    189

Disputatio de rhetorica et de virtutibus
    (Alcuin), 53
Dissenting Academies, 124, 130–131, 134
Divinity
    in colonial American colleges, 106,
        107, 138
    in Renaissance education, 110
Dominicans, 65–66
Donatus, Aelius, 71, 72
Drury College, 196
Du contrat social (Rousseau), 119
Duns Scotus, John, 76, 105

Earlham College, 216
Eaton, Amos, 146
Economics (Aristotle), 58
Edinburgh University, 105, 246
Educating Liberally (Hudson), 214
Education (Adams), 218
Educazione in europa, 1400/1600: Problemi
    e programmi, L' (Garin), 3
Efficiency in Liberal Education (Bowen
    and Douglass), 229
Eighth American Scientific Congress,
    159
Elective system
    in American education, 166–167, 177,
        178
    rejection of, 177, 178
    scientific research and, 167
Elizabeth I, queen of England, 99
Emile (Rousseau), 119, 122
Emory University, 216
Enchiridion militis christiani (Erasmus),
    88
Enfield, William, 249
English (language)
    in colonial American education, 135
    in post-revolutionary American
        education, 149
English education
    Catholic scholars driven from, 99
    Enlightenment universities in,
        123–125, 126–127, 129–132
    gentlemanly ideal in, 108–110
    humanism in, 86–87, 99–100, 207
    "New Humanism" in, 174–175
    in Renaissance, 86–87, 99–100,
        108–110, 123–127, 129–132
    research ideal in, 171, 174

English education (*continued*)
    uniform liberal education in, 99
    Victorian, 170–176
Enlightenment
    American colleges insulated from, 136
    American institutions responsive to,
        136–137
    critical skepticism in, 121–122, 137
    decline of universities in, 125–126
    ethic of individualism in, 122
    freedom as understood in, 115, 120
    liberal studies in, 123–126
    New Philosophy embraced in, 119
    reason sovereign in, 120, 121, 123
    scientific societies established in, 127,
        136–137
Erasmus, Desiderius, 87–90
Erfurt, University of, 83, 84, 90
Erlangen, University of, 127
Ermenric of Ellwangen, 45
Essay Concerning Human Understanding
    (Locke), 129, 250
Essays on a Liberal Education (Farrar,
    ed.), 171
Ethics. *See* Moral philosophy
Ethics (Aristotle), 58
Etymologiae (Isidore), 46, 60
Etymological English Dictionary, An
    (Bailey), 132
Euclid, 24
Euripides, 21
*Evolving Liberal Arts Curriculum: A
    Historical Review of Basic Themes,
    The* (Rudy), 7
Experimental College, University of
    Wisconsin, 177
Experimental science, 115
    in antebellum American education,
        153, 155, 156
    excluded from liberal education, 131
    included in liberal education,
        133–135, 153, 156, 225
    liberal-free ideal and, 219
    meaning of "experimental" in, 252
    modern world shaped by, 117
    moral guidelines for, 237–238
    secondary position given to, 156
    spurned by colonial American
        colleges, 133–138
    Renaissance as beginning point of,
        117–118

Faba, Guido, 70
Feltre, Vittorino da, 76, 80
Ferrara, University of, 80, 83
Florence University, 80
Florida, University of, 192
"Folklore of Liberal Education, The"
    (Horn), 1
Forum on Liberal Education, 208
Four-School Study Committee, 4, 227
Fourth Lateran Council, 62
Foxe, Richard, 100
France
    decline of Renaissance universities in,
        98
    humanism in, 85, 98, 207
France, Collège de, 99
Franciscans, 65, 76
Franeker University, 93
Franklin and Marshall College, 191,
    224–225
Frederick the Wise, 84
Freethinkers, 116, 120, 217
Fund for the Improvement of Post-
    secondary Education (FIPSE), 4, 229
Furman University, 225

Galen, 30
Galileo, 118, 128
General College, University of
    Minnesota, 194
General education
    integration stressed in, 194
    liberal education distinguished from,
        192, 204, 213
    liberal education equated with, 193
    meaning of, 193
    modern recommendations for, 212
    objectives of, 195, 200
    rationale for, 213
    three axes of, 194–195, 200
    vocational education in, 194
General Education in a Free Society (Buck
    et al.), 233–234
General Idea of the College of Mirania, A
    (Smith), 135, 140, 141
Geneva, 94
Gentlemanly ideal
    in American colleges, 110–113
    humanism in, 108, 110, 173, 207
    in Renaissance education, 107–110

Geography
  in colonial American education, 105,
    107, 134
  in post-revolutionary American
    education, 147
  in Renaissance education, 108, 109
Geometry
  in colonial American colleges, 105,
    106, 138
  in Greek education, 23
  in medieval education, 14
  in post-revolutionary American
    education, 147, 149
  in Roman education, 36
Georgia, University of, 145
Gerbert, 57
German education
  artes liberales accommodation in, 153
  free research in, 146, 150, 161–162
  historicocritical method developed in,
    176
  humanism in, 82–85, 207
  specialization in, 161
Goethe, Johann Wolfgang von, 8
Gonzaga family, 80
Gorgias (Plato), 17, 18, 19
Gorgias of Leontini, 17, 24
Göttingen, University of, 127
Goucher College, 197
Grammar
  in colonial American colleges, 103,
    107, 138
  de-emphasized by philosophers,
    25–26
  in Greek education, 24, 25–26
  humanism's influence on, 96–97,
    99–100
  logical rules sought for, 71
  in medieval education, 16, 46, 49, 52,
    54, 70–71, 72, 73, 75, 207
  "petty" instruction in, 96, 99–100
  in post-revolutionary American
    education, 147
  in Renaissance education, 78, 82, 90,
    96–97, 101, 109
  in septem artes liberales, 14, 59–60, 206
  in study of logic, 70–71
Grammar schools
  in colonial America, 106, 133
  in Enlightenment, 124, 133
  humanist trend in, 99–100

  liberal arts taught by, 97–98
  in post-revolutionary America, 144
Grammatica (Alcuin), 51
Grammatica speculativa, 71–72, 92
Gravesande, William J., 249
Greek (language)
  in antebellum American education,
    155
  in colonial American colleges, 103,
    104, 105, 106, 138
  in Enlightenment, 130, 138
  in post-revolutionary American
    education, 144
  in Renaissance education, 108, 109
Greek education
  dominant rationale in, 14–15, 16–18
  dominant theory of, 14–20
  "gymnastics" in, 21, 23
  Isocrates vs. Plato in, 18–19
  liberal education originating in, 10,
    14–29
  "music" in, 21, 23, 24
  orators vs. philosophers in, 18–19
  septem artes liberales in, 23–29
  sophists vs. philosophers in, 17–18,
    25, 34–35
  specialization in, 28–29
Greenwood, Isaac, 134, 139
Greifswald, University of, 93
Gresham College, 131
Grinnell College, 184
Grosseteste, Robert, 65
Guarino da Verona, 76, 80, 115
Guilds of masters, 62, 65
Guilford College, 184
Gymnasia
  colleges vs., 164
  liberal arts taught by, 97–98
  trivium taught by, 96, 97

Halle, University of, 127
Hamilton College, 197
Harper's, 170
Hartlib, Samuel, 126, 130
Harvard report, 233–234
Harvard University, 3, 154, 220, 244,
  246, 249, 251
  curriculum of, 104, 133, 134, 156
  Divinity School of, 215
  educational innovations and, 134, 146,
    150, 161, 166, 213, 147–248

Harvard University (*continued*)
elective system at, 161, 166, 167
elitism of, 110, 112
faculty of, 134, 161, 166, 177, 255
foreign influence on, 103, 106, 146,
150
Hebrew (language)
in colonial American colleges, 104,
105, 106
in Renaissance education, 97, 100
Heidelberg, University of, 75–76, 83, 90
Helvétius, Claude-Adrien, 141
Hendrix College, 225
Henry IV, King of France, 98
Higher Learning in America, The
(Hutchins), 180
Higher Learning in America, The (Veblin),
182
Hippias of Elis, 17, 27
Historicocritical method, 176
History
in antebellum American education,
155
in colonial American colleges, 107,
112, 134, 138
in post-revolutionary American
education, 147, 149
in Renaissance education, 78, 82, 96,
108, 109
in *septem artes liberales*, 206
Hobart College, 156
Holland, New Philosophy embraced in,
130
Hollins College, 213–214
Holy Cross, College of the, 204
Homeric poetry, 16, 17, 19
Honors programs, 191, 200
Huguenot colleges, 94, 98
Humanism. *See also* "New Humanism"
artes liberales ideal and, 78, 79, 87–89,
90, 173, 207
artes liberales program of, 78, 80, 82
Christian ethics and, 88–89, 206, 207
classical literature studied in, 76–78,
80, 81, 236
classical vs. scientific training in,
132–133
college tutorial system and, 86–87
in colonial American education, 105,
107, 133, 207

deficient in philosophical speculation,
78–79
definitions of, 81–82
encouraged by pluralism, 84
in England, 86–87, 99–101, 207
as forerunner of Enlightenment, 81
in France, 85, 98, 207
in gentlemanly education, 108, 110,
118, 173, 207
in Germany, 82–85, 207
grammar influenced by, 96–97
in Iberian peninsula, 86, 207
in Italy, 76–82, 207
literary culture revived by, 76–77
mathematical-mechanical world
model and, 118
north European scholars influenced
by, 83–85
opposed by English churchmen, 99
oratorical tradition in, 78, 91–92, 207
as paragon of liberal education, 173
Protestant Reformation related to,
91–92
Roman orators admired by, 77
scholasticism opposed by, 91–92, 101
secondary education influenced by,
82
septem artes liberales reinterpreted by,
80
universities influenced by, 80, 81, 82,
100–101
Humanists
ancients related to, 116
early scientists allied with, 117–118
freedom as understood by, 115
Luther vs., 91

Iberian peninsula, humanism in, 86,
207
Idea of a College, The (Trueblood), 216
Illinois, University of, 163, 201
Individualism
as characteristic of liberal-free ideal,
122, 196, 258
as characteristic of liberalism, 256
in general education, 194, 195
in liberal education, 217
Ingolstadt, University of, 83
*Inquiry Concerning Human
Understanding, An* (Hume), 121

Institute for Advanced Studies,
Princeton University, 190
Institutiones (Cassiodorus), 44
Institutio oratoria (Quintilian), 33, 37, 76,
80
Institutio principis christiani (Erasmus),
87, 88
Introduction to Natural Philosophy, An
(Olmsted), 251
Iowa, University of, 184
Ireland, as repository of liberal studies,
49–50
Italy
humanism in, 76–82, 207
New Philosophy embraced in, 130

Jacksonville, University of, 212
Jefferson, Thomas, 141, 142, 146
Jena, University of, 93
Jesuits, 95, 98, 174
Johns Hopkins University, 161, 164, 167,
173, 182
Jones, Howard Mumford, 249
Jones, Hugh, 105–106
Jordan, D. S., 161
Journal of Higher Education, 159
Juniata College, 211

Kalamazoo College, 202
Keane, J. J., 161
Kenyon College, 210
Kepler, Johannes, 118
King's College. *See* Columbia
University
Kingsley, J. L., 150
Knowledge, pursuit of
as highest happiness, 17
skepticism about, 18
for own sake, 5, 15, 122
through philosophical dialectic, 17, 18
progressivist view of, 182–183
Knox College, 196, 203
Königsberg, University of, 93
Krakow, University of, 76, 83, 84

Lafayette College, 183, 197
Lake Forest College, 213–214
Land-grant movement, 156

Language arts. *See also* Modern
languages; Vernacular languages
in medieval education, 45–46, 51
in *septem artes liberales,* 206
trivium as term for, 51–52
Lao-tzu, 10
Latin (language)
in antebellum American education,
155
in colonial American colleges, 103,
104, 105, 106, 112, 135, 138
in Enlightenment, 130, 135, 138
in post-revolutionary American
education, 144
in Renaissance education, 108, 109
Latin schools, 93–94
Latitudinarians, 129
Law, study of
Italy as home of, 69
in medieval education, 108, 110
rhetoric and, 70, 73
rooted in *trivium,* 69–70
Lawrence College, 193, 200
Leibniz, Gottfried Wilhelm, 127
Leipzig, University of, 76, 82, 84, 93
Lessing, Gotthold Ephraim, 122, 126
Leyden, University of, 93
Liberal
etymological roots of, 13, 115, 160
meanings of, 115, 132, 142–143, 144,
148, 158–160, 182
Liberal arts
in colonial American colleges, 104
developed in English universities,
100–101
diminution of, 73, 75
as gentleman's education, 108–109,
110–111, 112, 113, 132, 173
in medieval education, 73, 75
unaffected by New Philosophy, 130
*Liberal Arts College: A Chapter in
American Cultural History, The*
(Schmidt), 6
Liberal College in Changing Society, The
(Johnston), 188
"Liberal culture" movement. *See* "New
Humanism"
Liberal education
academic standards for, 190–191
American Revolution and, 141

Liberal education (continued)
a priori definition of, 4, 8–9
artes liberales ideal in, 175, 176, 177,
  215–216
balance of ideals needed in, 239–241
"basket" definition of, 4, 7, 195, 227,
  229
chaotic state of, 237–238
classical curriculum persistent in,
  138–141, 173–174, 197
classical letters as indispensable to,
  150–151, 172, 202, 219–221, 223
committed to oratorical tradition, 141,
  151
definition lacking for, 208–209
discipline needed in, 238
in Enlightenment, 123–126
experimental science excluded from,
  131
experimental science included in,
  133–135, 153, 156, 225
first description of, 5
general education vs., 192, 193, 213
historical appeals in definitions of, 5,
  9–11
humanism as paragon of, 173
improvement possible in, 239–240
individualism and, 217
intellectualism vs. egalitarianism in,
  178–179, 225
as "liberating education," 4, 8–9, 158,
  213–215
meaning of term for, 3, 9–11, 158–160,
  203, 224, 229
modern social issues in, 202
modern subjects as foundation of, 187
natural sciences in, 172, 187, 201, 225
operational definition of, 4, 6–7, 229
oratorical tradition accommodated by,
  151, 152–153, 156, 175
philosophical vs. oratorical traditions
  in, 171
political liberalism and, 235, 236,
  255–256
post–World War I, 201–204
purposes of, 132, 152, 171, 172–173,
  177–178, 204, 216
quadrivium in, 198
recitation method used in, 250
research vs., 164

Roman origins of, 29–39, 206, 222
scientific discipline useful for, 201
theological perspective on, 210–211,
  216
trivium in, 198
uniform pattern for, 95
unifying philosophy needed for,
  186–196, 210, 233–234
as "useless" education, 231
utility and, 183–184, 202, 204, 230–232
vocational education in, 183, 229–230,
  235
wartime technical needs and, 201
Liberal Education (Van Doren), 197–198,
  208
Liberal Education and a Liberal Faith, A
  (Thwing), 173–174
Liberal Education for Free Men (Woody),
  7
Liberal Education: Or, a Practical Treatise
  on the Methods of Acquiring Useful
  and Polite Learning (Knox), 132
Liberal Education Re-examined (Greene et
  al.), 203
Liberales
etymology of, 13, 15–16, 214, 231
social position and, 13
used in regard to education, 13
Liberal-free accommodation
absoluteness and, 226
aristocracy vs. democracy and,
  224–225
elitism and, 188–189, 190, 224
institutionalization of research and,
  188, 199, 208
New Science and, 187
precursors of, 186–188
scientific discipline valuable to,
  200–201, 225
unifying principle for education and,
  191–192
utility and, 199–200, 208
Liberal-free ideal
artes liberales ideal allied with,
  183–184
artes liberales ideal congenial with, 156
characteristics of, 119–122, 228, 258
in Enlightenment, 119–123
first appearance of, 207, 208
in general education, 194

latent elitism in, 188–189, 190
liberalism and, 161, 255–259
pioneered by scientific societies vs.
  academic institutions, 127,
  136–137, 147–148
pragmatism and, 169, 198
progressivism and, 194, 198
skepticism central to, 120–121, 219
universities infiltrated by, 124–125
utility opposed by, 182–184
Liberalism, 255–259
ancient roots of, 258–259
characteristics attributed to, 256
liberal-free ideal and, 161, 255–259
meaning of, 255
names associated with, 256
political, 161, 235, 236
*Liberalism and American Education in the
  Eighteenth Century* (Hansen),
  158–159
Liber de septem artibus liberalibus (Seneca
  the Younger), 45
Licentia docendi, 62, 63
Lindsley, Philip, 145–146, 149
Lisbon, University of, 63
Literary societies, 154
Literature and the American College
  (Babbitt), 174
Logic
in colonial American colleges, 104,
  105, 106, 107, 138
in Enlightenment, 130, 138
grammatical arguments introduced
  into, 70–71
as heart of *artes liberales*, 67, 73
liberal-free ideal and, 219
in medieval education, 64, 67, 72, 73,
  207
as philosophy's primary instrument,
  57
in Renaissance education, 97, 101,
  108, 110
rhetoric favored over, 36, 91, 92, 206
in *septem artes liberales*, 14, 206
Louisiana State University, 182
Louisville, University of, 159
Louvain, University of, 85, 86, 93,
  98–99
Lutheranism, students driven from, 93,
  94

Lyceums, 153

McPherson College, 210–211
Madison, James, 146
Magdalene College, Cambridge
  University, 102
Maine, University of, 217
Manhattanville College of the Sacred
  Heart, 216
Mantua, 80
Manuale scholarium, 84
Marischal College, 105
Marsh, James, 145–146, 149
Martin, Benjamin, 249
Massachusetts Institute of Technology,
  187
Mathematics
in antebellum American education,
  153, 155
in colonial American colleges, 133, 140
decline in study of, 165
in Enlightenment, 130, 140
in Greek education, 23, 27
as liberal arts foundation, 57
liberal-free ideal associated with, 217,
  219
in medieval education, 45, 46, 49, 51,
  64, 68, 73, 207
in post–Civil War American
  education, 165
in post-revolutionary American
  education, 149
in Renaissance grammar schools, 97
in Roman education, 31
in *septem artes liberales*, 206
Mather, Increase, 136
Mead, George H., 169
Medicine, in medieval education, 63,
  68, 73
Medieval education
antiqui vs. *moderni* in, 60
artes liberales ideal in, 52–55
character building as goal of, 53
decline of, 49, 50
educated elite created by, 53–54
elementary curriculum used in, 50
good citizenship as goal of, 53
influenced by Greek philosophy, 58
institutions for, 49–51
intellectual activity stimulated in, 57

Medieval education (*continued*)
liberal arts disseminated through, 50
liberal arts vs. Christianity in, 44–46
new knowledge not sought in, 54–55
oratorical tradition challenged in,
58–59
oratory vs. philosophy in, 46–47,
58–60, 207
philosophical tradition in, 55, 58–60
scholasticism in, 57, 58, 207, 230
texts used in, 52, 53
trivium in, 51–52, 56
ultimate learning assumed in, 54
Melanchthon, Philipp, 90, 92–93, 94, 96
Meno (Plato), 24
Mental discipline theory, 151, 166, 167,
175, 176, 178
Mercer University, 154
Merryweather, John, 102
Metalogicon (John of Salisbury), 61
Metaphysics
in colonial American colleges, 105,
106, 139
in Enlightenment, 130, 139
in post-revolutionary American
education, 149
in Renaissance education, 110
Miami University, 160
Michigan, University of, 146, 156, 161,
163, 211, 229
Michigan State University, 225
Middlebury College, 183
Milton, John, 126
Minnesota, University of, 186, 192, 194,
199, 202
Minto, Walter, 137
Modernist views, 244–254
evidence presented for, 249–250
prejudicial language used in, 247–248
standards of comparison used in,
245–246, 248
on traditional historiography, 245,
249, 254
Modern Language Association of
America, 166, 202
Modern languages
accepted in liberal education, 156
increase in study of, 166
rejected by universities, 126, 153, 154,
155
Monasteries, 45, 49–51

Monte Cassino monastery, 49, 56, 69
Montpellier, University of, 63
Morale scolarium (John of Garland), 71
Moral philosophy
in antebellum American education,
155
in colonial American colleges, 105,
106, 107, 135, 139
decline in study of, 167–168
in Enlightenment, 130, 139
medieval divisions of, 110
in post–Civil War American
education, 167–168
in Renaissance education, 105, 108,
110
Morgan State College, 212
Moriae encomium (Erasmus), 87
Morrill Land Grant Act, 156, 181
Music
in Greek education, 21, 23, 24, 27, 36
in medieval education, 47–48, 60, 207
in Renaissance education, 110

Naples, University of, 63, 67
Nashville, University of, 145–146, 149
National Academy of Sciences, 148
National Council of Religion in Higher
Education, 211
National Education Association, 183
National Project IV: Liberal Education
Varieties and Their Assessment, 4,
229
National Society for the Study of
Education (NSSE), 4, 183, 191, 193,
213
Yearbook Committee on General
Education in the American
College, 194
National Youth Administration, 10, 160
Natural philosophy (physics)
in antebellum American education,
155
in colonial American colleges, 105,
106, 133, 134–135, 138, 139, 140
in Enlightenment, 130, 138, 139, 140
in medieval education, 64, 68, 75
modern science equated with, 252
as philosophical speculation, 249
in post-revolutionary American
education, 149
in Renaissance education, 97, 105, 110

Natural science
  in antebellum American colleges,
    244–254
  in colonial American colleges,
    244–254
  "experimental" component in, 252
  fundamental to liberal education, 187,
    201, 225
  liberal-free ideal associated with, 217,
    244
  liberalism and, 256–257, 258–259
  New Philosophy and, 244
  recitation method used in, 250, 253,
    254
  scientific equipment used in,
    250–251, 254
"Neo-Classical Revival," 221
"New Humanism," 173, 174–180
New Jersey, College of. See Princeton
  University
New Liberal Arts, The (Koerner, ed.),
  9–10
New Philosophers, 125–126
New Philosophy
  clergy opposed to, 128
  conventional beliefs challenged by,
    118
  liberal arts unaffected by, 130
  natural science and, 244
  rejected by universities, 127–130, 154
  schools as viewed by, 125–126
  schools responsive to, 130–131
  spurned by American colonial
    colleges, 133–138
New Republic, 184
New School for Social Research, 197
New Science
  character formation strengthened by,
    187
  critical method used in, 118, 121
  liberal-free accommodation and, 187
  schools as viewed by, 125–126
Newton, Sir Isaac, 118, 120, 128, 134,
  139, 208, 253, 256–257
Nicomachean Ethics (Aristotle), 17
Nisbet, Charles, 137–138
Nominalism, 75–76
North American Review, 170
North Carolina, University of, 138, 145
Notre Dame, University of, 154, 185
Nott, Eliphalet, 145, 149

Nouvelle Héloïse, La (Rousseau), 122
Novum Organum (Bacon), 111
Nuremberg, University of, 84

Oberlin College, 154, 187, 199
Observations on Liberal Education in All
  Its Branches (Turnbull), 140
Occam, William of, 75–76, 111
Of Education Especially of Young
  Gentlemen (Walker), 131
Ohio State University, 202–203
Ohio University, 145
On Liberty (Mill), 256
On the Origin of Species by Means of
  Natural Selection (Darwin), 156, 171
Oratorical tradition
  accommodated by liberal education,
    151, 152–153, 156, 175
  in American Revolution, 142
  challenged in medieval education,
    58–59
  discipline required by, 238
  in humanism, 78, 91–92, 207
  liberal education committed to, 141,
    151
  Protestant Reformation and, 91
  research discouraged by, 165
  specialization criticized by, 165
Oratorio (Celtis), 83
Orators
  grammar elevated by, 25
  Greek education dominated by, 18–19
  humanists' admiration of, 77
  as philosophers, 18
  philosophers vs., 18–19, 26, 33–36,
    46–47, 58–60, 207, 234
  rhetoric as viewed by, 18–19, 26–27
Oratory
  in colonial American colleges, 112, 138
  Erasmus's allegiance to, 89
  as index of understanding
    philosophy, 35
  knowledge essential to, 36
  in medieval education, 58–59
  as philosophy, 18, 28
  in Renaissance education, 109
  sophistic deterioration of, 39
Ordre du Collège (Calvin), 96
Oresme, Nicholas, 117
Orientation courses, 184–185
Origines (Isidore), 46

Orléans, 63, 72, 241
Oxford Classical Dictionary, 15
Oxford University, 63, 71, 86, 112, 151
  curriculum of, 67–69, 70, 75, 100–102,
    104, 105, 129–130, 132, 170, 246
  nominalism at, 75–76
  scholastic-humanist tradition of, 73,
    127–128, 129, 131, 176

Padua, University of, 63, 68, 70, 79, 80
Paedologia (Mosellanus), 84, 95
Paine, Thomas, 141
Paris, University of, 63, 85, 241
  faculty of, 94
  grammar at, 14, 70–71, 72
  humanism and, 98
  liberal arts at, 67, 68, 69, 72, 73
  nominalism and, 76
Pavia, University of, 83
Peacham, Henry, 109
"Pedagogical century," 14, 16, 18
Pennsylvania, University of, 133, 135,
    141, 145, 149, 152, 155, 186
Petrarch, 76
Phaedrus (Plato), 18, 19, 34
Phi Beta Kappa Society, 202
Philosophers
  criticized by orators, 33
  grammar de-emphasized by, 25–26
  as orators, 18
  orators vs., 18–19, 26, 33–36, 46–47,
    58–60, 207, 234
  rhetoric as viewed by, 18–19, 26
  sophistry suspected in, 34–35
Philosophiae Naturalis Principia
    Mathematica (Newton), 118, 139
Philosophy
  confirmation of, 35
  criticism identified with, 116
  distinguished from sophistry, 34–35
  elevated above septem artes liberales,
    73
  in Greek education, 28
  meaning of, 212
  in medieval education, 46–48, 58–60
  oratory as, 18, 28
  quadrivium as path to, 47–48
  in Renaissance education, 78, 90, 97,
    101
  in Roman education, 32
  scriptural truth mistaken for, 56

Stoic-Augustinian-Isidorian divisions
    of, 66, 67
Stoic division of, 42
  systematic classification of, 58–59
  theology related to, 64, 65–66
  thirteenth-century divisions of, 67, 73
Physics. See Natural philosophy
Pius II, 82–83
Plan of Education (Cooper), 139
Poetry
  in colonial American colleges, 138
  in Renaissance education, 78, 82, 96,
    108
Poland, humanism in, 84
Politics (Aristotle), 29, 58
Populist party, 169
Positions (Mulcaster), 111
Pragmatism, 168–170, 179, 180, 198, 216
Prague, University of, 75–76, 83
Presidential Commission on Higher
    Education, 4
Princeton University, 133
  educational innovations and, 137, 145,
    182
  faculty of, 137, 154, 182
  liberal arts at, 134, 148–149, 182, 210,
    212
  traditional studies at, 140, 166
Priscian, 71, 72
Prodicus of Ceos, 17, 24
Progressive Education Association, 196
Progressivism, 179, 180, 243
  individualism and, 194
  liberal-free ideal and, 169–170,
    182–183, 198
  pragmatism and, 168, 169–170
  utility supported by, 182–183, 199
Project QUILL: Quality in Liberal
    Learning, 208
Proposals Relating to the Education of
    Youth in Pennsylvania (Franklin),
    135, 140
Protagoras, 17, 24, 27
Protagoras (Plato), 18
Protestant Reformation
  humanism related to, 91–92
  moral philosophy important to, 92
  Roman orators admired by, 91
  scholasticism opposed by, 91–92
Prudentius, 84
Pythagoras, 23–24, 47

Quadrivium, 51
  in colonial American colleges, 107
  in liberal education, 198
  origin of, 47–48
  preparatory to natural philosophy, 68
  in Renaissance education, 90, 97, 101
Québec, Collège de, 110
Queen's College, Oxford University, 102
Queen's College. *See* Rutgers University

Randolph-Macon College, 154
Ratio studiorum, 95
Recitation method, 250, 253, 254
Reductio artium ad theologiam
  (Bonaventure), 66
Reed College, 184, 191
Reformed Church schools, 94
Reforming of General Education, The
  (Bell), 234–235
Remigius, 55–56
Renaissance
  artes liberales program in, 78
  as beginning point of experimental
    science, 117–118
  gentlemanly ideal in, 107–109
  grammar schools in, 96–97
  universities in, 82–86, 97
  unphilosophical leaders of, 77
Rensselaer Polytechnic Institute, 146,
  149, 156
*Report on Medical Education in the United
  States and Canada* (Flexner), 190
Republic (Plato), 176, 223
Research ideal
  discouraged by oratorical tradition,
    165
  "New Humanism" opposed to, 174
  progressivist view of, 182–183
  undergraduate majors and, 193
  in Victorian English education, 171
Reuchlin, Johann, 83
"Revisionism," 243–244
Rheims monastic school, 56, 57
Rhetoric
  in antebellum American education,
    155
  in colonial American colleges, 106, 138
  favored over logic, 36, 91, 92, 206
  in Greek education, 24, 26–27
  law studies and, 70, 73

  in medieval education, 45, 46, 49, 51,
    52, 54, 60, 69, 71, 73, 207
  New Philosophers' approach to, 126
  origins of, 24
  philosophers' vs. orators' views of,
    18–19, 26
  in Renaissance education, 78, 82, 90,
    96, 97, 100, 101, 108, 109
  in Roman education, 31, 32–33
  in *septem artes liberales*, 14, 24, 36, 206
Rhetoric (Aristotle), 19, 24, 34, 58
Rhode Island, University of, 140
Rise of Liberalism (Laski), 255
Rochester, University of, 156
Rollins College, 159
Roman College, 95
Roman education
  artes liberales ideal in, 36–39
  classical texts used in, 38
  course of study in, 36
  curriculum variability in, 30
  good citizenship as goal of, 37
  Hellenistic influences on, 31–32
  liberal education originating in,
    29–39, 206, 222
  oratory vs. philosophy in, 33–36
  septem artes liberales in, 16, 29–31
  specialization in, 36
Rome, University of, 80
Rostock, University of, 93
Rousseau and Romanticism (Babbitt), 174
Royal Society of London, 126, 127, 136
Rush, Benjamin, 135, 141, 142
Rutgers University, 133, 134, 140, 146,
  149, 201

St. Gall monastic school, 51, 56
St. Ignatius of Loyola, 95
St. John's College, 192, 202, 212, 220
St. John's College, Oxford University,
  132
St. Paul's School, 99
St. Peter's College, 209
Salamanca, University of, 63, 86
Salerno, University of, 68
Sarah Lawrence College, 5, 192
Saturday Review, 227
Saturday Review of Literature, 175
Scholasticism
  "artificial logic" of, 97
  deterioration of, 207

Scholasticism (continued)
dialectical method used in, 57
in Enlightenment liberal education,
123
humanist opposition to, 91–92, 101
influenced by Greek philosophy, 58,
207
in medieval education, 57, 58, 207,
230
Protestant Reformation opposed to,
91–92
universities infiltrated by, 127
Scholemaster, The (Ascham), 100
School for Social Studies, 178
School of Political Science, Columbia
University, 163
Scientific research
discouraged by oratorical tradition,
165
discouraged in American education,
162
elective system and, 167
encouraged in American education,
161–162
liberal education vs., 164
specialization encouraged by, 163
utilitarian vs. free, 182
Scientific societies, 127, 136–137,
147–148, 153
Scientific Thought in the American
Colleges, 1638–1800 (Hornberger),
244
Scotland, universities in, 130
Scribner's, 170
Secondary schools. See Grammar
schools
Septem artes liberales (seven liberal arts)
Christianity's adoption of, 41, 44
in colonial American colleges, 140
decline in study of, 165
Erasmus's recommendations for,
89–90
formulation of, 22–23
in Greek education, 23–29
humanist reinterpretation of, 80
in medieval education, 14, 66
in need of new philosophical
divisions, 66–67
"New Humanist" program drawn
from, 179
normative program for, 24–25, 29, 36

philosophy elevated above, 73
in post–Civil War American
education, 165
purpose of, 206
rationale for, 31
in Renaissance education, 90
resistance to changes in, 66
in Roman education, 16, 29–31
Sermon on Education, A (Peters), 140, 152
Sheffield Scientific School, Yale
University, 176
Sidney, Sir Philip, 132
Siena, University of, 63, 83
Silliman, Benjamin, 146, 246–247, 250,
251
Alfred P. Sloan Foundation, 9–10
Smith, Adam, 141
Smith, William, 135, 140, 141
Smith College, 202
Social Science Research Council,
199–200
Societas Regia Scientarum, 127
Society of Jesus, 95, 98, 174
Socrates, 2, 5, 8–11, 19, 36, 222
oratorical confirmation of philosophy
and, 35
as sophist, 34–35
sophists as viewed by, 24
truth pursued by, 15, 17–18, 33
Some Thoughts Concerning Education
(Locke), 126
Sophism, Roman oratory deteriorated
to, 39
Sophists
in development of septem artes
liberales, 24, 25
Isocrates vs., 17–18
persuasion vs. truth important to, 17
philosophers regarded as, 34–35
Plato vs., 17
rhetoric as viewed by, 18–19, 26–27
South, University of the, 201
South Carolina, University of, 145
Southern Association of Colleges and
Secondary Schools, 195–196
Southern Illinois University, 211, 216
Southwestern at Memphis, 159, 191, 201
Southwestern University, 210–211
Special Committee on Liberal Studies,
208
Specialization, 161

in American education, 163–165, 210
criticized by oratorical tradition, 165
encouraged by research, 163
in Greek education, 28–29
"New Humanism" opposed to, 174
in Roman education, 36
in *septem artes liberales*, 206
Spencer, Herbert, 168
Spinoza, Baruch, 128, 256
Springfield College, 186
Stanford University, 161, 165
Stiles, Ezra, 138
Stillingfleet, Edward, 128
Strasbourg, University of, 94
Studia, 62, 63, 64, 73, 75
Studia humaniora, 78, 96, 123
Studia humanitatis, 78, 96, 123
Sturm, Johannes, 93–94, 96, 100, 117
Sumner, William Graham, 168
Survey courses, 184–185
Swarthmore College, 190–191, 201
Cooper Lectures at, 221
Syracuse University, 184

Teachers College, Columbia University,
159, 198
Terence, 84
Theology
in colonial American education, 135
dialectic applied to, 75–76
five-step program leading to, 67
philosophy related to, 64, 65–66
symbolic vs. dialectical, 57
Third Lateran Council, 62
Timaeus (Plato), 47
Tomlinson, Gideon, 150, 152
Toulouse, University of, 63, 70, 71
Trinity College, Cambridge University,
101
Trivium, 56
in Carolingian era, 51–52
language arts as, 51–52
law studies rooted in, 69–70
in liberal education, 198
in Renaissance education, 61, 90, 96
Truth, pursuit of
artes liberales ideal and, 216, 234
through critical rationality, 217
experimental method used for, 225
through free research, 190
ignored in medieval education, 48

liberal education as, 171
liberal-free ideal and, 234, 237
orators critical of, 33
for own sake, 226
Platonic view of, 17, 33
public expression and, 238
by Socrates, 15, 17–18, 33
Tübingen, University of, 90, 93
Tucker, W. J., 165
Turnbull, George, 140
Tutors, in Enlightenment, 124
Two Treatises of Government (Locke), 119

Union College, 145, 149
Union Theological Seminary, 186
Universities. *See also specific universities*
bourgeoisie and, 82, 84, 85
Catholic, 185
diminution of ecclesiastical power in,
82, 84, 85
Enlightenment alternatives to, 124
Enlightenment decline of, 125–126
founding of, 62
general requirements of, 63–64
graduate faculties of, 63, 73
humanist inroads into, 80, 81, 82,
100–101
humanists vs. scholastics at, 82
Melanchthon-influenced reformation
of, 93
New Philosophy embraced by, 130
New Philosophy rejected by, 127–130,
154
nominalists vs. realists at, 75–76
post-revolutionary American, 145–153
in Renaissance, 82–86, 97
Universities—American, English, German
(Flexner), 190
Utility
individual judgment and, 257
liberal education and, 183–184, 202,
204, 230–232
liberal-free accommodation and,
199–200, 208
as matter of contention, 181–184, 202,
204, 216, 230–232
progressivists supportive of, 182–183,
199

Valla, Lorenzo, 80, 92
Valladolid, University of, 63

Vanderbilt University, 197
Varro, Marcus Terentius, 27, 29, 30, 31, 32, 37, 38, 40, 42
Venice, University of, 80
Vergil, 84
Vermont, University of, 145, 146, 149
Vernacular languages, 153, 155–156
Vespasian, emperor of Rome, 32
Via moderna, 75, 76
Vicenza, University of, 63
Vienna, University of, 83
Vincent of Beauvais, 66
Virginia, University of, 146, 150
Vivarium monastery, 44, 45, 49
Vocational education
  general education and, 194, 196
  liberal education and, 183, 229–230, 235
Voltaire, 8

Wake Forest College, 247
Washington, George, 142
Washington College, 145, 215
Watson, Richard, 130
Wayland, Francis, 146
Webster, Noah, 142
Wells College, 191
Wesleyan College, 156
Western Reserve University, 174, 183
White, A. D., 161
Whitgift, John, 109
William and Mary, College of, 208–209
  British influence on, 103–104, 106, 249

educational innovations of, 133–134, 139, 145, 148, 246
  entrance requirements of, 103–104
  founding of, 105
Williams College, 202
Winthrop, John, 134, 136, 139
Wisconsin, University of, 192, 201
Witherspoon, John, 134, 140
Wittenberg, University of, 84, 90, 93
Worcester Polytechnic Institute, 225

Yale, Elihu, 104
Yale Corporation, 152
Yale Reports, 150, 175
Yale University, 103, 150, 215, 249
  arts curriculum at, 104, 106–107, 138, 213
  conservatism at, 139
  elitism at, 110
  founding of, 106
  recitation method used at, 250
  science studies at, 134, 146, 156, 246–248, 251
  specialization at, 163
  traditional studies and, 164, 166
Yearbook of the International Institute of Teachers College, 175
Yearbook of the National Society for the Study of Education (NSSE), 159

Zurich, 94

About the Author

BRUCE A. KIMBALL, who is Dean of Morse College at Yale University, received the A.B. from Dartmouth College, the M.Div. from Harvard Divinity School, and the Ed.D. from Harvard Graduate School of Education. He has edited a small volume, *Selected Essays in Liberal Theology, 1975–1985,* for *The American Journal of Theology and Philosophy* and published articles in *Educational Theory,* the *Journal of Higher Education,* the *Journal of Law and Education, Liberal Education, Teachers College Record, Religious Traditions, Religious Humanism,* and other journals. He is currently doing research as a Liberal Arts Fellow at Harvard Law School.

DATE DUE

6. 10. '87	
JUN 15 1987	
JUN 15 '87